RENEWALS: 691-4574

DATE DUE

DEC 4			
DEC 12			
GAYLORD			PRINTED IN U.S.A

VENICE

The Golden Age 697–1797

VENICE

The Golden Age 697–1797

Alvise Zorzi

ABBEVILLE PRESS · PUBLISHERS · NEW YORK

Opposite title page: Scene from the Pala Feriale *by Paolo Veneziano, 1345, showing the miraculous discovery of the body of St. Mark in one of the columns of the basilica. Museo Marciano, Venice*

Title page: Detail from Vittore Carpaccio's Lion of St. Mark, *Doge's Palace, Venice*

ON THE JACKET
Detail of *The Square of Saint Mark's* by Canaletto.
National Gallery of Art, Washington, D.C.
Gift of Mrs. Barbara Hutton.

Translated from the Italian by Nicoletta Simborowski and Simon Mackenzie

Copyright © 1980 Arnoldo Mondadori Editore, S.p.A., Milan
English translation copyright © 1983 Arnoldo Mondadori Editore, S.p.A., Milan

First published in Italian under the title *una Città, una Repubblica, un Impero Venezia 697–1797* by Arnoldo Mondadori Editore, S.p.A., Milan

First American Edition

Library of Congress Cataloging in Publication Data

Zorzi, Alvise.
  Venice.

  Bibliography: p.
  Includes index.
  1. Venice (Italy)—History. I. Title.
DG676.Z596 1983   945'.31   83-6432
ISBN 0-89659-406-8

Printed and bound in Italy by Arnoldo Mondadori Editore, Verona

Contents

"Venetiae Caput Mundi"

"The Venetians now plan to found a new monarchy and so vindicate the fate of ancient Rome . . .": words spoken by pope Pius II. The Venetians "have set their hearts on creating a monarchy just like the Romans," continues Master Niccolò Machiavelli, the author of *The Prince*. They are "determined and stubborn, their mouths always agape to snap up signory . . . so as to satisfy their hearts' desire to dominate Italy . . ." The speaker is the duke of Milan, Francesco Sforza. But king Louis XII of France goes even further: according to him, the Venetians would like "kingship and dominion over the whole world."

We are at the height of the Renaissance, but rumours like these have already been passing between court and chancery for quite a while. In medieval times Paduan, Ferrarese, Genoese and Greek chroniclers hurled such accusations; they re-echoed in the words of Florentine poets and Byzantine princesses. The Venetians spoke of themselves in a different tone, harsh and proud:

"King of kings, corrector of laws:" so reads a stone in the atrium of St. Mark's basilica, referring to the doge Vitale Falier. In the church of San Giorgio Maggiore another stone declares that the doge Domenico Michiel is "terror of the Greeks," the "lament of Hungary". The Lion of St. Mark, that proud heraldic beast which holds the Gospel with one paw and brandishes in the other a naked sword, proclaims:

"I am the great Lion: I am called Mark – whosoever resists me will be put to flight."

Venice, today. A winter's evening, when the mist muffles the soft lapping of the tide, and in the silent alleys, only rarely does someone pass, chilled to the bone. A summer's day, when at all hours, from canal to *campiello*, the multicoloured, carefree panorama of international tourism wends its way. All through the year, the comings and goings of an unhurried way of life: the glass of white wine in the local bar, the sharp wit of the housewives threading pearls, all the easy-going commonplaces with which, following Goldonian traditions, current opinion decks out the daily routine of the lagoon city. Another angle shows a nobler vision, though just as closely-linked with preconceived ideas: the velvety atmosphere of a cultured and sophisticated world, drifting between concerts at the Fenice theater and study groups on the island of San Giorgio, between the Carpaccios in the Scuola degli Schiavoni and the Galleria dell'Accademia. Otherwise, there remains the myth of international society life, blessed by the legend of Hemingway; or else the mythology of decay, celebrated by Thomas Mann and Maurice Barrès, given new life by Luchino Visconti and stereotyped by books and films for the masses. Certainly the grandiose remains of a great history still exist, but they are not enough to link the Venice of today with the overbearing entity which aroused hatred and suspicion, worry and fear; and which, in the eyes of men of great power, evoked the menacing shadow of universal monarchy.

By conjuring up this shadow which the Renaissance had clothed in the ancient grandeur of the Rome that was (and the Venetians for their part were flattered by it: "*Roma caput mundi, Venetiae secundi* . . ."), the other European powers ended up by forgetting their differences and forming a united front against the city which seemed to embody it.

To someone sipping an aperitif in the plush

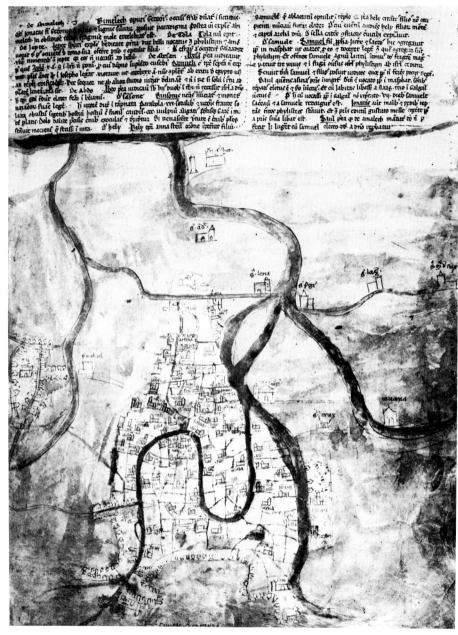

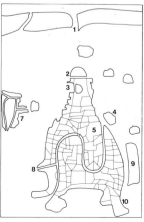

Above: the earliest map of Venice is preserved in the Biblioteca Marciana, in a manuscript of 1346, which shows that the main outlines of the city were already fixed at that time. The marshes had been filled in to restrict the waters to the canals and the lagoon. The map is oriented with East at the top. The simplified diagram alongside shows how the sinuous course of the Grand Canal stands out from the houses and districts of the city. The numbers refer to the following places:

1. *The Lido harbour.*
2. *San Pietro.*
3. *The Arsenal.*
4. *The island of San Giorgio.*
5. *The Piazza and the San Marco area.*
6. *The Rialto quarter.*
7. *The island of Murano.*
8. *Cannaregio.*
9. *The Giudecca.*
10. *San Nicolò.*

and slightly decadent salons of the café Florian, beneath the arcades of the Procuratie Nuove, it may seem impossible that, at the beginning of the 16th century, the thorny problem of Venetian expansion was being tackled by the various governments in the shape of a European coalition. Venice seen in the same terms as Napoleon! But to find a similar example of such solidarity, we have to come right up to the years when Europe, thrown into confusion by Bonaparte's victories, united in order to resist his attacks. In the year 1508 the kings of France, Spain and Hungary, the pope, the German emperor and the archduke of Austria formed an alliance called the League of Cambrai, after the French town in which it was signed. These were the greatest powers in Europe: other lesser powers aligned themselves with them, such as the dukes of Mantua and Ferrara, Urbino and Savoy; while others such as the king of England staked a claim on the future partition of the Venetian territories.

Venice took up the challenge. The inland territories, the Veneto and Lombardy were lost in less than no time. From Santa Marta, San Nicolò dei Mendicoli and Cannaregio, the Venetians could see the glow of the enemy encampments little more than a stone's throw away, and could hear the thud of artillery fire. No one thought of surrender. Instead they recalled other, no less dramatic occasions, such as the time in 1380 when the Genoese naval forces gathered at Chioggia with the armies of the lord of Padua, the patriarch of Aquileia and the king of Hungary, and all would have been lost if Carlo Zeno's galleys had not suddenly arrived from the East. Or they could think of the time the Hungarians entered the lagoon itself in their little skin-covered boats and there met defeat and death; or how when, in 810, the Franks under Charlemagne's son king Pippin penetrated so far into the labyrinth of canals as to end up hacked to pieces between the banks of the canal which ever since has been called the Orphan canal after the terrible massacre. ... Hemmed in on all sides, passed off as finished, dead and buried, Venice emerged from the adventure of the League of Cambrai more powerful and free than ever. A French minister wrote:

"The strength of the Venetians is indeed great, when those who dared to lie in wait in open country for the four most powerful princes of

St. Mark's basin with the Molo, the Doge's Palace, the Piazzetta, and the Campanile, from an engraving by Erhard Reuwich in Breydenbach's Peregrinatio, *15th century. The large number of ships gives an idea of the volume of Venice's trade in her golden age.*

An impression of Venice from a 15th–century codex, Bodleian Library, Oxford. Venice's fame was at its height in the 15th century. It is clear that the artist had never visited the city, but based his drawing on accounts of merchants and statesmen returning from the Republic.

Christendom and, with banners unfurled, fought close battle, must certainly be esteemed and judged most powerful men. . . ."

In fact it is difficult for anyone to realize the extent of power gained by Venice in the long years of her greatest splendour (more than four centuries, from 1100 to the end of the 1500s). Most of all, it is difficult for us to visualize the vastness of her territorial expansion, the extent of the territory which she eventually ruled (directly or indirectly) for an even longer period, not to speak of her unlimited mercantile and financial resources. Official Italian history taught in schools either does not mention this or speaks of it merely in passing. Other legends and traditions have precedence in the story of Italian unity, and the greatness of Venice's past has been erased by a series of prejudices, old and new, as well as the lamentable circumstances which accompanied the fall of the Venetian Republic, aggravated by cunning propaganda that was organized by the very forces that had toppled it. Historical accounts remain on the whole restricted to those directly involved in research, and imagination in its noblest as well as lowest forms, has preferred the theme of decadence to that of grandeur, in accordance with the by now inescapable tradition of a romantic Venice.

Nevertheless, for a long time the name of Venice aroused all over the world echoes of power comparable to those awakened by Victorian Britain at the height of its empire. The comparison is also apt with regard to the mass of objections,

hatred and prejudice stirred up as a counterforce. Certain anti-Venetian Renaissance pamphlets recall, almost to the letter, themes in anti-British propaganda towards the end of the British empire. The humanist Platina, in the Rome of the Venetian popes Eugene IV Condulmer and Paul II Barbo, was savage in his criticism of the arrogance he attributed to the fellow-citizens of these two pontiffs and he also credited the second of these with the charge of arrogance. Already in the Constantinople of the 12th century, public outcry was provoked by the fact that the Venetians controlled commerce and armaments to far too large a degree, that they claimed special customs tariffs and that (just like the English with their Shanghai "concession" right up to 1939) they had at their disposal a privileged sector with a church, square, foundry and well-equipped docks. All this resulted in the mass arrest and subsequent exile of the Venetians.

To further irritate public opinion and to humiliate the pride of the Byzantine emperor, there had been the ostentatious display of power and riches afforded by the naval cortege that escorted the Venetian ambassadors. When Manuel Comnenus, the emperor of Byzantium, ordered the arrest of all the Venetians resident in his empire, Venetian merchants spread from the extreme edge of western Europe to the East and Asia; and a good 150 years had already gone by since the doge Pietro Orseolo II had achieved, in the course of a triumphant crusade, the submission of the principal cities and islands of Istria and Dalmatia. Yet the borders of the motherland, the city-state of Venice, did not even reach as far as the funnels and cranes of today's Porto Marghera. The Venetians were nothing more than the inhabitants of a modest, scattered archipelago, protected by a thin strip of coastal islands, in the part of the lagoon that goes from the source of the Isonzo to the source of the Adige: from Grado to Cavarzere, if we want to use the official delineation of what had been a remote Byzantine province, then a frontier dukedom, and was to become a republic with unique characteristics, and which would have power capable of standing up victoriously to the great powers and superpowers at the time of their greatest assertiveness.

Origins and Development

"Once, Venice was a deserted place, uninhabited marshland. ..." Tradition and legend (the narrator here is a Byzantine emperor, Constantine Porphyrogenitus) surrounds the founding of Venice in a mythology which is almost reminiscent of the Biblical account of the origins of the world. From deserted marshland to the splendour of a great metropolis straddling East and West, this can be relived today (were it not for the sound of the aeroplanes coming into Marco Polo airport) by anyone entering from the remotest part of the lagoon, around Lio Piccolo and Lio Mazor, towards the lagoon fish hatcheries, amid the islets thick with blue-green or russet grasses, along little canals which peter out in shoals and marshland. Tradition and legend attribute the birth of the lagoon community from which Venice originated, to the barbaric invasions, and above all to the raids of Attila, "The Scourge of God". The story goes that in order to escape the Huns, the inhabitants of the various Roman cities inland took refuge on the islands amid the lakes and canals, taking with them their holy relics and few belongings salvaged from the onslaught of the invaders. But in reality, the lagoons that stretch from Isonzo to the Po have never been the totally deserted region that Porphyrogenitus and other chroniclers describe.

Grado, which is very near the metropolis of Aquileia, then the capital of the Roman empire, was a small fortified city with considerable port facilities; there was also a Roman colony at Chioggia, and undoubtedly some kind of Roman settlement, however modest, at Torcello. In addition there were probably forts on the islands which make up the present-day historical center of Venice: at Castello or maybe San Marco, and Altino was actually an important town situated just on the edge of the lagoon.

As far as Attila, *flagellum Dei* is concerned, the locals attribute a certain sculpted stone chair at Torcello to him. (Legend claims that he lies buried along with boundless treasure beneath the island called Monte dell' Oro.) However, although we know that he ravaged Altino, he cannot be either blamed or credited for the mass migration to the lagoon.

Neither can Alaric and his Goths be blamed,

though one famous medieval legend fixes the date of the founding of Venice in that era (25 March, 421 A.D.). The migration of the inhabitants of the towns of the Roman Veneto (many and prosperous, ranging from Padua to Concordia Sagittaria, and Altino to Oderzo, to name but the nearest) did not take place all at once. But it is more than likely that the raids of the Goths and Huns had prompted those who had the means to do so to relocate themselves swiftly somewhere where the Goths and Huns could not reach them, having no marine base. The really major event which prompted a migration destined to last some while was undoubtedly the arrival of a particularly aggressive, primitive Germanic tribe, the Longobards. Unlike the Goths and Huns, they had come to Italy with the firm intention of staying for good.

In this way, over a period of centuries, against a background of violence and strife, the newly-arrived "barbarians" and the surviving traces of the Roman world represented by Byzantine authority (the western Roman empire had crumbled and the only Roman emperor left had his court in Byzantium), peoples and their institutions moved into the lagoon territories, lands not far from the mainland but protected by stretches of water.

Near Grado, which had become a religious center, and Torcello, now (as Porphyrogenitus says) "a great emporium," new towns came into being, such as Cittanova and Eraclea based on a lagoon that has now vanished, or Metamauco and Malamocco, on the edges of what is now the Lido. In 639–40 the cathedral at Torcello was founded. A stone in its walls proclaims the authority of the patriarch of Ravenna, the greatest representative in Italy of the emperor himself, and mentions the presence of the "soldiers' master" Marcellus, army commander and local governor. This shows that the refugees had made a specific political choice: in preference to the new Longobard regime they opted for the ancient Roman order as represented by Byzantium; in short, they wanted to remain faithful to the old Venetian-Roman traditions, with their age-old roots on the mainland.

The years went by, and amid changes of attitude that pointed to closer bonds with the Longobard kingdom and sometimes to tighter links with

Byzantium, the lagoon province, "maritime Venice," veered more and more towards independence. After a certain stage, in a turmoil of bloody events, it was decided that the *duca* (later he would be called the doge), the ruler of the province, should be an elected ruler. His residence and the capital of what was by now a small confederation, moved from Cittanova to Malamocco. It was around Malamocco in the fateful year of 810 that a decisive event took place, the attack by Charlemagne's son which we mentioned earlier.

Once more it is Porphyrogenitus who tells us that king Pippin, "who ruled Pavia and other kingdoms," swooped down upon the Venetians "with all his strength and a powerful army," with

the intention of reaching "with all his horsemen" the island of Malamocco. The Venetians prevented him doing so by blocking the port with rows of pikes, and from their ships "attacking him with arrows and javelins" and so stopped him in his tracks. They answered king Pippin's claim: "You are my subjects because you belong to my lands and my kingdoms" with the words: "We are subjects of the emperor of the Romans, not of yours."

According to local chroniclers, Pippin's fleet was stranded in the lagoon shallows and suffered severe losses in being driven back; according to the Frankish chroniclers, Pippin succeeded in imposing his rule on the Venetians. Whatever the truth, the fact is that Pippin and his father Charlemagne were obliged to do without maritime Venice, which remained outside the Frankish kingdom and instead preserved a directly dependent relationship with Byzantium. In this way Venice avoided a future of agriculture and feudalism, and affirming its severance from the mainland, turned East, towards the sea. However, links with the Frankish empire, formalized by an agreement with Constantinople and later renewed directly between doges and Charlemagne's successors, become such as to make Venice the natural and official go-between for dealings between the two powers. In this way Venice's role as bridge of communication between East and West was firmly established.

Contemporary documents add another element to this scene. The boundless world of Islam, with its huge, overcrowded cities, its wealth and poverty, had entered into a close business relationship with the tiny lagoon nation. In this way the triangle was formed on which Venetian economic expansion was to be developed, the prelude and the basis for its future greatness: the Byzantine East, the Moslem East and the European West.

Readers may have noticed that we are no longer discussing "maritime Venice," but simply Venice. The fact is, that as an extraordinary and wonderful consequence of Pippin's attempted invasion, and from the events of 810, the entity which we now know as Venice came into being. Malamocco was abandoned, and the ruler and his government transferred to the Realtine islands which form the setting for the historical center of Venice today. In

all probability it was already the most important center even then; it was certainly the safest, right in the midst of deep waters and relatively distant from both the mainland and the mouths of the port. It was also the most suitable point for harbouring merchant-ships, along the tranquil, meandering Grand Canal. A few years later, in 829, Venetian merchants loaded with booty purloined the corpse of St. Mark the evangelist from Alexander of Egypt. According to a deeply-rooted legend of the Roman-Venetian world, he was the founder of the patriarchate of Aquileia. The chroniclers, clearly moved, describe a scene of unanimous enthusiasm, but above all this marks the establishment of a specific political and moral identity. From that moment Venice possessed all the ingredients necessary for becoming an independent entity and a force capable of expanding: she had her own ruler, own people, own capital and own saint. On the site where those bones so laden with significance were set down, was to be built one of Christendom's most beautiful and famous churches.

For many long years Venice continued to maneuver between Eastern empire and Carolingian empire (later the Holy Roman Empire), without in effect depending on either. But gradually the ancient relationship with Byzantium altered and modified. A series of decrees issued by the Byzantine emperors confirmed the position of privilege of the Venetian merchants, those Venetians that the courtly Constantinople tongue insisted on calling "dearest friends and subjects"

Opposite: view of the lagoon towards Burano and Torcello, detail from Jacopo de'Barbari's famous Pianta Prospettica *(perspective map), 16th century.*
Above: view of the lagoon from a painting by Canaletto, engraved by Berardi. This fascination with its natural surroundings is a constant reminder that Venice owed its fortune to its situation. When the newly revived cities of the Veneto were sacked in the great barbarian invasions, their inhabitants took refuge on the many islands scattered over the lagoon. Here a community arose which came to look on the water as its natural source of livelihood. Protected from human threats on the landward side by marshes and stretches of water, and from the force of the sea by long sandy strips of land, this community found the right conditions to begin its thousand year-long history.

the fourth crusade in 1204, the conquest of Constantinople and the partition of the lands which constituted what remained of the eastern Roman empire, an act known in the Middle Ages (and even nowadays, by specialists in the field) as *partitio Romaniae*.

We will come back to the *partitio Romaniae*, the sharing of the divided property which Venice was able to get hold of, and what she was able to preserve. For the moment, suffice it to say that from 1205 onwards Venice, already a great mercantile power, became a great colonial force.

How did Venice become a great mercantile power? The barren and meager lands on which the Venetians had perched, like the seagulls that perch on the posts in the canals, were capable of only an inadequate agricultural production: there were some woods and a few vineyards (such as on the island still known as "Le Vignole") where there were underground springs of fresh water. Some vegetables were grown, a few cows and horses raised, but nothing else. However, though the canals and lagoons provided plenty of fish, the seawater also contained an element essential to the survival of men and animals: salt. Salt-works had swiftly been built all over the place, right from earliest times (they certainly already existed in Roman times), and they were particularly numerous among the Realtine islands and Chioggia. This precious mineral, as vital to the civilization of the Middle Ages as oil is to ours, could be produced limitlessly and sold wherever it could be transported by ship (or rather by barge). Already at the time of the Goths, vessels could be seen setting sail over "infinite horizons" – that is, crossing the Adriatic in search of corn and wine on the Istrian coast.

The salt was sold along the Adriatic coast, but also and probably to a far greater extent, on the Italian mainland, which was reached by means of other barges, often drawn by hand from the towpath, along the waterways of the Po valley. A tenth–century Pavian customs official expresses his amazement faced with "these people [that] neither plough nor sow, but can buy corn and wine everywhere." Soon other more sophisticated products appeared on the scene (though salt was for a long time the primary basic essential). These included fabrics, perfumes, the feathers of exotic oriental birds and another ancient product of the

Tombstone of Paolo d'Altino, first bishop of Torcello on the floor of the cathedral in Torcello (15th–century bas relief, dating from a period after the death of the bishop). The see was moved to this site in about 640 from the coastal city of Altino under the pressure of the Langobard conquests. In spite of the crisis which engulfed the Byzantine province of the Veneto, the unified and centralized government of the exarchate remained unaffected, and the local bodies which gradually grew up still depended on the Byzantine governor. Thus the association of islanders which eventually found its political center around the Rialto in the ninth century was thoroughly Byzantine, a fact which was to leave a permanent mark on Venice. These links with the East can be seen not only in Venice's commercial, political, and social relations, but also in its art. The finest example of this is St. Mark's basilica. Facing page: mosaic over the door of Sant'Alipio, executed between 1260 and 1270, showing the facade of St. Mark's as it appeared at that time.

whereas they figured more and more as friends and masters. The seizure of all the Venetians in the empire, ordered by the emperor Manuel Comnenus in 1171, confirms the violence of the situation: the "dearest friends and subjects" were in despotic control of the Byzantine economy, had at their disposal military forces far superior to those of Byzantium and, as the ancient eastern empire was not economically viable on its own, once the Venetians were gone its livelihood had to be sought elsewhere.

Unfortunately (for Comnenus), as far as navigation and commerce were concerned, only Italians were of any significance in the entire Mediterranean basin: these were mainly Genoese and Pisans, as the people from Amalfi had been wiped out some time before and those from Ancona and Gaeta were too weak to withstand competition. In breaking the ancient relationship of privilege with the Venetians, which had given them a virtual commercial monopoly in the Byzantine world, Comnenus laid the basis for the other major event in Venetian history, which in its turn laid the foundations for the Venetian empire:

lagoon culture, glass. It would seem that for a very long while no one was capable of making glass except in Venice, where production was so plentiful that the furnaces were ordered to be moved to the island of Murano, to avoid poisoning of the atmosphere with the smoke from their chimneys.

Salt and glass were also transported by land, particularly to Styria, where they were exchanged for iron. This, together with timber, the only other abundant product of the lagoon area as it would float there in enormous quantities on the tide of the Piave and Adige, would then be sent on its way to the Moslem East, which was very short of both commodities. Wood and iron were considered strategic materials, and popes and emperors (East and West) did all they could to obstruct this trade. The ferocity and mobility of the Saracens kept the whole Mediterranean basin in a constant state of crisis. But the Venetian merchants went on undaunted, taking no notice of threats and repudiations. They also sold slaves, but the main aim of all this trade with Islam was the handling of a particular and highly expensive commodity which the western world considered as precious as salt: spices. Pepper figures very early on in Venetian records. It was the principal but not the only drug known to a world that had no other stimulants (tea and coffee had not yet appeared on the scene as European beverages, liquor was a rarity and tobacco was still *in mente Dei*). Nor were there any means of preserving food or making it palatable when no longer fresh (gentlefolk preserved game in urine; and snow, transported at great cost and preserved with difficulty, was brought from the mountains and used to cool drinks. The principal beverages were wines mulled with cloves, cinnamon, ginger, coriander and every kind of wizardry . . .).

In spite of many incongruous features, in a world in which money was still a rarity and where ships' anchors were either hired or inherited, all this trade brought about a process of social evolution which spawned a new class of the rich (besides the old property-owning families, who also had been very keen to run the risks of trade and armaments): these were the businessmen, merchants and craftsmen. The aristocracy was always a significant presence right from earliest times in Venice, and it expanded. In the govern-

ment assembly, which appears to have been the basis of Venetian politics for a long while, it is difficult to decide how much the common people counted, and on the other hand, how much power was held by the ever extended and revitalized aristocracy. The concentration of power within a restricted circle of nobles (merchants in fact, but almost all merchants were nobles and all nobles merchants) in any case seems a rather old-fashioned situation, in spite of the intermittent voice of the popular assembly which went on electing the doge and approving the basic decisions of the government. Later however, the common people were gradually and quite openly pushed into second place, and reduced to a role of passively approving the decisions of others. The climax of this situation in which, by the middle of the 13th century, power had settled decisively with about ten families, came in a kind of coup d'état (but which was officially accomplished with the seal of parliamentary approval). This was the *serrata*, "locking," of the *Maggior Consiglio* or Great Council in 1297.

This episode, which has so enraged historians of a liberal and enlightened mould and which even now makes Marxist noses wrinkle, was part of a series of causes and consequences which must not be evaluated by today's yardsticks, but in the light of the circumstances of its own time. At first, as the historian F. C. Lane has noted, no more than about 40 people were necessary for settling political decisions (the principal businessmen, adds another historian, Yves Renouard). Later the power to make decisions passed to a sovereign assembly, the *Maggior Consiglio*, which eventually numbered 2,000 members. But all these members belonged to a single social class that would later take on definite outlines and be called "patrician," embracing rich and poor, descendants of ancient families and those of lesser dynasties of craftsmen and merchants.

For all those making up the particular class to which the exercise of political power was entrusted for the next 500 years, the only necessary requisite was that they or their ancestors should belong to an elected political assembly. This phenomenon is as extraordinary as it is unique, like all the political manifestations of Venetian civic life. It hardly seems to have been inspired by the idea of the dominance of one particular

At the side of St. Mark's basilica stands the Treasury tower. The corner of this building is decorated with a 4th–century Syrian porphyry sculpture of the tetrarchs, the four joint emperors who held power during the reign of Diocletian. The wall is decorated with slabs of coloured marble and carved plutei from the 9th to 11th century. The base is decorated with two putti in the teeth of two dragons, dating from the end of the 13th century. St. Mark's basilica grew with Venice's power, its facade being gradually enriched over the centuries as the city expanded and conquered its maritime empire. This process reached its height in the 12th to 13th century, when marble, columns, sculptures, and capitals, booty from the great buildings of the East flowed into the city's harbours.

but as soon as he returned, he was obliged to take part in political life, which was not restricted to the legislative functions of the *Maggior Consiglio* (which met as a rule every Sunday), but also extended to vast responsibilities in central and peripheral government, to embassies, governorships and military commands. As time went by, the duties of service became less flexible and more oppressive: the patrician of the seventh and eighth centuries, as soon as he reached the age of majority (25) entered the machinery of the *cursus honorum*, with no means of escape apart from becoming a priest (ecclesiastics of every grade were rigorously excluded from political life) or paying heavy tolls, which became increasingly punitive as centuries went by.

The effective result of the "locking" of the *Maggior Consiglio*, however one views it, was that while Genoa, Venice's great rival, suffered a constant change of rulers, sometimes local and sometimes foreign, Venice itself preserved total independence from outsiders for a good 500 years, and even internally rejected systematically any kind of domination whether individual or dynastic. These two features make Venice virtually unique in Italy and Europe. They are also the anchor and the focus of an original, self-derived civilization which had no counterpart in Italy or Europe. Bearing in mind Venice's deliberate insistence on specifically "Italian" characteristics in an Italy exposed from the late Renaissance onwards to all kinds of outside influences, this is no meager originality.

economic class (it should be stressed that among those "locked" into the *Maggior Consiglio* were wealthy financiers, traders, shipowners and entrepreneurs, but also wretchedly poor people who were already a social problem). It seems rather to have been inspired by the idea of political specialization, whereby the role of politician becomes handed down. This (in terms of recent Italian events) is as far removed from anti-populist politics as can be imagined.

Did politics then become a "job"? It did not, but it became a duty. For those who belonged to the patrician class, the only ones with the right to belong to the *Maggior Consiglio*, there were no alternatives. The medieval patrician could trade, sail the seas and pass long years away from Venice,

A Unique Reality

The gradual process of stripping the popular assembly of all its prerogatives had taken place over a long period of time and practically painlessly. Meanwhile, the "locking" of the *Maggior Consiglio* had brought about particularly serious repercussions. Certain "great" citizens, who were accustomed to being important but in fact were so no longer (owing to the institutionalizing of the inheritance of power in the parliamentary class) had instigated the uprising of 15 June 1310, which subjected Venice to the risk of becoming a personal dominion.

The candidate for the *Signoria* belonged to a

great family which had already supplied two doges, father and son, and had been on the brink of supplying a third: he was called Baiamonte Tiepolo and was known as the *gran cavaliere*, "the great knight." His father, Jacopo, had enjoyed widespread popularity with all classes, and this had taken him to the threshold of the *dogado* or dogeship; but the friends, supporters and henchmen of Baiamonte were all nobles of ancient houses and were all famous and jealous of their own prestige, such as the Querini and Badoer families. His attempt to overthrow the system to his own advantage was thwarted precisely because he lacked real popular support, whereas among those who flocked to the aid of the doge Pietro Gradenigo in order to stop his path, were many craftsmen and common folk who demonstrated clearly that they preferred the political monopoly of the aristocracy to the personal dictatorship of a single great man. The affair had a lengthy aftermath, but the main consequence was the institution of a magistrature which was destined to play a large part in Venetian life, and gave birth to a dark legend almost as grim as the Spanish Inquisition. This was the Council of Ten, which features in infinite works of romantic literature, poetry, theater, music and even the cinema.

Another attempt to overthrow the system was tragically thwarted in 1355, when the doge Marino Falier took part in a conspiracy which this time was conceived and directed by authoritative members of the so-called *popolo grasso*, the wealthy bourgeoisie which practically all over Italy had brought to power princes or despotic rulers who were hated by the noble classes. The plot was discovered, and he paid for his failed attempt to rule "with a rod of iron" by decapitation. This time too, the common people refused to take the part of the conspirators, and indeed flocked to St. Mark's square together with the patricians in response to the urgent appeal launched by the government.

After this tragic affair (exploited fully by poets, musicians and painters such as Byron, Donizetti and Delacroix) the Venetian system of government took on a definite stabilized form. The Venetian state reached the height of its power in the first half of the 15th century, at the same time as the climax of its economic prosperity. Its internal systems went on developing even after

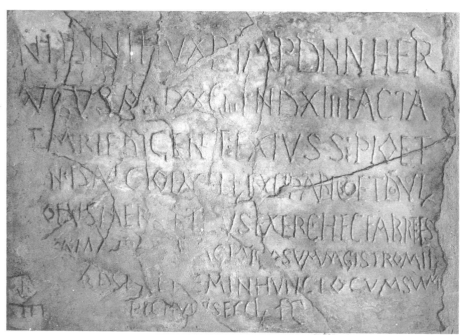

The stone carvings illustrated on this page are some of the earliest records of Venice's history. Above, left: the Lion of St. Mark with his closed book and his wings framing his head. This work dates from the 13th century, and is one of the earliest representations of the Venetian symbol. It stands at the base of the campanile of Sant'Aponal. Above right: detail of one of the columns from the ciborium in St. Mark's basilica. This piece is of unknown date and provenance, but according to tradition it was brought to Venice by doge Pietro II Orseolo after the Dalmatian expedition of 1000. Below: the original foundation stone of the cathedral of Torcello, bearing the inscription, "In the reign of Heraclius Augustus, by order of Isacius. exarch and patrician." This is the oldest Venetian historical document (639 A.D.).

Above: the Chair of St. Mark (St. Mark's Treasury). Alexandrian work, sixth to eighth century. Above, right: Attila's Chair at Torcello. Right: Alexander transported into heaven (St. Mark's, 12th century). Below: capital from the Doge's Palace. Below, right: pluteus with peacocks from the iconostasis of the cathedral of Torcello (10th to 11th century).

this, but no longer under the pressure of external events of varying degrees of dramatic intensity, instead by means of a lengthy process of debates, discussions, motions, orders of the day, arguments and voting sessions. In effect, the *serrata* had in no way put a block on what had been demonstrated since earliest times as the typical characteristic of Venetian politics: government by means of an assembly. Instead, once the *Maggior Consiglio* had been "locked," the Venetian Republic assumed even more broadly and comprehensively the characteristics of a republic that was first and foremost parliamentary.

But we must consider whether it is possible to confine by an all-embracing definition an organized reality as multicoloured and multiform as that of the republic of Venice. From Charles Diehl's "patrician republic" to Frederick C. Lane's "mercantile republic," modern historians have undertaken, without success, an attempt at schematization which eluded even theoricians and historians of the past, Venetians and others. In truth, just as Venice the city is something unique, which perhaps can be compared to others in certain details but as a whole has no counterpart, so Venice the Republic is also unique and defies categorization and analogy.

The city is as unique as the structure of the Venetian state, and there is a subtle resemblance between the two. Nothing gives such an impression of disorder as a map of Venice or a glance at the infinite stylistic, urban, topographical and physical details of the lagoon city; and yet the overall result is deeply harmonious. The same sensation of disorder and confusion – picturesque to a greater or lesser extent – is provoked by a glance at the Venetian system of government in the centuries during the height of its maturity; and yet the overall result is a harmony which, while perhaps not reaching perfection, at least represents one of the best achievements by a collective body towards the attempt to find a balanced and lasting constitution. Lasting indeed: in the history of Venice time has to be measured in large doses, and the Venetian Republic along with the Byzantine empire still holds the endurance record among all the European states.

The Keys to Power

At the head of the Republic, or rather, the most Serene Republic, as it was to be called in later centuries, surrounded by all exterior manifestations of sovereignty, the doge embodied the majesty of the state. He wore sumptuous garments, mantles of brocade and ermine, of gold and silver damask or scarlet silk, according to the season and the occasion. On his head he wore the doge's crown, the *corno*, or cap: there was one particularly precious version, the *zogia*, or jewel of independence, with which he was crowned at the top of the Giants' steps in the Doge's Palace, but he wore it only once a year, on Easter Day when he visited the church of San Zaccaria. Ordinarily he would wear a less opulent version, the *corno d'uso*, over the *camauro* or *rensa*, a characteristic kind of bonnet made of Rheims cloth. When he appeared in processions on the great liturgical feast-days such as Corpus Domini or Palm Sunday, or on the occasion of the innumerable solemn visits to a church or monastery (there were enough of these visits to span the whole year: January 6 to the cathedral of San Pietro di Castello for the feast of San Lorenzo Giustiniani, first patriarch of Venice, January 31 to Santa Marina in memory of the recapture of Padua against the Cambrai confederates in 1512, February 2 to Santa Maria Formosa in memory of the recovery of the Venetian brides carried off by the Narentine pirates in 935, and so on, almost daily) he would be preceded and followed by the insignia of the Byzantine royalty: silver trumpets, naked swords, the *cero*, chair, cushion, damask canopy, eight silk standards carrying the Lion of St. Mark, two of which were white, two red, two violet and two blue, symbolizing respectively peace, war, truce and allegiance. His image, on his knees before

Mark the evangelist, figured along with his name on coins; the same design was stamped on the signet ring on his finger, but where once was written *voluntas ducis*, the will of the doge; now, significantly, *voluntas senatus*. Stately and majestic as a Caesar or a pope, on Maundy Thursday he would preside at the celebrations in the Piazzetta, standing between the two red columns of the colonnade of the Doge's Palace. These celebrations were in commemoration of the defeat of the patriarch Ulrico of Aquileia, and culminated in the decapitation of a bull and 12 pigs, an irreverent allusion to the prelate and his ministers. On board his superb galley, the *Bucintoro*, a mass of carved and gilded decorations and rowed by a hundred workers from the Arsenal, he could be seen escorted by gondolas and boats of all kinds, all sumptuously adorned, crossing St. Mark's basin amid the sound of all the city bells and the thunder of all the artillery of the fleet; he would cross to San Nicolò di Lido, to the mouth of the port and the open sea, and there would toss into the waters of the Adriatic a wedding ring, while pronouncing the famous words: "We wed you, o sea, as a sign of true and perpetual dominion."

But when the doge died, he was seen to lie in state on the bier in the hall of the Piovego, with the doge's cap on his head, the rapier by his side and spurs on his feet, and was then followed by an enormous cortege (besides statesmen, ambassadors and patricians, there were all the priests and monks of the city: at the funeral of doge Giovanni Corner II there were as many as 6,000 people). From the Piovego the body was taken to the church of St. John and St. Paul for the funeral mass. But the body that in front of St. Mark's basilica was raised high nine times by

CANONICI · SCVDIERI DEL DOGE · CAMERARII SERENISSIMI PRINCIPIS · TROMBE PIFEARI · TVBÆ ET BARBITON · SERVITORI DELL'IMBASCIATORI · ORATOR. FAM.

seamen in deep silence, save for the cry "Misericordia!" repeated nine times, was but a dummy, with the doge's features modelled in wax. "*Sacco de pagia e mascara de cera/El cadaver la' del Serenissimo ...*" ("Sack of straw and mask of wax/That corpse of the most Serene ..."). The actual remains of the doge would have already been buried by night, in strict privacy, in his own family vault.

This extraordinary custom, which began with the death of the doge Giovanni Mocenigo in the early 16th century (though it seems to have

originated not from political motives but from the fear of contagion in times of plague) is profoundly significant. Respect, devotion and honour were due to his office; to office indeed, but not to the person. From a more or less absolute governor, as in the first few centuries, the doge had gradually become a magistrate, through a lengthy constitutional evolution. He was the first magistrate of the Republic but a magistrate whose powers, in order to avoid undesirable monarchial revivals, were limited – extremely limited in fact – and at every succession they were circumscribed yet

The Procession of the Doge on Palm Sunday. *The original engraving is four meters (13 feet) long, and was executed by Matteo Pagan between 1556 and 1559 (Museo Correr, Venice). The doge was the living symbol of the state's grandeur and dignity. The procession illustrated in the print was led by six silken standards decorated with the Lion of St. Mark. Next came silver trumpets and bugles, then the doge's chamberlains, canons vested in copes, the*

L'ILLVSTRISSINA · SIGNORIA · ILLVSTRISSIMVM · DOMINIVM · LA SPADA ENSIS · AMBASCIATORI VARII PRINCIPI · ORATORES DIVERSOR. PRINCIPVM · OMBRELA · IL SERENISSIMO · PRINC.

TROMBE | DI ARZENTO | SEX | TVBÆ ARGENTEÆ | COMANDATORI | PRÆCONES | GLI OTTO | STENDARDI | OCTO VEXILLA

patriarch in his pontifical vestments, the clergy and the secretaries. The dogeʼs crown, the golden chair and the golden cushion were borne by equerries. Behind the doge dressed in a robe of gold and ermine came the ambassadors, the sword-bearer and the Signoria in robes of velvet and damask.

further by the *correttori* to the dogeʼs oath, advisors who were punctually elected the day before every election to the supreme office. In fact the doge, though one of the very few Venetian magistrates without a time limit on his mandate, was also one of the very few Venetian magistrates to exercise his mandate alone. He was elected, once his predecessor had died (in the last 600 years of the Republic, only one doge, Francesco Foscari, abdicated, in 1457), by all the patrician members of the *Maggior Consiglio* in a procedure which in its complexity had no equal anywhere

else in the world. It consisted of a series of stages, in which voting by ballot alternated with selection by chance, and nominations alternated with eliminations: it began with a line-up of all the patricians (more than 1,000, and sometimes 2,000) before the voting urn, in which were the same number of brass marbles as the number of voters, and of which 30 were gilded. The "ballot-boy," a child of between eight and ten years of age and in theory selected at random, fished out the marbles without looking and one by one handed them to the nobles as they passed in front of him. The 30

IL CANTITIER GRANDI | SECRETARII | CORNO | CORNV | LA CANDELA | CERIVM ALBVM | PATRIARCA

CONSCIOUS SUPREMACY: THE MARRIAGE WITH THE SEA

"Desponsamus te, mare, in signum veri perpetuique dominii," We wed you, o sea, as a sign of true and perpetual dominion: with these words the doge threw a golden wedding ring from the *Bucintoro* into the sea on Ascension Day. This proud assertion of Venice's maritime power may have its origins in a *benedictio maris* (a blessing of the sea) at the time of Pietro II Orseolo's expedition against Dalmatia in 1000, to which the *desponsa-* *tio* was added when the legends surrounding the meeting of pope Alexander III and the emperor Frederick I at the peace of Venice in 1177 had taken shape, in order to confer legitimacy on Venice's control of the Adriatic.

The ceremonial route (1) began in the Piazza with the procession of the doge (2, from a painted panel of 1515), and after meeting up with the patriarchial barge finished at the Lido port (3), where the doge threw the ring into the sea. On its way out the *Bucintoro* passed through St. Mark's dock, returning via the Riva degli Schiavoni (4, from a painting by Francesco Guardi), stopping for Mass at the church of San Nicolò di Lido (5, also by Guardi).

The marriage with the sea was connected with the legend of the gift of a golden ring to the doge (6, detail of a canvas by Paris Bordon) by a fisherman who received if from

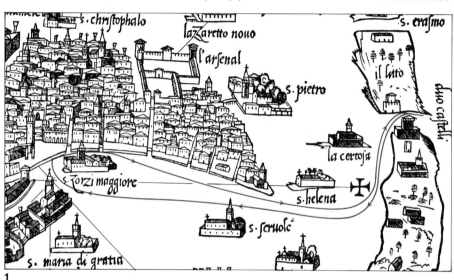

1

2

4

3

St. Mark on the tragic night in the reign of doge Bartolomeo Gradenigo on which Satan threatened the city with a fearful hurricane. By the end of the Republic, the ceremony was a colourful spectacle rather than a national event.

5　**6**

people who had received a gilded marble, the *balla d'oro*, remained, while the rest went away. In addition, every time a patrician received a gilded marble from the child, his name was cried out by the ushers, and all his relatives had to leave as well, because the remaining 30 had to belong to different families and be unconnected with one another in any way, whether by birth, marriage or business. Of these 30 chosen members, 21 were eliminated by chance methods, and it was up to 9 survivors to fill voting-papers with the names of 40 electors, which were instantly reduced to 12 by another selection of *balle d'oro*, the gilded marbles. The 12 chosen, who had to have a minimum majority of 9 votes, elected 25 new electors, 16 of whom were eliminated immediately at random, and the 9 left had to elect 45 new electors, of whom 11 were selected by the *balle d'oro* as those who would choose the electors of the doge. The 41 chosen electors (who could not have been among the 11, the 9 or the 11 chosen in the earlier stages) had the task of electing the *Serenissimo Principe*, the Most Serene Prince. This was carried out in a conclave which could last a very short while (such as the one for Pietro Grimani, elected at the first ballot in 1744) or a very long time (such as that for Carlo Contarini in 1655, when 68 ballots were needed). There could be several candidates, or, as in the case of the celebrated writer and historian Marco Foscarini, elected in 1762, a single candidate. Once elected, with a majority of at least 25 votes, the chosen man was the subject of a veritable apotheosis: he was presented to the people in St. Mark's basilica, taken round the square in a kind of sedan-chair carried by workmen from the Arsenal, tossing money to the crowd. Then there was the coronation and feasting which went on for three consecutive days. However, the most important act was the swearing of the *Promissione*: this was a document containing all the laws regarding the prerogatives of the doge, and above all, the limitations of his prerogatives.

By perusing the richly illuminated and bound copies of the *Promissioni ducali* which are kept in the Venetian archives, it is simple to discover how much was forbidden to that highly decorative personage who very often began at his coronation a long career of service to the Republic on the sea, in embassies, in the governing of colonies and subject cities, in the administration of justice, but above all in the exhausting and never-ending activity of parliamentary government. In the first place, he could not propose measures which would increase his own powers, nor could he abdicate unless asked to do so. He could not receive anyone in his official capacity without his advisors present, nor could he give private audiences. In public audiences, such as when he received foreign ambassadors (this was one of his prerogatives), he had to agree his replies with his advisors. If anyone, in any circumstances, spoke to him alone on matters of state he was obliged to change the subject. The doge could not display his own coat of arms in public, nor raise canopies over his throne. Neither he nor his associates could for any reason give or receive gifts except between very close relatives. He could not allow anyone to kiss his hand or kneel before him: Agostino Barbarigo allowed this and was the object of such hatred that when he died, as one chronicler notes, "it was amazing to hear the curses heaped on him by all." Lorenzo Celsi, who kept lions and leopards in the palace and had a page precede him carrying a kind of scepter, risked ending up like Marino Falier, if he had not died first (of a broken heart, it was said, after a councillor had snapped his ill-omened scepter before his very eyes and the Council of Ten had started a legal action against him). He could only leave the palace in official guise (though in the 18th century, several doges would go out secretly in disguise, to go to the *Filarmonici* 'club' at the end of the square, where a room was kept for the use of the Most Serene). He could not go to the theater, to a café or attend *conversazioni*. In order to leave the city for a holiday he had to ask permission and prove that it was necessary for his health. A number of restrictions were imposed on his family, children and brothers too: they surrendered the right to vote in constitutional assemblies, and could not accept benefices or ecclesiastical honours. It is no wonder that some respected politicians viewed the prospect of the threat of election as doge with horror.

A vast spirit of self-sacrifice was needed to submit to all the restrictions which invaded private and family life (we have quoted only a few examples) and to bear the strain of a diary packed with engagements. Some of these would be in his

The "lion's mouths" or "mouths or truth" situated in the streets or on the walls of magistrates' palaces allowed the people to influence public affairs and justice by placing secret denunciations in them. Such denunciations had to be signed by at least two witnesses before they could be taken up, unless the chiefs of the Council of Ten and the Dogal Councillors voted by a five-sixths majority that they concerned a matter of state.

representative capacity, but some were quite taxing, such as obligatory participation in more or less all the meetings of the constitutional assemblies and the collective offices to which the exercise of power had been delegated. It is even less surprising that the relatives of many a candidate for the *dogado* should be troubled when presented with the possibility that their kinsman might reach the winning-post: apart from everything else, there was the risk of a gross reduction in the family's wealth as, if a fairly heavy civil list was conferred on the doge, the list of expenses for which he was personally liable was much more substantial: in later times, three years of the civil list were hardly enough to cover the cost of feasting for the elections, and besides, there was the expense of all the sumptuous vestments and cloaks which alone were worth a fortune. He was also obliged to make expensive gifts to the basilica of St. Mark, and yet was forbidden to pursue any commercial, industrial or financial activity engaged in before his election to the throne, though his privileges did not include tax exemption. Once the doge was dead, the funeral ceremonies over and the funeral orations uttered, there was the *redde rationem*: the *inquisitori sul doge defunto* (the "investigators of the late doge") nit-picked their way through the documents of the deceased to ascertain the legitimacy of expenses incurred and collected income, and if they found any irregularity, it was up to the heirs to take the consequences. A great doge like Leonardo Loredan, the life-blood of the resistance against the Cambrai confederates, was the subject of a *post mortem* inquiry lasting over two years, concluding with an injunction for the heirs to refund 2,700 ducats considered to have been illegally appropriated as income. (It was true that the doge and his family had contributed vast amounts towards the expenses of the war, but these were voluntary contributions and did not cancel out the alleged illegality.)

However, it is true that when the "most excellent Forty-one" elected as doge some not inestimable person but a shrewd and skilled parliamentarian, limitations or not, the *Serenissimo* could count, and count heavily too. Not all were found out with regard to their ambitions or projects, like Agostino Barbarigo, or Andrea Gritti, a courageous general who hungered after

The Hall of the Maggior Consiglio *in the Doge's Palace during a plenary session, engraving by Paolo Forlani, 1566. The* Maggior Consiglio *was the sovereign body of the Venetian state, in which all the officers of state met. Here laws were passed, and elections to the high posts in the Republic held. It consisted of all the patricians of more than 25 years of age. Inquiries were undertaken by small commissions which were entrusted with the preparatory work, votes taking place in the plenary assembly. At such times the doge sat on the* Tribunale, *also known as the* Bancale di San Marco, *flanked by the* Serenissima Signoria. *Members of the council occupied the seats along the walls and the double rows of benches which were placed back to back.*

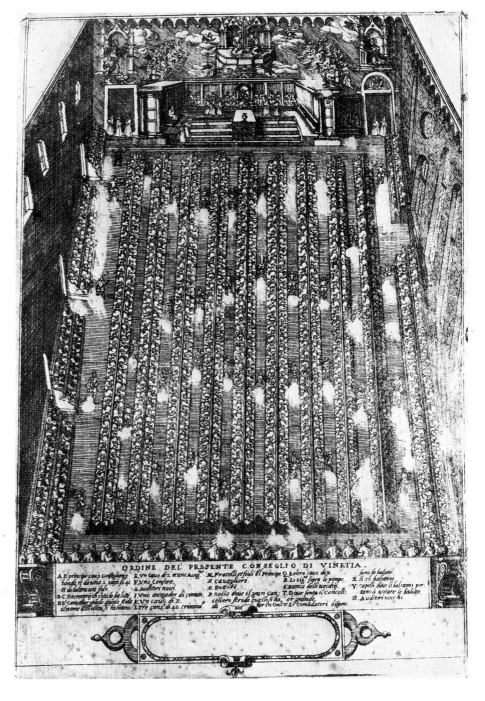

ARBORE SIMBOLOGICO
Nel quale apertamente si scorge il Modo facile, e sicuro di elegger il Serenissimo Doge di Venetia

IL SERENISSIMO MAGGIOR CONSEGLIO PROPONE E CONFERMA

Il Serenissimo Maggior Conseglio

A Con Balle d'Oro nu. 30. cavate à sorte ellegge 30 Nobili del medemo, che restano parimente à sorte n. 9.
B Con 7. Balle, e non meno del predetto n.9. vengono eletti n 40., che à sorte restano questi n.12.
C Con 9. Balle, e non meno del predetto n.12. vengono eletti n 25., che à sorte restano questi n.9.
D Con 7 Balle, e non meno del predetto n.9. vengono eletti n 25., che à sorte restano questi n.9.
E Con 9. Balle, e non meno del predetto n.9. vengono eletti n 45., che à sorte restano n.11.
F Con 9. Balle, e non meno del predetto n. 11. vengono eletti n 41., che con il quale s'aumano anivanza al Trono Ducale, il Nobile fortunato, & eletto.

At first the doge was elected by the popular assembly, but later on the elections became indirect, and fell into the hands of a closed group of people. The electoral process evolved gradually until it was codified in a law of 1268. In order to eliminate corruption, lottery and voting alternated, until the 41 members of the conclave had been chosen. The first process was for a boy called the ballottino to draw ballot-balls at random, giving

The Most Serene Republic

Who were then the real holders of power in the Venetian constitution at the height of its maturity? We have already pointed out that the doge was in effect unable to carry out any act of government alone: he could not even open letters from ambassadors or governors of cities and provinces – though according to custom, these were formally addressed to him. For any of his acts to be legitimate, the presence of the dogal advisors was indispensable. The doge, together with his councillors, constituted an organ of government which in itself was the figurehead of the state as a whole. There were six Dogal Councillors, one for each of the *sestieri* or quarters into which the city of Venice is divided. These are Castello, Cannaregio, Dorsoduro, San Marco, San Polo, and Santa Croce. Altogether they make up what was first called the *Minor Consiglio*, *Consilium Minus*, an obvious contrast with the great legislative assembly, the *Maggior Consiglio*. The six councillors, together with the doge and the three heads of the *Quarantia Criminal*, the major judiciary magistrature, formed *la Serenissima Signoria*, the Most Serene Signory, the apex of the Venetian state.

Let us join the councillors as they meet, awaiting the doge in the great hall of the palace, still known as the "hall of scarlet" after the colour of their gowns. They could not be related to the doge, stayed in office for eight months, and were elected by the *Maggior Consiglio* at random dates, three at a time. Once their period of office was up, they remained in the Senate a further two months retaining the right to vote. Their origin is closely linked with the progressive limitation of the monarchic power of the doge: they had already made an appearance (but as small fry at that time) in 1033, alongside the doge Domenico Flabianico; and in 1204, when the marshal of Champagne, Geoffroy de Villehardouin, introduced himself to doge Enrico Dandolo in order to request Venice's help for what would be the fourth crusade, the councillors were already enthroned in full capacity beside the Most Serene Lord, rather to control and discipline than act as advisors in the true sense of the word.

It was in fact specifically part of their duties not just to collaborate with the doge, but to curb and

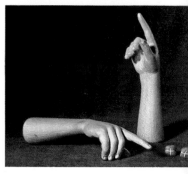

power and in order to impose his point of view had to pretend to support the opposite opinion. The observance of the *Promissione* did not prevent Francesco Foscari from getting Venetian expansion under way on the mainland, as leader of a militant political party, nor Leonardo Donà dalle Rose from commanding in extremely dramatic circumstances the struggle against pope Paul V in defense of the sovereignty of the Venetian state. However, not all doges were of the caliber of Silvestro Valier, "great statesman, perfect politician," or of Francesco Dandolo or Nicolò Contarini, to mention but a few of the most notable of the 120 doges that held the office up until 1797. For long periods in the 15th, 16th and 17th centuries, the doge's seat was occupied by venerable old men whose decrepitude was usually coupled with immense wealth and a neutral personality which was incapable of creating as much as the shadow of a problem. Under such conditions, the doge was the splendid incarnation of power held and manipulated by others.

control his actions. At least once a year, in the first week of October they had to read the *Promissione* to the doge so that he would not forget it, and it was their duty to admonish him whenever he seemed to be deviating from it. We have already mentioned the councillor that snapped Lorenzo Celsi's scepter in front of him, because the unfortunate doge, otherwise a most worthy, cultured and patriotic person and a respected friend of the poet Petrarch, had insisted it be carried before him. There are other examples which may be less dramatic but are equally significant when councillors intervened instantly and occasionally with extreme severity towards the doge. In 1464, for example, Cristoforo Moro was to assume command of the fleet for the crusade which pope Pius II wished to organize against the Turks. However, as he was no expert in naval matters, apart from being old and feeble, he did not want to go. The councillor Vettor Cappello replied sharply that "it is necessary for you to go, for our land cannot do without your services in these times of need." Two centuries later, the doge Domenico Contarini, as popular and well-loved as Moro had been unpopular and disliked, introduced into a speech in reply to an ambassador a note of authoritarianism. The

one to each member of the Maggior Consiglio over 30 years of age. The 30 members who drew a golden ballot ball in this lottery were then reduced to 9, again by lot, who then in turn proposed 40 names. At this point voting entered the process, as each of the 40 had to obtain 7 out of the 9 possible votes in order to be confirmed. These 40 were then reduced to 12 by a further process of lottery, who then chose 45 electors by vote, who were in turn reduced by lottery to 11. These were the electors of the electors of the doge, who selected the 41 members of the conclave by vote. These 41 finally put forward the candidates for the position of doge. These names were then voted for with crimson ballot-balls, which were deposited into as many urns as there were candidates. In order to be elected doge, a candidate had to obtain at least 25 votes. Opposite, far left: engraving from the Venice State Archives showing a symbolic representation of the complex electoral process.

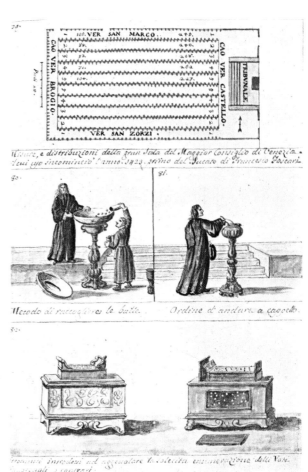

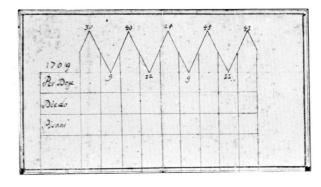

Facing page, above right: the ballottino *(from* Varie Venete Curiosità Sacre e Profane *by Jan (Giovanni) Grevembroch, 1755–1765). Center: a voting-urn. Below: wooden hands used by the ballottino to count the ballot-balls in the final vote (Museo Correr, Venice). Left: another page from the State Archives explaining the electoral system. Above: plan of the* Maggior Consiglio *and illustrations of the voting procedure. Below: one of the* ballot-papers used in the election of 1709 in which Giovanni Corner was elected doge.

MODO DELL' ELEZIONE DEL SERENISSIMO PRINCIPE DI VENEZIA.

Tutti deuono passare le eta d'Anni. 30

Morto il Doge, i Configlieri, ed i Capi di Quaranta a' quali appartiene tutto il Governo della Città, vanno ad abitare nel Palazzo Ducale, e chiamafi gran Configlio, e fi eleggono cinque Correttori della Promiffione del Doge, e degli Ordini del Palazzo, e fimilmente tre Inquifitori delle operazioni del Doge morto: il che fucede in tre, o quattro giorni, e fatti li Funerali a fi chiama gran Configlio, folamente con quelli, che eccedono Anni trenta, e viene letta, e confirmata la Promiffione predetta. Si mettono poi in un Cappello numerato il Configlio, tante Balle, quanti Gentiluomini fono nel Configlio, delle quali ne fono trenta d'Oro, e tutte l'altre d'Argento. E vanno un Configliero il più giovane, ed un Capo di Quaranta in Chiefa di S. Marco, e trovano un fanciullo, dimandato il Ballottino, e quello conducono nel Configlio, e vengono chiamati a Cappello tutti i Nobili del Configlio. Il fanciullo, per ciafcuno mette la mano dentro il Cappello, e fe piglia Balla d'Oro, quello per cui l'ha tolta, riman eletto; frattanto ufcendo del Configlio alla pubblicazione di ciafcheduno eletto il Padre, Figliuoli, i Fratelli, i Zii di lui, e tutti della fua Famiglia; ma fe la Balla è d'Argento fi parte. Onde quelli, a i quali toccano le dette trenta Balle d'Oro, tratti però di diverfe Famiglie, e uno per Famiglia, che non vi fia Parentela alcuna, nè congiunzione di fangue tale, che come fi dice) fi fcacciano di Cappello, fono detti i primi trenta, e tutto il refto del Configlio fi parte. Poi mettendofi nel Cappello Balle trenta delle quali nove fono d'Oro, l'altre d'Argento; e per ognuno il fanciullo ne piglia una. Quelli a' quali toccano le nove d'Oro rimangono eletti, gli altri fono licenziati. Quefti nove rinchiufi, eleggono 40. con fette Balle delle nove, a quefto modo, che gettate le Teffere di primo, fecondo, ec.

ai 4. primi tocca la elezione di 5. per ciafcuno, ed agli altri cinque tocca folamente di 4., che tutto fanno il numero di 40. i quali eletti, chiamafi di nuovo gran Configlio, e fono pubblichati i predetti 40. e gli altri fi partono, e mettonfi 40. Balle nel Cappello delle quali 12. fono d'Oro, ed a cui toccano, reftano eletori, gli altri fi partono. Quefti 12. eleggono 25. con nove Balle in quefta guifa, che al primo tocca la elezione di tre, ed agli altri, e due per ciafcuno, che fanno il numero di 25. Fatta quefta elezione chiamafi gran Configlio, e pubblicano li 25. e gli altri partono. Poi mettono 25. Balle nel Cappello delle quali nove fon d'Oro; quefti a chi toccano, reftano elettori, gli altri fono licenziati. E detti nove eleggono 45. con 7. Balle, in tal maniera, che ne toccano 5. per ciafcuno, che fanno il numero di 45. è chiamato gran Configlio, fi pubblicano li 45. eletti, gli altri fono licenziati. Si mettono poi 45. Balle nel Cappello, delle quali 11. fono d'Oro, ed a cui toccano refta 11man eletori, e gli altri fi partono. Quefti undeci fono quelli, che eleggono il Quarantuno con nove Balle a quefto modo, che gettate le Teffere come di fopra, a primi otto toccano cinque, agli ultimi tre, tocca di tre folamente per ciafcuno, che tutti fanno il giufto numero di Quarantuno. Fatta quefta elezione è chiamato gran Configlio, anco con quelli, che non arrivano a trenta Anni, e fono condannati da quefto. Ora, creati li Quarantuno, udita la Meffa dello Spirito Santo, e dato loro il giuramento, fi ferrano, e con Balle di Scarlato fegnate di Croce Gialla, eleggono il Doge con Balle 25.

councillor Piero Basadonna intervened with these chilly words: "Your Serene Highness speaks as a sovereign prince, but should remember that we are not lacking in the means to punish you when you err from your duty." Apart from controlling the doge, the most Serene Signory also had guard-dog functions with regard to the electors of the doge: when they dallied too long in the intricacies of the conclave, the Signory could present itself in all its majesty on the doorstep and peremptorily invite the "most excellent Forty-one" to hurry up. Besides this role of vigilance, the Signory had many other, more positive duties. It had the task of settling the organization of elections to the various offices and magistratures and controlling the process; the *consiglieri* had to take weekly turns at the presidency of the *Maggior Consiglio*, and the councillor on duty had to answer the *eccitamenti* or queries first, and open and close the parliamentary debates. Together with the doge, the councillors sat on all the legislative and executive councils including the Council of Ten. Each one in turn took part in the dreaded tribunal of the State Inquisitors, and when the doge was on

holiday, the Signory took charge of governing, and one of its members assumed (in cases where the doge was absent from Venice) the title and functions of vice-doge.

However, this high-level committee was likewise subject to limitations and controls. While it was true that the doge could not leave Venice without two councillors at his heels, it is also true that no councillor could leave Venice for so much as a single day without the permission of the doge. Though the doge could not reply to ambassadors without his councillors, they could not do so either without the authorization of the Senate; the Signory needed the consent of the Senate to take any decision involving public expenditure, or if they wanted to allocate any kind of office; its every interpretation of the laws was subject to revision by the Senate. Elected by the *Maggior Consiglio*, the *scarlatti* or *rossi*, "reds" as the common people referred to them, had authority and scope, but this was limited and controlled by the doge and the Senate.

Now the Senate came into its own in all its authority: it was an assembly which, according to Francesco Maria della Rovere, duke of Urbino, was the wisest head in the world, since, as written in the study carried out by Federico Badoer in 1582, a politician but also a highly sophisticated humanist, it was a perfect body in that it was composed of categories of members: the young, daring by nature, the old, made cautious and suspicious by experience, and middle-aged men who were therefore at the height of their perceptive faculties and balanced and sure. Instituted in around 1255, the *Consiglio dei Pregadi* (*consilium rogatorum* because the members were "begged" to convene) normally referred to simply as the *Pregadi*, originally consisted of 60 members. Later, these 60 members of the *Pregadi* were supplemented by another 60 who were called the *Zonta* ("addition") and the election of all 120 members was entrusted to the *Maggior Consiglio*, However, gradually the 120 were joined by numerous magistrates, who took part in the assembly with or without *balla*, that is the right to vote: at the fall of the Republic, the Senate, that is, the *Pregadi* plus the *Zonta* plus the other magistrates with or without the right to vote, numbered 275, all elected, all with a limited time in power (one year for the members of the *Pregadi* and *Zonta*,

The dogaressa *(the doge's wife) flanked by two ladies. Engraving from Giacomo Franco's* Habiti d'huomeni et donne venetiane, *1610 (Biblioteca Marciana, Venice). The* dogaressa *was also charged with solemn honours and duties which were laid down in the dogal* Promissione *or oath, and included prohibitions against accepting gifts, recommending people for offices, or entering into trade. In compensation she was solemnly inducted into her duties with lavish ceremony. She was escorted from the* Bucintoro *by the Grand Chancellor and four councillors, and received in the basilica by the canons where she swore the* Promissione *and heard the* Te Deum. *Then she made her entry into the Doge's Palace escorted by a long procession of gentlemen and patricians, where she was received by the members of the craft guilds who exhibited their most precious wares in her honour: carpets, tapestries, glass and arms.*
Opposite: engraving by Giulio Goltzio in G. G. Boissard's Habitus, *1581, showing the doge and* dogaressa *in their rich state attire. Both the doge and* dogaressa *as well as their parents, who also lived in the Doge's Palace, were exempt from the sumptuary laws. As a mark of her exalted position, the* dogaressa *had the right to wear the* corno, *the dogal crown, although hers was smaller than the doge's.*

and varying lengths of office for the other magistratures) – apart from the doge and the nine procurators of St. Mark, who held the only lifelong offices in the Venetian patriciate.

"Land Senate" and "Sea Senate"

The miles of cupboards containing the acts and debates of the Senate in the enormous Venetian state archives, divided into two great classifications, "Land Senate" and "Sea Senate," give some idea of the vast scope of the powers held by this parliamentary assembly, which combined legislative and executive powers, but which nevertheless is perhaps closer than any other body in the Venetian constitution to what we nowadays call the government. This was a government of 275 members! We mentioned right from the start that one of the characteristics of the Venetian political scene was the emphasis on government by assembly. In fact, this government of 275 members was responsible in the most difficult times for crucial decisions, main-line policies, and oper-ational directives; and it has been said many times that this represents one of the principal reasons for many mistaken decisions and much indecision and evasion. This is true. On the other hand, if we consider that between the institution of the *Consiglio dei Pregadi* and the fall of the Republic of Venice, there are a good 542 years, it does make one realize that this kind of government by assembly has proved more efficient than many individual governments.

In the jungle of duties assigned to the Senate, the direction of foreign affairs figures prominently. For the Venetian state, foreign politics were vital. In earliest times Venice's survival depended on her knife-edge relationships with Byzantium on the one side, and the Longobard kingdom, the Carolingian empire and then the Romano-Germanic empire on the other. As the net of Venetian commerce gradually spread wider, as new roads opened up, struggling over the great land-masses of the Alps, down into the huge valleys of central Asia, through the snows of Pamir, the sands of the Trans-Jordan or the rocks of the Gobi desert, as new routes were ploughed

Above: a procurator of St. Mark from a miniature in Paolo Belegno's Capitolare, *1362. The office was instituted in the ninth century, when a single procurator was appointed to administer the basilica. Later the number of procurators was increased to nine, entrusted with the administration of the state's revenue, and from the 13th century with the duties of legal guardians and commissioners for oaths. They were nominated by the* Maggior Consiglio, *and the festival in honour of their appointment lasted for three days, ending in a solemn procession from the church of San Salvador to the basilica.*

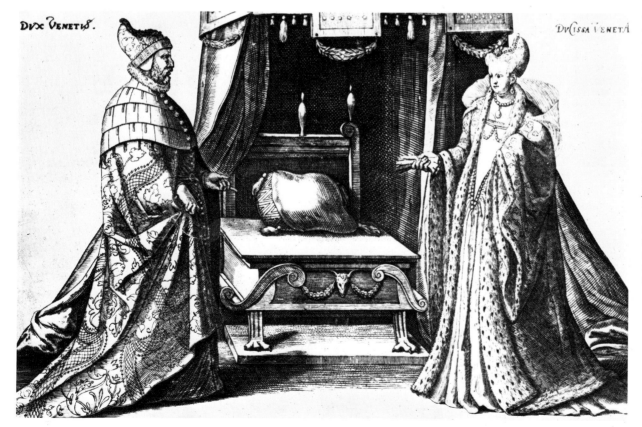

the famous reports which represent for the modern scholar the richest existing sources for dates, details, judgements and evaluations concerning most of the great European states and many eastern countries. They are extraordinary documents not only because of the meticulously collected information, but also because of the lucidity of analysis. These reports would be sent to the Senate daily by each ambassador starting from the moment he set out from Venice right up until his return. The despatches are so detailed that some have felt that in their precision (and no item of news is neglected, however intimate or private it might be, regarding kings and queens, ministers and their favoured women and everyone concerned in the power structure of the country to which the ambassador was attached) they reflect the Venetian passion for gossip. But in the Senate they became precious tools for the task of interpretation and evaluation. We will often have cause to return to the question of the action and effect of Venetian diplomacy, to which must be ascribed an indisputable priority as far as the institution of permanent diplomatic representatives in various courts is concerned, and which was hyper-active right from earliest time. There are particular Venetian ambassadors whose personalities will always be models of capability and wisdom as well as showing a spirit of devotion to duty that occasionally reached the level of heroism. The most extraordinary was possibly Alvise Contarini, first made ambassador at the age of 25. He spent all his life constantly abroad, engaged on an unending series of missions, each more delicate than the last, and culminating in the lengthy, complex and wearing negotiations for the drafting of the Westphalian peace (1648) which re-established, mainly through his efforts, European equilibrium after the tragedy of the Thirty Years' War. When plenipotentiary in Constantinople in 1638, he was imprisoned on the orders of the sultan who was enraged because of a serious incident (the *provveditore* Marino Cappello had sunk 15 Algerian pirate ships in the Ottoman anchorage of Valona, Albania). Even in that unpleasant and dangerous situation he was able to maneuver in such a way as to avoid catastrophic consequences for Venetian-Turkish relations. The Constantinople embassy was in any case traditionally risky: the Turks were quick to arrest,

Left: page from the Promissione *of Andrea Dandolo, 1342 (Museo Correr, Venice). This was the doge's oath of office, which defined his powers and prerogatives. Above: the Grand Councillor, head of the dogal chancellery, before doge Antonio Venier. Miniature from the* Cronaca *of Raffaino Caresini (Biblioteca Marciana, Venice).*

A councillor, from the Capitolare dei Consiglieri di Venezia *in the Museo Correr, Venice. Opposite: the entrance to the Arsenal.*

by the processions of mercantile ships from the West to the East, from Southampton to Alexandria in Egypt, Bruges to the Azov Sea, so the net of Venetian diplomacy had to extend and widen in order to conclude agreements and contracts, to secure privileges, negotiate better prices and defeat rivals. Skilled diplomacy was indispensable right from earliest times in order to cover and guarantee a developing economy and an independence that had been won with difficulty amongst powerful and dangerous neighbours. The ability to negotiate successfully became ever more essential as, with the gradual growth of prosperity and power, the jealousy, envy, greed and hostility of other peoples also increased. With the founding and establishment of great national states such as France and Spain, and the emergence in the West of a great multi-national power such as the Ottoman empire, these dangers became more and more threatening so that to control and defend herself from them, Venice had to use ever more refined forms of dialogue.

It was in the Senate that Venetian ambassadors, on their return from their assignments, would read

THE ARSENAL: THE HEART OF NAVAL STRENGTH

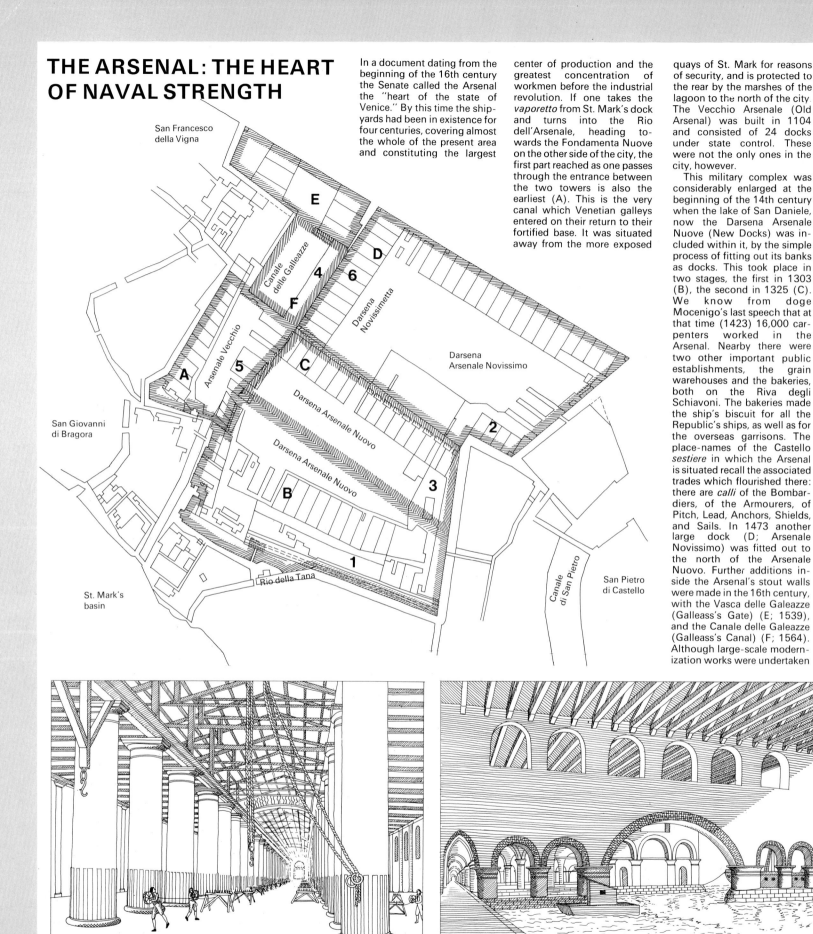

San Francesco della Vigna

San Giovanni di Bragora

St. Mark's basin

Arsenale Vecchio

Canale delle Galeazze

Darsena Novissimetta

Darsena Arsenale Novissimo

Darsena Arsenale Nuovo

Darsena Arsenale Nuovo

Rio della Tana

Canale di San Pietro

San Pietro di Castello

In a document dating from the beginning of the 16th century the Senate called the Arsenal the "heart of the state of Venice." By this time the shipyards had been in existence for four centuries, covering almost the whole of the present area and constituting the largest center of production and the greatest concentration of workmen before the industrial revolution. If one takes the *vaporetto* from St. Mark's dock and turns into the Rio dell'Arsenale, heading towards the Fondamenta Nuove on the other side of the city, the first part reached as one passes through the entrance between the two towers is also the earliest (A). This is the very canal which Venetian galleys entered on their return to their fortified base. It was situated away from the more exposed quays of St. Mark for reasons of security, and is protected to the rear by the marshes of the lagoon to the north of the city. The Vecchio Arsenale (Old Arsenal) was built in 1104 and consisted of 24 docks under state control. These were not the only ones in the city, however.

This military complex was considerably enlarged at the beginning of the 14th century when the lake of San Daniele, now the Darsena Arsenale Nuove (New Docks) was included within it, by the simple process of fitting out its banks as docks. This took place in two stages, the first in 1303 (B), the second in 1325 (C). We know from doge Mocenigo's last speech that at that time (1423) 16,000 carpenters worked in the Arsenal. Nearby there were two other important public establishments, the grain warehouses and the bakeries, both on the Riva degli Schiavoni. The bakeries made the ship's biscuit for all the Republic's ships, as well as for the overseas garrisons. The place-names of the Castello *sestiere* in which the Arsenal is situated recall the associated trades which flourished there: there are *calli* of the Bombardiers, of the Armourers, of Pitch, Lead, Anchors, Shields, and Sails. In 1473 another large dock (D; Arsenale Novissimo) was fitted out to the north of the Arsenale Nuovo. Further additions inside the Arsenal's stout walls were made in the 16th century, with the Vasca delle Galeazze (Galleass's Gate) (E; 1539), and the Canale delle Galeazze (Galleass's Canal) (F; 1564). Although large-scale modernization works were undertaken

1

2

in the last decades of the Republic to bring the yards technically up to date, it was only under Austrian rule that the perimeter of the surrounding walls was further enlarged. This great state enterprise was administered by a council, the *Eccellentissima Banca*, which consisted of three Senators, the *Provveditori dell'Arsenale* and three *patroni*, who were members of the *Maggior Consiglio*. These men had a tour of duty lasting a fortnight in the course of which they had to sleep in the Arsenal, keep the keys of the warehouses and workshops, and inspect the guard during the night.

On the technical side, the head of the Arsenal was the *magnifico armiraglio* who commanded the different *protomagistri* or *proti*, from whose ranks the *armiraglio* was chosen. These were the heads of the different groups of specialized craftsmen such as the *marangoni* (carpenters), caulkers, oar-makers, smiths, sawyers and the saltpeter or gunpowder workers. The Arsenal in Venice fulfilled all the functions performed by any modern arsenal. It was a protected naval base, a maintenance and refitting station, and a repository of equipment, provisions, and armaments. It was also a shipyard in which the state's vessels were built, kept in working order and armed. In 1597, when the Turks attacked Cyprus, 100 galleys in all were put in fighting order in two months, part newly built, part refitted with arms. The drawings on these pages illustrate the diversity and complexity of work in the yards. The rope-factory played a very important part: here all ropes were made from hemp.

Until the introduction of iron in the 19th century the main raw materials used in ship-building were hemp, pitch and timber. The Tana or Casa del Canevo (Hemp Shop) was a feature of Antonio da Ponte's reconstruction of 1579-83, measured 315 metres (1,033 feet) in length, and was divided into three naves of 84 columns (1). Da Ponte was not the only great Venetian architect to work in the Arsenal: Sammicheli built the stocks for the *Bucintoro*, and Sansovino designed the two functional but elegant covered wet-docks called the *Gaggiandre* (2; 1573) in the the Arsenale Novissimo. The artillery stores were known as the "iron garden" by the distinguished visitors whom the Republic admitted for propaganda purposes and for reasons of prestige (3). At the fall of the Republic the Arsenal contained 5,293 fire-pieces. The building stocks occupied almost all the banks of the basins (6). The sail-shops (5), where sails were cut out and stitched were as important as the oar-shops. The constant efforts of the state to ensure that the Arsenal remained efficient is illustrated by the construction of the timber workshop in 1778 (4). Here the timber for the latest type of vessel, the line-of-battle ship, was laid out in full scale and cut.

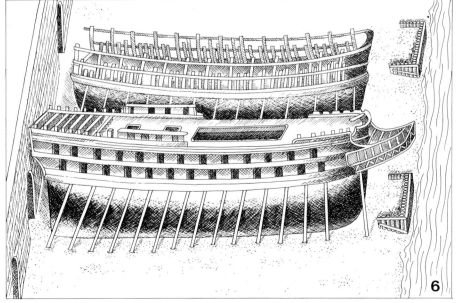

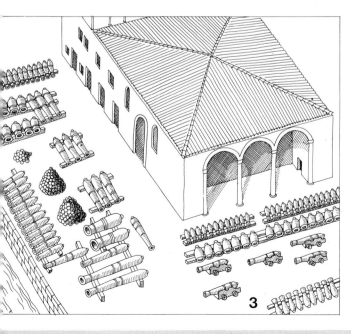

Above: illustration of a dockyard worker, after Grevembroch. These men formed a large and privileged body in the Republic. They worked in the docks and in the port, kept watch for fires, and were the only citizens permitted to work in the mint.

Below: plan of the Arsenal dating from the 16th century (Museo Correr, Venice).

and casual with the scimitar. Marcantonio Barbaro learnt this to his cost. He was the cultured humanist patron of Paolo Veronese (who also continued to negotiate from the tower in which he was imprisoned) and Giovanni Soranzo who was dragged in chains through the streets of Constantinople, a butt of ridicule, after his interpreter (or *dragomanno*) Giannantonio Grillo had been assassinated in prison in 1648. The ambassador Giovanni Cappello, also an exceptional man, died from virtual humiliation and deprivation in the castle of Adrianople in 1652, and his secretary Giovanni Ballarin was also to perish there after eight years' imprisonment, during which time he was constantly trying to reopen diplomatic negotiations. Other Venetian diplomats, such as Caterino Zeno and Giosafat Barbaro, in the course of their missions, explored remote, unknown regions, establishing contacts which could later prove useful in economic dealings. However, it would be a mistake to imagine these indefatigable negotiators as smiling diplomats, honey-tongued and quick to compromise at any cost: when pope Julius II, a notorious hot-head, ranted and raved that he would reduce Venice to the fishing-village it actually was, the ambassador Giorgio Dolfin replied, stony-faced, that the Republic would

reduce the pope to the status of "any village curate."

On the same level as foreign policy, the Senate also dealt with economic and financial affairs. In its ranks were the magistrates engaged in the exaction of direct taxes and the up-dating of the register (*governatori delle entrade, dieci savi sopra le decime, provveditori sopra camere*), the apportioning of the money gathered (*camerlenghi di comun*), the collecting of customs duty (*provveditori sopra dazi*), government accounts (*uffiziali alle rason vecchie, uffiziali alle rason nove, provveditori sopra conti*) and the controlling of the banking system (*provveditori sopra Banchi*). However, the Senate also elected a number of other very important magistrates who took no part in their cabinet, but were directly responsible to it. These were the three *deputati alla provvision del danaro*, (delegates for the provision of money) and the *savio cassier* (literally the wise cashier), who together formed the Ministry of Finance. Then there were the *scansadori alle spese superflue*, a kind of "axe commission" permanently engaged on the reduction in public spending, and the magistrates who supervised the mint with regard to issuing money and the preservation of public and private deposits of precious metals, including the men that looked after the state mint's activities in its functions as a savings bank, and those who controlled its activities as an investment bank for state deposits. Finally, they also elected the *depositario al Banco Ziro*, that is, the governor of the state bank, founded in 1619.

As well as these, there was a string of offices concerned with food supply, stores and price control (carried out in exemplary fashion, judging by the rare shortages in comparison with what happened in the rest of Europe). The Senate also nominated five *savi alla Mercanzia*, to whom was entrusted research into the means, routes and facilities which could favour expansion of Venetian trade in the world, and which could nourish and revitalize it. The magistrature of the *inquisitor alle Arti* was employed from 1707 onwards in the same task with regard to industry and crafts, and it should be noted that during the last phase of the Venetian economic decline both institutions busied themselves with all kinds of studies, conferences and proposals to combat extrava-

Above: naval architect. Below: the Armiraglio of the Arsenal (after Grevembroch). This officer oversaw the yards and had large and independent powers in directing and maintaining them. Below: the Arsenal bridge, from a painting by Canaletto (Duke of Bedford collection. Woburn Abbey). The bridge could be raised to allow vessels to pass.

gance, even though unfortunately the lucidity of the diagnoses, clarity of ideas and intelligence of the proposals were not always backed by equal tenacity and energy in their realization. One of the most prominent political personalities of the last phase of the republic was one of these "inquisitors for the Arts." This was the procurator Andrea Tron, whose reports to the Senate can still be read with great interest, so lucid and accurate are his analyses and deductions. However, in reality, the application of remedies did not fall within his power, nor those of the Senate. In such a situation, by then totally compromised and weakened, it was not only the Venetian economy that went by the board, but Venice herself that drifted towards an end that was by now inevitable and close at hand.

Another field in which the Venetian state demonstrated a legislative acumen which in this case survived its general decline, was that concerning control over waterways and defense and exploitation of the land. Water was a vital feature for this amphibious capital, which depended in several ways on the lagoon surrounding it, but also on the mainland, broken up with its quantity of rivers, some large such as the Po and the Adige, some shorter, like the Piave, the Sile and the Tagliamento, but all capable of sudden fury, and many, such as the Piave, Sile, Brenta,

Bacchiglione, Musone and so on, opening on to the lagoon. The question of hydrographics took its place in the body of the Senate in the form of three *esecutori alle Acque* ("water executives"), but all other magistrates were also directly involved and together formed the *Collegio delle Acque*: there were three *savi* and one *aggiunto inquisitor*, plus the three *provveditori all'Adige*, who specialized in looking after the most troublesome of the rivers of the Veneto. Care of the lagoon, as well as all problems to do with drainage and ecological balance (swamps, land reclamation, etc.) fell to another magistracy elected by the Senate, the three *provveditori ai Beni Inculti*. All these state bodies concerned with matters which today are often neglected (particularly in Italy), with sometimes catastrophic results, employed the best consultants and technicians that could be found. This technical skill was matched by a broadmindedness and sharp vision on the part of the acting magistrates and the Senate when tackling the problems, and is demonstrated by the grand scale of the operations undertaken. Just a few years before the fall of the Republic, the architect Bernardino Zendrini realized the ambitious project of the embankment of the lagoon on the Adriatic side with the famous "murazzi" or dykes which line the coast of Malamocco and

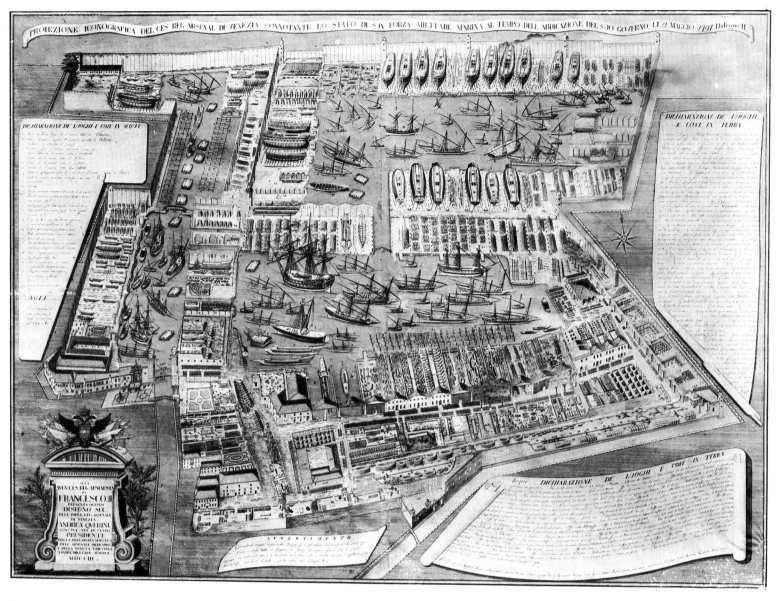

Pellestrina. This was a mammoth task for the times as there were no cranes or other machinery for shifting the great masses of Istrian sandstone, transported by sea from the opposite coast of the Adriatic.

Yet even in the Middle Ages, man had influenced the natural conditions of the lagoon by means of all kinds of contrivances, including the blocking and diverting of rivers so as to avoid flooding, and to maintain her only fortification, the instrument of her good fortunes, that vast, sheltered, impenetrable port. A notable part of the Senate's activities was concerned precisely with the eternal question of the lagoon's equilibrium, nowadays handled with dangerous approximation by too many supposed scientists who respond not so much to science as to political stimuli, and economic and corporative interests. We should not imagine that such interests did not exist then too: in a parliamentary state such as Venice, every interest made itself felt in political assembly, then as now. However, it would seem that for final

Above: plan of the Arsenal by abbé Giammaria Maffioletti (18th century), naval writer and master in the Scuola dell' Arsenale. Below: the exterior of the Arsenal as it appeared in the first half of the 18th century, engraving by Michele Marieschi. According to tradition, this huge complex was founded on two small islands called the Gemelle (the Twins) by doge Ordelaf Falier in 1104. It was several times enlarged. At the peak of its prosperity as many as 16,000 workers were employed there.

decisions, the seriousness and independence of the experts were held in higher regard than they are today.

The *provveditori ai Beni Inculti* and *provveditori ai Beni Comunali* bring us back to another activity handled by the *Pregadi*: the supervision of agricultural policy. Agricultural problems on the Veneto mainland had always been acute and the Senate was just as fearful of famine as of recurrent disease. Disease was gallantly combated by the magistrature of the *provveditori alla Sanità*, which was so efficient and enlightened as to be considered exemplary even by such a declared enemy of Venice as Napoleon Bonaparte. Enormous grants and extensive cultivation initiated with state support had dealt with the chronic shortages of cereals (corn, then maize, and rice) which had nearly always been imported. However, farming had been neglected, and this had been indispensable for the supply of wool for the clothing industry, for a long time extremely important to the Venetian economy. The Senate therefore set up a special commission which made a number of recommendations, many of which could not be put into action because of the fall of the Republic; but some of them were swiftly implemented and were truly enlightened gestures, such as the printing at public expense of a technical handbook for farmers which was to be circulated to thousands.

Public education was handled by three *riformatori allo Studio di Padova*, who were also responsible to the Senate. They had care of the state university, one of the oldest and most famous in Italy, as well as direct jurisdiction over all other state schools – and the printing industry, always one of the most prosperous and flourishing industries in Venice. Their obsession with taking the best teachers from Padua university enriched the scientific faculties in particular: students could be taught by exceptional professors, such as Mercurialis, Vesalius, Fallopius, Fabricius of Acquapendente, Morgagni, Vallisnieri and Galileo, and the results reflect this, if we remember that one of the students was none other than Nicolaus Copernicus. On the other hand, the desire not to lose the scholars that flocked from the Germanic and Slav world encouraged the *riformatori* to neglect ideological limitations, ignore the warnings and criticisms of the Inqui-

sition and extend a welcome to heretics and the persecuted. Indeed it is true that both before and after the Council of Trent, one of the strongest influences against ideological dependence on Rome, apart from the importance of the interests of the publishing industry, was the traditional Venetian spirit of independence with regard to the curia. As far as the Inquisition was concerned, the Republic traditionally found them something of a bane: the Senate itself would elect three *savi all'Eresia* who were a real thorn in the flesh of the Roman popes, having as they did the duty to stand by the Inquisitor fathers of the Holy Office and control their activities, in practice curbing and opposing their excesses.

Senato Mar. Navigation and its connected problems also concerned the state directly, the merchant navy above all, but also the maritime industry. The state Arsenal, the very one which had so enraptured Dante as to make him draw the famous comparison with hell, did not only make men-of-war, nor was the Venetian state uninterested in the merchant fleet, quite the contrary. Originally there was great confusion between the public and private sectors. Many of the galleys which took part in the great expeditions of the fourth crusade and the conquest of

Above: scribes of the doge and Signoria *(from Giacomo Franco's* Habiti*). Below: the doge and the* Signoria *(engraving by L. Ziletti, 1575). The* Signoria *was the highest rung on the political ladder, both restricting and complementing the power of the doge. It attended all the sessions presided over by the doge. From the 13th century it consisted of six councillors (one for each* sestiere*, with a term of office of eight months), and three heads of the* Quaranta al Criminal.

Venetian patricians, from a painting by Francesco Guardi depicting the Corridor of the Hall of the Maggior Consiglio *(private collection, Bergamo). Here the patricians met between sessions of the* Maggior Consiglio. *Alliances were made and broken, and agreements determining the outcome of votes in the assembly entered into. Below: detail from the manuscript of* Livy's First Decad, *illustrated in the 14th century by the Venetian artist Giannino Cattaneo, who reproduced the clothes and manners of his fellow-citizens. This miniature gives an impression of the Venetian patricians of the 14th century (Biblioteca Ambrosiana, Milan).*

Constantinople were private property. In the middle of the 13th century, the maritime policing of the very jealously guarded Gulf of Venice, the Adriatic, was in fact entrusted to a private citizen, the owner of an armed galley. But on the other hand, state galleys were put up for auction every season and assigned on contract from one voyage to another to the highest bidder. The barges (probably like the *bragozzi* of today) and small sailing-boats, which acted as coasting-vessels, were in fact superseded at the latest from the end of the 12th century, by other kinds of ships, far more capacious, sturdy and swift: this was the great age of the galley, fast and nimble for use in either war or commerce, equipped with sail but powered mainly by oars. The oarsmen were not the "galley-slaves" or condemned criminals of popular imagination, and as was to happen later: these were volunteers, not recruited overseas in Dalmatia or Greece, but natives of Venice itself, who hoped to add to their pay with some side benefit from the flood of business negotiated by the great contractors in the East and the West. These galleys were eventually superseded by the galleass, and these in their turn, because of conditions on the Atlantic routes, by the cog, *cocca* and carrack, transport ships with sails which eventually spawned the galleons and vessels of the centuries of Venice's decline. Over all this picturesque world of adventure shone the power of the Senate, filtered through the various magistratures. As far as the Arsenal was con-

Two paintings by Gabriele Bella. Above: the Sala della Bussola, *the antechamber to the Council of Ten. Here the Missier Grande or chief constable and guards waited with those who were to be tried by the Council of Ten. Below: the* Supreme Tribunal, *a college of State Inquisitors consisting of three members, two chosen from the Council of Ten, and one from the dogal councillors. This tribunal took charge of matters which concerned the defense of the state. The Republic was an oligarchy in which the nobility held all power. They met in the Doge's Palace, where they were the only true masters of the house, to debate and vote on the Republic's laws and to do justice. All noblemen belonged to the* Maggior Consiglio, *and the holders of all offices were chosen from among them.*

cerned, it had a flock of ruling members, *provveditori, inquisitori, patroni* and so on, who acted as supervisors, while the workers, divided into their various categories of caulkers, carpenters and rope-makers, and holding various privileges (some merely nominal, some actual), took orders from a number of skilled foremen and engineers under the authority of the admiral (*armirag-lio*) who, while not a patrician, when the newly-elected doge was carried in triumph around St. Mark's square, stood next to him in the chair holding the dogal standard, and commanded the *Bucintoro* in the solemn annual ceremony of wedding the sea.

Since war had also become the province of the *Pregadi*, the top military and naval offices were answerable to the Senate, from the *provveditore generale da mar*, who lived in Corfu and commanded the fleet in times of peace, to the *provveditore generale* at Palma, who, from his great, star-shaped fortress (built at the end of the 16th century on the Friuli border) supervised the military defense of the borders on land. There were the *presidenti alla Milizia da Mar*, or the *governatori alle galere de'condannati*, who dealt with the crews (alas, from the middle of the 16th century onwards, the galleys were rowed by criminals or Turkish or Barbary prisoners of war). There were the *provveditori alle artiglierie* and the *provveditori alle fortezze*, but the most extraordinary factor is that in times of war, the Senate expected to assume corporate command.

THE DOGE'S PALACE: THE POWER CENTER

The monumental entrance to the palace, the Porta della Carta (1) takes its name from the decrees which were posted there, or perhaps from a repository of documents, the State Archives, which once stood nearby. The arcade on the ground level (2) is 75 meters (246 feet) long, and has 18 arches.

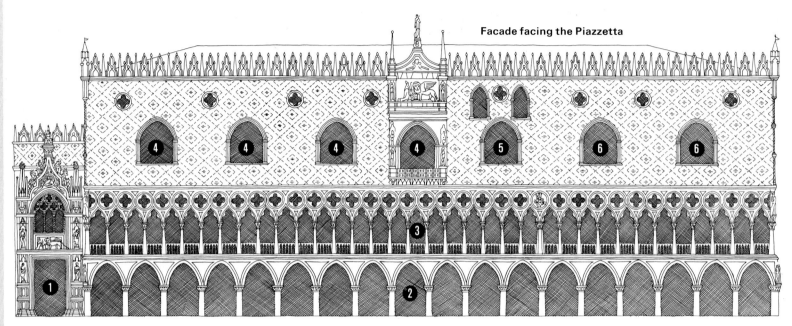

Facade facing the Piazzetta

The Doge's Palace is the largest municipal building in Venice. It grew gradually over the centuries and was the heart of the Venetian state, containing the doge's apartments, the seat of government, and the assembly rooms of the collegial magistratures, the most important of which was the *Maggior Consiglio.* Council chambers, armouries, tribunals, and even prisons were housed under its roofs.

Here some hundred doges were invested with power, and just as many died here; one of them being Marino Falier, beheaded for treason.

Often restored, its walls have looked down on a thousand years of history. From here the Venetian patriciate masterminded the conquest of an empire, confronted the pope, made war on Turkey, administered, gave judgment, endured through their shrewdness and wisdom and finally, in May 1797, abdicated.

The first building was begun in 810 but the palace took on its present appearance at the end of the 15th century, with the reconstruction of the east wing. The two attractive facades facing on to the Piazzetta and Molo had already been built. The chronicles record five famous and serious fires, in 976, 1105, 1483, 1574 and 1577.

At the coronation of the *dogaressa* the Guild Corporations held exhibitions in the Loggia Foscara (3). According to tradition, death sentences were read out from the ninth arch from the left.

The votes of the *Maggior Consiglio* were counted in the Sala del Scrutinio (counting chamber, 4), in which the commissions responsible for electing the doge and other magistrates also met.

The Sala della Quarantia Civil Nuova (5) was the assembly room of the magistrature of this name, which judged appeals on civil cases concerning mainland and overseas possessions.

The last two windows nearest the lagoon gave on to one of the short sides of the Hall of the *Maggior Consiglio.*

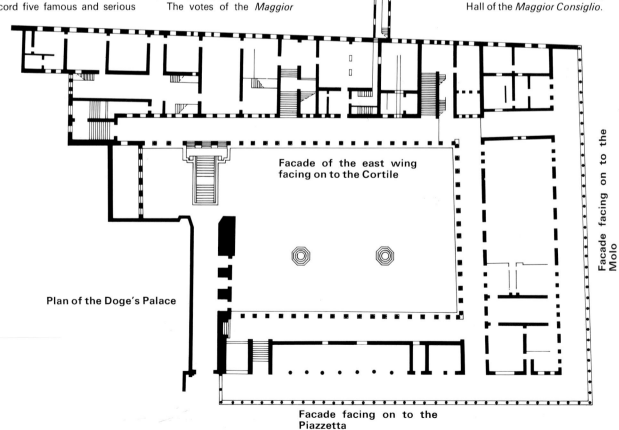

Plan of the Doge's Palace

Facade of the east wing facing on to the Cortile

Facade facing on to the Molo

Facade facing on to the Piazzetta

The facade facing on to the Molo is the palace's oldest. The arcade measures 71.5 meters (234 feet) in length, and has 17 arches. Here galley captains recruited their crews and paid them their advances.

Behind the central arches on the level of the Loggia (8), from the 14th arch from the left to the 26th was the assembly room of the magistracy of the Piovego, which was entrusted with affairs concerning Venice's domains. Here the bodies of dead doges were brought to lie in state for three days.

The largest hall in the palace is the Hall of the *Maggior Consiglio*, measuring 54 meters (177 feet) by 25m (81 feet), by 13.4m (44 feet) high. (9). Here sat the patricians in whom all power in the Most Serene Republic was vested.

The doge, flanked by the *Signoria*, presided over the patricians seated on benches running the length of the chamber.

Facade facing the Molo

Off the corridor leading to the *Maggior Consiglio* (10) was the Armaments' Room, where ammunition was stored, and the Sala della Quarantia Civil Vecchia, which adjudicated civil causes of more than 1,500 ducats in value from the city and duchy.

The Bridge of Sighs (11) connected the palace to the prisons. The legendary sighs were those of condemned prisoners.

From the top of the majestic Scala dei Giganti in the east wing (12) the newly elected doge swore obedience to the laws and received his dogal cap.

On the level of the Loggia in the east wing were the dogal chancellery (13), the magistrature of the *Milizia da Mar* (14) which recruited members of the navy, the *Avogaria* (15) which prepared cases to be brought before the *Quarantia* and registered patricians in the Golden Book, and the Censors (16) who watched over the patricians' morals and attempted to prevent electoral malpractice.

Facade of the east wing facing the Cortile

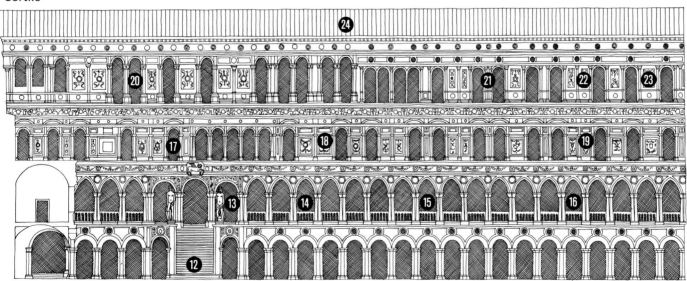

The doge's apartments were on the first *piano nobile* on the side facing the Rio del Palazzo. The Sala Grimani (17) was used as the doge's private audience chamber. The doge's councillors and other high dignitaries met to attend on the Most Serene Prince in the Sala degli Scarlatti (18). In another room (19) the *Quarantia Criminal* met to adjudicate serious crimes commited in the city and duchy.

The second *piano nobile* housed some of the most powerful bodies in the state. The *Signoria* met in the Sala del Collegio (20), behind which lay the Senate chamber. Other rooms housed the three heads of the Council of Ten (22) and the three very powerful State Inquisitors (23). An inner stairway led to the torture chamber, and the *Piombi* (24), prisons built in the roofs and so named because the roof was covered with lead ("piombo") strips.

The "Quaranta" and the "Dieci"

The Senate therefore had a hand in every area of Venetian life: politics, economics, war, diplomacy. ... It was even involved in the judiciary, though the *Pregadi* had no actual power in that sector. Among the Senate's members however where the three *avogadori di Comun*, a very particular magistrature with many functions, including the duty of guarding the Golden Book of the patriciate and checking the titles of the candidates for the *Maggior Consiglio*, but most important, the position of procurator general. The members of the *Quarantia Criminal* and Council of Ten were also members of the Senate.

The *Quarantia* or *Consiglio di Quaranta* (Council of Forty) came into being between 1207 and 1222 as a political assembly. One of its most important acts was the institution in 1284, under the doge Giovanni Dandolo, of the golden ducat or *zecchino*, the dollar of the Middle Ages and the most authoritative currency in the Mediterranean right up to modern times, remaining stable for 500 years as regards its denomination and weight. This magistrature gradually became predominantly judiciary, and branched out into three distinct sections, the *Quarantia Civil Vecchia*, which judged civil cases concerning sums in excess of 1,500 ducats and acted as court of appeal for civil sentences passed by the lesser tribunals of the city; there was the *Quarantia Civil Nova*, which judged appeals from courts in Venetian territories; and the *Quarantia Criminal*, which judged penal sentences in appeal from lesser courts while being primarily an assize court for the more serious crimes committed in the city or in the *dogado* (the oldest center of the Republic, from Grado to Cavarzere: the borders of the ancient Byzantine province, belonging to the ancient Venetian *dogado*).

The members of the *Quaranta* first took part in the *Civil Nova*, then, after eight months, they passed *en bloc* into the *Civil Vecchia*, and again after eight months, they all moved on together into the *Criminal*. The three heads of the *Criminal* were members of the *Serenissima Signoria*. However, automatic rotation started earlier, from the election to the *Collegio dei XV*, empowered to judge civil cases involving between 200 and 800 ducats, and this opened the doors to the *Collegio*

Opposite: the whimsical facade of the Doge's Palace facing the Molo. This is the oldest side of the building which housed the government of the Republic, dating back to the 14th century, although it was partly restored after the disastrous fire of 20 December 1577. This devastated the Hall of the Maggior Consiglio, *which was finished in the middle of the 14th century and decorated by the Paduan artist Guariento. Above the* Tribunale *he had painted a fresco of* Paradise, *the remains of which are reproduced on this page, above. Today they are preserved in another part of the palace. Guariento was summoned to Venice after establishing his reputation with his decorations of the Reggia Carrarese in Padua. Below: detail of the armed angels from the chapel of the Reggia Carrarese, now preserved in the Museo Civico, Padua.*

dei XXV, empowered to pass judgement in cases where higher sums were involved.

On a lower level was the jungle of Venetian penal and civil courts, which is perhaps best left unexplored, so complex and intricate were its spheres of influence, from the *Signori di Notte*, "Gentlemen of the Night" (a kind of police court) to the *Giustizieri, Vecchi e Novi* and the *Giudici del Piovego*, who had exercised very important powers, particularly in the Middle Ages, with regard to the waters of the lagoon; or else there was the little group of magistratures dealing with private rights (the judges known as the *Giudici del*

Petizion, del Procurator, del Forestier, dell'Esaminador and *del Mobile*) or else the *Auditori Vecchi, Novi* and *Novissimi*. Finally at the apex stood, in all its fearful majesty, the *Eccelso Consiglio di Dieci*, the Most High Council of Ten, if we are to give it the pompous, official title it held until the fall of the Republic.

We have not mentioned that among the judiciary magistratures elected in the Senate were the Censors, who had jurisdiction over the rigging of elections, but also, curiously, over "salaries and goods of servants" as well as "those boatmen that make money on their masters' boats … and … start brawls when clients are on board." There were four *Esecutori alla Bestemmia*, executors for blasphemy: these held office for a year and punished "blasphemers and profaners of Temples and Sacred Places," swindlers, seducers of maidens ("… obliged either to marry the deflowered damsel or bestow on her a suitable dowry") as well as jurisdiction over obscene prints and publications. Even in the bland, easy-going atmosphere of 18th-century Venice, the Executors clamped down harshly on offenders: readers may recall Pandolfo, the playwright Goldoni's gambler from the *Bottega del Caffè* who was betrayed by the inopportune gossip of the slanderous Don Marzio, and publicly whipped. In harsher times the punishments were much more severe. In the last decade of the 15th century, the nobleman Giovanni Zorzi, found guilty of horrible cursing had his tongue cut out and his right hand severed (though it is true that besides swearing, he "exported" *i.e.* carried off a nun from a convent in Treviso). In the 16th century, foul-mouthed priests were exposed to the elements in an iron cage attached to an outside wall of the Campanile; one example was the priest Agustino, a gambler, womanizer and protagonist of a very unusual rhyme written at the beginning of the century (however, some managed to escape, even from the cage).

Let us return to the Most High Council: "In the year one thousand three hundred and ten – in the midst of the month for harvesting grain – Baiamonte passed over the *ponte* – and so was formed the Council of Ten." So runs a popular rhyme. The Council of Ten was set up as an emergency magistrature to judge the partisans led by Baiamonte Tiepolo. This *Consiglio di Dieci*

Opposite, far left: two pages from the famous Golden Book. *At the beginning of the 16th century the division of the populace into patricians, who were allowed to participate in government, and the common people, who were not allowed into the high offices of state, received its official sanction in the* Golden Book. *This was a kind of state register of the patriciate, and consisted of the* Book of Patricians' Births, *begun in 1506, and the* Book of Marriages, *begun in 1526. The book was kept by the Avogaria until the fall of the Republic, and the rules for inclusion were strict. Opposite, right, and on this page, above and right: drawings inspired by Venetian patricians from the 14th century codex of Livy's* First Decad, *illuminated by Giannino Cattaneo.*

(not "*dei*" Dieci: there had already been several councils and committees with ten members, and not only in Venice – it should be sufficient to recall the Florentine *Dieci di Balia*) had turned into a permanent institution with jurisdiction over crimes of high treason, gradually extended to cover all matters which were thought to be secret and then other crimes such as sodomy, falsification of currency, crimes committed with firearms, or on board ship or by masked persons, and perfidious or corrupt administration on the part of governors of cities or provinces. Some of these duties had been conferred on the Council of Ten by the *Maggior Consiglio* or the Senate, others they had taken upon themselves: in its 487 years of existence, the *Eccelso* displayed on several occasions a deplorable tendency to meddle in the province of others, and more and more often the Venetian system had to react and bring it round to exercise milder judgements, restructure it and generally exert influence over it.

In reality, the importance and authority of the Council of Ten lay in its essential duties: the judgment of crimes, offences and infringements committed by the patrician class. It was founded at a crucial point for the establishment of the Venetian political aristocracy, indeed, at the very moment of the birth of the patrician class as the only class invested with political power; and so the Council of Ten, the direct, immediate expression of that same class and the instrument of its definitive seizure of power, also instantly became its harsh and conscientious curb. This has no precedent in any European constitution, and in itself illustrates at least two other facts: the integrity of the Venetian political world, unwilling to stand by and watch an oligarchy be set up in the bosom of an extended legislative body, as was the *Maggior Consiglio* once it had been "locked" compared to how it had been in the past, and the double-check on the oligarchic origin of Baiamonte's uprising, as the council had been created specifically to repress this rebellion. The fact that later, the Council of Ten took advantage of its own extraordinary powers in order to attempt, more than once, to form an oligarchy of its own within the body of the dominant class, is something that those who initiated the council and gave it its authority had not foreseen. But there is no doubt that the elasticity and speed of response

Head of the Council of Ten. The three Heads of the Council of Ten were elected in rotation each month. They had the responsibility of opening letters and convening Council meetings.

Capitan Grande or Missier Grande. This officer was the chief constable of Minister of Justice (from Cesare Vecellio's Habiti*).*

THE PATRICIANS: BORN TO RULE

Whilst in the rest of Europe there were barons, earls, marquesses and so forth, high-born members of the Venetian nobility were not distinguished by rank among themselves. A Venetian aristocrat's title was simply N.H., *Nobilomo* (Nobleman), a "Patrician of Venice" and no more.

Even before the 11th century, the most famous families claimed descent from the ancient noble Roman families which had sought refuge on the lagoon from the barbarian invaders. Later, they tended to claim descent from the tribunes which had governed the city before the creation of the doge. There were 24 "old" families, to which were added the "new" families, those officially included in the nobility at the time of the *serrata* of the *Maggior Consiglio* in 1297. There was a third group of *novissimi* who were admitted on payment at the time of the Genoese wars in 1381, and others were admitted on payment at the end of the 17th century in order to cover the costs of the war of Candia. In the 14th century there were 120,000 inhabitants in the city, whilst the adult male patricians, members of the *Maggior Consiglio*, numbered about 1,200, from hardly more than 150 families. In the middle of the 16th century the *Maggior Consiglio* reached its greatest number of members with 2,050 out of a population of 15,000 souls. After this the nobility fell into both relative and absolute decline, in spite of the admission of new houses. In 1797 the Golden Book had only 1,030 nobles registered in it, some 3.2 per cent of the population, from 111 families. All power was legally concentrated in the hands of the patricians, and

the body through which they exercised their power was the *Maggior Consiglio*. This was the sovereign body in the Most Serene Republic which elected the holders of every high office of state. Male patricians of more than 25 years of age descended from legitimate marriages duly recorded in the Golden Book were eligible for this, the largest assembly. Under this age, only 27 young patricians who drew a golden straw by lot on Saint Barbara's day were admitted.

Sessions were held in the hall in the Doge's Palace (1), in crowded gatherings of more than 1,000 members. The course of an official career was determined by a number of factors, not the least of which was the financial status of a man's family. Although all nobles were *de jure* equal, many of the offices demanded huge sums of money. Before they took on duties of state, poor young patricians were helped by the Republic to complete their studies at the Academy of Nobles or at the University of Padua. Young men often gained their first experience in trade, voyaging on ships belonging to their families or to the Senate (5, Venetian traveller). Later they would enter offices of state, but not necessarily abandon trade or finance.

If his family could afford it, a young patrician (7, young patricians) would begin his career in state service as a *savio agli ordini* which would allow him to attend meetings of College and Senate and gain experience in various state offices. But the main advantage of wealth was that it

5 **6**

allowed a man to defray the expense of the more important *reggimenti* and to take on ambassadorships (8, Venetian ambassador). In between he would take on other duties and gain further experience, such as acting as a *savio di terraferma* and as a member of the Council of *Pregadi* (10) or of the Council of Ten (4). This led to higher offices such as Dogal Councillor, or *savio del consiglio*, from where he might eventually reach the heights of becoming a procurator of St. Mark (9), playing a part in the Senate. Those from slightly less wealthy, but still well-off families could enter the judicial magistratures, leading to the Council of Forty. From here they might become Head of the *Quaranta al Criminal Superior*, and thence a member of the *Signoria*. Less rich men

than these began in the humbler magistratures, in the Grain Office or the Customs House. Then came lesser *reggimenti* or minor offices in the more important *reggimenti*. Alternatively, they could follow the career of a lawyer, which could lead eventually to the *Avogaria di Comun* (2, *avogador*), and to the Forty. Anyone could enter a military career, which started in the lowest ranks (*nobile di nave, di galera*) and could lead to the highest rank of *provveditore generale da mar* (6). Some came to a military career from politics becoming, for instance, *provveditori generali* in Dalmatia or Albania.

These careers were more or less interchangeable, and it was common for men to transfer from one to another. Soldiers might become suc-

cessful diplomats, merchants, great captains, with the versatility that belonged to the Venetian patriciate. Patricians who chose a career in the church were excluded from the *Maggior Consiglio* and had to obtain the permission of the state in order to become bishops or cardinals (3).

10

of the Venetian political system was always able to prevent it establishing a proper internal dictatorship, as it was tempted to do on more than one occasion.

Many foolish things have been said and written in connection with the Ten, probably more than of any other constitutional body. There has been talk of grim, shadowy rites, inhuman prisons, and even today the legend of the "lion's mouths" still prospers and flourishes: the sinister post-boxes designed to receive secret denunciations sufficient to make the difference between life or death for innumerable innocent folk, sacrificed to the pride of the patrician class.

These are all literary inventions or propaganda without a single grain of truth. Certainly, the Council of Ten in its role as special tribunal with wide-ranging powers (it was made up of 17 members in all, ten titled members, the doge and the six Dogal Councillors) was harsher than the other Venetian courts, and was cloaked in the strictest secrecy and brooked no interference. Certainly, following a practice that was normal at the time of its institution and even more so in the centuries that followed up to the end of the 17th century, it never shrank from ordering the suppression of any dangerous element (such was the fate of the "great knight" Baiamonte Tiepolo, who, after the failure of his *putsch*, went on weaving anti-Venetian plots from his exile in Slavonia): it is worth remembering that such methods, which are so repellent to our democratic moral sense, are the habitual resort of many governments represented today at the United Nations. However, as judges, the Ten displayed an integrity which is certainly absent among the magistrates of many countries nowadays. It should suffice to point out what happened to the secret accusations posted in the notorious "lion's mouths:" if they were anonymous they were examined by three Heads of the Council (these were elected month by month and it was their duty to initiate proceedings and conduct trials). In conjunction with the six Dogal Councillors they had to decide, by unanimous vote, whether the denunciation was to be presented to the council. If so, the council had to vote in favour, with a majority of five to one, of passing it for a second examination, after which another majority of four to one was necessary before any action would be

Above: the Pisani family *painted by Pietro Longhi. Left: detail of Titian's* Pala Pesaro *(Pesaro altarpiece), depicting Jacopo Pesaro, who commissioned the work, with members of his family. The Venetian patriciate did not consider their rank as a privilege but as a service due to the Republic, consisting of magistratures and offices. No nobleman could escape this service, and the* cursus honorum *was extremely onerous. The wealth of the great houses was accumulated through trade from the earliest times, and it was considered to be a noble occupation. Even the doges indulged in commerce until they were forbidden to do so by the* Promissione *in the 16th century.*

taken. We will not go on with the description of the complicated procedures of the "rites of the Most High," which it can only be repeated, offered the accused far more guarantees than are available according to the legal processes of many countries today. Apart from anything else, the defense (which could be merely written) had a specific magistrate (the *avvocati dei Prigioni*), an institution established right from 1443 for the free legal protection of the accused who were poor, and no trial by the Ten was valid unless at least one member of the three *avogadori di Comun* was present. These had the power of intervention, that is, suspension and appeal on any sentence. (The sentences too were decided by majority vote, as were the penalties; right up to the last minute, any member of the council in any doubt could reopen the trial and bring about a revision before it was too late.)

As far as the prisons were concerned, the *Piombi*, which no longer exist, were nothing less than the attics of the Doge's Palace (Balzac made the witty comment that for such attics there were people in Paris who were willing to pay a fortune in rent). The notorious *Pozzi*, which some people are still writing about, basing their evidence on the false witness of the rogue Giacomo Casanova, were below the water-level of the *rio*, but on the same level as the offices in which, until about 30 years ago the president of the Biennale had his base. Still, *Piombi* and *Pozzi* were part of the deterrent weapon wielded by another tribunal, even more ill-famed, and a direct expansion of the Ten and successor to the Ten once they had suffered the umpteenth restructuring: the so-named *Tribunal Supremo*, that of the State Inquisitors.

Legend has also grown up around the Inquisitors. In reality, this magistrature, made up of two members of the Council of Ten and one Dogal Councillor, in office for a month, came into being in 1539 with the specific mandate to stem the disclosure of state secrets, one of the worst habits of the Venetian political scene, a consequence no doubt, of the assembly-method of conducting affairs. As time went on, the dramatic nature of the Republic's actual position, squeezed as it was between the Hapsburg territories so that its independence was constantly under attack and it was obliged to defend itself tooth and nail in

direct battle against enemies that were so much stronger and more powerful, all reinforced the tribunal's authority, and it surrounded itself in secrecy and operated far more swiftly and efficiently than the Ten. In this way, the State Inquisitors gradually became a determining factor on the Venetian political scene and were able to intervene directly in a variety of matters, could

correspond directly with ambassadors and *rettori* or governors (the Ten had also been responsible for this in the past) and could in effect almost completely replace the Ten in the last years of the Republic, as far as controlling the patriciate was concerned.

Strict as it was in the exercise of its prerogatives, the Supreme Tribunal enjoyed vast popularity, even when it over-reached itself or abused its power. This is difficult to believe, but a good indication is the behaviour of the common people during the great dispute between the *querinisti* and *tribunalisti*, which was one of the *Maggior Consiglio's* last great parliamentary battles. The *avogador di Comun*, Angelo Maria Querini, had intervened concerning a sentence passed by the *Tribunal Supremo*, and had been arrested and imprisoned on the orders of the Inquisitors. This gave rise to an enormous scandal and the *Maggior Consiglio* reacted polemically, deferring the vote for the renewal of the Council of Ten; in consequence five *Correttori* were nominated by vote to take on the task of reviewing the rules and regulations governing the different councils and

committees. Naturally, two factions formed: the *querinisti*, who, in the name of the *avogadore* who had been unjustly arrested, fought a battle to limit the powers of the State Inquisitors; and the *tribunalisti*, who upheld the thesis that the excessive power of the Inquisitors was necessary, and that their dread reputation acted as a curb on possible abuses perpetrated by the nobles and was a guarantee of liberty for all. In the confusion of the situation created by this debate, in which all the stars of parliamentary oratory figured prominently, headed by two future doges, Marco Foscarini, leader of the *tribunalisti*, and Paolo Renier, front-liner for the *querinisti*, as far as public opinion was concerned the positions appeared to be completely the reverse of what one

might expect. Those who maintained that the advocate Querini had been arrested illegally and based their arguments on Montesquieu and ideas of enlightenment, found themselves considered by the mob thronging St. Mark's square and awaiting the results of the voting, as supporters of the liberation of the patrician class from any constraint and therefore as supporters of patrician despotism. On the other hand, those who were proposing the full endorsement of the Inquisitors' powers were held to be defenders of the people against the patrician thirst for tyranny, and were applauded. Later, when the *Maggior Consiglio*, after a memorable discourse by Paolo Renier which lasted five hours, and Marco Foscarini's reply, approved the decision of the three "tribu-

Busy Rialto traffic from an 18th–century engraving. Below: right and left: gondolas of the 15th and 18th centuries by Carpaccio and Guardi. The gondola was developed to suit the narrow, shallow canals. Originally they were painted a variety of colours, only becoming black by order of the Senate in 1562. Opposite: detail from Gentile Bellini's Miracle of the Cross. *The young negro is not merely a picturesque touch, but reflects the mixed Venetian society of the 15th century.*

THE LAGOON: A THOUSAND YEARS OF DEFENSES

The lagoon of Venice is a delicately balanced living organism. Without man's intervention, it would long ago have disappeared under the assault of the sea eroding the outer string of islands and from the action of the alluvial deposits carried down by the fresh watercourses which gradually fill it up. In order to safeguard the lagoon's existence, the Republic undertook various protective measures. The tides were allowed free play, which kept the city canals clear with their ebb and flow, and permitted the watercourses to drain properly. The lower courses of the rivers which debouch into the lagoon were altered, and dams were built and other protective measures taken. Every effort was made to prevent the area of the lagoon from diminishing in order not to obstruct the tides. To this end it was forbidden to fill in any part of the lagoon, salt pans were closed down, and canals, the so-called Garzoni cuts, were dug. However, the largest-scale works were those which over the course of the centuries diverted the fast-flowing watercourses out of the lagoon. The chief stages in this undertaking are indicated on the map. The river Bacchiglione which originally debouched into the lagoon of Chioggia through the Montalbo canal (2) was diverted into the Toro canal (1) in 1540, from where it flowed into the open sea. In 1324 the mouths of the Brenta which until then lay just opposite the city itself were moved farther south by means of a canal (3). This was extended into the Malamocco lagoon in 1452 with the Corbola canal (4). In 1541 the course of the Brenta was further altered with the Mira diversion (5). Through

this and the Corbola canal the waters of the Brenta could be directed into any part of the lagoon at need. In 1507 yet another Brenta canal was cut, turning off from the main course at Dolo, and flowing via Conche into the lagoon of Chioggia through the Montalbano canal. In 1613 the New Cut and the Nirano Cut (7) were completed. These carried the waters of the Brenta, the Botinico, the Lusor, the Brentella and the Musone away from Venice into the lagoon of Chioggia. These waters were subsequently led right away from the lagoon down to Brondolo Harbour through the Toro canal (1) which already carried the waters of the Bacchiglione. The Osellin Canal was another large undertaking, diverting the Marzenego, the Zero and the Dese to the East of Venice (1505–07). In 1683 the waters of the Sile which debouched into the lagoon near Burano were led through the Sile Cut (9) into the old bed of the Piave, the waters of which had already been diverted elsewhere. In 1534 St. Mark's Dyke (11) was constructed to protect the lagoon from the Piave floods.

The Piave was diverted in 1579 through the King's Cut (Taglio di Re) into the Nuova Cava Zuccherina, whence it flowed into the sea. In 1683 it broke its banks at Landrona and formed a new bed which flowed into the sea at Cortellazzo (14).

It was only in the 18th century that sea walls were built (15) against the encroachments of the sea.

Today the lagoon is connected to the sea by three mouths or ports. These are protected by dykes, the need for which was foreseen as early as 1551, but which were built only in the 19th and 20th centuries.

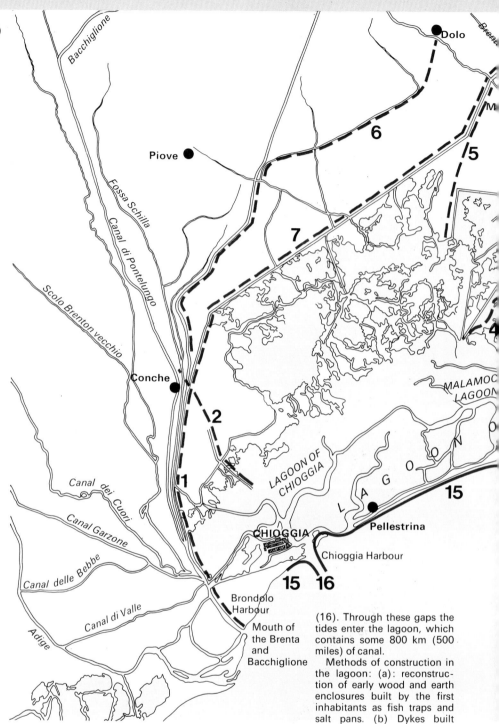

(16). Through these gaps the tides enter the lagoon, which contains some 800 km (500 miles) of canal.

Methods of construction in the lagoon: (a): reconstruction of early wood and earth enclosures built by the first inhabitants as fish traps and salt pans. (b) Dykes built

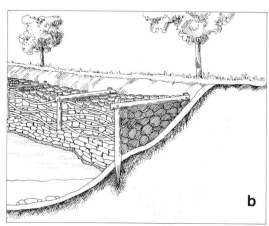

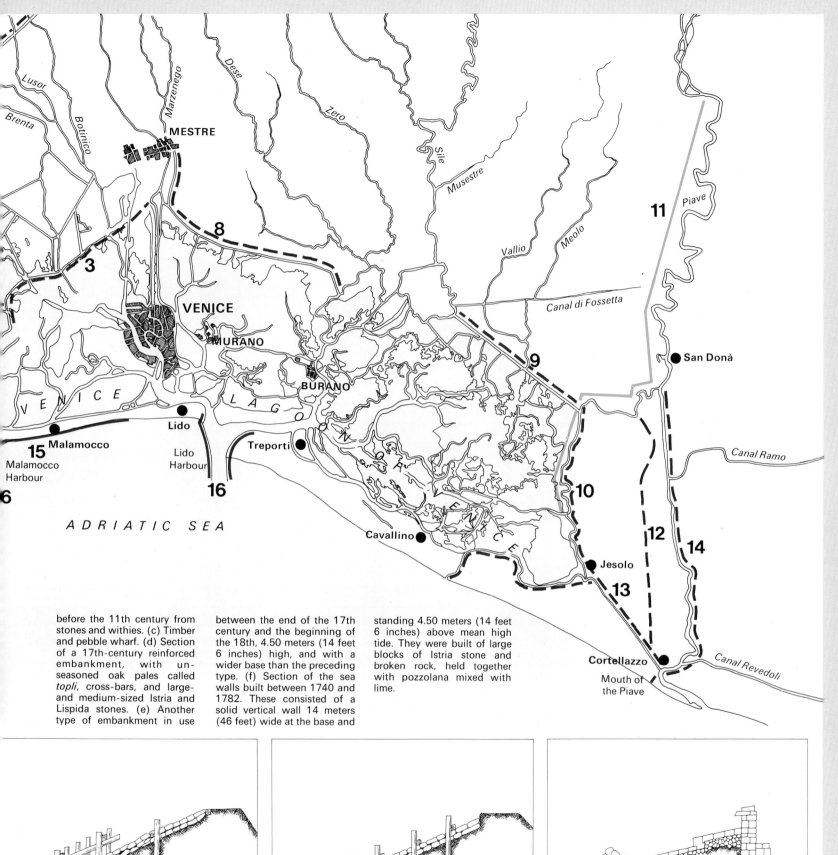

MESTRE

8

3

VENICE

MURANO

BURANO

Lido

15 Malamocco
Malamocco
Harbour

Lido
Harbour

16

6

Treporti

V E N I C E   L A G O O N

Cavallino

ADRIATIC SEA

Lusor

Brenta

Botinico

Marzenego

Dese

Zero

Sile

Musestre

Vallio

Meolo

Piave

11

Canal di Fossetta

9

● San Donà

Canal Ramo

10

12

14

13

Jesolo

Cortellazzo

Mouth of
the Piave

Canal Revedoli

before the 11th century from
stones and withies. (c) Timber
and pebble wharf. (d) Section
of a 17th-century reinforced
embankment, with un-
seasoned oak pales called
topli, cross-bars, and large-
and medium-sized Istria and
Lispida stones. (e) Another
type of embankment in use

between the end of the 17th
century and the beginning of
the 18th, 4.50 meters (14 feet
6 inches) high, and with a
wider base than the preceding
type. (f) Section of the sea
walls built between 1740 and
1782. These consisted of a
solid vertical wall 14 meters
(46 feet) wide at the base and

standing 4.50 meters (14 feet
6 inches) above mean high
tide. They were built of large
blocks of Istria stone and
broken rock, held together
with pozzolana mixed with
lime.

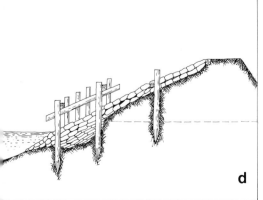

d

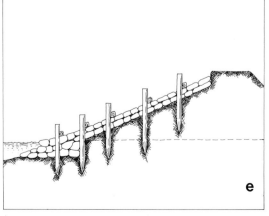

e

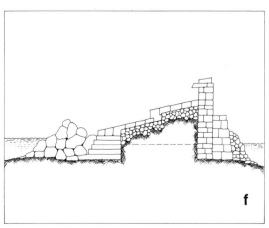

f

nalist" *Correttori* by a majority of just two, a crowd of more than 6,000 people. acclaimed the supporters of the *Tribunal Supremo* and threatened to besiege the homes of those who, according to today's reckoning, should have been considered liberals.

The episode clarifies to quite a significant degree (even taking crowd hysteria into account) the relationship between the people and the patriciate, and between the people and the political system. The ordinary people that hailed the State Inquisitors, acclaimed a tradition that was five centuries old of restricting the patrician class in any field not concerned with the legitimate exercise of judiciary power. No one could claim that Venetian society was egalitarian, quite the opposite: even such a man as Gasparo Contarini, a future cardinal and leader of a profound reform within the Catholic church that was a good 400 years ahead of its time, expounded his theories in terms of the rigid stratification of social categories; and those *beaux esprits* of the 1700s who displayed admiration for the Turkish social system, where there were no intermediate privileged classes between monarch

and people, were doubtless expressing dissatisfaction with a situation where there were too many privileged classes. However, the stringency with which tribunals and magistrates controlled the patriciate guaranteed what was the Venetians' dearest possession at that time: the legal system. One scholar, R. Guerdan, wrote perceptively that the motto of the *Serenissima* could have been the same as the French Republic, with a single basic alteration: instead of *Liberté, Egalité, Fraternité* – *Liberté, Legalité, Fraternité.*

The whole Venetian system was based on this principle: to prevent any single organ of the state from prevailing on any other; and to prevent the politically privileged social class from extending its own privilege into other fields of civil society. Baiamonte's plot had shown the risks which could arise from the excessive power of the noble classes; Marino Falier's plot had underlined the damage that could be derived from certain forms of noble dominance, if it were true that one of the *condottieri* of the failed bourgeois revolution, Isarello Bertucci, had been persuaded to join the conspiracy by the blows rained on him by a certain

The view of Venice from the island of San Giorgio is almost theatrical in its magnificence. From here the city seems to defy the years, appearing in all its past glory. From left to right: the dome of the church of the Salute, the point of the Dogana (customs house), and the mouth of the Grand Canal, which could once be barred and defended by an immense iron chain. Next are St.

Mark's basin, the Zecca (mint), the Libreria Sansoviniana, the Campanile (the paron de casa*), the Piazzetta with its two monolithic columns surmounted by a lion and the statue of St. Theodore, first patron saint of the city, and the colourful walls and airy fretwork of the Doge's Palace, with the Bridge of Sighs beside it.*

Dandolo. Therefore, the Venetian system, though directed by the patrician class, made it a point of honour to force the patricians to set an example of the strictest adherence to the law. Offences were punished with greater severity than for non-patricians. Occasionally, the doge and the Ten would almost seem to turn savagely against fellow members of their own class, as if to make examples of them at all costs.

The case of the doge Antonio Venier is very well-known: his son Alvise was found guilty of playing a trick considered to be vulgar, though in fact little more than high-spirited, regarding a certain Dalle Boccole: he had attached to this man's door, according to one story some horns (implying cuckoldry) and according to another story, a goat's head (implying stupidity). He was imprisoned while awaiting trial and fell ill in gaol: the judges had proposed that he should be set free provisionally but his own father was against this and let the boy die in prison. This terrible episode in fact provoked the doge's death shortly afterwards, as he was afflicted with a serious form of depression. However, this incident was considered

a valuable example in the face of the licentious behaviour of far too many young nobles. The incident regarding the patrician Gasparo Valier is equally well-known. He was condemned to death by the Ten in 1511 for the murder of a poor tax collector in Treviso: handsome, rich and of a great family, he had every kind of support. The patriarch of Venice came to beg for clemency and was "sent away with the words, the Council of Ten must continue its deliberations. ..." Even the three *avogadori di Comun* came along, though they had originally brought the charge, to ask for a suspension of sentence. They actually went down on their knees before the three heads of the Council of Ten, only to receive the chilly reply: "You are no longer worthy of this magistrature, however, you may rise ..." after which they were immediately demoted from office with a perma-nent veto on their re-election. This kind of behaviour, which persisted throughout the existence of the Republic, though not always in such an extreme form, is not the least surprising aspect of the characteristics of the Venetian system we are attempting to outline here.

Above: fashionable wedding clothes of the 15th century (Fieschi manuscript). Below: merchant's wife (after Giacomo Franco). Opposite: Portrait of a Lady by Carpaccio (Rijksmuseum, Amsterdam). Venetian ladies lived in an atmosphere of luxury and elegance, adorned with jewels and cosmetics.

"El paron de la Repubblica"

To continue our search for a hypothetical holder of maximum power, let us take up once more our review of the organization of the Venetian state. Attached to the Senate and a kind of half-way house between a parliamentary commission and a ministry, the *Pien Collegio* held its meetings in a hall which communicated directly with the senate-hall. Its president was the doge, and it comprised, apart from the *Serenissima Signoria*, 16 members, the *savi* (sages). This title, also used for other magistratures, represented varied but extremely important functions. There were the five *savi agli ordini*, who were originally concerned with naval affairs, and lost some of their authority in the last stages of the Republic, but were always a most useful springboard for anyone wishing to start on a political career at a high level. There were the five *savi di terraferma*: the *savio cassier*, concerned with finance, the *savio alla scrittura*, war minister, the *savio alle ordinanze*, responsible for the organization and efficiency of mobile territorial forces, the *savio ai cerimoniali*, who looked after

official visits of princes, ministers and foreign ambassadors, and the *savio ai "da mo'*," who took care of very urgent arrangements, whose report always began with the words "*E da mo'*," the shortened form of the phrase: "*La parte che ando' mo ...*" meaning, more or less, "the law that has just been voted in." Finally there were the six *savi del consiglio*, or *savi grandi*, a cross between parliamentary commission, presidency of the Council of Ministers, Ministry of Foreign Affairs and many other things besides: generally these were great men, worldly-wise, shaped by the heaviest of responsibilities and the greatest and most prestigious official positions. Like all the rest, they were elected on random dates, in threes, so that there would always be some alternation, and they were not renewable for six consecutive months.

Every morning, in the doge's apartments, the *Signoria* and *Collegio* would meet to examine the business in hand and to prepare the proposals to be presented to the Senate, which met in its turn usually on Thursday and Saturday. This gives some idea of the importance of the *Collegio*, but also gives a clue as to the progressive degeneration of this institution. In the last years of the Republic, the meetings between the *Collegio* and *Signoria* in fact ended up excluding the Senate from most of the most important decisions; in the very last months, the *consulte negre* ("black conferences" because the *savi usciti* also took part, and these were *savi* who no longer held office and wore a black cloak, while those still in office wore violet) ended up by taking upon themselves all the determining decisions. This was the end of the Republic, because the system that had been built up with such wisdom in the course of five centuries, on the pretext of urgency and secrecy, was set aside and dismantled. However, we are running ahead too fast: we have yet to consider the definitive, final example, the keystone of the system, the sovereign body, the *paron de la Repubblica*, the *Maggior Consiglio*.

We have said that a popular assembly presided in earliest times over the most important decisions taken by the government, starting with the election of the doge. The first clear appearances of the assembly go right back to the eighth century, after a series of doges had been removed from the throne by disputes between different factions,

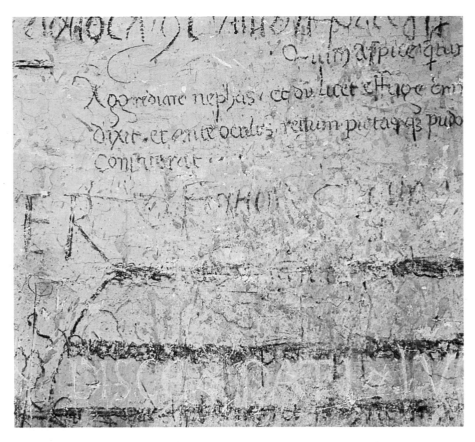

whose exact political orientations are difficult to establish. (Often, in accordance with the cruel Byzantine custom, the eyes of the deposed ruler were put out; later, the gentler custom prevailed, probably introduced from France, of tonsuring such doges and shutting them up in a monastery.) At this point, all the free men in the dogate, from Grado to Cavarzere, elected doge Maurizio, traditionally known as Galbaio. The tendency of the doges to form family dynasties was soon replaced by election. (The last dynasty was that of the Orseolo family, who were shipwrecked shortly after the year 1000.) From Pietro Flabianico onwards, doges were elected by the assembly, the *arengo*, in which the nobles occupied a distinctive position from remotest times, and whose powers were soon limited to basic decisions. The crowd that filled St. Mark's basilica (not much different then from now) and applauded the decision of the doge Enrico Dandolo to participate in the fourth crusade, constituted the *arengo*, which voted and decided by acclaim. However, by 1143, a new assembly had already assumed the task of virtually directing Venetian politics: the *Consilium Sapientium*, or council of sages, which, at the beginning of the 13th century, had only 35 members, not elected by popular assembly, as may have happened before, but by a college of three electors, selected in turn by three of the *trentacie* into which the population was divided.

Later, the *Consilium Sapientium*, now commonly referred to as the *Maggior Consiglio*, increased in number from 35 to 100 members, and gradually it was supplemented by the members of the *Quarantia* and the *Consiglio dei Pregadi*. However, it was made up almost exclusively of noblemen, from the ancient aristocracy derived from ancient tribunes in the days of the first maritime Venetian communities, and more recently, the nobility originating from the growth of power among seamen, artisans, merchants and financial operators in general, who had come into prominence through their wealth. The operation of the "locking" of the *Maggior Consiglio*, carried out at the suggestion of the *Quarantia* by the doge Pierazzo Gradenigo in 1297, both extended and restricted the composition of what was by then the true decisional assembly: it extended the Council numerically, but restricted it to those who were part of it, or had been part of it by election, and to

the descendants of those who had been part of it
for the last 125 years (always by election), apart
from the co-option of new men from a suitable
electoral college. In this way, from the 586
members counted in 1297, the *Maggior Consiglio*
increased to more than 1,000 in 1311 and more
than 2,000 in the 16th century. But, once the
arengo had been deprived of power and eventually

eliminated, it became a council of nobles, the
members of which, along with their families,
constituted the patrician class. Little by little, the
patriciate became more and more enclosed. The
Golden Book which was looked after and kept up
to date by the *avogadori*, registered the births and
marriages, and these marriages, in order to be
approved, had to be between people of equal
social standing, otherwise the children lost the
right to be part of the *Maggior Consiglio*. (No
wives from the servant or plebeian class were
permitted: parity was agreed only with patrician
wives, or the daughters of secretaries of the
Senate, lawyers, notaries, doctors and apoth-
ecaries, mainland nobles or master glass-blowers
from Murano.)

Boys born of a legitimate marriage and approved legally had the right to enter the sovereign
political assembly, the *Maggior Consiglio*, at the
age of 25. This was their right, but also their duty
unless the young man became a priest, since
political life was strictly forbidden to the clergy,
even though the *Maggior Consiglio* and Senate
interfered radically in church matters by electing

the bishops. Moreover, the young man would
belong to the council until his death, as the
stubborn Venetian bureaucratic organization
envisaged a suitable office (naturally, concurrent
with others) even for men over 80, that of the
Decano d'Età.

If we were looking for a decisional center or
nucleus of the complicated Venetian political

system, we have at last found it. The *Maggior
Consiglio* was a kind of valley of Jehoshaphat, in
which all the patricians came together, all
theoretically equal (and actually equal as far as the
right to vote was concerned), from the doge to the
senators, the Ten to the *Quaranta*, the very rich
and the wretchedly poor, the influential and the
unknown, descendants of ancient lines and those
who were humbly born. The *Maggior Consiglio*
elected by the electors of the doge, the 60 members
of the *Pregadi*, the 60 members of the *Zonta*, the
Ten and the *Quaranta*. Moreover, within the
Maggior Consiglio, the vote of one member was
worth as much as the vote of another, a poor
man's vote had the same weight as the vote of the
savio grande or the Dogal Councillor.

This had a number of negative consequences:
for instance, there was a certain trade in votes.
"He who desires honour should give money to
impoverished gentlemen . . ." noted the chronicler
Marin Sanudo in the early 1500s; and in the 18th
century, even a universally respected figure such as
the highly-cultured doge Marco Foscarini sank
funds into obtaining the votes of the poorer

nobles, who were afterwards nicknamed the *Barnabotti* after the houses conceded to them free of charge by the state in the San Barnaba district. In fact, the *Broglio* (meaning 'kitchen garden'), that is, the part of the square directly in front of the Doge's Palace, has always borne this name because originally it was part of the garden of the nuns of San Zaccaria. The patricians would stroll here in the intervals between parliamentary sittings and here the candidates for the various offices would introduce themselves, and so it became synonymous with the practice of trading in votes. However, the system also had very positive aspects: there was no tyrant, no senator, nor any decemvir that could not be thwarted by a single vote, and potential tyrants were constantly on display, always risking failure and loss of status, so they were consequently more scrupulous and careful not to abuse their power.

Once in a while, almost casually, the *Maggior Consiglio* remembered its sovereign prerogatives. The Council of Ten paid the price once when it had pushed too hard to gain extra authority, and so the *Maggior Consiglio* deferred the elections for

its renewal; in the years when it was at the height of its powers, the Ten formed an addition for itself, the *Zonta*, made up of the most influential people in the city, and saw it suppressed in practice even before being suppressed legally towards the end of the 16th century, by means of the usual system, that of not electing anyone out of those who had presented themselves as candidates. On other occasions, the *Maggior Consiglio* had reacted drastically towards overbearing politicians by electing them, for example, to rather modest posts which were beneath them; and they were obliged, in order not to submit to the humiliation of going for instance to be *podestà* in Camposampiero or governor of Quero, to renounce the office, by paying a fee and "atoning by default;" in other words, they could not be elected to another post for the whole duration of the rejected office.

Under normal conditions, the *Maggior Consiglio* was called to determine or ratify the most important measures proposed. As we have seen, it also had to elect incumbents for all the main offices, including ambassadors and the *capitani generali da mar*, supreme commanders of the fleet. It also had to elect a veritable army of magistrates of greater or lesser importance, and this task was split among its members. These positions included political, administrative, judiciary, naval, commercial and victualling offices, plus the *reggimenti* – the important, the lesser and the extremely minor governors on land and sea, as well as all the military officials, starting with the *sopracomiti*, the galley commanders, and the *governatori di nave*, commanders of sailing-vessels.

However, the *Maggior Consiglio* was also the setting for the great political debates. Meetings took place in the enormous hall which, before the fire of 1578, had been decorated at the hand of Titian, Carpaccio and the Bellinis, with a huge fresco of the *Coronation of the Virgin* by the Paduan Guariento as a background, behind the tribunal of the doge and the *Signoria*. This hall had on the odd festive occasion, such as the solemn state visit of Henry III of France and Poland in 1576, been transformed into a ballroom and banqueting hall, but in the days of turmoil in May 1797 it was also the scene of the riotous voting which marked the end of the thousand year independence of the *Serenissima*.

Left: members of the Scuola dei Mercanti, the Confraternity of Merchants, painted by Tintoretto (Galleria dell'Accademia, Venice). The picture shows the members wearing their ceremonial garb; two patricians are depicted in the foreground, protectors of the confraternity. These confraternities (scuole) were a feature of Venetian civil, religious and social life, which began as mutual aid associations. All the trades, even the most humble, had their own scuola, in which the artisans and tradesmen of the middle classes and common people came together to protect themselves against the patriciate. Patricians were only rarely enrolled in the scuole, and then only in exceptional circumstances. In 1501 there were 215 scuole, illustrating both Venetian industriousness and the great number of crafts practised in the city as a result of the economic impetus provided by maritime trade and wealth from the East. Some of these crafts are shown opposite, taken from Jan (Giovanni) Grevembroch's Varie Venete Curiosità Sacre e Profane (1755–65), (Museo Correr, Venice). From above, left to right: mirror-maker, wax-refiners, fishmonger, firemen (a duty delegated by the Senate to the Arsenal workers), the doge's tailor, and a fustian-maker.

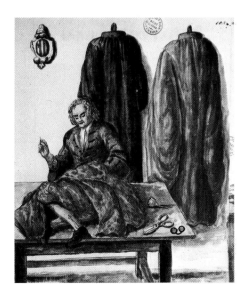

Followers of the pope thrown out . . .

It has been stated repeatedly that the Venetians of the golden age considered Venice to be above and beyond all else first Venetians, then Christians.

It was said at one time that the Venetians believed deeply in St. Mark, quite a lot in God and very little or not at all in the pope.

The pope then was first and foremost a temporal ruler, one of the Italian princes whose territories bordered with Venice's lands. This was more than sufficient to justify a certain diffidence regarding the successors of St. Peter, who controlled ports on the Adriatic and encouraged sailors, merchants and shipowners there to compete with Venice. There had been some friction with the pope concerning Comacchio, a rival town vying for the business along the rivers of the Po valley, mainly to do with the export of salt. This little town of the Romagna was attacked twice and the second time brutally eliminated from the contest by the deportation of its inhabitants. (This happened in 932, under doge Pietro II Candiano.) It became the focal point of a bitter conflict with the apostolic see. Then there was the case of Ancona, which gradually had to give up in favour of Venice all hope of trade with the East. Then again, in the late 1500s, the port construction works promoted by pope Clement VIII in Goro, in the Polesine district, were so hindered by the Venetians that the pope threatened to change from a "lamb" to a "lion" and to go in person to smash the so-called "Po Cut", built by the Republic to divert the waters of the Po. In over a thousand years countless disagreements had spoilt the relationship between Venice and the Roman pontificate, even though at the time of the great clash between the German emperor Frederick Barbarossa and Alexander III the Republic had supported the pope, and with his good offices had made the peace between him and his powerful rival. The last and most serious conflict came about in 1606 when, following the arrest of two priests found guilty of common felonies, pope Paul V, who claimed for the priests the right to immunity from secular law, attacked Venice with the most dread of spiritual weapons, the interdict. Venice rejected the interdict as null, invalid and canonically illegal, and there followed

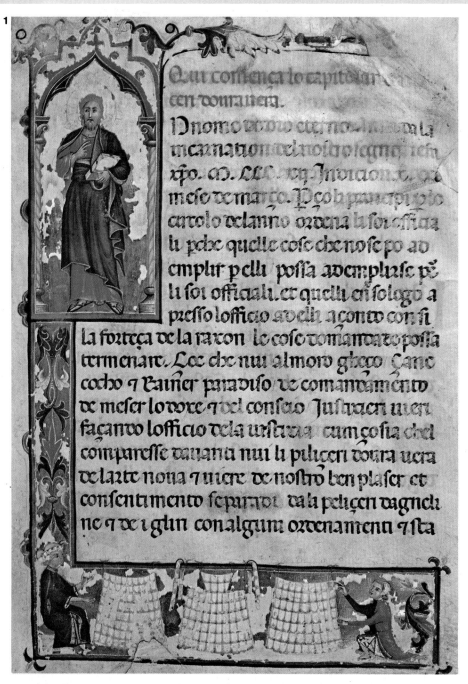

CONFRATERNITIES AND GUILDS

The first associations or *scuole* were not primarily professional bodies, but religious and mutual aid societies. People of different trades could join them, and they were connected with a particular monastery or church, with permanent meeting-houses. These early forms provided the model for the craft guilds in which members of the same profession came together to look after their own interests. They were thus associations of the labourers and middle classes who had no part in political power, and were able by these means to assert their importance and the role of their guild in the community. As early as the 11th century we have records of associations of workers giving free labour in the workshops; by the 14th century there were some hundred religious, trade and craft associations, small and large. Venice was renowned for the diligence of its workers and for its specialized artisans. The central arch of St. Mark's basilica is decorated with Romanesque bas reliefs depicting the craftsmen (5, smiths; 6, carpenters; 7, bakers; 8, vintners), as if in homage to the flourishing guilds which contributed so much to the city's greatness. The guilds enjoyed a large degree of freedom, and were regulated by statutes or *mariegole* (1, page from the *mariegola* of the furriers) which controlled the life of the society and dealt with trade abuses such as unfair competition, poor workmanship, over-long hours (especially night-work) and defective raw materials. Some of these consortiums were powerful

2

3

enough to fix the price of their goods, and on several occasions the *giustizieri*, the three state officials created in 1173 to oversee the markets, had to intervene to prohibit such unilateral fixing of prices and enforce a fair charge by ordinance (9, butchers' price list). The *mariegole* were drawn up by the society's officials approved by the plenary session of the guild, and ratified by the *Giustizieri*. In general a society's officers were annually elected and consisted of a president, vice-president and various members of the board who formed the council, as well as a treasurer, secretary, fund-raiser, two auditors and one or more

5

6

7

8

9

1

assessors whose duty it was to make an equitable division of the charges. Only master craftsmen voted in the elections, journeymen and apprentices being excluded. In its meeting-house the society would keep its banner with the image of its patron-saint, the emblems of its trade (10, panel of the Guild of Furriers), its seals (2 and 3, seals of the Guild of Masons and of the Guild of Oil-sellers), and its chest. The assemblies and the annual banquet for the elections to the offices were held in the hall and the refectory (4, the main hall of the Scuola di San Rocco). All decisions taken by the assembly had to be ratified by the *Giustizieri*. New members had to promise honest practice and a responsible attitude to the trade. Apprentices had to be 12 years old, and spent five to seven years in training. After two or three years as labourers they could be examined for the title of master craftsman, and had the right to open a shop. Members paid the society an annual impost, recompensed the officials and paid a tax on their revenue. They were charged to be ready to settle quarrels between members of the same confraternity, and to ensure the loyalty of the society to the state of Venice. The confraternities played a very important social role, giving financial assistance to the poor and infirm and pensions to widows, looking after orphans and founding alms-houses. From 1539 it was obligatory for all craftsmen and workmen to belong to a corporation. Members had both honours and responsibilities. They provided conscripts for the galleys, and played an active part in religious festivals and public ceremonies, when they appeared with their emblems and banners.

almost a year of *quid pro quo* before the gaze of an astonished Europe until it was all over and Venice was seen to be substantially the victor.

The principal protagonist of this extremely important episode both on the theological and judiciary plane was the monk of the Servite order, Paolo Sarpi, councillor of the Republic. However, in spite of pressures and threats of all kinds (Venice had already been struggling with all her might for about 80 years to free herself from the Spanish influence which by now hung heavy over the whole of Italy) the most active section of the Venetian political class had supported and fostered a resistance which eventually ended up focussing on the major exponents, doge Leonardo Donà, Nicolò Contarini and a few others, who appealed to everyone's sense of patriotism, whatever their actual convictions.

In his inopportune curial and inquisitorial zeal, the Borghese pope had in fact awakened the chronic, irrepressible, civic pride of the Venetians, that intransigent patriotism which has given rise to a number of anecdotes, similar in many respects to those attributed to Victorian England under the

ensign of the famed, proud, stubborn motto: "right or wrong, my country."

At that time, few nations practised such spectacular, solemn state Catholicism; fewer still defended their civic rights with such confidence in the face of church authority. The relationship between church and state was extremely tense: the doge officially attended more religious functions than even the bishop, but the bishops were nominated by the Senate. (The Senate often selected bachelor senators, diplomats or parliamentarians who, amazingly, generally became exemplary bishops.) The sentences handed out by ecclesiastical tribunals had to be ratified by the lay tribunals, ecclesiastics had no say on political matters, and when the *Collegio* discussed church problems or anything to do with links with Rome, the "papists," that is, anyone who had relatives high up in the church or were in any way beneficiaries of the Roman papal court, were ejected; the official minutes would contain the note *Cazzadi i papalisti* ("followers of the pope having been removed").

Yet it is said that the state professed orthodox Catholicism (more orthodox than in Rome, as someone has pointed out). Social life was permeated with a full-blooded devotion, and the city was crammed with churches, pious foundations and cult-figures among the faithful. However patriotism always had the edge on all other sentiment and permeated every social sector. There is a famous anecdote about the senator and cosmographer, brother Mauro Camoldolese: he had presented a senator with his magnificent planisphere, which is still in the Biblioteca Marciana. "Where is Venice?" asked the senator immediately. When brother Mauro showed him, he was amazed and angrily asked why he had made it so small. The monk launched into a scientific explanation: compared with the extent of the world's lands and seas, Venice had to be very small. "*Strenze' el mondo*," exclaimed the senator indignantly, "*e fe' Venezia piu' grande!*" ("Reduce the size of the world and make Venice bigger"): if the tale is not true it is still a good one. Even though John and Sebastian Cabot sailed on behalf of the king of England, when they discovered Newfoundland their first act was to raise the banner of St. Mark. "Because," notes the chronicler simply, "they were Venetians."

The importance of the role of the scuole and their achievements can be seen not only in their grand halls, but also in the illustrations of their trades and the duties which they were assigned on solemn occasions. The chief processions are depicted in the fine Romanesque bas reliefs in the central arcade of St. Mark's basilica (left: shipbuilders). Opposite: during the doge's coronation, he ascended the pozzetto, a kind of chair in which he was carried around the piazza by 50 strong workers of the Arsenal at great speed, throwing handfuls of money to the crowd (from Franco's Habiti). In this way Venice achieved a happy modus vivendi between the classes. According to a calculation made by Gaetano Cozzi in 1586 there were 150,000 inhabitants. Of these the nobility accounted for 6,039, the "citizenry" 7,600, and the people 19,000. There were 2,507 monks, 1,205 friars, 447 beggars, 1,111 poor people in almshouses, 536 priests, and 1,694 Jews. Manservants accounted for 3,680, and maids for 6,000.

Two pictures from the series of Venetian crafts in the Doge's Palace, preserved in the Museo Correr, Venice. Above: the Barbers' Guild (detail), showing a barber shaving the doge's beard. Below: the Guild of the Peateri, *owners of goods barges.*

The chosen people: that was how the Venetians of the golden age saw themselves. They were the descendants of the Romans that had opted for the freedom of the seas and lagoons rather than bend to the will of barbarian monarchs: history, legend and tradition stressed this every day. The patrician class then, wielders of the power exercised within the "locked" *Maggior Consiglio* in their turn saw themselves as the elite of the chosen people.

They were fiercely proud of their pedigree, which, for many families (such as the houses of Marcello, Valier, Venier, Gradenigo, Falier and

many others) was undoubtedly Romano-Venetian, going back to the dawn of time. Within their own circle there were long-standing subdivisions based on the greater or lesser antiquity of their origins. The *case vecchie* ('old houses') already existed before the ninth century, and 12 of these, known as the "apostolic" houses, were supposed to have participated in the legendary election of the first doge in the year 697 (Badoer, Barozzi, Contarini, Dandolo, Falier, Gradenigo, Michiel, Morosini, Memmo, Polani, Sanudo and Tiepolo). The *case nuove* ('new houses') had entered the ranks of the nobility after the ninth century but before the "locking" of the *Maggior Consiglio*. The *case novissime* ('brand-new houses') had been assumed to the patriciate on merit during the last stages of the conflict with Genoa in 1381, and there were also various families of great lords from the mainland, who had also been admitted in recognition of various good qualities in the course of the Middle Ages. Since every male patrician, as a member of the *Maggior Consiglio* was theoretically eligible for the doge's throne, all members were considered of princely status: *tot nobiles veneti, tot reges*. However, all this vanity and pretentiousness was sacrificed totally to patriotism: when the Turkish sultan in the 12th century decided to take Crete for himself, and a bitter war drained the Republic's finances and decimated the ranks of the patriciate, the patricians themselves took the very serious decision to put themselves up for sale.

On 16 February 1646 it was proposed that a law should be passed opening up access to the patrician class and therefore to the *Maggior Consiglio*, to whoever, in Venice or on the mainland, could offer financial support for a thousand soldiers for one year or else 60,000 ducats in cash. This proposal, defended by the dogal *consigliere* Giacomo Marcello, using arguments that would still be relevant now, was not approved, but the *Maggior Consiglio* nevertheless occasionally accepted the petitions of several families who offered the Exchequer 100,000 ducats for the costs of the war: neither did they quibble over refinements, receiving into the *Maggior Consiglio* not only the Zaguri family, nobles from Zara, but also the Labia family, rich merchants of Florentine origin, the Correggios, fur-traders from San Giovanni Crisostomo, the

FV FATTO LANNO 1517 SOTTO MISIER ZACHARIA D'ANTONIO GASTALDO DE MARANGONI D'NAVE D'LARSENAL
FV RINOVATO D'LANNO 1753 SOTTO LA GASTALDIA DI FRANCESCO ZANOTTO GASTALDO E COMPAGNI

Plaque of the Guild of Arsenal workers, restored in 1753 (Museo Correr, Venice). The name marangoni *included master-carpenters, joiners, and all woodworkers. The guild of the* marangoni *was one of the busiest and most famous in the city because wood was so much in demand for the construction of ships and buildings in Venice.*

Tascas, clothiers at the sign of the Golden Tree and the Lombrias, descendants (it was said) of the Rolla family's cook. So it went on, even when Candia had been lost, in order to finance this time the victorious campaign in which, a century before the fall of Venice, Francesco Morosini routed the Turks and conquered the Peloponnese: in this way there was a mixture of professional and merchant families, self-made men, all fresh from the plebeian ranks at a time when ancestry was painfully important. Mingling with the descendants of ancient tribunes, the newly elected members took part on equal footing in political life and had their share of offices and magistratures, married the daughters of noble patricians, who in their turn took the daughters of the new members into their families as wives. All this somewhat reduced the standing of the Venetian patriciate in the eyes of European nobility to whom the Venetians had always considered themselves superior; but the interests of the state were more important.

Patriotism and civic solidarity did not however prevent the patricians from disagreeing among themselves and having little arguments and conflicts, sometimes quite openly. A plot between some *nuove* and *novissime* families, referred to for

this reason as dogal (*ducali*) families, blocked for more than two centuries, from the death of Michele Morosini to the election of Marcantonio Memmo, the selection of the doge from among 16 families (Barbarigo, Donà, Foscari, Grimani, Gritti, Lando, Loredan, Malipiero, Marcello, Mocenigo, Moro, Priuli, Trevisan, Tron, Venier and Vendramin). The conflicts between 'long' and 'short' lines (old and new houses) reached breaking-point more than once, and later on, in the 17th century, there were even more violent outbursts between the *vecchi* (the conservatives, linked with the Roman court and ardent supporters of the Counter Reformation) and the *giovani*, followers of a livelier, more adventurous policy which supported wider participation in decision-making and less formalized religion, but a harsher, more austere style. The main exponents of this stance were the doges Leonardo Donà and Nicolò Contarini. Even later, in the 1700s, the friction within the patriciate focused on rich and poor: the Venetian custom of burdening its nobles with enormous expenses connected with the carrying out of their political and diplomatic roles, the impoverishment of a part of the patrician class and the concentration of wealth in relatively few families, had all ensured that in

1

2

3

4

6

There is no doubt that the aristocratic regime which ruled Venice during the Renaissance and after used sports and festivals as an instrument of their power. Such events brought the whole community together in joyous celebration of Venice itself, and helped to create a national spirit. One strange feature was that some of the sports, such as the "wars" fought on the bridges between rival sections of the population with fisticuffs (2) or staves (3: both from engravings by Franco) continued the memory of the communal strife which Venice had overcome politically by putting power in the hands of the patricians, who formed a very large "political class." It is therefore not surprising that these mock battles were later banned on the grounds of public order.

7

FESTIVALS AND SPORTS

In the festivals of Venice the city itself or part of it became a stage, and the people were both protagonists and spectators. Some of these Venetian festivals still continue today. The queen of festivals was the regatta (1, on the Riva degli Schiavoni, from a 17th-century drawing, 4, on the Grand Canal, from an engraving of 1740 by Zucchi, showing the winning "machine"). In this event the Venetians expressed their close links with the sea. Civic ceremonies were just as important, such as the various visits of the doge to different places in the city and different institutions, or the marriage with the sea, as were specifically religious feasts (9, the festival of the Redeemer, and the bridge of boats to the Giudecca, from an engraving after a painting by Canaletto). There were also various entertainments. Several of these are depicted in an illustration by Franco (5): killing a cat with a shaven head; catching a duck; catching a goose; and bull-chasing, in which women also took part (7). Balancing acts included the *forze d'Ercole*, a kind of human pyramid (6, from an 18th-century engraving) and "Turkish tightrope walking" (8), shown taking place between the Campanile and St. Mark's basin.

5

8 9

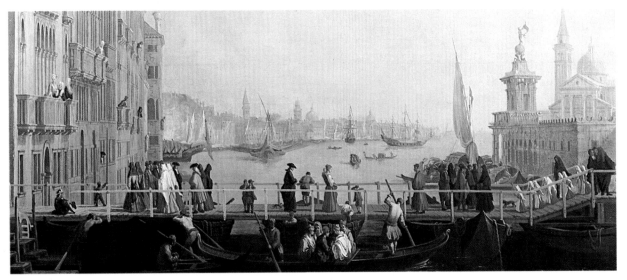

The Votive Bridge for the Celebrations in Honour of the Madonna della Salute *by Luca Carlevaris (Wadsworth Atheneum, Hartford, Connecticut). This feast is still celebrated on 21 November in memory of the vow of 1630, by virtue of which the Senate decided to build a great church in honour of the Virgin for delivering them from a dreadful plague. On the anniversary of this feast a pontoon bridge is built between the two banks of the Grand Canal so that the church can easily be visited. Salt mutton, the so-called "castradina", is served in inns and at home. Opposite: gilded wooden sculpture, a fragment of the last* Bucintoro *built in 1729 (Museo Correr, Venice). The* Bucintoro *was a highly carved and gilded state barge on which the doge and his retinue performed the "marriage with the sea," the greatest of the many joyful Venetian ceremonies.*

practice decision-making always fell to the well-off. This situation gave birth to the last great parliamentary battle in the *Maggior Consiglio*. The protagonists were the patricians Carlo Contarini and Giorgio Pisani (neither very rich nor very poor, but both brilliant lawyers). They wanted a reform that would give every member of the patriciate an opportunity and would suppress the monopoly of power concentrated in the hands of the rich and the "great." The tragic end to this long parliamentary contest heralds the imminent fall of the Republic: the State Inquisitors had the two leaders of the opposition arrested, and the *Maggior Consiglio*, which just a few years earlier had become so heated over the arbitrary arrest of the *avogadore* Querini, and had found no peace until he was released, the same *Maggior Consiglio* which in the previous century had supported the opposition against the abuses of the "great" in the person of the doge Giovanni Corner and his family, now kept silent, then approved and finally actually voted a motion of congratulation for the State Inquisitors. The system had broken down and did not function properly any more. (So much so that, in order to get his own way, the doge Paolo Renier who had moved into the ranks of the "great," made a celebrated speech in which he cunningly applied the screw of patriotism and conjured up the bogey of intervention by European powers worried by the Republic's internal problems which were weakening and tiring her . . .).

Right up to the very last moment however, the duty of the patriciate was clear: to serve the state from the age of 25 until death; this was an unbreakable commitment. The growing number of very rich men who, in the 1700s, preferred to burden themselves with enormous fees rather than take on their duties, or poorer people, who would become priests in order to escape the *cursus honorum*, symptomizes this decadence, though it was not as widespread as has been suggested.

N.H., *Nobilomo*, "nobleman" was the title given to a patrician, the only title permitted, with the appellation *ser* before the Christian name (*missier* for the procurators of St. Mark). His uniform was a long cloak fastened at the waist with a belt. In winter it was edged with fur, red for the Dogal Councillors, blue or violet for other magistratures, and black for patricians who held no particular office. On their shoulders they wore the *stola* or *bàtolo*, a kind of stole, edged in gold for the knights. The procurators of St. Mark (nine in all: three *de supra*, the direct guardians of St. Mark's basilica and its treasures; three *de citra* and three *de ultra*, tutelary judges for widows and wards, as well as testamentary executors for the commissioners in the quarters on both sides of the Grand Canal): the latter wore purple cloaks with very wide sleeves, *alla ducale*, "in dogal style." For the whole of the 18th century, which was in many ways a more frivolous century than the others, there was a lengthy tug-of-war between the patricians, who did not want to have to wear these garments all the time and be on display, and the State Inquisitors, who were against the patricians wearing the ordinary *tabarro*, or cloak, a garment

Below: a puppet stall, a common sight in the squares of Venice (from Grevembroch).

One classically Venetian spectacle was the regatta. Women also took part in these "to the delight of all beholders" according to a caption in Giacomo Franco's Habiti (1610, above). Below: the ballad-singers' platform, from an 18th–century engraving.

they said that was not in keeping with the "patrician character," though in fact it was most useful for blending in with the crowd. Why should they want this? Because while local and foreign citizens could do more or less what they liked, provided they kept out of politics, a keen watch was always kept on the patrician class. The blessed "patrician character" had to be preserved and class status was not to be prejudiced. There was too the ancient obsession with spying and the spreading of state secrets, an obsession which plagued the rulers of a Republic that had always been surrounded by hostile powers.

The most glaring manifestation of this obsession was the tragic Foscarini affair, brought to its climax by a number of shadowy episodes (one such was that the influential senator Angelo Badoer, a *savio di terraferma* was exposed as a spy, and the Spanish ambassador, the Marquis of Bedmar, spied quite openly). The knight Antonio Foscarini was a senator from a great family and ambassador to France and England. He was arrested, tried, condemned to death and hanged on a gallows between the columns of St. Mark and St. Theodore in the Piazzetta in 1622 for "having met privately and in secret with princes' ministers ... and having revealed to them verbally and in writing the most intimate secrets of the Republic," and being paid for his service. Later, however, the Council of Ten discovered that Foscarini was innocent, the victim of a professional spy who had falsely accused him. With exceptional civic courage, the high assembly solemnly proclaimed its error in a circular to all the courts of Europe, restoring the condemned man's good name. Even in easy-going 18th-century Venice, it was dangerous and prohibited for a patrician to associate with foreign ambassadors.

The Law of Balance

At this stage we have completed this survey of the basic structures of the Venetian state. But it remains to examine one particular center of absolute and definitive power: the *Maggior Consiglio*. We have already said that it was the sovereign body, the assembly which approved fundamental laws and elected all organs of state, including those who were required to fulfil other

The bailiff of the Nicolotti. The populace of Venice was divided into two factions, the Nicolotti and the Castellani. The Castellani included the inhabitants of the sestieri *of Castello, San Marco, and Dorsoduro, whilst the Nicolotti comprised the inhabitants of Santa Croce, San Polo, and Cannaregio.*

electoral and legislative duties. The patricians who were its members, however, were subject to the scrutiny of the Council of Ten and the State Inquisitors – whom they themselves elected. The Senate undoubtedly represented executive power, as did the *Pien Collegio*, its direct expression but itself responsible to the *Maggior Consiglio*. The doge and the *Signoria* were also answerable to the *Maggior Consiglio*, were elected by them and had too a reciprocal measure of control over them. The Council of Ten's power was limited by the *avogadori di Comun* (but the *Signoria*, which was actually part of the Ten could also contain and control it). In effect, the whole structure consisted of reciprocal controls, each cut in with the other so that none could have indisputable dominance.

We have already seen that several times one or other of these bodies tried to climb to absolute and definitive power. Among the doges, Marino Falier paid with his life, Lorenzo Celsi (who probably never even tried) paid with humiliation, Agostino Barbarigo with posthumous execration (and once he was dead, the *correttori alla Promissione ducale* introduced all kinds of cautionary measures so as to prevent his successor "making himself omnipotent like Missier Augustin Barbarigo"). As for the Ten, the *Maggior Consiglio* progressively limited and restricted them with the threat of not electing anyone else to the dreaded Council and so allowing it to die out. It was only in the last few decades of the Republic that the knot loosened and the State Inquisitors were able to arrest the heads of opposing parliamentary parties with impunity. Soon the *Pien Collegio* no longer bothered to inform the Senate of the dispatches addressed to it or of the reality of the situation. This brought about the catastrophe, consummated by means of a series of illegal discussions in assemblies or conferences that were illegal both in their composition and their authority. Even the last vote carried, the one which closes the chapter of the independent Venetian Republic with the abdication of the *Maggior Consiglio* on 21 May 1797, was illegal: there were not the number of voters required by law. The magic circle, Liberty, Legality, Fraternity, had broken; it was the end.

In effect, the constitution of the aristocratic Republic, as we said earlier, was based wholly on a parliamentary system that relied on balance, and while this balance was healthy it was able to absorb the attacks and counter-attacks such a form of government attracts. This system can be defined as one whose foundations are not determined by electoral suffrage, but whose every movement beyond that is based on suffrage. As such it was an extremely egalitarian system within the power-holding class. Venetian politicians were delighted whenever they could give examples of patrician egalitariansm in effective action. This is expressed in the ceremony accompanying every candidature: the candidate for whatever office it was, escorted by relatives and *piezi* or guarantors, would go down into the *Broglio* in the Piazzetta and introduce himself to the electors, *sbassando stola*, that is, bowing so that his stole (or *bàtolo*) would slip from his shoulders to be caught in his hands. In one of his famous discourses, Marco Foscarini narrates one of these episodes and attempts to draw from it an edifying moral:

"I cannot strike from my memory something I read in my youth by a writer from the last century. A high-ranking Spanish gentleman came to Venice ... he had been here many years earlier in the battle of the Curzolari ... and for this reason had come to know closely that great man Sebastiano Venier ... who used to go about in public with a cortege of a hundred or more nobles, all under his command. When asked ... what he had seen in our city that had seemed to him most worthy of admiration ... he replied 'for me the greatest wonder has been to observe Sebastiano Venier shortly before the elections to the procuratorship in the pose of a supplicant, and how a humble Greek who had served on the fleet during the war could pass before him without even removing his hat' – and he concluded: 'Oh! blessed city! Oh divine laws, as worthy of respect as the ways of any sovereign power ... on my return I pray I will be able to imitate such a civilized, moderate way of life!'"

It is a haunting image, that of the victor of Lepanto submitting to the rules of the parliamentary game, even though he had exercised an enormously wide and absolute power. It is also perhaps one of the keys to correct understanding of the mentality of the Venetian political class, and therefore of the Venetian constitution. Moreover, within this constitution, however aristocratic it may have been, there was also room for the other social categories.

VENICE'S UNIQUE DEVELOPMENT

Venice's existence is due to an accident of geography, the presence of the Realtine islands, which are more sand-banks than solid ground at the center of the waters, reeds and mud that make up the changing face of the lagoon. Without the skill and foresight of its inhabitants, however, who successfully adapted the environment to their needs, the city could never have become what it is. The city's development is illustrated in the center superimposed on an outline map of modern Venice. The yellow patches indicate the probable position of the islands in the seventh century, taken from the foundation dates of the earliest churches. These together with the areas in pink show the probable situation in the ninth century,

when the seat of the duchy was transferred there from Malamocco. The light green areas are additions up to the 11th century. The extent of the city in the middle of the 12th century is indicated by these colours with the areas in brown. By this time Venice had assumed more or less its present shape. Expansions up to the 16th century are shown in blue, by which time the present city had evolved, apart from some differences in the East and on the side facing the Fondamenta Nuove. This impression is confirmed by an examination of Jacopo de'Barbari's famous perspective view, parts of which are reproduced here to illustrate some of the city's historical quarters. Venice's commercial center and markets have been

in the Rialto (1) since the ninth century. Here Venice's only bridge, still made of wood, and which opens, joined the two parts of the city separated by the Grand Canal. Beneath the arch of San Giacomo were the counters and books of the money-changers, later the bankers.

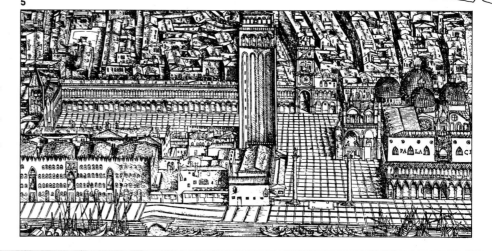

The shore in front of the Piazzetta is still called the Molo, recalling the historical heart of the port of Venice. The harbour originally extended up to the Riva degli Schiavoni and the Grand Canal until this thoroughfare became a luxury residential area, and up to the Zattere on the Giudecca Canal. The warehouses of the Dogana Marittima (3), the Customs House were thus naturally situated on the point dividing the Grand Canal from the Giudecca Canal. The salt warehouses stood nearby.

Venice's political and spiritual center is on the site of the Porteciaci's *palatium*. In

de'Barbari's perspective view, the Doge's Palace, the basilica, the Procuratie Vecchie, the Piazza and the Piazzetta all have their present appearance. The Piazzetta was originally an arm of St Mark's basin, and the Piazza was crossed by a *rio*. The Mercerie lead from San Marco under the Clock Tower directly to the Rialto, joining up the political and business centers.

Crafts, industries and even work yards were scattered over the city. Before the Jews settled in the ghetto in Cannaregio, for example, there were foundries on the site. With the creation of the Arsenal on the eastern edge of the city, this area became the industrial heart. In illustration 2, the lake of San Daniele is already turned into the Arsenale Nuovo, and the Docks of the Arsenale Novissimo are protected by a wall, though the banks are not yet fitted out.

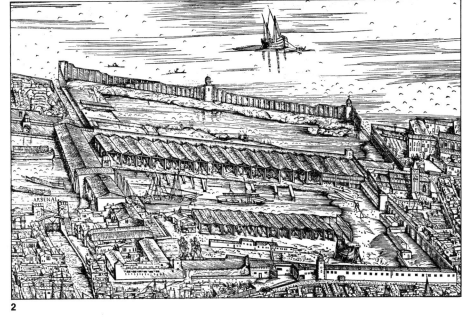

2

A characteristic feature of Venice is its double system of canals and *rii* by water, and *calli*, *campi* and *fondamenta* by land. The city is divided in two by the double bend of the Grand Canal, so that the Rialto, where until the 19th century the only bridge linking the two halves stood, naturally became the nerve center for land traffic. Like all medieval cities, Venice was not divided according to wealth. The patrician palaces adjoined the dwellings of the artisans and commoners, so that the city formed an organic whole. But this was not the case everywhere, and in some areas, Castello for example (4), there were rows of houses for the common people, some of which belonged to the state and some of which were intended for sailors.

The religious center of the

4

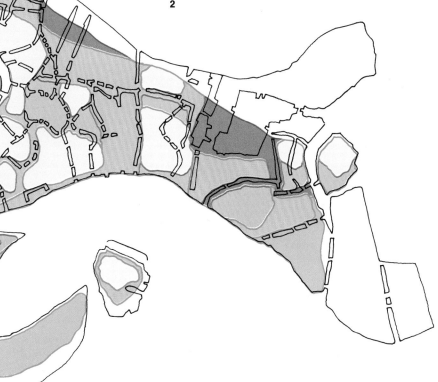

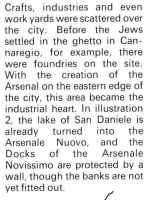

Plan: The Realtine Islands in the seventh century:

Extensions up to the ninth century

Extentions up to the 11th century

Extensions up to the middle of the 12th century

Extensions up to the 16th century

6

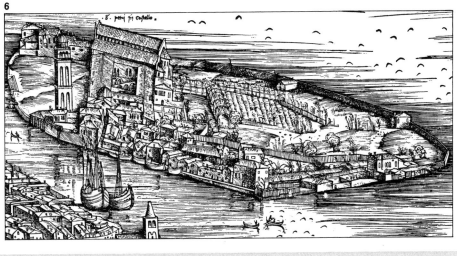

city (6) was the island of Olivolo or San Pietro di Castello off the eastern edge of the city, where there must have been a fortified castle in the early Middle Ages. This was the seat of the bishop, perhaps from 775 when Obeliebato installed himself there, and from 1451 of the patriarch, when the title was transferred from Grado to Venice. Only in 1807 after the fall of the Republic was the patriarchate removed from Castello to San Marco. The 16th-century map shows empty ground, pergolas, and walled gardens.

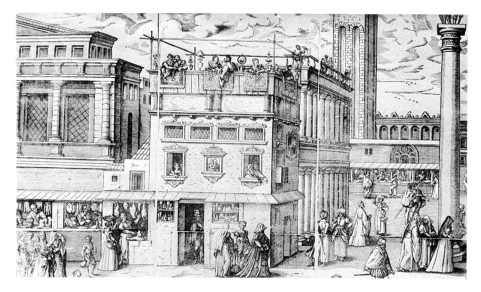

Venice's uniqueness lies in more than the mere appeal of its numerous canals. Its unique style of architecture is also determined by the environment, the difficulties of which were turned to advantage in imaginative architectural solutions. Above: the Piazzetta in the second half of the 16th century, as it was left by the architect Sansovino, with the Libreria still incomplete, and the Zecca (mint) only one storey high. Opposite: view of the Piazzetta dei Leoncini towards the Clock Tower (detail of an engraving by Michele Marieschi). Note the belvedere on the right, a typical feature of Venetian architecture.

Besides the doge and the procurators of St. Mark, the other life-long post was that of *Cancellier Grande*. Although he was not a patrician, this particular man would be called knight of the golden stole (*Stola d'Oro*) and wore a purple mantle with the wide 'dogal' sleeves: he was the head of ministerial bureaucracy which was recruited (just as the magistratures were recruited exclusively from the patricians) from a particular class, that of the *Segretari* or secretaries, a word describing a precise social category, that of the *cittadini originari*, founding fathers.

When past Venetian writers have tried to define this category, they have spoken of a "people's nobility." In reality, this was not a true noble class, but rather a specific bourgeoisie, to which the tendency to "nobilize" all privileged classes, experienced all over Europe in the 16th century, had attributed some form of noble standing. The foundation of these families, so eager with their coats of arms, was the medieval subdivision between citizens *de jure*, *de gratia*, *de intus* and *de extra*. The last three categories came into being to encourage a form of graded immigration: those who though born elsewhere had lived in Venice for more than ten years at a stretch became citizens *de intus*, and had the right to assume certain public offices and exercise certain crafts, including the most esteemed. After six more years they could acquire citizenship *de extra*, which authorized them to "sail under the protection of the banner of St. Mark," *i.e.* to practise the "noble art" of commerce with the aid of all the patronage,

diplomacy and military force guaranteed by the state. Citizens became *de gratia* (subject to approval by the *Maggior Consiglio*) if they had been resident in Venice for at least 25 years, engaged in non-manual work or with a private income. Towards the middle of the 14th century, in order to replenish the city whose numbers had been decimated by disease, *de intus* citizenship was granted to all those who had moved to Venice with their families and had registered with the *provveditori di Comun*. Already, earlier still, the silk-weavers from Lucca, who had fled because of internal domestic unrest, had been welcomed in Venice with every honour and made *de gratia* citizens: they brought with them a new industry, destined to prosper rapidly, and some of them found fortune and actually became part of the patriciate. But the *de jure* citizens were those who had been born in the city of a legitimate marriage between two citizens, and who had never done manual work: merchants, entrepreneurs, lawyers, notaries, doctors, chemists and landowners. Their ranks were swelled automatically by those descendants of patrician families who had lost, through a marriage not approved by the *Avogadori*, that cherished "characteristic" which gave access to the *Maggior Consiglio*: among these were members of the families of Barbarigo, Contarini, Gradenigo, Foscarini, Bragadin, Venier, Celsi, Foscolo, Tron, Zen, Zorzi, Querini and Dolfin.

When the Republic fell there were 286 families of *cittadini originari* (and 176 patrician families). There were varying degrees of renown: some of the greatest were of extremely long lineage, with such names as Alberti, Zon, Dardano, Imberti, Busenello, Giacomazzi, Sanfermo and Tornielli. Many had acquired noble titles and arms outside Venice; they were generally disdained by the patricians. Some very well-to-do families vied with the patricians as to the splendour of buildings or art collections. An example is the Coccina (or Cuccina) family who built themselves the magnificent palace later called Tiepolo-Papadopoli on the Grand Canal not far from the Rialto, and had their portraits painted by Paolo Veronese – two famous canvases which now hang in the Dresden Gallery. There were also the Amadi (or Amai), whose palace at Santa Croce was the object of a visit in 1576 by the cardinal of Lorena so that he

Above: the round chimneys with their flared conical pots are a common but original decorative feature of Venice. Those illustrated here are from the Palazzo Dario on the Grand Canal. Opposite: hull-shaped wooden roof of the church of San Giacomo dell'Orio, dating from the 14th century, which vividly illustrates the need for light roofing; the experience of the near-by Arsenal carpenters was able to satisfy this requirement. Such hull-shaped roofs were common in the city, and the roof of the Hall of the Maggior Consiglio *must have been of this type before the fire of 1577.*

could admire its collection of classical antiquities and musical instruments. Their showrooms, so to speak, were the *Scuole Grandi*, the greatest among the numerous Venetian confraternities, where no expense was spared to secure the greatest painters, sculptors and architects available (a good example is the *Scuola di San Rocco* with its series of masterpieces by Tintoretto). However, their most prestigious field of activity was the *Cancelleria Ducale*, the dogal chancellery: this was directed by the *Cavallier Grande*, Grand Knight, and divided into four categories, the secretaries of the Council of Ten, the secretaries of the Senate and the *nodari* or notaries, who were described as *Ducali* (dogal), *Ordinari* and *Straordinari* ('ordinary' and 'extra-ordinary'). The four secretaries of the Council of Ten and the 24 secretaries of the Senate had the title *circospetto* ('prudent') and the others, 72 in all, *fedelissimo* ('most faithful').

All these men held extremely sensitive posts, from the secretary of the *Maggior Consiglio*, the *Pregadi*, the *Collegio*, the Ten and the State Inquisitors, to diplomatic commissions in the least important states, such as the duchy of Mantua, the grand-duchy of Tuscany and the kingdoms of Sardinia and Naples, or else the secretariat of the high naval command and the major regiments, and of the Republic's ambassadors. These functions were traditionally carried out very conscientiously: Marc'Antonio Busenello (later to become *Cancellier Grande*) was taken prisoner by the Imperialists, since he was a Venetian resident in Mantua, and swallowed his code-book rather than let it fall into enemy hands. Giambattista Ballarin, secretary of the *bailo* in Constantinople, died while a prisoner of the sultan in 1666, and the very day before the fall of the Republic, the *circospetti* Sanfermo and Giacomazzi did all they could from their diplomatic vantage-points of Basle and Turin, sending out unheeded alarms and gathering valuable information. On the other hand, on more than one occasion certain of the more committed Venetian politicians such as Ranieri Zeno and Nicolò Contarini, had alerted the Ten, the Senate and the *Maggior Consiglio* to the risk that this silent and omnipresent class represented: while the Venetian magistratures changed constantly (the longest lasting offices never exceeded two or three years), this class never changed and too often exercised an excessive

influence on business, pressurizing the politicians through their experience, sometimes tinged with a little arrogance. It is the eternal battle between politicians and bureaucracy all over again; someone had suspected that behind the political and personal catastrophe of Antonio Foscarini lay the hidden guiles of this secretarial caste: the unfortunate ambassador who was condemned to death had clashed with bureaucracy several times and, according to the story, the bureaucrats took their cruel revenge.

We mentioned earlier the *Scuole Grandi* (these were the six largest with citizen confraternities: their headquarters were sumptuous and can still be admired, though the state of preservation varies. They are St. Mark's, with its splendid Renaissance facade in Campo SS. Giovanni e Paolo, San Rocco, San Giovanni Evangelista, San Teodoro, Santa Maria della Misericordia, now reduced to a gymnasium and Santa Maria della Carità, the present site of the galleries of the Accademia). There were an infinite number of *scuole*: at the fall of the Republic there were more than 300. Many of these institutions had a devotional, charitable basis, but most were based on co-operative, mutualist principles.

There were also national *scuole*, which were really clubs where foreigners or people of foreign extraction could meet: these were the *Scuole degli Albanesi* and *degli Schiavoni*, both famous because of the marvellous series of canvases by Carpaccio, the school at Volto Santo dei Lucchesi, or *dei Milanesi* under the invocation of saints Ambrose and Carlo, and the *Scuola dei Greci*, the 'Greek' school. There was also the *Scuola dei Zotti*, for invalids and war veterans. But the vast majority of *scuole* served to gather together people who were already linked in a guild or corporation, with functions that were mutualist and self-supporting, and affiliated with the specific functions of the corporations *i.e.* to control apprenticeships and the exercise of various crafts, professions and trades. If the headquarters of the various *scuole* display a constant vying for beauty of adornment, a symptom undoubtedly of substantial prosperity apart from a sign of innate good taste, their story, which has not yet been written by anyone (so far, only the statutes of a certain number of medieval guilds have been published) it would constitute an extremely important chapter in the history of the

VENETIAN BUILDING METHODS IN THE LAGOON

Venice's natural environment led to several unusual features in its building methods. Constructions had to be light and flexible in order to survive on the unstable floor of the lagoon. Foundations consisted of a number of piles driven into the earth (1) until they reached the bed of sand and clay known as *caranto* (2, pile-drivers at work, after an 18th–century engraving by Grevembroch). The piles were either arranged in several rows (5) around the edge of the building, or covered the entire surface area (4), if the building was to be very heavy. On top of these was placed a raft of planks which supported the foundations of Istria stone, and the walls above ground. Wood was used in large quantities, including its employment in tie-beams, a technique which may have originated in ship-building.

The wooden *reme*, horizontal wooden courses placed at regular intervals in the walls to distribute the weight of the floor-beams evenly are an example of the structural use of wood. Used for its lightness, wood appears in the typical Venetian dividing wall. A row of timber offcuts was reinforced with joists (*cantinelle*) running horizontally (7b, 7c) or diagonally (7a). The whole structure was then plastered over.

The use of wood as a structural material is also illustrated in the projecting buttresses (6) which can be seen on a number of Venetian buildings, sometimes along whole *calli*. Using a row of wooden corbels, it is possible to allow the facade of the building to project beyond the ground floor.

In monumental buildings, the mainbeams were crossed by joists which bore the floor-planks (8). In other Venetian buildings, however, the floors rested on beams running across the shorter side of the room. These beams were either fitted straight into the wall above a *rema* (3), or rested on a beam running parallel to the wall, and supported by wooden corbels. This technique prevented the floor-beams from weakening the walls and allowed them to absorb less moisture. The ceiling was either covered with plaster on a base of woven reeds, or the beams were left exposed.

1 brick wall / foundations of Istria stone / plank raft / piles / bed

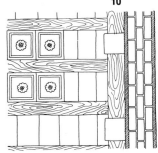

2

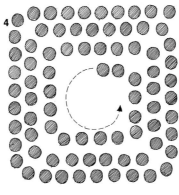

4

5

3

wooden courses or *reme*

7b

offcuts

7a

7c

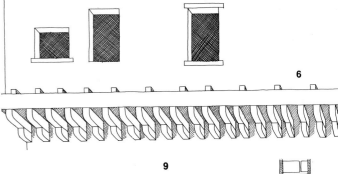

6

8

9

10

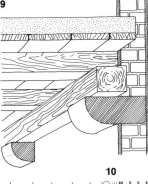

11

Functional elements were happily combined with aesthetic design in other areas of Venetian architecture as well. In the central windows which pierce the palace facades, the need to reduce the weight of the facade is combined with the need to give light to the main room. This became the principle decorative element of these buildings, especially in the Gothic period, while other points of interest such as external staircases (18, from a drawing by Jacopo Bellini), and *liagò* (covered loggias, 12, also from a drawing by Bellini), could be reserved for the courtyard. One picturesque feature of the Venetian sky-line are the chimney-pots (15). Even in smaller buildings the windows often consist of a graceful double arch closed with folding shutters (13). Shop-fronts (14) have their wooden architraves supported by a row of stone pilasters.

Wellheads are much decorated (16, showing re-used ninth or tenth century material), and were a very popular feature in Romanesque art, being found in courtyards, *campi* and *campielli*. The wellheads themselves are merely part of a complicated and quite functional installation, designed to provide drinking water. The well stands in the center of a cistern (17) with impermeable walls, which fills with rain-water through gutters placed around the well. The water was filtered through sand on its way into the well.

To complete this outline of Venetian building methods we append an example of the plan of a dwelling-house. This is a small palace dating from the second half of the 15th century, on Castello, later converted into popular rented accommodation. There are three floors, of which the plans of the ground (19) and first (20) floors are illustrated. The front looks out on to the *calle* (below). Each house has an entrance on the ground floor and a staircase leading to the upstairs rooms. Both have six rooms and at least one chimney. At the back is a courtyard with a well, and two external staircases.

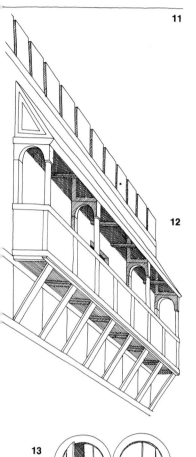

12

13

14

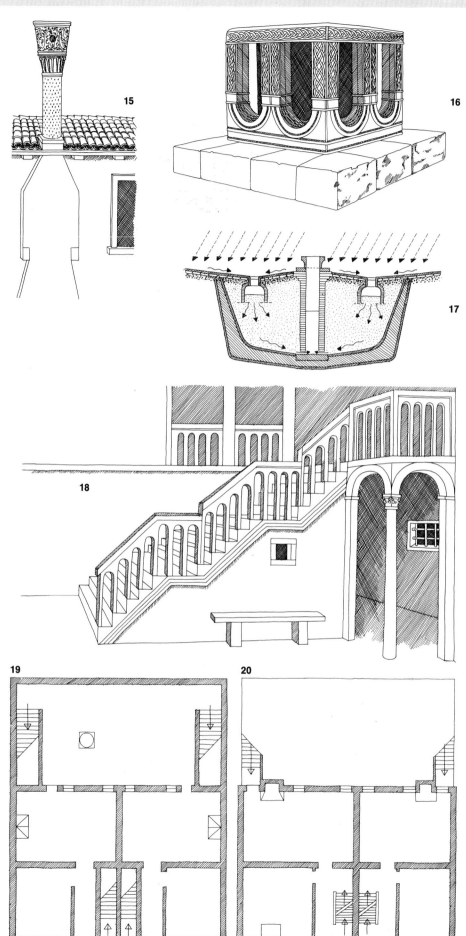

15

16

17

18

19

20

The Ca' Da Mosto on the Grand Canal. This is a typical Veneto-Byzantine building of the 12th to 13th century, which acted both as a dwelling-house and a warehouse for goods, thus fulfilling the needs of the Venetian nobles who were traders and sailors. Although the Venetian houses of this period were inspired by the rich palaces of Byzantium, a new and developed aesthetic conception makes itself felt, even in their very functionalism, and they fitted completely into the environment.

common people of Venice: that marvellous people, so full of courage and strength, hardworking and generous, a people that constitutional evolution gradually stripped of all political power.

The *scuole* and the *arti* (guilds), numerous as they are, chart the extraordinary variety of the work undertaken by the Venetians. Craftsmanship, which flourished right from the early Middle Ages, was still in full flower right at the end. In spite of merciless competition, shifts in fashion and general decadence, Venice's refined and elegant products, displayed in the great annual fair called the *Sensa* (Ascension Day) when St. Mark's square would be filled with pavilions, were always much sought after and greatly revered all over the world. Industry had its ups and downs – particularly the textile industry, which after an extraordinary peak in the 15th century, declined alarmingly until the 18th century, when it became really quite negligible. The same was true of the ancient industry of shipbuilding, which was spread all over the city in the Middle Ages (there were even shipyards on the

Grand Canal) but later concentrated in the huge state Arsenal. Though shipwrights' pay might seem rather modest compared to the enormous dividends that real estate paid out throughout the history of Venice (leaving aside commerce for the moment), nevertheless the workers at the Arsenal were a privileged sector of the working-class. The most privileged were the glass-workers; to these the Republic offered every blandishment to avoid their leaving and taking with them the secrets of their trade. Where master-craftsmen were concerned, this respect could reach the stage of open flattery, as for example, the disposition which allowed access to the *Maggior Consiglio* to the sons of a marriage between a patrician and the daughter of a glass-maker from Murano.

Ample documentation, particularly from the 1500s on, points out notable social and economic differences between classes, but it would be a mistake to underestimate the standard of living of workers in the city. The peasants on the mainland were much worse off. Their uncomfortable conditions were shared, at times of economic crisis, by the gardeners and vine-dressers from the estuary: in particularly bad winters, they would pour into the city and sleep clustered together under the bridges in the freezing weather. Worse still were the living-conditions of the fishermen and seamen; worse even than for the sailors, was the plight of the galley-crews, the people who rowed the galleys, who were often actually defrauded by the state, which would dock their salaries or endlessly delay payment on agreed contracts. So it is not surprising that there were often riots provoked by oarsmen who had not been paid or who had been enraged by delaying tactics and capricious modifications to their conditions of employment. Sometimes, the discontent of seafarers erupted into real mutiny, as in 1437 when a furious mob besieged stalls and shops and killed or injured guards, and were only placated by the intervention of a greatly respected commander, Captain Jacopo Loredan.

Naval employees were badly paid, badly treated and often badly recruited; anyone choosing the trade of a galley worker, particularly that of an oarsman, was usually the kind of person who could not find anything else or was not capable of any other work. They could also display dangerously violent attachments and devotion to any

Above: Campo di San Boldo. Below: two Gothic palaces; on the left, the Palazzo Giustinian and on the right, the Ca'Foscari, one of the most beautiful of the ogival

buildings of Venice. Venetian architecture adopted ideas from the East and produced an entirely indigenous style using central windows to pierce and lighten the facade. This came

to constitute the basic decorative and architectural feature of all Venetian Gothic buildings.

respected commander who was a little more loyal and humane. During the conclave which produced doge Carlo Contarini in 1655, the sailors of the fleet raised a violent mob because they wanted as doge "our Foscolo," the very popular *provveditore generale*, Leonardo Foscolo. Four centuries earlier, the election of Lorenzo Tiepolo had aroused the enthusiasm of the crews, who wanted to bring the galleys right up to the quay of St. Mark's square so that the doge could hear their cheering in his honour. On the other hand Giovanni Sagredo, the diplomat, politician and historian, had to face violent resistance from the common herd when, at the news of his election in August 1676, they crowded into the square crying, "Don't choose Sagredo, we don't want him!" In this case however the sailors were of no importance: the riot had been organized by Sagredo's political rivals. The *Signoria* took fright and cancelled the list of the 41 great electors who had been in his favour and as a result someone else was elected as doge.

Any picture of Venetian society would be incomplete if it failed to mention, at least in passing, other components which were more or less marginal for various reasons, but nevertheless present, and important in many respects.

First of all, the clergy: in the first centuries of Venice's existence, the patriarch of Grado, the main city of the province (the title of patriarch was later combined with that of bishop of Castello, and together they formed the patriarchy of Venice), the bishops of the lagoon dioceses and the abbots of the chief monasteries, had a front-line position in political assemblies. However, they were gradually excluded from any activity that was even vaguely connected with politics. The same was true also for the *primicerio*, the prelate, endowed with many episcopal prerogatives, who had care of St. Mark's basilica and all the church's parishes and estates. (It must be stressed that St. Mark's was never Venice's cathedral: it only became such in 1806 under Napoleon Bonaparte. The actual cathedral was San Pietro di Castello, while the basilica was the dogal chapel and state church, under the patronage of the doge.) The lay clergy, whose members in earlier centuries often acted as notaries, was numerous, but the regular clergy was even more so: convents and monasteries were bursting at the seams. Among the bad

THE VENETIAN PALACE: HOUSE AND BUSINESS PREMISES

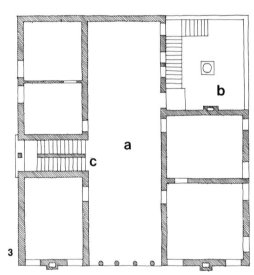

The splendid palaces which front on to the Grand Canal making it one of the world's most beautiful thoroughfares, and telling the story of Venetian architecture, also betray the mercantile and entrepreneurial activities of the Venetian ruling-classes. Although these palaces tended to develop into ever more glittering stately residences, especially from the Renaissance period on, they never completely lost all traces of their origins. They began as combined residence and merchant's factory. This factory-residence, and hence the palace, had two entrances, corresponding to the Venetian environment. One was from the water, and was used by goods as well as visitors: this was the *riva* or quay, and was a basic part of any such building (6). The other entrance was from the land, often leading into a courtyard with a well and external staircase. The court and the spiral staircase of the Contarini palace (1) are famous examples of these, and although their style is unusual, they perfectly embody the imaginative spirit of Venetian architecture. Another feature which the palace preserved from the medieval factory-residence was the three-fold division of both plan and facade. Inside, a large rectangular room was flanked by two series of smaller rooms, whilst the central hall corresponded to the multiple windows of the *piano nobile* on the facade (5, 15th century Gothic). Until the Renaissance it was usual to place the windows of the side rooms at the corner of the facade, giving rise to the abundance of corner windows (2). The relationship between the various pierced spaces was always delicate and original, and this effect was heightened by the Istria marble used in the cornices and on the surfaces of the walls.

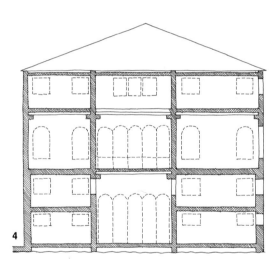

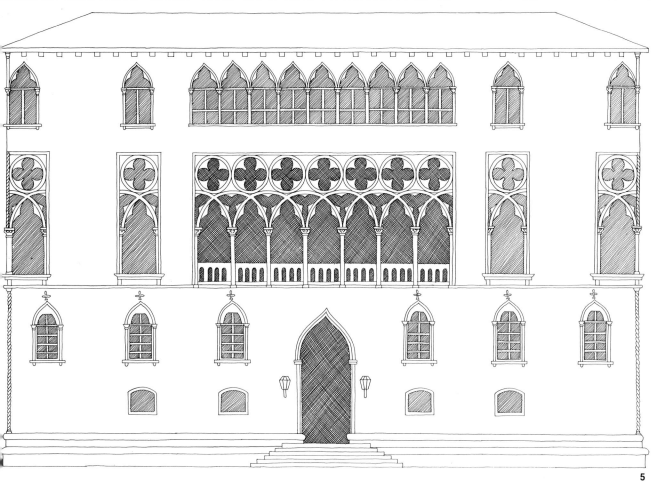

Ca' da Mosto on the Grand Canal (see p.84) and the Gothic period; see for example the Ca' Foscari on p.85, and the palace illustrated here (5), until the middle of the 15th century the palace retained its basic pattern although it became increasingly elegant and sumptuous. With the coming of Renaissance ideas to Venice, considerable changes were made. Interesting examples of this are the Palazzo Vendramin-Calergi (8), begun by Mauro Codussi from Bergamo and finished by Lombardo in the first decade of the 16th century; the Palazzo Manin (9) built for the Dolfin family by Jacopo Sansovino in the middle of the 16th century in mature Renaissance style; and the Palazzo Pesaro (10) begun in 1652 by Baldassare Longhena, the great Venetian Baroque architect. These examples show how an architectural language of classical derivation was varyingly interpreted between the Renaissance and Baroque periods, surviving with measured elegance into the neoclassical period. A large proportion of the palaces along the Grand Canal date from the last four centuries of the Republic, when the society of the merchant-traders who created the city's wealth and developed the factory-residence was left farther and farther behind. In spite of this they remain faithful to the spirit of Venetian architecture, forming a kind of shimmering ensemble of walls, light and water.

5

Plan (3) and elevation (4) of a palace which closely resembles the original type of factory-residence in its design. The function of the building is apparent. The ground-floor hall (a) could be entered from the canal and from the court (b). Here goods were loaded and unloaded; later this became the monumental entrance-hall. The staircase (c) led to the drawing-room on the first floor. The rooms on both sides were store-rooms.

By dividing the two wings on each side of the entrance-hall half-way up, a mezzanine floor (mesà) was created where the merchant had his administrative offices. The large central room on the first floor or *piano nobile*, the *portega*, was the state room for receptions and festivals. In the factory it was also the place where samples were exhibited to clients. The rooms to each side were the merchant's living quarters. The top storey was originally in-

habited by dependents and servants, clerks and men employed by the merchant in his business. The arrangement of the windows on the facade (5) reflects the functional character of the factory-residence, with multiple windows in the center and single windows at the sides, small windows on the ground and mezzanine floors, and the largest of all on the *piano nobile*. This tripartite division of the plan and facade which we have described in its

mature 15th-century form descends from the "*torresele*" type of building, with a central block and portico and loggia set between two towers. This late Roman model can still be seen in the Turkish factory (Fondaco dei Turchi, 7), which was built in the 12th to 13th century and belonged to the dukes of Ferrara, the Priuli, and the Pesaro before becoming the Ottoman emporium in 1621. After the period typified by the Turkish factory and the

8

9

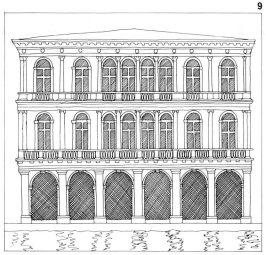

10

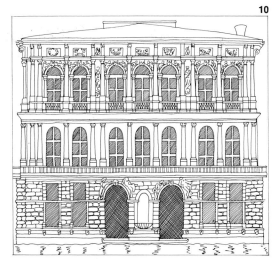

habits of Venetians of all classes was that of earmarking their daughters for the convent so as not to lose money in dowries, and the frequency of forced entrance into an order is one of the causes, and possibly the main one, of the corruption rampant in Venetian cloisters, and which neither the Ten, nor the patriarchs, nor apostolic nuncios ever succeeded in rooting out.

Then there were the Jews: first they were relegated to the island of Giudecca, then to Mestre and then again to the island of the *sestiere* of Cannaregio, which was named after an ancient foundry and called Ghetto (the name which was to be given to one of the most tragic institutions of Western civilization). Jews were obliged, in accordance with the church's laws, to wear some distinguishing mark. Now favoured, now ill-treated, they were always the object of blackmail: the enormous sums of cash at their disposal (since they were forbidden to invest in property) awakened the greed of all the world's exchequers, including that of Venice. In practice however, the Jewish colony in Venice found itself in the right conditions to develop exceptionally well, so that it took pride of place in Jewish culture, and the Venetian Ghetto was crowded with sumptuous places of worship.

Another group of people were not enclosed in a ghetto but were instead obliged to concentrate their activities in one place: the *Fondaco dei Tedeschi* was the base for the commercial operators who came from Germany, Austria and neighbouring areas. They too improved their business center where they also had their homes and ate together. They were responsible for the abundance of frescoes by the fashionable painters Giorgione and Titian at the beginning of the 16th century, on the outer walls of the *Fondaco*. The Germans were the main contingent of the countless highly-coloured throngs that frequented the Rialto, the business quarter, where the most important banking, insurance and commercial operations were carried out against the background of the noisy, bustling local markets for vegetables, fish and meat.

The Rialto, with its lodging-houses, inns and taverns, was the center too for an activity which thrived on the edges of the constant comings-and-goings of businessmen, sailors and tourists, always numerous in this unique city: prostitution.

The city seen through paintings. Left: detail of Carpaccio's Dismissal of the English Ambassadors *from the* Legend of St. Ursula *cycle. Although the building is imaginary, it shows how cautious the Venetians were of accepting the spirit of the Renaissance in their architecture. The inhabitants of the lagoon had developed an innate desire for wealth of decoration and variety of line and colour, and they resisted the simple balance of surface and proportions which constituted the theoretical basis of Renaissance art. Opposite: detail of Gentile Bellini's* Procession of the Cross in St. Mark's Square *(Gallerie dell'Accademia, Venice). In this painting the urban background is realistically executed, with a corner of the Piazza, the Doge's Palace, and the shaft of the Campanile with the Ospizio Orseolo backing on to it. This was knocked down in 1582 to make way for Scamozzi's Procuratie Nuove.*

Rows of houses on the Rio della Tana, along the southern edge of the Arsenal. From the Middle Ages on, the Republic erected rows of houses for the Arsenal workers. Public housing was unknown elsewhere at this period.

much sought after as concubines for great lords, but a more usual custom in the houses of patricians and merchants was that of keeping elderly slave women to look after the pantry and wardrobe. The phenomenon disappeared during the course of the 16th century, and eventually the name of slave was given to prisoners brought back from the Turkish wars, who were condemned to row Venetian galleys just as Venetian prisoners were condemned to row Turkish galleys.

Vagabonds and gypsies were particularly troublesome during the 16th and 17th centuries. In the 17th century, there was a rash of *bravi* and *buli*, professional toughs and hooligans, who could be put to use by unruly and arrogant nobles. There were few of these, admittedly, in comparison with what was going on in Spanish-dominated Lombardy for example, but the bullying bravos too often went unpunished. The Turkish wars eventually absorbed much of this misdirected energy, and the problem had died out by the end of the 1600s.

The Venetian Civilization

Prostitution had spread more or less everywhere in Venice, but it was controlled by the state, which tried every way to confine it to a precise sector of the Rialto, the Castelletto, as it was called. But its efforts were in vain. As the Renaissance flourished, the prostitutes deserted the Castelletto and while most of them occupied the old houses of the noble Rampani family in the *contrada* of Sant'Aponal (known as the Carampane), the better-class ones spread out through the city and brought into being that most Venetian phenomenon of the "courtesan" who sold company as well as love, often refined and elegant company, sought after by painters and princes, politicians and poets alike. The law struggled to restrain the phenomenon, if not repress it, but when king Henry of France came to Venice on a state visit, he demanded to spend a night with Veronica Franco, a professional courtesan and talented poetess.

Then there were the slaves. Venice bought and sold them, at least from the tenth century on, and in the city Negro and Tartar slaves could be seen rowing gondolas and waiting at table. Female Circassian slaves, who were very beautiful, were

Towards the end of this brief survey, let us take a last glimpse at Venice itself. This city, from the famous year 810 and from king Pippin's ill-omened attack onwards, became the capital of first the province, then the duchy, then the municipality, then the signory – in short, capital of the Republic. It was formed gradually around two original nuclei, probably the doge's fortified palace and the bishop's cathedral. Little by little it attracted inhabitants from the other islands, which progressively declined in favour of Venice itself. After centuries of silting-up and dredging, it gained the tiny islands of the archipelago around the Grand Canal. These then were over-run by an intensive urbanization operation, which sent property values rocketing. Alongside the Doge's Palace the state basilica soon made its appearance and became the shrine for the national symbol, the body of the evangelist, St. Mark.

Venice's enormous prosperity, achieved by the year 1000 and preserved for more than 500 years, is revealed in the large number of buildings that were redesigned according to new fashions, improved and embellished using every means

The Lagoon Frozen Over, by Francesco Guardi (Ca'Rezzonico, Venice). This is a rare event in Venice, and the natural exuberance of the Venetians seems stronger than ever in the figures in the canvas.

available (this obsession went on right through the years of the city's decline: these were the most frenzied years of artistic activity). When circumstances (in particular Bonaparte's lightning-strike campaign against Italy, his unexpected victories and his even more unexpected agreements with the Austrian empire) deprived Venice of her independence, the victors – the first in more than 11 centuries – found themselves face to face with the most monumental jumble of artistic riches that has ever existed.

But (and this is another key to the understanding of the Venetian civilization), however splendid the works of art realized by private citizens, patricians, religious orders, merchants or guilds of craftsmen, the greatest effort of all went into ensuring that nothing could rival the state in beauty, sumptuousness and majesty. A great deal of what Venice achieved by this effort no longer exists: at one time, there was no public office, no headquarters of magistrature or public administration that was not a precious work of art. Nowadays, although stripped at least in part of their decorations, the Doge's Palace and St. Mark's basilica retain their magnificence, and

together are the fulcrum of what has been for centuries the reality of Venice.

No single architect can be accredited with either of these two buildings. In effect, the global conception of the two works is the result not of a single but a collective personality. St. Mark's as we see it now can be attributed to the doge Domenico Contarini and the people who gave him their support towards the rapid reconstruction of a monument that had been already once destroyed. As far as the palace is concerned, its global conception must be attributed to a social class in its full maturity, the patriciate, who wished to make it their monument as well as the foundation stone of the political system. Nearly all the stages of its construction, its reconstruction and its decoration, are the result of collective decisions taken in the various constitutional assemblies.

The overall impression gained from this is disconcerting: it represents the superiority of collectivity over individuality, of the public over the private. In this, leaving aside any moral judgement, we can perhaps glimpse one of the reasons for Venice's exceptionally long life-span.

The Venetian Empire

The year 1000. Ascension Day, and a Venetian armed fleet takes to the waters. Doge Pietro Orseolo II is personally in command, and his destination is the opposite coast of the Adriatic. Venetian ships had for centuries had plenty to do with that particular coast, but this time, the aim was a military expedition in high style. At Ossero, both Latin and Slav inhabitants solemnly swore allegiance to the doge. The same scene took place at Zara, where representatives from the islands of Arbe and from Veglia had also gathered. These were peaceful, festive ceremonies, but things went differently with the Slavs in Dalmatia. The doge forced the inhabitants of the Pasman and Vergada islands into submission, and near to the island of Cazza, captured a convoy of Narentine Slavs, for centuries Venice's traditional enemies. Then he wiped out the island of Curzola which had tried to resist him and that of Lagosta, a haven for pirates. From there the doge made his way back in triumph along the whole length of the Dalmatian coastline.

Venice had been due for a reckoning with the Slavs for a long while, particularly with the Narentines, who were hardened pirates. Perhaps the rape of the Venetian brides, supposed to have happened during a collective marriage ceremony in Santa Maria Formosa in 946 or 948 was only a legend, but it is true that in 912 Serbian pirates had captured no less than Pietro Badoer, the son of the ruling doge and himself a future doge, on his way back from a diplomatic mission to the Orient. It is also true that doge Pietro Candiano lost his life in a skirmish with the Slavs from the Narenta in 887. The Saracens too had turned their dangerous attentions towards the north Adriatic, but had been driven away repeatedly in no uncertain terms.

The doge Orseolo's expedition was nothing more than the most spectacular episode in Venice's long struggle for right of way in the Adriatic, the route all Venetian seafaring traffic was obliged to take. Tradition has it that from that particular time Venice had dominion over Istria and Dalmatia (the doge ever after assumed the title "duke of the Venetians and the Dalmatians"). This dominion was contested for centuries, and as far as Dalmatia was concerned, only actually definitive from 1420, after interminable uprisings, revolts, skirmishes and warfare – particularly against the king of Hungary, once the Hungarians had also conquered the kingdom of Croatia.

However, eight years earlier, in 992, Pietro Orseolo II registered a victory of even greater import, by obtaining from the emperor of Byzantium a "golden warranty" which recognized in substance Venetian dominance in maritime traffic between Italy and Constantinople and which virtually entrusted to Venice control of the route. The Venetian "colony" on the Bosphorus was not yet mentioned, even though Venetians increased their paternalist investments in a form which for financial profits were far more favourable to themselves than to their rivals from Amalfi and Bari. In any case, the 90 years that followed point the way to Venice's definitive self-assertion, and constitute the basis for the future fortunes of the lagoon city.

What happened in those 90 years in the Mediterranean basin could almost have been deliberately engineered to favour the development of the privileged relationship Venice had always enjoyed with Byzantium. The Venetian alliance enabled Byzantium to stem the Arab advance. The enormous, blond Normans poured down

from the misty north: they won victory after victory, and soon the whole of southern Italy was in their hands. Their vanguard turned to the Dalmatian coast and their greed vented itself on the Byzantine territories. In the inevitable military clash, the Venetians fought side by side with Byzantium. The poet-chronicler Guglielmo di Puglia, though celebrating the glory of his lord, the Norman Robert Guiscard, notes the awe inspired by the intervention of "that populous city, flowing with men and means" and "her people, so expert in naval warfare, so courageous," people that in their homeland "cannot pass from one house to another save in a boat" and have no equal as far as fighting on the sea is concerned.

The whole account of the war is very confused in the chronicles. However, we know that Guiscard did not succeed in defeating the eastern emperor, and that the emperor issued a new "bolla d'oro," "golden edict," in 1082, which besides increasing the fiscal exemptions conceded to Venice in 992, extended them to a number of internal ports and cities of the empire, where the Venetians would then be able to trade with full customs franchise. The list stretches from the lower Adriatic to the Mediterranean and the Aegean: Durazzo, Valona, Corfu, Modon and Corone in the heights of the Peloponnese, Nauplia at the foot of the Peloponnese in the bay, Corinth bestriding the isthmus, Athens and Thebes, Negropont, Demetrias in the bay of Volos, then Thessalonica, Chrisopolis, Peritherion in Thrace, to Abydus and Adrianople, Rodosto, Selymbria on the Sea of Marmara, up to the splendid imperial capital itself. It did not stop in the domes and bazaars of Constantinople, but spread instantly to the Asiatic coastline along the shores of Asia Minor, from Phocaea to Ephesus, Chios, Strobilos and Antalya, Tarsus, Adana, Mamistra, to Antioch and Laodicea. It did not matter if not all these places were still under the empire: the principle had been established and sealed. Sealed also was the commercial doom of the inhabitants of Amalfi who were too dependent on the Moslem world to be able to align themselves with Byzantium against the Arabs (and by now had been absorbed by the hated Normans into their southern Italian empire).

But here there is a fact of still greater im-

Opposite, above: a Byzantine emperor, ninth-century patera from the Campiello Angaran. Venice was at first more or less dependent on Byzantium, but gradually asserted her independence as her commercial and naval might grew during the ninth and tenth centuries. With her new strength came demands for her help and friendship. In 1094 the emperor Henry IV came as a friend to the consecration of the basilica. Treaties were entered into with the Holy Roman emperors: (opposite, below: charter of Henry V, June 1111; below: charter of Frederick Barbarossa. September 1177. State Archives, Venice). In 1177 the city welcomed pope Alexander III and Barbarossa when they met to agree to the reconciliation between the Empire, the papacy, and the Communes.

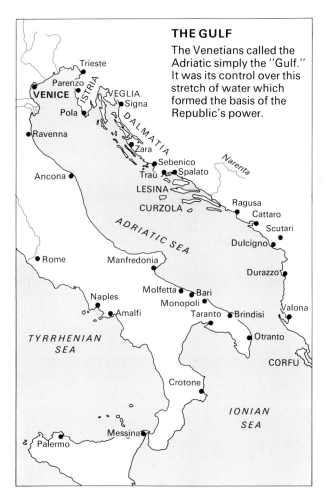

THE GULF

The Venetians called the Adriatic simply the "Gulf." It was its control over this stretch of water which formed the basis of the Republic's power.

portance. The golden edict of 1082 recognized the existence of a Venetian quarter right in the heart of Constantinople. There were two churches there, St. Nicholas "de Embulo" and St. Acindino, near which were kept the weights and measures used when buying and selling oil and wine. There was also a mill, a bakery and two shops. The act of donation of St. Acindino to the patriarch of Grado, signed by doge Ordelaf Falier in 1107, picturesquely describes the church as *"cum toto suo thesauro,"* with its decorations and books, and mentions also the *ergasteria* or goods depot. We know that the Venetians had their own wharfs or landing-stages, with freehold warehouses in which they could store and sell their merchandise without the Byzantine excise having any possibility of interfering.

This arrangement, which is not exactly a colony, but rather a concession, complete with all the above-mentioned accoutrements plus a fresh water supply and possibly a mill and public baths, was to be repeated some years later in another part of the Mediterannean basin. Pope Urban II launched the crusade for the recapture of the holy lands of Syria and Palestine occupied by the Moslems. The western feudal world responded with enthusiasm, and knights from Lorraine and France were soon joined by the Normans, unable to believe their luck in resuming their drive towards the East. There were also two Italian Republics, Genoa and Pisa, that perceived in the holy undertaking the possibility of enormously lucrative gains. Venice hesitated at first: the emperor of Byzantium regarded with great suspicion this armed expedition which was not over-subtle and made little distinction between what belonged to the Arabs and what was Byzantium's; Venice, thick as thieves with Byzantium, watched and waited for opportunities of mutual gain.

The first state to come forward was Genoa. She had been rewarded for her collaboration in taking Antioch with the donation of an entire quarter, with church, square and 30 houses: Antioch was in theory Byzantine territory where the emperor had conceded to Venice the privilege of commercial exemption. However, after a violent clash with the Pisan fleet in defense of Byzantine interests in Laodicea, Venice came forward too, and in exchange for the promised regaining of the coastline from Acre to Tripoli obtained from the king of conquered Jerusalem, Godfrey of Bouillon, church, kiln, well, warehouse and market in each of the cities that were to be taken, plus the entire city of Tripoli, with exemption from all tariffs.

The Venetian navy's failure to reach agreed targets meant that the realization of the pact fell through, but a right was nevertheless established. First, the Genoese took the lion's share; but in 1124 the conquest of Tyre, with Venice's determined participation, won for her the possession of a third of the city plus a third of the city of Ascalon. This time, along the entire coast, from one city to another a proper colonial system took hold. The basic structures of protection of commercial activity were now linked with concrete jurisdictional privileges.

The origins of the Venetian colonial system are right here, though for the moment it was no more than the Genoese, the first-comers, had achieved for their state and their private shipowners. There was also a Pisan presence; and however extended and lasting the Venetian interests were in the Syro-Palestinian zone, it was elsewhere that the future empire of the *Serenissima* was to be formed.

Venice and Byzantium

The most lively and active center of Venetian trade was, more than ever, Constantinople. In the prestigious capital and throughout the rest of the Byzantine empire, though other Italian traders had been admitted, Venetian activity represented the greater part of mercantile interests. The presence of rivals was cause for ill-feeling and tension, but it was Venetian-Byzantine relations that deteriorated rapidly. A violent crisis exploded in 1124, when the emperor John Comnenus became reluctant to renew the privileges accorded in 1082; and the doge Domenico Michiel, in order to persuade him, laid waste Rhodes, Samos, Lesbos, Modon and Cephalonia, where he established a military base from which he could attack Byzantine territories until the monarch decided to renew the decree.

Military solidarity between Venice and Byzantium resumed almost automatically when the Norman Roger II of Sicily attempted an attack on

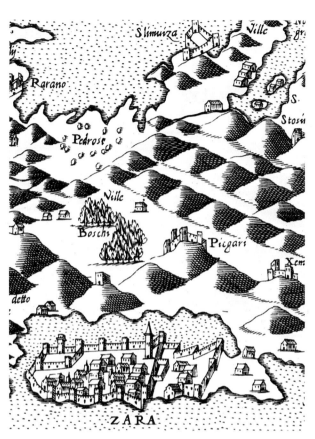

the Eastern Empire. However, the relationship had been poisoned. The Byzantine chroniclers Cinnamus and Nicetas were the mouthpieces of an ill-feeling that became ever more widespread among the Greeks. Of course the Venetians were great navigators, great seamen: they doffed their caps to them. But, if they appeared to be defenders or even saviours of the Byzantine empire, they certainly charged dearly for their intervention. Even the last military campaign against the Normans gained enormous advantages for them: freedom of trade over all the empire, with total exemption from all excise duty – including what the Byzantines still had to pay. And their arrogance was increasing out of all proportion: with each concession they gained, they became more haughty, more demanding. They had literally invaded the empire, and by marrying Greek women had introduced themselves into homes and families. Yet they affected disdain for the Greeks, whom they overshadowed with their riches.

In fact the Venetians were everywhere. There were thousands in the empire; in Constantinople itself there were a number scattered throughout all the city's various quarters, since their "empire" was only a commercial center where they did not actually live (and the same was true in the other cities where Venetians had citizenship and religious bases, above all, the patriarchate of Grado, St. Mark's basilica, and the abbey of San Giorgio Maggiore). Yet nowhere could these be said to constitute proper "colonies:" the privileges which so enraged Cinnamus and Nicetas never included any of a judicial nature.

Certain figures stand out, such as Romano Mairano, the incarnation of the breadth of vision and entrepreneurial spirit of the great merchant ship-builders of medieval Venice, or Domenico Mastrocoli and Dobramiro Stagnario (the latter clearly had Slav blood in his veins): they bought huge olive oil shares in Corinth. Olive oil played an important part in these merchants' business, as they traded not only with the West, but also within the empire from port to port and market-square to market-square. Among the products they exported from Constantinople silk also figured prominently, while imports included wool-cloth from Venice, wrought metals, carpentry, arms, and also spices and cotton purchased in Palestine

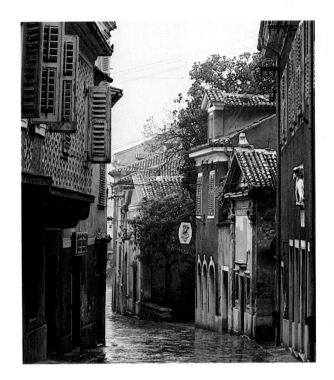

(the nobles, Colomanno Bembo and Marino Michiel, for example, did heavy trade in these commodities on the Venice–Jerusalem–Constantinople circuit).

Then international and internal tensions reached crisis point. Venice's refusal to support the emperor Comnenus' attempts at recapturing territories in the Adriatic basin, served to detonate resentments and jealousies. Assured of Genoese support, on 12 March, 1171, Comnenus ordered the capture of all the Venetians in the empire. This was a huge police operation, carried out very skilfully and took the Venetians by surprise. Only a few succeeded in escaping on a ship belonging to Romano Mairano, and prisons all over the empire could not house all the people arrested. Naturally, all Venetian property was confiscated. It was a disaster, and the naval campaign that was immediately organized in retaliation ended in serious failure, aggravated by plague. For many years, Venetian commerce had to take other routes. However, Venice was to win the final round: in 1182, under Andronicus II, the population of Constantinople massacred all Latin residents, and the Venetians could not help rejoicing at the fate that had befallen their Pisan and Genoese rivals who had stayed in the East.

These events formed the basis for the undertaking which, about 20 years later, gave rise

Left: two views of Capodistria. Below: the Town Hall. Above, left: one of the streets with the Totto palace on the right. Above: view of Pirano from the sea. Opposite: facade of the "lassa pur dir" house in Pirano in pure Venetian Gothic style. The industrious Venetians moved into the seaports which fell into their hands as the logical consequence of their trading policies. Venice's motives can be summed up in the accurate popular saying "Coltivar el mar e lassar star la terra." (Cultivate the sea, and leave the land be.) As the photographs on these pages show, Venice left its own ineradicable and frequently brilliant mark on the ports which it conquered.

to the birth of the Venetian colonial empire of the Levant. An agreement set up in 1198 put an end to the Venetian-Byzantine wrangling and opened other markets to the lagoon merchants: other regions, such as Yannina in the Epirus and Castoria in western Macedonia, Skopje in the Macedonian interior, Zagoria in Bulgaria, Philippopolis in Thrace, the Cyclades, Crete, Zante and Levkas plus, in Asia, the islands of Samos and Mytelene, Rhodes and Cos, as well as Philadelphia and the whole of Lydia in Asia Minor. There was also some compensation for the damages brought about by Comnenus's attack in 1171. However, business failed to return to its former prosperous proportions, and there were still difficulties, uncertainties and worries. Meanwhile Venice, thanks to her shrewd western policy, had gradually acquired great importance on the European scene.

The Fruits of a Good Contract

This political importance, thrown into relief by her successful intervention in the serious dispute between pope Alexander III and the emperor Frederick Barbarossa, was the underlying reason for the visit by a group of potentates from the feudal world, mostly French and Flemish, but including some Germans who came in search of an agent to transport their troops, horses, arms and siege weapons for a new expedition, a new crusade born of the passionate preaching and no less passionate ambition of a great pope, Innocent III, Lothario of the counts of Segni.

The aim of the crusade was, of course, the recapture of the kingdom of Jerusalem, lost after the Moslem victory of Hattin. The assembly (according to the chronicler Geoffroy de Villehardouin, who was present at the scene) in St. Mark's basilica in April 1201, attracted 10,000 Venetians and was carried away on a wave of mystical and warrior-like enthusiasm, but what the doge stipulated with the representatives of the crusaders was only a contract for transport or passage: Venice would supply the ships to transport by sea 4,500 horsemen, 4,500 horses, 9,000 grooms, and 20,000 foot-soldiers, as well as victuals necessary to keep the armada for a whole year; she would also arm 50 galleys at her

The crusades provided an opportunity which the practical Venetians could not afford to let slip. When the leaders of the fourth crusade assembled with their troops, their cavalry and their arms, they needed ships to transport their huge army. The crusaders' envoys asked for the help of Genoa and Pisa, but both cities refused. When they came to Venice, the doge, as a chronicler tells us, listened attentively, and said that "he wished to consult his councillors: the matter merited reflection." Since it was a question of business, the mercantile spirit of Venice triumphed yet again. The terms of passage demanded by the doge were extremely advantageous, and so huge was the price that the crusaders could only pay by rendering Venice the service of capturing Zara (Zadar). The capture of Constantinople was partly due to this also, although there were other motives as well. Above: soldiers bound for the Holy Land on board ship, 11th century French miniature. Below: pilgrims disembarking at Jaffa en route for Jerusalem.

own expense. In exchange, the crusaders had to pay 85,000 silver marks plus a half of the profits realized on the expedition. The ships were to be ready by 29 June, 1202, in the port of Venice. The objective of the crusade was not specified in the contract, but it emerges from Villehardouin's testimony that it must have been Egypt, rightly considered the heart of the Moslem empire.

By June, 1202, everything was ready, according to the pact: the ships, supplies and also some special ships which opened up for the disembarkation of the cavalry and were known as *uscieri*. In other words, Venice had kept her part of the bargain. On the crusaders' side, a number of people were missing, princes or barons who had preferred to march on foot or take other routes, as well as a quantity of money, at least 34,000 silver marks. What was to be done? After much consultation, the heads of the crusaders approved Enrico Dandolo's proposition: in exchange for the unpaid sum, they would help Venice to regain the city of Zara which had rebelled and had gone over to the king of Hungary.

The fact that Zara and the king of Hungary were Christian did not seem to the crusader barons a good enough reason for refusing, nor a reason for the papal legate, cardinal Pietro Capuano to oppose the plan. Only Innocent III flew into a rage and excommunicated the Venetians. Everyone else, however, thought the slight diversion to be well worth the trouble, so that the crusade could finally get under way.

But during the stop at Zara, something far more

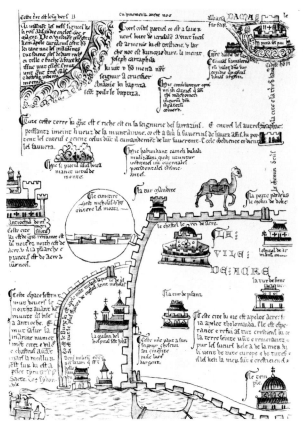

A page from Matthew Paris's Historia Anglorum, *13th century, showing the route from London to Jerusalem, with the city of St. John at Acre, now Akko on the coast of Israel. This city was besieged and taken by storm by the crusaders in 1189–91. and became the crusaders' most important stronghold in the Holy Land. Below: crusaders and Saracens in the Holy Land, miniature from the* Liber secretorum fidelium crucis *by Marin Sanudo the Elder, compiled in Venice in 1321.*

serious happened. On their journey from their bases to Venice, the crusaders had already had occasion to meet the Byzantine prince Alexius, son of the emperor Isaac Angelus, who had been dethroned and imprisoned by his brother Alexius III, at that time ruler of Byzantium. The prince had asked for their support in order to regain the throne for his father and for himself, and the main

Mosaic from the pavement of the church of St. John the evangelist in Ravenna, dating from 1213, slightly later than the fourth crusade, of which it depicts an incident, with attacking Latins.

they thought they could resume their path afterwards with greater chances of victory. The pope himself, deep down, looked favourably upon the prospect of the re-uniting of the Greek and Roman church, and indeed, no one really thought of conquering the Byzantine empire. But it is clear that the doge and the other representatives of the Venetian government saw the crusaders' favourable attitude and thought that, after all, the restoration of the old man Isaac Angelus and the enthronement of the young Alexius would not be a bad thing, and that, if this were due to Venice, the two would be certain to give Venice certain concessions once the throne had been regained. The ease of the operation, apart from anything else, scotched any scruples anyone might have had. Alexius III's resistance was rapidly overcome and it seemed there was nothing else to do besides extract from the two Angelus what had been agreed and resume the expedition as soon as possible.

It was Byzantine national sensitivity that changed the course of events radically. The usurper, Alexius III was neither particularly popular nor well-loved as a sovereign, but Alexius IV, the new sovereign, installed using a foreign army's force was, in the eyes of the Byzantines, a puppet king, manoeuvered by the crusaders and the Venetians, a traitor and a lackey of foreigners. Unpopularity, enmity and hatred enveloped him on all sides, and, realizing this, he personally asked the crusaders to remain in Constantinople until the spring of 1204. It is patently clear that the Venetians were not at all pleased with this decision: the armed and equipped fleet represented a heavy investment which risked remaining unproductive for far too long, and the doge and his colleagues knew the Byzantine mentality far too well not to expect huge problems as a result of that armed presence in a great and hostile metropolis.

This hostility broke out after a very short while. First of all Alexius IV himself, hoping to regain respect and support from the population, turned against his protectors. But his volte-face did little good. A rebellion deprived him of the throne, and in the wake of a blaze of patriotism he was replaced by an exponent of Greek national resistance, Alexius V, Ducas Mourtzuphlos, who immediately demanded the dismissal of both

leaders of the crusade had not openly declined the offer. Venice knew nothing at all about it: in fact she was laboriously trying to improve her relationship with Alexius III in order to benefit trade. Now, at Zara, the envoys of the young pretender and his brother-in-law, the powerful German prince, Philip of Sweden, put forward concrete proposals: in return for support for the restoration, they would give 200,000 silver marks in cash, would unite the Greek orthodox church with the Roman church and would supply a contingent of 10,000 men for the fight against the Moslems. This was in the first week of January, 1203.

It is currently accepted that it was doge Dandolo's cunning that brought about the absurd deviation which led the huge expedition to Constantinople instead of Egypt, to fight against the Christian Byzantines instead of the Moslem Arabs. The truth is that the surviving barons of the crusade, headed by Conrad of Monferrato and Baldwin of Flanders, were tempted by the idea of the huge monetary gains and, in all good faith,

Venetians and crusaders. There had already been one attack after another, the Venetians had needed courage to save their fleet from fire, and another conflagration had devastated the best quarters of the city and obliged the Latins to take refuge in the outlying area of Pera. Now, there was nothing else but to fight to save the fleet – and their own skins.

Once more, it is a false commonplace which claims that the Venetians instigated the military conquest of the city. In fact the opposite is true: Enrico Dandolo took upon himself the task of last-minute negotiations with Mourtzuphlos, and only when he persisted in his intransigence did hostilities break out. Before launching the attack, however, the doge and Conrad of Monferrato, supreme commander of the crusading armies, signed an agreement which revolutionized the aim of the crusade and paved the way for a radical change in the constitution, structure and life-style of the Byzantine empire. This empire was to have a Latin emperor; elected by Venetians and crusaders in equal proportions, and would be organized not according to traditional Byzantine structures but in keeping with the criteria of western feudalism. Byzantium's territories were to be divided among the future emperor, the crusaders and the Venetians. The patriarchate of Constantinople, obviously part of the Roman church, would fall to crusaders or Venetians, depending on whether the emperor was Venetian or crusader. Having fixed the terms by which temporal and ecclesiastical fees would be divided, the agreement bound the signatories to remain in Constantinople until the end of March 1205 and threatened defaulters with excommunication.

After a furious battle, the fabulous city, devastated by another fire, was at last conquered. On 12 and 13 April 1204, the victors subjected it to systematic sacking from which it would never recover. Art treasures were destroyed or looted. Precious relics (protected by equally precious reliquaries) made their way to Venice together with the four bronze horses from the hippodrome, destined for the façade of the state basilica. Horrified chroniclers describe the orgy of violence and pillage that rocked what had been the most beautiful, richest and most splendid city in Europe.

The most extraordinary aspect of this whole

Above: the serpent and the eagle, detail of the mosaic pavement from the imperial palace in Constantinople. Left: the earliest map of Constantinople from the beginning of the 15th century, showing the extraordinary combination of natural and artificial defenses which the crusaders had to overcome.

affair is that chance alone had led the expedition to results that no one could ever have dreamed of, let alone foreseen. Venice least of all: it was a city of less than 50,000 inhabitants, and the borders of her original state, the *dogado*, had been limited to the narrow strip of lagoons which lies between the Adriatic and the mainland from Grado to Cavarzere. However, faced with what had happened, the city of merchants and sailors did not draw back. Venice was ready to accept the destiny dictated by events, and proposed to reap from it the maximum advantage possible.

Division of the Eastern Empire

The *partitio Romaniae* is the document which authorized the subdivision of the territories of the Byzantine empire between the conquerors and brought into being the new Eastern Latin Empire. Venice emerged as owner of a huge slice of the land which at one time had belonged to the powerful sovereign state to which she herself had been subject. It was such a large slice that the doge henceforth was to be entitled "ruler of a quarter and a half of all the Eastern Empire" – more than was due to the Eastern Latin emperor, who was credited with direct rule of only one quarter of the

The Capture of Constantinople by the Crusaders, 1204, by Palma il Giovane, from the Doge's Palace. The surprising outcome of the fourth crusade assured Venice a string of bases stretching from the lagoon to the Black Sea, which proved indispensable to the development of her trade with the East. Stunning the world with her opportunism, Venice started from these remarkable beginnings and went on to become one of the strongest nations in Europe. Now that she was mistress of all the Cyclades and a large part of the Aegean archipelago, Venice's empire could be said to have taken shape. The islands were divided between the patrician families on the condition they colonized them. The old doge Andrea Dandolo who had been the mastermind behind this strange crusade, wisely refused the crown of the Latin empire, but assumed the title of "Lord of a quarter and a half of all the Eastern Empire," borne by his successor in Venice, and in Constantinople by the podestà, a kind of viceroy. Venice was now at the height of her power.

Right: the ancient walls of Constantinople which date back to the time of Theodosius. Below: an early map of the city on the Bosphorus. On the upper part of the map is the Pera peninsula on the northern shore of the Golden Horn, which was for long a Genoese commercial quarter. The Venetian factories were built on the south bank. Among the many advantages which Venice drew from the fourth crusade was the exclusion of all her trade rivals from the whole of the Eastern Latin Empire.

empire. The doge had refused to be elected emperor so as not to offend the barons (though he did see to it that instead of Conrad of Monferrato, who was too friendly with the Genoese, Baldwin of Flanders was elected emperor). But he was given great honours, special short boots in purple, and exemption from paying homage to the emperor. But this counted less than the territories, adroitly distributed along the Venice–Constantinople route, selected to be assigned to the *Commune Veneciarum*.

First of all, they held three-eighths of the capital, with the best landing-places of the Golden Horn. Then they had the province of Adrianople, Rodosto and the coast right up to the Dardanelles, the ports of Oreoi and Karistos in Euboea, the islands of Aegina and Salamis in the gulf of Athens, and the western coast of the Peloponnese with the fortified ports of Modon and Corone, Patras on the Ionian sea and Kalavrita in the bay of Corinth. Inland there was Sparta and all her territories. There were also the Ionian isles, Corfu, Levkas, Zante and Cephalonia, and all the territory west of the mountain chain of the Pindus, *i.e.* the Epirus, Aetolia and Aroania. It was a huge territorial kingdom to which the doge in his farsightedness had added the island of Crete, acquired from Conrad of Monferrato who had in his turn received it in fief from Alexius IV.

Besides these territories Venice was also given other extremely important privileges. The patriarchate of Constantinople was given to a Venetian, and the clergy of the Hagia Sophia was also

Venetian: Venice therefore was responsible for the spiritual leadership of the new empire. Finally, the Venetians could demand the exclusion of their commercial rivals from the whole of the Eastern Latin Empire.

This last clause was the source of the greatest satisfaction in Venice. The wise merchants who ran the Venetian state, did not share the euphoria of their fellow-citizens in Constantinople, even

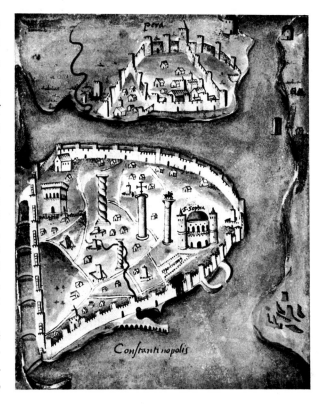

though the prestige of doge Dandolo constituted a guarantee, appreciated according to its correct value. Nor were they entirely wrong: much of the territory assigned to Venice was irrecoverable, in the hands of the Greeks, and the Greeks had no intention of letting it be taken from them; furthermore, the body of the crusaders as a force did not seem at all sufficient to occupy, control and maintain an empire, even though it was far smaller now than before the conquest. Also, the forces of the *Commune Veneciarum* seemed disproportionate to the Republic, for though powerful and well equipped for sea warfare, they could not fight inland on treacherous, mountainous, rough territory such as that in Thrace and Greece. These doubts were soon justified by the invasion of the Bulgars, who conquered Adrianople and took the emperor Baldwin prisoner. What was to be done?

Wise Venetian pragmatism solved every problem in the most opportune manner. Current opinion is convinced that conflict had developed between Venice and the Byzantine Venetians which only the doge Pietro Ziani, elected in 1205 after the death of the great Dandolo, was skilful enough to succeed in containing and calming, though even he was unable to resolve it completely. Proof of this can be seen in the election by the eastern Venetians of a ruler who also took the title of doge, "ruler and sovereign of a quarter and a half of the empire." He made certain decisions, agreements with the emperor, confirmation of fiefs to the Venetians, the concession of Adrianople to a Greek ruler, and even conceded Corfu to the Venetian state.

It is more likely that there was a division into two camps intent on avoiding the direct involvement of doge and *Commune* in a number of embarrassing and complicated matters. These included the refusal of goods conceded by the *partitio Romaniae*, the sanction of certain situations such as that of the Venetian feudal lords or, in general, the very relationships with the heads of the empire, an empire that had been born maimed. Indeed, dogal sanction always came in after the event to legalize the decisions of the ruler, until, 20 years later, the Venetian colony of Constantinople returned to strict obedience in both actual and official terms.

We called the Venetians feudal lords. It was

After the conquest of the legendary capital of the eastern world, Venice was flooded with gold, marble and art works. Booty of nearly 800 years ago is stored in St. Mark's Treasury. The tenth-century Byzantine icon of St. Michael illustrated on the left is a relief on enamelled gold plate. The perfume burner (opposite, above) dates from the 12th century and shows Arab-Byzantine influence, but it may have been made in northern Italy. Inside the basilica the Madonna Nicopeia (Bringer of Victory) is venerated, so-called because such images were carried at the head of Byzantine emperors' armies (below, left). On the front of the basilica are four superb bronze horses which once dominated the hippodrome in Constantinople (perhaps Greek-Alexandrian work of the fourth to third century B.C.).

precisely from Constantinople that an expedition set off composed of Venetian nobles and commanded by no less than the nephew of Enrico Dandolo, Marco Sanudo, the man who had negotiated on behalf of the doge for the acquisition of Crete. Marco Sanudo was no ordinary private citizen. He had held the post of judge in the Venetian colony of Constantinople; and more important, he had undertaken a long and difficult journey to Venice in order to inform the doge Ziani of his intentions, and had apparently received his blessing. So, having taken part as a regular member of the Venetian forces in the capture of Corfu, Modon and Corone, Sanudo set sail with a group of friends in a small private armada and turned his helm towards the Aegean islands. He introduced himself to the Greek islanders as protector against the raids of the Genoese and Turkish pirates that infested those waters, and with the support – or at least the benevolent neutrality of the population – he and his friends took over a number of islands of greater and lesser importance and made themselves feudal lords of these territories. In this way there came into being, alongside the *de facto* official colonialism, a second colonial system made up of feudal lords who considered themselves feudal vassals but who, in accordance with agreements settled by Marco Sanudo with the doge Ziani, were pledged not to concede their fiefs save to other Venetians.

In this way Sanudo personally set up for himself and his descendants the duchy of Naxos, or the Archipelago, which included much of the Cyclades: Naxos, Syra, Sifnos, Paros, Amorgos, Milos, Ios. Marino Dandolo installed himself on Andros, Andrea and Geremia Ghisi at Tinos, Mikonos and the boreal Sporades (Skiros, Skopelos, Skiathos, Alonissos); Giacomo Barozzi took for himself Santorini and Giovanni Querini took Stampalia. All these were vassals of the duke of the Archipelago, except Philocalos Navigajoso, who made himself lord of the large island of Lemnos and took the title of grand duke directly from the emperor. One Venier and one Viaro were direct vassals of the Republic for their fiefs of Cerigo and Cerigotto.

In looking after its own interests, the Republic had not been inactive, but neither had it been very lucky. Modon and Corone, the two fortresses on

the peaks of the Peloponnese (known as the "eyes of the Republic") remained squarely in its possession, but though the Genoese pirate Leone Vetrano had been dislodged from Corfu, the island was seized in 1214 by the Greek despot of the Epirus, Michael Angelus, who had already taken over the whole of the Pindus area, apart from Durazzo. (Venice eventually made him an ally.) As for the other Ionian islands, the Republic was unable to secure them for herself. Sparta and the western coast of the Peloponnese was a precious source of oil and silk, and this territory was grabbed by Geoffroy de Villehardouin, the grandson of the chronicler of the fourth crusade: however, Venice was to achieve a relationship of feudal supremacy and of protectorate as far as he was concerned, and he took Venetian citizenship.

There were also the Euboean strongholds: Oreoi in the north and Karistos in the south. Apparently not trusting sufficiently to its own strength, the Republic agreed that the large, oblong island should be divided into three fiefs, assigned to three Veronese knights, the *terzieri*, Pegoraro dei Pegorari, Gilberto da Verona and Ravano dalle Carceri. But it maintained supreme sovereignty so as to take formal possession later.

Finally, there was Crete. A dangerous intruder, the Genoese pirate, Enrico Pescatore, count of Malta, had installed himself on this enormous, mountainous island, rich in corn and wine. This pirate, with the aid of another Genoese buccaneer, Alamanno da Costa, repulsed a military expedition commanded by Ranieri Dandolo, son of

The Pala d'Oro behind the main altar of St. Mark's basilica is a sumptuous work, glistening with gold, jewels and enamel. It is one of the richest pieces of the goldsmith's craft in existence. Three panels from the Pala d'Oro are illustrated opposite, showing St. Mark the evangelist, the discovery of the relics of St. Mark, and Christ appearing to St. Mark.

the doge Enrico, in 1207, and stayed there undisturbed until the following year. But just when he was thinking of assuming the title of king of Crete, a new expedition engaged his attention and Genoa, herself engaged in disputes with Pisa and Marseilles, failed to support him. Greedy as he was, he left in 1212 in exchange for a large sum of money. Only five years later, a Venetian-Genoese treaty got rid of Alamanno da Costa too, who was stirring up the islanders with the support of half the population.

The Eastern Latin Empire was not to last very long. The treaty of Nymphaeum, agreed in 1261 between Genoa and the Greek emperor of Nicaea, marked its end, after less than 60 years of struggling miserably to survive. Gradually, the feudal *signorie* instituted by the crusaders died out. But Venice lasted longer than the others. Two and a half centuries after the crusaders' expedition and the *partitio Romaniae*, her dominions had grown and strengthened in all the Levant.

The "dominio da mar" and the mainland

We should now take an overall look at the various areas of dominion of the Republic of the *Serenissima*, starting with the *dominio da mar*, the sea. It must be borne in mind once again that in the centuries of greatest expansion, the Venetian state in Italy was limited to the city and the *dogado*, the original nucleus based around the lagoons of the northern Adriatic, from the Po to the Isonzo and with a few modest projections on to the mainland. In order for the *Serenissima* to gain a real foothold inland in the Veneto, she had to wait until the acquisition of Treviso in 1338. Nearly six and a half centuries had passed since the presumed election of the first doge, a little more than five centuries since the transference of the capital from Malamocco to Venice itself, and 134 years since the *partitio Romaniae*.

Let us first of all examine the network of Venetian merchant bases. The pattern was much as described above, and the basic model was the Venetian quarter in Constantinople. In spite of innumerable adversities, there was always to be a Venetian quarter in Constantinople. It was to survive even the Turkish conquest; and later, the

The present framework of this magnificent work was designed by Gian Paolo Boninsegna in 1342 combining enamels from several periods from the 10th to the 12th century, some of which came from the sack of Constantinople, and some from the first Pala d'Oro, ordered from Byzantium by doge Pietro I Orseolo, and enriched in the 12th century by doge Ordelaf Falier, and in 1209 by doge Pietro Ziani. It is 3.48 metres (11 feet 5 inches) wide and 1.01m (39¾ inches) high, and contains more than 80 enamels.

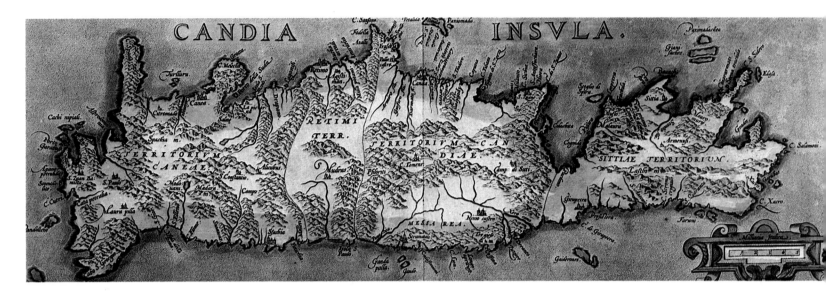

Above: the island of Candia (Crete) from Abramo Ortelio's Theatrum Orbis Terrarum *(1570). Left and below: the cities of Candia and Khania from Angelo Oddi's* Città, fortezze ... del regno di Candia *(Cities, fortresses ... of the kingdom of Candia) (1601). Both Venice and Genoa fought over Crete, but the island fell to the Venetians shortly after the fourth crusade. It was a very important strategic base until 1671, when it passed to the Turks in the peace following the long war of Candia.*

judiciary aspects which gave the Venetian community the characteristics of a "colony" were to survive until 1797. The *bailo* was the permanent representative of the Republic, first of all at the court of the Greek emperor of Byzantium, then for the sultan, but as successor to the Venetians in Romania, his judiciary role continued to be associated with diplomatic functions. This representative had a palace in the vineyards of Pera (the quarter which the Turks now call Beyoglu, "prince's son," in memory of *messer* Alvise Gritti, the illegitimate son of the doge Andrea, a great Ottoman lord). From here he went on exercising governmental powers over all the Venetian settlements of the eastern Mediterranean.

He also governed the Black Sea area. Here too commercial centers and privileged quarters had sprung up. At Tana (present-day Azov), the base-camp for Asian caravans and supply-point for a number of products of great economic importance, a consul held jurisdictive and administrative powers over his compatriots from 1313, with the aid of 12 councillors elected by the Venetian commercial collective. The quarter assigned to the Venetians by the Khan of the Tartars, Usbek, was to be sacked by Tamerlaine in his devastating attack in 1395, but it survived in spite of many setbacks until 1475. Other bases were situated on the coast of present-day Rumania (at Cetatea Alba) and on the Asian coast at Trebizond, where for a while another *bailo* exercised independent functions with regard to his colleague in Constantinople.

The Venetian centers on the Sea of Marmara and in the Dardanelles (where the Dandolo and Viaro families had taken possession of Gallipoli, and the two brothers Querini of Lampsacus) did not survive the crisis of the fall of the Latin Empire. Like the signories of Tarsus and Samothrace, they were later reoccupied by Venice for a brief period in the second half of the 15th century. The same is true of the great fief belonging to the Navigajoso family, Lemnos, which later passed into the hands of the Genoese family of Gattilusi before being swallowed up by the Turks. The island fortress of Tenedos, however, remained in Venetian hands from 1204 to 1261, then in spite of the Genoese, from 1364 until 1400, and again for one brief year, at the time of the war of Candia, from 1656–57.

Venetian dominion over Thessalonica was to be rather short-lived: it lasted 14 years in all, during which the Republic spent enormous sums building fortifications which did not prevent the city being conquered by the Turks in 1436. Setting out from the important Macedonian port where the Venetians had always been in evidence, one of the merchant routes followed the coast of continental Greece, in sight of the Thermopylae pass, well guarded by the massive fortress of Vonitsa. Then it passed close by Euboea and the fertile Negropont, which the Venetians considered the pearl of their kingdom and which, according to a later traveller, produced "an extraordinary abundance of all things," corn, vegetables, wine, oil, silk, cotton, wax, sheep "and other animals, particularly oxen." When Venice lost it, in 1470, she was as stunned, and a chronicler faithfully recorded the sense of annihilation that struck the rulers of the *Serenissima* at the news of the fall of her capital, which, but a few years earlier, had still maintained the picturesque air of a Venetian fortified city.

The fact that, barely two years after the fall of Negropont, the Venetians secured for themselves the control of the kingdom of Cyprus, the prelude to a total assumption of power which was to take place in 1489, is just one more demonstration of the flexibility and quickness of reflex of the collegiate bodies that ran the politics of the Republic. We will speak later of the nuances of diplomatic and financial operation that brought Cyprus into the sphere of Venetian possessions. For now, suffice it to say that from the official

Above: the fortress built by the Venetians to defend the port of Candia, the modern Iraklion. Venetian rule over the island of Crete was punctuated by bloody rebellions, which the Republic overcame by imposing its rule over the large local landowners and allying itself with the latter against the populace. The territorial arrangement of the island reflected the divisions of the city of Venice; it was divided into seven parts, one of which was reserved for the Comune as a whole, while the other six took the names of the six Venetian sestieri.

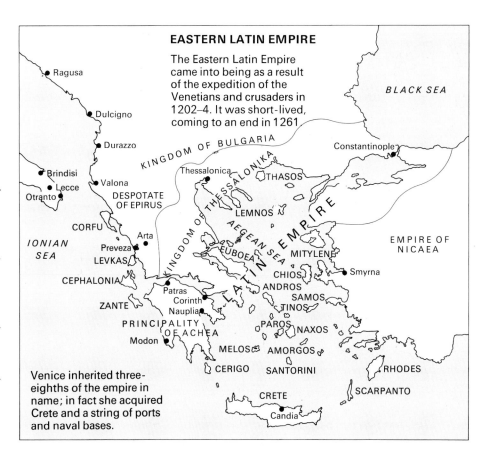

EASTERN LATIN EMPIRE

The Eastern Latin Empire came into being as a result of the expedition of the Venetians and crusaders in 1202–4. It was short-lived, coming to an end in 1261.

Venice inherited three-eighths of the empire in name; in fact she acquired Crete and a string of ports and naval bases.

In the two centuries after the fourth crusade, incalculable riches poured into Venice from its new trading-posts, as the volume of trade increased. It has been estimated that in the middle of the 15th century the volume of business was worth at least ten million ducats, on which the Venetians netted a clear 40 per cent profit. Money circulated freely, and the Exchequer was able to pay off a public debt of four million ducats in a mere ten years. Illustrated above is the office of the procurators of St. Mark, from a miniature in the Register of Landed Property of the Monastery of San Maffeo on Murano, 1391 (Seminario Patriarcale, Venice). The city was gradually adorned with splendid palaces, and the sumptuary laws were unable to check the age-old Venetian passion for luxury (see the mosaic of Salome from St. Mark's basilica opposite).

handing-over of the kingdom to Venice to its definitive fall into Turkish hands, an entire 82 years were to pass.

Another great Mediterranean isle was also a Venetian kingdom: Crete, or Candia as the Venetians called it. It was to remain in their possession for no less than 450 years, and when the Turkish menace threatened here too, they defended it in hand-to-hand combat against the aggressors in an interminable and bloody war, which in 25 years of battle drained the finances of the state and the life-blood of the patrician class.

From Candia, the Venetian dominion radiated out into the Aegean. It was an indirect but effective dominion, represented up until 1540 (but some lasted even longer) by the island fiefs founded by Marco Sanudo and his companions: they were myriad islands, scattered all over the Aegean as far as the northern Sporades. But, the direct navigatory route to Venice avoided the stormy area of the Cyclades, buffeted by wind, and touched on at the fortresses of Modon and Corone, in Messenia, passing via the islands of Cerigo and Cerigotto, both, apart from a brief interlude, constantly Venetian from 1205 to 1797.

Navarino and Patras on the Peloponnese coast were temporary possessions. There was a time when the whole of the Peloponnese was Venetian:

this was in the years following the military campaign on land and sea directed by Francesco Morosini, until the peace of Passarowitz (1718) which marked the beginning of the real decline of the Republic. This courageous and able general had demonstrated, little more than a century before the fall of the Republic, that the lion's claws had not yet been blunted. He solemnly embarked on board his captain's galley on 8 June 1684, and by 7 August had already conquered St. Maur (Levkas), and by 29 September held the stronghold of Preveza. The following summer he had recaptured Corone and stripped the Turkish general (the *seraschier*) of the standard bearing three horses' tails, the symbol of his office, and this was deposited with great rejoicing in the Tolentini church. In the campaign of spring-summer 1686 he regained Modon and Navarino and recaptured Nauplia and Argos, territories that had been lost two centuries earlier. A year later Patras, Lepanto, Rumelia, the bay of Corinth, Athens and Aegina fell into his hands. Venice replaced the lost crowns of Candia and Cyprus with the kingdom of Morea.

This victory lasted no more than 20 years. Venice lacked sufficient means to rule and recolonize such a vast territory, so depopulated and impoverished after the long Ottoman reign. However, even in the short period that Venice was ruler, she managed to launch a series of enlightened systems for the area's agricultural reform and its repopulation, while at Argos, Acrocorinth and Naples in Romania, she built new, powerful fortresses. In no other place does the disproportionate grandiosity of achievement, as against the relative modesty of the state which had initiated and realized this achievement, strike one so forcefully.

Of Morosini's conquests only the Epirote strongholds of Arta, Preveza and Vonitsa, together with the island of Levkas were to remain Venetian until the end. The Ionian isles also remained Venetian, as they had been since remotest times: these were Zante, the most southern, Cephalonia, Ithaca, Paxos and Corfu. The latter was the key to the Adriatic: for this reason, there was permanently stationed there, on the orders of the "captain of the gulf," a naval squadron whose specific duty was to block any armed force which might attempt access to the

gulf of Venice. Even now Corfu retains certain typically Venetian characteristics, and is a kind of picturesque annexe to Venice inserted into a hauntingly Greek setting. For centuries, officers and seamen of the fleet had their permanent residence there. Local society often married into the Venetian patriciate, and the same happened, to a lesser extent, in Cephalonia and Zante. As far as Paxos was concerned, the island nearest Corfu, and recently discovered by international tourism, Venetian domination did not equip it with fortresses as had happened elsewhere but covered it instead with olive groves.

Though Scutari had been lost after a lengthy siege conducted by Mehmed II, Venice's Adriatic domain began in Albania. From there, the coast was entirely Venetian right up to the Velebit mountains. There was Budua, the sleepy little town with an oriental flavour. There was Cattaro, nestling, along with Perasto and Castelnuovo, in the winding ravines of its Straits, at the foot of the craggy Montenegro mountains, a marvellous natural mooring, inferior in the Mediterranean basin only to the bay of Navarino. Then, ascending again, and leaving aside Ragusa, a small republic which by means of all kinds of cunning had managed to preserve its independence, there was Macarsca and Almissa, Spalato and Traú, Sebenico and Scardona, and the rocky outcrops of Clissa and Imoschi, wrenched from the Turks who had advanced their threat even on these lands which boasted the most ancient bonds with Venice. A little north of Zara, the capital of Dalmatia, west of Nona, was the continental frontier; but the chain of islands which begins with Cazza, Lagosta, Meleda and Curzola, opposite Ragusa, and continues with Lissa, Lesina, Brazza and Solta in front of Spalato, up as far as Pago, in front of Nona, widens into the gulf of Quarnero with Arbe, Veglia, Cherso, Ossero and Lussino. Beyond lay Istria, Pola and Rovigno, and the wood of Montona, whose administration was directly dependent on the Council of Ten, as well as Pirano and Capodistria. Beyond the gulf of Trieste stretched the lagoons, the *dogado*, and the capital.

On the Italian coast of the Adriatic, beyond the Po, Venice had taken possession of Cervia, Ravenna, Bertinoro, Faenza, Rimini, Forlimpopoli, Sant'Arcangelo, Fano and Montefiore, all

Right: Venetian merchants of the 14th century; below: their rounded cogs which could carry a large cargo with a small crew. Center: the Gulf of Lepanto in the 17th century, crowded with Venetian galleys.

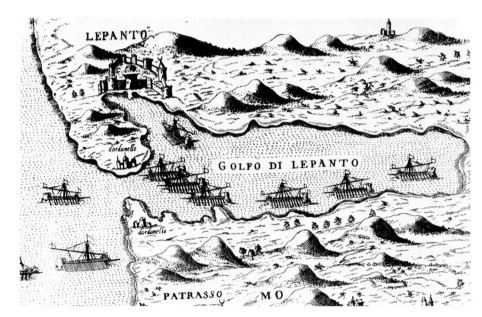

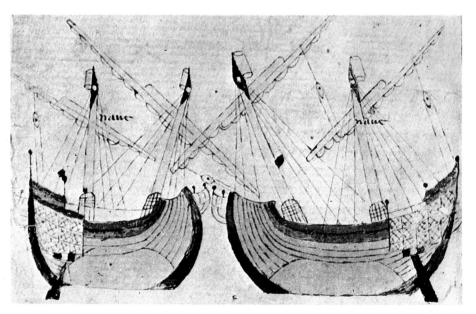

papal cities, the possession of which seriously damaged Venice's relationship with the Holy See. Her reign lasted longest at Ravenna: it was thanks to one of Venice's *podestà* that there is a monument in memory of Dante there, and the fortress built by the Venetians can still be seen, the walls liberally dotted with winged lions. Farther south Venetian rule had for some time and on various occasions, fallen on Bari, Brindisi, Monopoli, Lecce and a few other places. The Apulian ports, which at one time had been Byzantine and then Norman, would have been most useful in further barring entry to the Gulf, but the dictates of politics and war obliged their restitution to the kingdom of Naples, under Spanish sovereignty.

The cities of the Romagna region are part of the complex of Venetian possessions on the mainland. These were dominions, if not colonies: as we shall see farther on, in annexing the Veneto, Friuli and part of Lombardy, Venice in no way intended to ally herself with these regions, with their beautiful, ancient cities, rich in an ancient culture, from which Venice's own civilization drew its heritage. Venice intended to subjugate them, even though her dominion was far more mild and benevolent than that of Austria, Spain or the pope. In any case, it was a vast expanse of territory which, according to the borders established by the peace of Lodi in 1453 and not altered in any significant fashion later on, stretched from the Isonzo to the Adda; the "enclave" of Crema, Rovereto and Val Lagarina, annexed for a while, like Gorizia, were soon returned to Austria. But there remained an area of more than 33,000 square kilometers, including Polesine, Rovigo and the provinces of Padua, Treviso, Belluno, Verona, Bergamo, Brescia and Crema, each governed by a *capitano* elected by the *Maggior Consiglio*, chosen from among the Venetian patricians, as was the lieutenant of the *Patria del Friuli*, which had been taken from the patriarch of Aquileia. Istria and Dalmatia were to remain in Venetian hands until 1797, and they formed another territory of 18 or 19,000 square kilometers in all. The remainder of Venetian holdings at the fall of the Republic, *i.e.*, the Ionian islands plus Cerigo and Cerigotto and the naval bases of Arta, Preveza and Vonitsa, together made up an area of about 3,000 square kilometers. The overall extent of Venetian ter-

The illustrations from Paolo Minorita's Cronologia Magna *(Biblioteca Marciana, Venice) are a valuable source of information on the habits, clothes and activities of the 14th century. Top to bottom, left to right: sailing boat, judge, king, queen, tailor, merchants, doctor, judge, soldier, knight, tailor, shepherd, apothecary.*

ritory on land and sea in 1797 was about 57,000 square kilometers, including the capital and the *dogado*.

While thinking in terms of figures, it is valuable to work out the overall extent of Venetian holdings at the beginning of the 16th century (when Negropont had been lost, but the Turks not yet taken possession of the Aegean islands, and while Venice still had a firm hold on the kingdoms of Cyprus and Candia): it must have been about 77,000 square kilometers. This is perhaps the greatest area of control ever achieved at any given moment. When Cyprus had been lost together with Crete and the Cyclades, but the Peloponnese had been added after Morosini's conquests, Venice regained (before the Passarowitz treaty) more or less the same area of influence.

Any kind of evaluation in terms of population would be very complicated. In terms of productivity, the values alter according to the times and the circumstances. The information supplied by the historian Marino Sanudo for the period around 1464, speaks of an annual income of 698,500 ducats for the city of Venice, 317,400 for the mainland (the highest figures are 75,000 ducats for the province of Brescia and 65,500 for the province of Padua) and 180,000 ducats for the dominion *da mar*, on the sea. Forty years earlier, in April 1423, the doge Tommaso Mocenigo gave far higher figures in the speech he addressed to the

Signoria, sensing that he was close to death: he gave the income of the city of Venice as 774,000 ducats, that of the mainland as 464,000, and that of the dominion *da mar* as 376,000. Apart from the problem of evaluating the currency (which in this case was gold) the difference in the figures must undoubtedly be attributed to the deterioration of the Venetian economy in the 40 years after the death of the doge Mocenigo, precisely because of the assumption of power of the very person whose election this speech was meant to prevent: Francesco Foscari, the leader of the party for territorial expansion within Italy. There had been in fact a notable territorial expansion, but there had also been a state of constant warfare which, apart from the enormous cost, had brought about considerable damage.

Much later, in the 18th century, an estimate sets the total income of the Venetian state at 7,160,000 ducats (silver this time), of which 3,000,000 are for Venice and her *dogado*, 2,460,000 for the mainland and only 800,000 for the dominion *da mar* (there was also an extra million from the salt monopoly). The proportions have changed somewhat in favour of the mainland, but the scale of the contribution of the dominion *da mar* has remained more or less constant. It is clear then, that the income from the overseas colonies never constituted the main part of the Republic's wealth. The major source of the income of the

Thanks to a system of fortresses, support bases and other security measures, Venetian ships were able to sail freely wherever they wished. A naval squadron was permanently based at Corfu where strong fortifications guarded the entrance to the Adriatic (above, 17th-century view from the Museo Storico Navale, Venice), in order to prevent any armed force from attempting to enter the "Gulf." Farther out, the two fortified outposts of Modon and Corone on the south-west coast of the Peloponnese (opposite) were known as the "eyes of the Republic" because of their strategic importance.

The sculptures on the facade of the Doge's Palace form an elaborate symbolic and allegorical group, designed to provide the people with moral instruction. On the corner facing the Piazzetta the theme of sin is illustrated in the group of Adam, Eve, and the serpent. Above, the archangel Michael with his drawn sword protects men from the evil designs of the Tempter (left, above). On the corner facing the Ponte del Paglio is a group depicting the drunkenness of Noah, with his sons, two of whom, Shem and Japheth cover his nakedness, whilst the third, Ham, stands to one side. Above this group stands the archangel Raphael leading the young Tobias on the adventurous journey with which his father has charged him. The allegory of the angel guiding the weakness of humanity is plain. This angel gains special importance from his position on the corner facing out to sea, from where he extends his protection over ships departing from the harbour and greets those returning to it.

state was trade. Many of the Venetian colonies represented economic reserves of considerable value. Such is the case of Cyprus, which supplied the Venetian business world with expensive and sought-after goods such as sugar, cotton, salt and potash. The Peloponnese produced grain and silkworms; Crete proved a most reliable source of fine wines and corn. Also, while it is true that during the anti-Turkish wars the Venetian troops cut down the olive groves in Paros and a few other islands, so as to prevent the enemy getting supplies, it is equally true that the Venetian government was responsible for the introduction of highly productive agricultural enterprises in many areas of their empire. An example is Brazza, the Dalmatian island, where in 1565 the planting of olive trees was made compulsory and wild olive groves were given official recognition. At Cephalonia hitherto unknown crops were introduced such as cotton, indigo and coffee. At Zante, important draining operations were put into action to improve the healthiness of the region and the Republic also introduced the vine, a goldmine, even according to a traveller who was on the whole hostile, Saint-Sauveur: it fed the rich trade in Corinthian grapes, suitable for raisins, which the English market could not do without.

So the Venetian enterprising spirit revitalized and refreshed the economy in many parts of the colonial world of the *Serenissima*, in spite of its philosophy that the interests of the city took precedence over all other interests. In the best years, the balance-sheets of the colonies were heavily in the black: such was the case in Cyprus in 1491, when merely the income from the agricultural estates pertaining to the state, added to the income from the customs, covered all expenses and left a comfortable margin of 5,734 gold ducats. Not that this happy situation benefited the Venetians alone, nor that the forced introduction of certain forms of agriculture was to the detriment of the indigenous population's livelihood. The latter, on the contrary, always received some part of the profits. Venice did not drain her colonies of more than was reasonable, precisely because killing the goose that lays the golden egg is not part of the merchant mentality, and the Venetian mentality was that of the merchant.

The same scheme continues on the corner facing St. Mark's square. Here the judgment of Solomon is depicted, symbolizing human justice, whilst on the upper level the archangel Gabriel exemplifies divine justice and bears the tidings of salvation. All these sculptures were executed between the end of the 14th and the beginning of the 15th century. Although they are the work of different artists, they are remarkable for the unity of their composition.

The Love of the Subjects

"Our subjects must be treated as colleagues" said the doge Paolo Renier in a famous speech in the *Maggior Consiglio* in 1780. However, if the truth be told, other words were added to these noble and affectionate-sounding ones, which place the statement in a particular light: "Princes with no power must base their security on the love of their subjects." It is the reverse of the Roman "let them hate me as long as they fear me:" we must make ourselves loved since we have not the means to make ourselves feared.

When examining the activities of the Venetian administration in the territories which the Republic considered "dominions" (all of them besides the capital and the *dogado*), we should think carefully about such declarations, dictated by the desire to frighten the *Maggior Consiglio* with the specter of the extreme weakness of the state, so as to stifle any opposition on the pretext of the absolute necessity for unity.

As it happened, Venice did not present the same face in all places. In the cities of the mainland which were annexed to Venice along with their territories, but which in general had given themselves up – *i.e.*, had spontaneously delivered themselves into her power – she liked to offer the image of a strong government, vindicator and protector against the injustices and oppression of other rulers. In other cases, she might appear as the defender of a weak community against whatever outsider might wish to suppress and subjugate that community. Venice would therefore give wide scope to local autonomy and preserve statutes and customs; at most, in general, she might offer herself as protector of the less privileged classes. At the time of the annexing of the Treviso region, a great deal of publicity was given to the function of tutelage of the villeins entrusted to the Venetian ruler, to whom anyone who had suffered violence or injustice at the hands of the feudal lords, barons and land-owners could appeal.

Things were more or less the same in the cities of Istria and Dalmatia, all of which were annexed to Venice because they themselves had wished it (the glorious crusade of the year 1000 had been undertaken by the doge Pietro Orseolo II following an appeal that reached him from the Roman cities along the coast, which were being held to ransom and tormented by the Slavs on the basis of fiduciary contracts). But whereas in the mainland cities there were no uprisings, only occasional anti-Venetian plots (such as in Padua, not long after the annexing, which in this case had been forced on them after a long and harsh war), or else defections in periods of crisis (always, however, on the part of the local nobility); in Istria and Dalmatia there were proper revolts and heavy, repressive military interventions, such as in Capodistria at the beginning, and particularly in Zara.

With its seven rebellions, quelled by operations whose principal events are retold in some of the paintings by great masters which adorn the rooms of the Doge's Palace, Zara was a model of stubborn unruliness. At least it seemed so: for there is some doubt as to the spontaneity of those "rebellions." Between ethnic conflicts and judiciary conflicts, the eastern Adriatic coast constituted a perpetual problem, indeed a perpetual accumulation of problems, from the times of the Byzantine empire right up until the end of the last world-wide conflict; and Zara, a Roman city considered even at the time as one of the

121

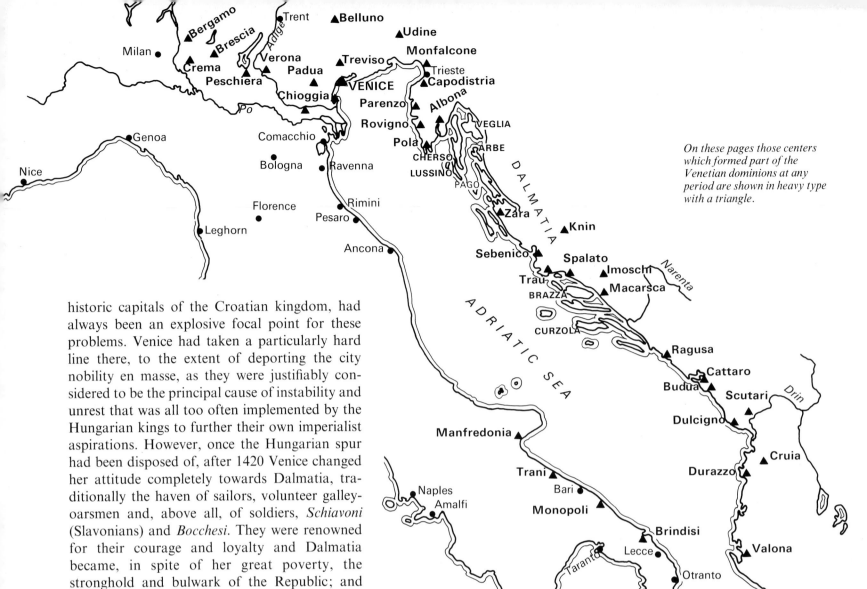

On these pages those centers which formed part of the Venetian dominions at any period are shown in heavy type with a triangle.

historic capitals of the Croatian kingdom, had always been an explosive focal point for these problems. Venice had taken a particularly hard line there, to the extent of deporting the city nobility en masse, as they were justifiably considered to be the principal cause of instability and unrest that was all too often implemented by the Hungarian kings to further their own imperialist aspirations. However, once the Hungarian spur had been disposed of, after 1420 Venice changed her attitude completely towards Dalmatia, traditionally the haven of sailors, volunteer galley-oarsmen and, above all, of soldiers, *Schiavoni* (Slavonians) and *Bocchesi*. They were renowned for their courage and loyalty and Dalmatia became, in spite of her great poverty, the stronghold and bulwark of the Republic; and when the Republic fell, the inhabitants of Dalmatia mourned her bitterly in scenes that were genuinely touching.

Crete was another story. It has been said that when the Venetians took possession of Crete they had never before controlled enormous territories nor been lords of agricultural lands, and so found themselves faced with totally new problems with neither the experience nor the vocation to deal with them. It has also been said that after the conquest of Constantinople and the partition of the Eastern Empire, Venice had become a territorial force virtually in spite of herself, and it is true that what concerned her above all was the economic aspect of the conquest, whereas the territorial side represented a burden which a city of 50,000 inhabitants could not take up without a certain measure of reservations. In Negropont and the Peloponnese, all had been resolved in a form of protectorate, but Crete had to be subjugated and governed directly. There too the Venetians had to deal with a structure originally based on great land-owners who were proper feudal lords, and a local population which, in agreement with its lords, had not the slightest intention of letting itself be dominated.

So Crete proved a real problem for the Republic. Once the Genoese pirates had been driven out (with great difficulty), it was the people's turn to rise up and organize partisan warfare from the high, inaccessible mountains of the interior. (The same was to take place against the Turks and, with particular success, against the Germans in the Second World War). For almost two centuries, Venice ruled with a rod of iron, though some of the ideas she had thought up to consolidate her sovereignty on the island backfired dramatically.

With a few exceptions, the Venetian empire in the Levant consisted of naval bases, staging-posts and trading-stations. The principal ones on the route to the great trading center of Constantinople are shown on this map. North of the Bosphorus, Venice held some important ports in the Black Sea up to the Crimea. East of Crete she held some important warehouses and colonies in the crusader kingdoms on the east coast of the Mediterranean and on the island of Cyprus, which was Venetian between 1489 and 1571.

In the rest of the Greek world, relationships were far less strained. It should not be forgotten that the feudal Venetians of the Cyclades and Sporades had been considered a blessing by the islanders, who had been left exposed by the decaying Byzantine rule to continuous raids from pirates and scavengers from the sea. Anyway, in all locations, the advantages of a correct and farsighted administration coupled with a judiciary system that was in general equally correct, tended to improve the quality of daily life.

This aspect of the Venetian presence is just as clearly visible in the land empire as in the empire *da mar*. Not even two centuries of systematic lynching of the memory of the *Serenissima* (a treatment that as far as the mainland is concerned has become harsher and more accentuated in these last 30 years) have succeeded in dismantling what is apparent to any observer. Everywhere the influence of the Republic was marked by evidence of civilization, dignified ways of life and sophistication of customs which still distinguish the places which were under her rule for a while from those which never experienced it. What remains of Venice in Nauplia, Crete, Naxos, Tinos and Corfu is obviously not to be compared with the wonderful flowering of the mainland Veneto under the protection of the *Serenissima*, but all the same it is clearly noticeable. In addition, the serenity and grace of the little Dalmatian and Istrian towns which Venice spared from catastrophic Ottoman rule, having extracted them from the Slavic grasp, is (or at least was, until a short while ago) a no less effective and significant testimony to this positive influence.

The Colonies

We should now examine how the Venetian colonial system was structured and how it worked. We have already seen how the commercial colonies, from the Sea of Azov to Syria, responded to a more or less identical structure. For some time, the size and importance of the colonies on the Syrian coast justified the presence of *baili* there too: one of them, Marsilio Zorzi, left a detailed study which is a mine of interesting information. Later, the trading posts established in the Arab world, having undergone Ottoman rule, fell once more under the authority of the ultimate *bailo*, that of Constantinople.

The first *bailo* of Negropont, *ser* Pietro Barbo, seemed to be already firmly installed in 1216, and he solemnly received each year from the *terzieri* 700 gold pieces and a gift of rich fabrics, all tributes destined for the doge and the *Serenissima Signoria*. The last, Paolo Erizzo, who held the office at the time of the Turkish attack (1470) met a horrible end: when, after resisting as long as he could, lack of naval support obliged him to capitulate, he was promised by sultan Mehmed II that his head would be safe. The savage conqueror kept his word: alive, his body was sawn apart between two wooden planks.

"Sight and hand directed by the Republic," the kingdom of Negropont passed completely under

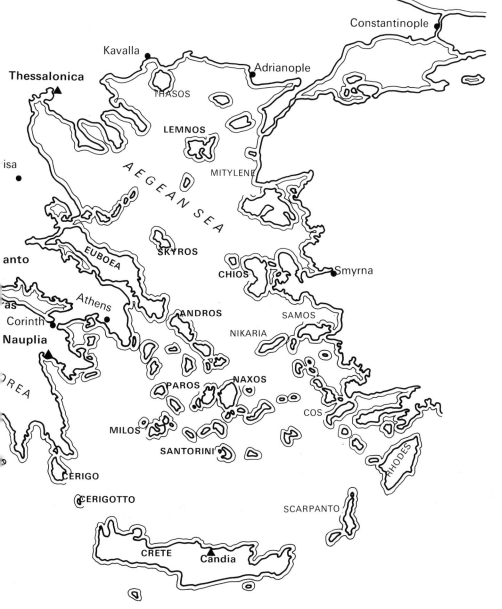

Venice's direct authority in 1390. The *Comune* set aside as its personal property the city of Chalcis, the seat of government. The rest of the island went on being divided into feudal jurisdictions, many of which, however, gradually became the property of the Venetian *Comune* too, which assigned them to trusted patricians. In this way a notable number of fiefs that had belonged to the Dalle Carceri family, in 1470 belonged to the Venetian patricians Zorzi. This was the same family for which the Republic had procured the great fief of Bodonice (present-day Mendenitza) at Thermopylae by marrying *ser* Nicolò Zorzi to Guglielma Pallavicino, widow and heiress of the marquis Zaccaria de Castro. (Venice never shrank from using the weapon of matrimony to consolidate her position, and in this way was to make certain European dynasties

great). The great strategic importance, as well as economic weight of Euboea, particularly after the fall of the terrible Catalans who had devastated Attica, meant that as far as possible, power and income was concentrated in the hands of the *bailo*.

Venetian colonial organization strove to be as centralized as possible. Administrative centralization appeared indispensable for maintaining the cohesion of a whole that was scattered, and at a distance from the mother-city that, for the times, was simply enormous. This characteristic recalls once more the comparison drawn earlier between the Venetian and the British empires, taking into account of course the different scale.

Centralization, that is, the direct dependence of local governors on the *Maggior Consiglio* and the Senate, gave communications a most important position: the prompt delivery of information and carrying out of directives sent out from the central government depended entirely on efficient systems of communication. F. Thiriet has made a study of the lengths of journeys in the Middle Ages from Venice to the various capitals of Venetian dominions in the Levant at that time. He compares them with the length of journeys from London to the various capitals of the British dominions at the beginning of this century, before air travel. We see that from Venice to Khania on the island of Crete, a month's sailing was necessary – the same as from London to Bombay 50 years ago; from Venice to Constantinople took seven to eight weeks, which was the same as from London to Hong Kong. As for the trip from

During the long centuries of Venetian rule, the east coast of the Adriatic was fortified with fortresses and naval bases. Sebenico (Sebenik) is still partly encircled by its Venetian walls, and is dominated by the fort of St. Nicholas (above, right), built by G. C. Sammicheli in 1546. The city boasts a large number of patrician houses in the Venetian style, such as the Orsini Palace (above, left), and the cathedral of St. James, reconstructed after 1431. Below, left: detail of the frieze, and opposite, the extremely fine side-entrance to the cathedral.

Above: Slavonic musketeers of the 18th century. Below: military uniforms of the 17th century (State Archives, Venice). The Slavonians were overseas regiments of soldiers from Slavonia. They were very loyal to the Republic, only abandoning it when its fate was finally sealed.

and the mother-city. At the beginning of the 16th century, the journey from Venice to the Holy Land lasted 50 days, and in 1608 it still took 44 days. F. Braudel has studied the time taken for news to be transmitted in the 16th century, and discovered a number of curious facts: the news of the fall of the capital of Cyprus, Nicosia, into Turkish hands, on 9 September 1570, reached Constantinople on 24 September and Venice only on 26 October. The news of the victory of Lepanto (7 October 1571) took exactly 11 days to reach Venice on board Onfré Justinian's galley (Spanish messengers took 24 days to get to Madrid), but the news of the Turko-Venetian peace, concluded secretly on 7 March 1573 and made known in Venice on 4 April, was already known in Rome on 6 April, in Naples on the 8th and in Madrid on the 17th. Dependence on weather conditions made maritime communications more chancy and variable than those carried over land, but it was impossible to carry news by land to Venice from Crete, Tinos or Cyprus. For this reason, dogal letters which communicated the decisions of the Senate to the governors of the colonies would take 20 to 30 days in the summer and up to 60 days in the winter to reach Candia; letters from the *bailo* to the Senate would take an average of three to four weeks to arrive from Constantinople, but it could happen that a Venetian ship might spend 18 days sheltering off the coast of Chios, as happened in August 1609. A sea as capricious as the Adriatic meant that for news to get from Zara to Venice could take a single day or six whole days.

The feat performed by the galley captain, *ser* Benedetto da Lezze between April and May 1447, is still the most exceptional: he was charged to arrest the Venetian duke (and governor general) of Candia, Andrea Donà, who had been convicted of high treason. He left Venice on 13 April, and by the morning of 28 May, the duke had already appeared, in chains, before the supreme Council of Ten, the *Eccelso*: 45 days in all, from departure, arrest of the duke, return and delivery of the prisoner to the governor of the dungeons of the *Eccelso*. However, the very special interest that Venice had in the city and port of Durazzo derived above all from the fact that this was the terminus of the ancient *via Egnatia*, which linked, via land, the Adriatic with Thessalonica and Constantinople: this was an excellent route for official

Venice to Tana or Trebizond, that lasted about three months, the same as the journey from London to New Zealand at the time of the empire.

Certainly, travelling was lengthy and dangerous (there was the treachery of winds and seas to contend with, summer epidemics and winter storms, and the innumerable, inevitable attacks of pirates and privateers who were the great, ineradicable plague of the Mediterranean). This did not help relationships between the colonies

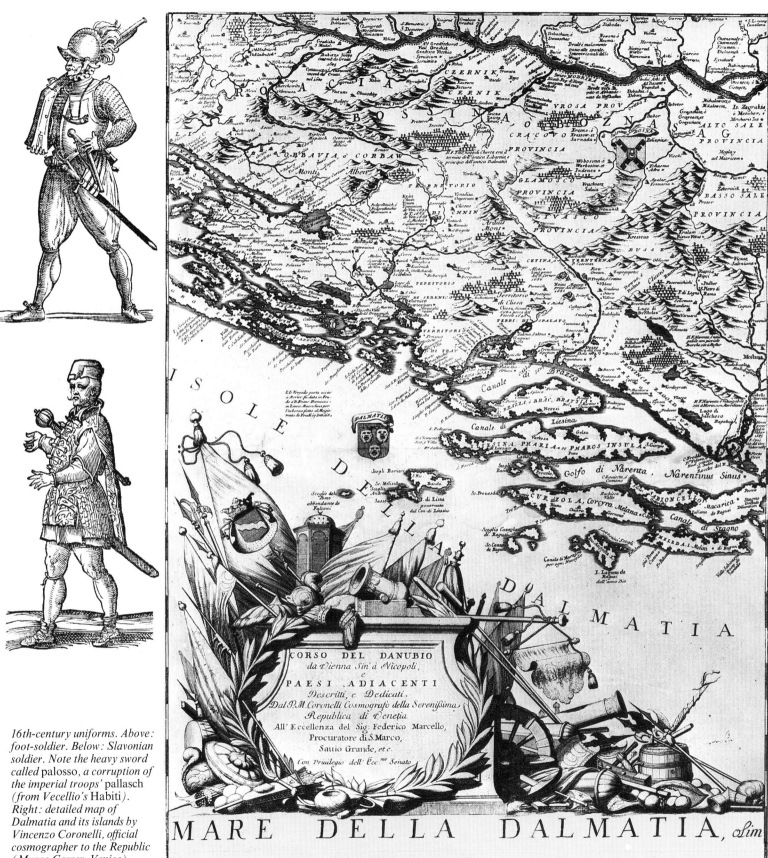

16th-century uniforms. Above: foot-soldier. Below: Slavonian soldier. Note the heavy sword called palosso, *a corruption of the imperial troops'* pallasch *(from Vecellio's* Habiti). *Right: detailed map of Dalmatia and its islands by Vincenzo Coronelli, official cosmographer to the Republic (Museo Correr, Venice).*

CORSO DEL DANUBIO
da Vienna Sin'à Nicopoli,
e
PAESI ADIACENTI
Descritti, e Dedicati,
Dal P.M. Coronelli Cosmografo della Serenißima
Republica di Venetia
All' Eccellenza del Sig: Federico Marcello,
Procuratore di S. Marco,
Sauio Grande, et c.
Con Priuilegio dell' Ecc.mo Senato

MARE DELLA DALMATIA, Sim

correspondence, until the Turkish occupation put an end to this to-ing and fro-ing.

It was also possible that in times of warfare no instructions at all would arrive from Venice. In such cases the dogal governors had to use their own initiative. Yet even after the event, their decisions were subject to ratification by the Senate, prior to examination by the *Pien Collegio*. In other words, Venice was still the ruler that administered her own dominions at first hand, and the running of these dominions would be inspired by the example of the central Venetian organization.

The office of *bailo* in Constantinople was, as has already been noted, still the most prestigious post of all. Even in later times it represented the peak of

a man's career, not least because the jurisdictive functions attracted a sizeable income, contrary to the normal procedure, particularly from the 17th century onwards, that laid the burden of a significant part of the expenses of public office on the private fortune of the person who held that office. In 1407, the remuneration of a *bailo* reached around 1,000 ducats: this is a remarkable figure for the times, equalled only by the income of the governor general of Crete. In April 1600 the Senate assigned to Agostino Nani, who had been elected *bailo*, the sums of 900 gold ducats for expenses, 300 for "steeds, coffers and coverlets" and 300 for unusual extra expenses. This last, however, was nothing other than an extra subsidy which did not have to be accounted for; in the "commission" containing the detailed instructions of the *Pregadi*, 2,000 *zecchini* extra are mentioned, plus various rights. The *bailo* was elected by the *Maggior Consiglio* by an overall majority, "with four election rounds," that is four examinations; he had to be of noble birth and over 25 years old, and, as soon as he was elected, he had to declare acceptance of the office and swear an oath. After this the Senate approved the "commission," *i.e.* the letter of instructions which established his duties: these were general, connected with the nature of the mission, and particular, dictated by the prevailing circumstances. The "commission" was often transcribed (at the addressee's expense) on a beautiful, illuminated manuscript: this was the custom for every office as a memento of the honour and obligation bestowed upon the man elected and his family. It was an honour and a burden; above all a burden for, although lucrative, neither this office nor any other, at least from the end of the 14th century, exonerated the incumbent from payment of taxes. Indeed, the first to be affected by special duties or extra contributions when times were difficult for the exchequer, were precisely the payments made to public officials, starting with the doge. Then there were the compulsory trappings of being the country's representative: the "commission" stated what the composition of the "family" should be, that is, the court which the *bailo* would have to take with him at his own expense, including servants, footmen and horses for everyone. Mercantile activity was strictly forbidden, both for himself and all the people that

Above: circumcision in the Jewish ghetto in Venice, from a painting belonging to the Baali Berit confraternity, the Venetian Jewish community. Below: interior of the Spanish or Western synagogue in the ghetto. Venetian Jews were of various extraction, German, Spanish, Portuguese, and were attracted to the city by the relative tranquillity of life there. Within the community they preserved the habits and manners of their different countries of origin, and of their different religious rites. Center: the Fondaco dei Tedeschi, from an engraving of 1740. These trading centers were not duty-free extra-territorial areas, but were built and owned by Venice and let out to foreign traders who used them as warehouses, shops and hostels, under the watchful eye of the state which levied duties on business transacted there. The German, Turkish and Persian centers were situated along the Grand Canal. The largest and most famous was the German, both for the quantity of its trade, and for the frequent cultural exchanges to which it acted as host. Albrecht Dürer stayed in Venice for a long time and painted the picture for the church of the German community, San Bartolomeo, near the Rialto. This painting, a detail of which is reproduced opposite, is now in the Národni Galerie in Prague.

accompanied him. In the Middle Ages though, a special deed was introduced which allowed him to invest on the spot during the last two months of his office any savings which he might have accumulated, and to sell his horses before embarking for Venice.

The collegiate nature so typical of all Venetian political structures is reflected in the Levant by the presence of two councillors, whose opinion was compulsory for any important decision. The councillors disappeared from the scene in Constantinople when the *bailo*'s jurisdictive duties began to give way to diplomatic functions. But they maintained a presence right until the end in all the most important seats of government of the Venetian empire.

A Centralized System

What has been said concerning the *bailo* in Constantinople applies to all the Venetian colonies – and not just the colonies. The duties of government normally fell to the *regimen*, a Latin name for what was usually referred to in administrative jargon as the *reggimento*, and comprised the *rettore*, or Venetian representative, who had different titles depending on the place and the times and, if the place were important there would

be a *consiglio*, generally consisting of two members. These (always assuming the place was of some significance) would be backed up by two *camerlenghi*, whose particular concern was finance. Sometimes there was a *capitano* to aid the principal *rettore*. In these cases, the man of a higher grade would take care of judiciary duties and co-ordination while the other would look after day-to-day government, public order and military command. However, the members of the *regimen* were always Venetian nobles, elected in Venice by the *Maggior Consiglio*, and the structure of local government would always be strictly modelled on the example of the Venetian government. This was so even when local circumstances called for very different practical solutions.

The most extraordinary case and also the most

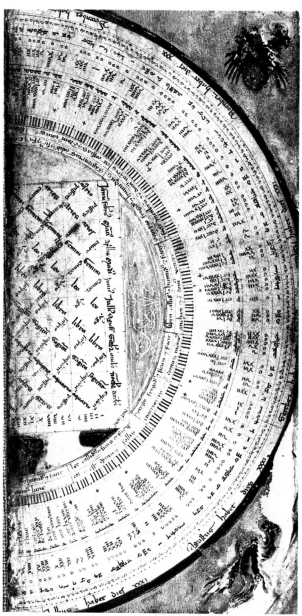

characteristic is that of Crete, the great island which the Venetians called Candia, like its capital city. The Republic (or rather the *Comune* as it still called itself in 1208) sent there the noble Jacopo Tiepolo with the title of duke, a man who was later to become *podestà* of the Venetians in Constantinople, and afterwards doge of Venice. With the support of the doge Pietro Ziani, this very talented and energetic man proposed, had approved and put into action, an arrangement which actually reflected the structure of the motherland even from the territorial point of view: the island was divided into seven parts, one of which remained *pars Communis*, the section reserved for the *Comune*, while the other six took the names of the six *sestieri* into which the city of Venice is divided. In this way, Sitia, Hierapetra and the upland plain of Lasithi with its windmills were incorporated in

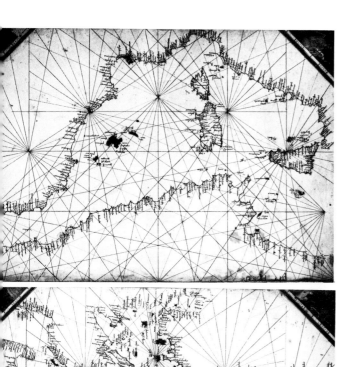

of knighthood, and 48 *sergenterie*, that is, fiefs for sergeants rather than knights, were given to 48 members of the ordinary Venetian populace. All *milites*, *i.e.* feudal lords, had to have a house in Candia, the capital of the island and of that section of the *Comune*.

The meager success of attempts to make peace, and the determination of the islanders to oppose Venetian colonization, in later times caused more men to be posted from Venice to Crete. In 1222 another hundred knights and sergeants were installed in as many fiefs, another nine joined them in 1233, and 45 knights and six sergeants settled on the northern coast in 1252. In all the Venetians transferred to Crete in this enforced "Venetianization" numbered about 3,500: a huge number if we consider the sparse population of the mother-city (about 60,000 inhabitants in the middle of the 13th century), but very few compared with the extent of the occupied territory.

Yet the *Maggior Consiglio* of Candia (for there was a *Maggior Consiglio* in Crete too) did not for this reason get out of hand: in fact not all the feudal lords had the right to belong to it. Every year, in December, the *regimen*, which in Crete was made up of the duke, the *capitano* of Candia, two *consiglieri* and two *camerlenghi*, assembled with a *zonta* of 25 nobles, in order to designate the members (from 250 to 300) of which it would be composed in the following year. Its duties were varied, but not of vital importance. Mainly, it was concerned with approving the decisions made by the Senate of Candia, known in Latin as *Consilium rogatorum Candidae*.

The Cretan colony, then, imitated the mother-city even in this: 90 *rogati* (i.e. begged, *pregadi*, in effect) took office for a year starting each January, and concerned themselves with foreign policy, or rather with what the Venetian Senate left for them to do, having given general guidelines in matters concerning relationships with foreign countries. On the whole these would be local affairs initiated by the delicate position of the island, such as the nomination of the ambassadors for the Great Master of the Knights of Rhodes or for some other neighbouring ruler, or their services might be required in an emergency. The Cretan Senate elected from among its own members a number of *savi* to examine specific problems and to take care of religious matters. Above all, it was the Senate

the *sestiere* of Cannaregio, the area south-east of the island in the San Marco *sestiere*, Castelnuovo and Priotissa, along with the fertile plain of Messara in the *sestiere* of Santa Croce, Rethimnon, Milopotamos and Arios in that of San Polo, and Khania, Kissamos and the whole of the western side of Crete in the *sestiere* of Dorsoduro.

The Venetian colonials summoned by the duke must then have felt a little more at home in this vast, rocky, hostile land, but which now echoed household names. They needed to, for the colonization conceived by the duke Tiepolo was a military regime, intent on suppressing Cretan resistance by breaking up the great estates still held by the archons, the local feudal lords. The properties assigned to the *Comune* and the church were set aside, then 132 fiefs were handed over to the same number of nobles, as *cavallerie*, or marks

Two pages from Pietro Vesconti's pilot showing the eastern and western basins of the Mediterranean. Such pilots showed the precise outline of coasts, ports and islands, all carefully named. Superimposed on this is a series of crossing lines issuing from eight centers lying on the circumference of an imaginary circle, and coinciding with the wind rose. The study of nautical matters was encouraged by business and trade voyages. Venice was especially famous for its school of cartography.

Left: ivory sun-dial on a column, made by Clemente da Venezia, 1638. Below, left: brass and bronze sextant, 17th century. Below: ivory sun-dial with magnetic needle by Lienhart Miller, 1612. Right: 16th-century armillary sphere (from the collection of antiques in the Museo Correr, Venice).

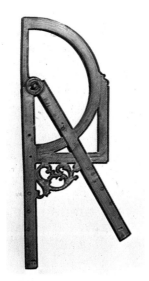

Top: compass with sun-dial in an ivory case, 17th-century. Above: astrolabe in brass and bronze by Descrolieris, 1571 (Museo Correr, Venice). Opposite: The Storm by Francesco Guardi (Castello Sforzesco, Milan). Venice lived by the sea; here the painter, a true Venetian, is both interpreter and participant in the perils of such a life.

that elected those sent to present to the doge and the *Signoria* the complaints and requests of the islanders, and it also discussed and approved what exactly was to be presented to Venice, and the "commissions" to entrust to those who would be the ambassadors. However, this Senate was not appointed by the *Maggior Consiglio* of Candia: its members were chosen by the duke and his *consiglieri*, who selected 30 each. Once more the principle of centralization comes into play: the element that decides and elects was the *regimen*, elected in Venice, guided by Venice, responsible only to Venice.

The procedure used to elect the *Maggior Consiglio* of Candia and the alternation it entailed also fulfilled a particular requirement: that of checking and rechecking, every year, the situation of all the feudal lords, so as to avoid the governing body being infiltrated by elements of the local population. The main preoccupation of the Cretan Venetians (few and far between in an area that was too large for them) was to dominate the population, which had been granted no rights of self-government. This was a crude principle, provoked by the violently hostile attitude of the population itself, and above all, of the local potentates; however, this principle was extremely negative in its effects, since the great Byzantine families, Cortazzi and Kalergis, Skordylis, Vlastos, Haghiostefanidis, kept the island in a topsy-turvy state and for decades blocked agricultural colonization. When the occasion occurred, they also lent their assistance to revanchist attempts by Greek sovereigns who, first of all from Nicaea, then from recaptured Constantinople, wanted to re-gain sovereignty of the island. Worse than ever, some of the feudal lords also took the side of the populace, and identified their own interests with local interests. The revolution of 1363, provoked by a tax that was thought excessive (though it was destined for the development of port facilities in Candia), had as its rebel leaders two Gradenigos and two Veniers: unmistakably Venetian names, and of great patrician families.

The revolt was crushed with extreme severity, but the Republic paused for thought. With her usual malleability, she set in motion a conciliatory policy which little by little modified the terms of her relationship with the island. We must point

out though, that this did not entail any greater general involvement of the populace in the government of the island, apart from the extension of certain privileges to landowners of Byzantine stock.

In Negropont and in the Peloponnese, Venetian policy was instead quite different, and far nearer to the principles preached by the doge Renier in 1780. In 1347, when the Greek villeins of Modon and Corone complained of the excessive weight of taxes, it was the two *rettori* (in this case, castellans) who, as soon as they had got back to Venice at the end of their period of office, presented the islanders' complaints to the Senate, which in the main accepted them. The same happened in 1362, and this time the Senate sent out dispositions to the castellans requiring them to prevent the exploitation of the poor peasants of Messenia. In Modon and Corone, the usual system applied too, castellan plus *consigliere* (the first paid 400 ducats and the second 200 in 1402). However, a sharp interjection from the Senate in Venice, deploring the excessive interference by the Council of Twelve of Modon in certain negotiations with the Greek despot of Mistra, reveals the existence of another consultative body, made up of 12 Venetian nobles, a kind of *collegio* to aid the *regimen* in its administrative duties. In Negropont instead, there was actually a *Maggior Consiglio* as in Crete and later in Corfu. Again and again the Venetian colonies modelled themselves, almost stubbornly, on their homeland.

As time went by, in almost all the Venetian colonies, just as on the mainland, the local aristocracy took predominance over local public office. There was no need to be disturbed by this: all decision-making at a higher level fell to the *regimen*, which continued to take orders from Venice alone. But as far as municipal offices and titles were concerned the nobles took precedence, particularly from the 16th century onwards, even where officially popular participation and representation had survived. In Tinos and Zante, there still exist today families that boast descent from those belonging to the ancient noble council of their islands, composed not of Venetian immigrants, as in Crete, but of genuine autochthons. The noble society which flourished in Corfu was to make a significant contribution at the beginning of the 19th century to the liberation and unifi-

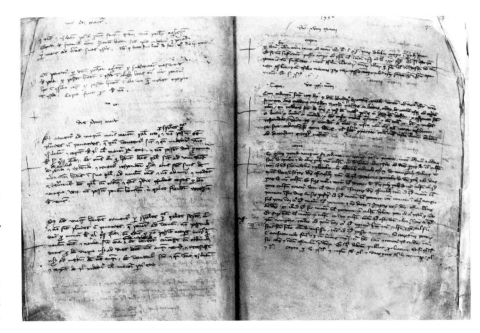

cation of Greece, and was to be a prominent section of the original nucleus of the Hellenic ruling class. It should suffice to call to mind the count Capodistrias, who was the first president of the council of ministers of the new-born kingdom, independent of Greece: his title of count had been conferred on his ancestors by the Venetian Senate, like the titles bestowed on the families of Theotokis, Bulgar, Petridin, and Lunzi, to name but a few. In Dalmatia, where the indigenous nobility was numerous and, at least from the beginning of the 16th century, somewhat poverty-stricken, the "populace" (which included a rich bourgeoisie, in the case of the Dalmatians, far richer than the nobles) did not always accept peacefully the supremacy of the aristocracy recognized in city councils. This strife was most painful on the island of Lesina where, between 1511 and 1514 there was actually a state of partisan warfare; and the Republic, which was going through a period of serious political and military crisis, did not listen to the many opinions voiced in the Senate supporting more benevolent solutions, and applied harsh, repressive measures. In this case however, the Republic was dealing with not so much a social problem as the security of an area that was extremely sensitive for the safety of the Gulf, at a time of great tension when she could not run risks of any kind.

To do "good and strict" justice

The colonial population, then, had various means by which it could make itself heard in Venice. We have already seen how the *rettori* of Modon and Corone took on the role of spokesmen for the peasants of Messenia. In fact, the inhabitants of all the lands in the Venetian empire, both on the mainland and *da mar* (with the exception for a long while of Crete, where only resident Venetians had the chance of making their voices heard in Venice), all had the right to send to the capital their own nuncios, ambassadors or delegates, to expound complaints and explain circumstances, and ask for justice. As the Venetian state expanded, the task of dealing with subjects' complaints against the administration was entrusted to the *avogadori di Comun*. This was a very important judiciary post which, as has been

pointed out elsewhere, combined the everyday functions of a procurator general with many other duties, such as that of suspending and appealing against sentences passed by a number of other magistratures, including *reggimenti*. Later, at the beginning of the 15th century, a specific magistrature was actually set up, the *auditori novi*, to hear appeals brought by the subjects of the mainland and Istria. Causes from territories *da mar* were presented to the *Collegio dei XX*. However, when we speak of ambassadors and nunciatures, these are not judiciary matters but proper missions appointed to set out broader and more general problems to the *Signoria*, *Pien Collegio* and Council of Ten. Gradually, these representatives were made permanent fixtures (*delegazioni*) and had a permanent base in Venice to carry out their duties. However, the main instrument at the disposal of subject populations, the best corrective to the power of the *rettori*, was another magistrature that was typically Venetian, the *sindici inquisitori*.

In the Venetian colonies, as in holdings on the mainland, the *regimen* was responsible not only for government but also for the administration of justice. The head of the *regimen* on the mainland normally had the title of *podestà*, translated in offical Latin documents by the word *praetor*. In the territories *da mar*, besides the *bailo* there was the duke, as in Candia, or the *provveditore*, of Zante, Cephalonia, Cerigo, Parenzo, Almissa, Capodistria, Cittanova and many other places. (The position also entailed that of military commander, besides offices of government and law.) Only in Istria and Dalmatia did the *rettori* of Arbe, Brazza, Cherso, Curzola, Lesina, Nona, Pago, Pola, Sebenico, Spalato, Traú and Zara bear the title of *conte* (count), of ancient Hungarian origin.

In smaller centers, the *rettore* administered the law personally, with the aid of a subaltern staff of chancery. In more important centers, the judiciary structure imitated on a smaller scale that of the mother-city. The basic law was Venetian. Local customs were taken into account more or less depending on the place, the circumstances and the times. In the Venetian colonies in Romania there were local magistrates that corresponded almost exactly to those in Venice: the equivalent of the *avogador di Comun* was the *advocatus* and the *signori di notte* acted as a police court like their Venetian namesakes. In Crete in the Middle Ages there were three *advocati*, just as in Venice, and four *signori di notte* responsible for public safety and, in certain respects, acting as coroners. (For example, among their duties was the unenviable task of taking charge of the corpses of the victims of murders and the retrieving of those injured in brawls). In larger territories such as Crete, the

regimen handled only the most important trials. The duke in person judged murder trials, *lèse-majesté* and treason trials, this last heading including embezzlement and theft of public funds. Lesser criminal trials such as brawling and theft were left to the *giustizieri* and *capitani* of the various cities, and in *castellanie* to the castellan. Four other *capitani* took charge of cases of banditry, but not as judges: they would listen to

Above: Curzola, "most loyal" island, whose inhabitants were granted Venetian citizenship for resisting the Turks in 1571. Below: detail of the mainland arch, and the fortress of Kamerlengo at Traú (Trogir).

complaints and then arrest the culprits – if they could catch them. The magistratures for commercial and private rights also mirrored the Venetian institutions, with the *giudici del proprio* and the *giudici del petizion*. In Crete once again it seems there was also a special magistrature of the *presoppi* or *prosopi*, which had to judge litigations in which Greeks or Jews were involved. The "commissions" written to the *rettori* of the colonies urged them in general to do "good and strict" justice to everyone, particularly the indigenous population, Jews and foreigners. The state recommended that these be treated on a par with Venetian citizens resident in the jurisdiction. In effect, although Venetian justice had a reputation for severity, it was felt to be far more fair than that exercised by the various Greek, Italian, Hungarian and Croatian potentates in their dominions, not to mention Moslem justice or that, often proverbially corrupt, of the many foreign sovereigns who held territories in Italy. An extremely strong sense of justice permeates Venetian civilization right from its beginnings, and this is reflected in the scrupulous punctiliousness of the central government bodies as regards peripheral governing bodies every time judiciary administration came into play. Perhaps we should remember at this point the conscientiousness, unheard-of under any other rulers, with which criminal trials were conducted even in turbulent, troublesome Crete. In 1290 the *Maggior Consiglio* sent out from Venice a sacrosanct disposition, valid for everyone, that forbade judges to inflict corporal punishment (then very common), however mild, on those under 14 years old and on the mentally sick.

The Senate of Candia itself ordered that torture, at that time part of the investigatory outfit of every state in the world, could not be used on a suspect unless prior authorization was gained from the Senate itself and the Council of Twelve. This was part of a system of guarantees which in many respects gave the accused a better deal than they endure even now under many systems in the western world, and which culminated in the principle of compensation of those found innocent, for damages sustained owing to unjust imprisonment.

Going back to the *sindici inquisitori*, we have spoken well of Venetian justice. But we should not

Right: statue of admiral Leonardo Foscolo, who tenaciously defended Dalmatia, Albania and Candia against the Turks; from the courtyard of the Papalic Palace in Spalato (Split). Below: the facade of the Sponza Palace, in pure Venetian style in Ragusa (now Dubrovnik).

imagine that all Venetian *rettori* were pillars of rectitude (though some of them were real gentlemen, such as Sebastiano Venier, duke of Candia and *podestà* of Brescia before winning the battle of Lepanto as general captain *da mar*. In one of his reports, he set out a principle that is still extremely relevant: "indulgence towards the wicked is tyranny against the good"). Neither should it be thought that the Venetian empire was a kind of earthly paradise. There were corrupt, unjust and inept *rettori*: the Republic was aware of this and had already foreseen problems, jùst as it had foreseen the possibility that the privileged classes in the colonies might try to corrupt the *rettori* in order to weigh the balance of justice in their own favour, and that the *rettori* might be subject to pressures or harbour ambitions contrary to the greater glory of the *Serenissima*, an aspiration officially only granted to the members of the patriciate.

For this reason, once the *rettori* returned to Venice, the details of their period of office were picked over meticulously by the Council of Ten, the *avogadori di Comun* and the relevant magistratures for financial control, and while still in office they could suddenly find themselves unexpectedly the victims of inspections which would review all aspects of their governmental activities.

Originally this duty too fell to the *avogadori di Comun*: a judiciary writer noted, curiously, that this office would only be given to those who "united talent with physical fitness, because in order for the work to be done well, the strongest constitution would be wearied." Even in 1410 an *avogador* was sent to Candia to investigate the

activities of a councillor of the *reggimento* and his brother. However, on 10 January 1363, shortly before the revolt of the feudal lords on Crete, in the face of a storm of pessimistic reports on the discontent of the islanders, the three heads of the *Quaranta* proposed to the Senate that three special *provveditori* should be sent to the islands, and the Senate approved. They were to visit Crete, Corone, Modon and Negropont. There, they were to gather the complaints of the inhabitants. The three were to remain together at all times, and could not conduct any business nor receive gifts. They were to meet to discuss matters and take decisions by majority vote. If they could not agree, on their return they were to appear before the Senate which would then decide on the basis of documents received. These three were elected from among the patricians who had never been *rettori* in any of the Eastern Latin Empire territories in the last ten years, and who had no relatives that were *rettori* or magistrates.

The inspection did not prevent the outbreak of the bloody rebellion in Crete, nor its repression, but it probably influenced the decision to change the navigational route which marked the peace made later between the Republic and her turbulent island realm. Anyway, from the end of the 1300s, those who by now were known as the *sindici di Levante* every five years set sail (unless there were serious reasons to oppose it) armed with the Senate's instructions, and headed for the colonies. They listened, read and investigated in Crete and Durazzo, Corfu and Negropont; and they did their job conscientiously. In 1432, as a result of the report made by the *sindici di Levante*, the Senate

"Fight which occurred on 19 April 1756. On the above-named day, the Venetian ship of count K. Marco Jvanovich of Dobrota and his brother K. Jeseppo with only 40 crew were attacked by a large sambuk 170 feet long and carrying 40 cannon, and with a crew of 360 Turks. The two above-mentioned vessels fought from noon to eleven p.m. exchanging fire the entire time, until the ship beat the said sambuk with the loss of K. Marco and eight of his soldiers. The next day the sambuk was fired, and the victorious ship sailed off to the Serenissima Dominante" (from the legend at the bottom of the painting by Vincenzo Chilone reproduced above, Museo Storico Navale, Venice).
Opposite: study of a galley attributed to Raphael (Gallerie dell'Accademia, Venice).

sentenced the nobleman Secondo Pesaro, a former *consigliere* in Candia, to pay a fine of 796 ducats, to spend two years in prison and to be permanently barred from public office, for being profoundly guilty of "selling right and justice as well as offices and fiefs of our Cretan kingdom by accepting gifts." Shortly afterwards the Senate conceded to the *avogadori* the right to take proceedings against *ser* Domenico Bembo, colleague and accomplice of Pesaro, and he was sentenced to the same penalties. At the beginning of the following year it was the turn of the former *rettore* of Rethimnon, *ser* Pietro Mudazzo. Later, Daniele Loredan, *bailo* of Negropont and an important figure, had the skeletons in his cupboard rattled by the *sindici* and was sentenced to a fine of 400 ducats, plus a year's imprisonment and five years of suspension from public office. These measures were taken on the basis of very detailed studies, in the course of which the populace had been given ample scope to express their complaints (and it should be noted that the accused, for their part, were given every opportunity to defend themselves). The effect of all this strictness, as the French historian F. Thiriet, an eminent authority on the Venetian Levant, has stated, was completely in favour of the peoples governed: rulers and colonial staff felt themselves carefully observed from the capital, which in this way had a very precise responsibility as patron of the subject populations. For this reason, when Paolo Renier claims that subjects were treated as "colleagues," he is not basically exaggerating at all from the point of view of Venetian political morality. Neither was another doge, Marco Foscarini, exaggerating when he proclaimed that the institution of the *sindici inquisitori* was inspired by "love of our subject peoples." Harsh in repressing rebellion, unbending in her demands of unconditional loyalty and total fidelity, at her peak Venice repaid the peoples under her rule with a justice that discriminated against no one. This explains far better than any arguments the reason why many cities and communities spontaneously allied themselves to the *Serenissima*, which found in the cult of justice the corrective to the imperfections and errors that are part of every form of government and rule.

The Territories of St. Mark

Venice's expansion in the East reached its height in the 13th century. Its colonial empire included the Ionian islands, huge stretches of Albania, Epirus, Attica and the Peloponnese, the Sporades, the Cyclades, many other islands of the Aegean, Crete and Euboea, the European coast of the Dardanelles and the Sea of Marmara, and three-eighths of the city of Constantinople including the arsenal. This chain of possessions and outposts formed a commercial empire, since Venice was more interested in widening the sphere of its trade than in territorial expansion.

Opposite: the triple enclosure of Acrocorinthos, the hill on which the ancient acropolis of Corinth stood. The situation of this city at the entrance to the two gulfs of the Peloponnese was of the greatest strategic importance, and the site was long contested by the powers striving to dominate this area of Greece. Venice successfully made herself mistress of it on several occasions against the Turks, holding it between 1687 and 1715; one of the surrounding walls was in fact built by the Venetians.

Readers who are familiar with the astonishing exploits of Sandokan, the Tiger of Malaysia and his constant companion and friend, Janesz the Portuguese, characters in the oriental saga created by Emilio Salgari, will remember the proud, disdainful figure of Sir James Brooke, the white rajah of Sarawak, the ever-thwarted enemy of the hero.

Sir James Brooke was no figment of the vivid imagination of the Veronese writer. He was a product of the versatility and courage of British society in the Victorian age, and of the flexibility and practicality of British rulers at the time when Britain reached the peak of her imperialist fortunes. Born in India of a family of English officials in 1803, James Brooke was an officer of the armed forces of the East India Company, and joined the service of the sultan of Brunei in Borneo to put down the Dayak tribe of Sarawak on the north-west coast of the island. He succeeded, but in exchange asked for the whole territory of Sarawak as a personal principality. As soon as he had obtained this and had become rajah, he immediately put himself and his state under the protectorate of the British Crown. The Crown named him consul general for Her Majesty in Borneo and at the same time governor of the neighbouring colony of Labuan. In this way, Sir James (created baronet in 1847) became a very useful pawn in the British power game in Indonesia because, from his semi-independent position, for ten years he was able to use the most brusque methods to dispose of the pirates that infested the Sound, without involving the British Crown directly (which could officially wash its hands of him). At the same time, he was able to found a dynasty which reigned for more than a

century, until, in a changed world, his great-grandson, Sir Charles Vyner Brooke, was obliged to abdicate in 1946.

There is no way of knowing whether Sir James Brooke had read the history of the Venetian Levant, but given the great interest the British have always shown in Venetian history, the possibility cannot be excluded. The parallel between the enemy of Sandokan and Marco Sanudo, the nephew of Enrico Dandolo who as we have seen, set up for himself and his descendants a feudal duchy in the Cyclades while his colleagues took over a number of islands and islets in the Aegean, is too close not to be surprising.

Having served the Republic as judge in the Venetian colony of Constantinople and later as a galley captain, Marco, together with a band of Venetian nobles from Constantinople, left for the conquest of the Cyclades and northern Sporades. First he made an agreement with the doge Pietro Ziani, who assured him of the protection of the *Comune* of Venice. The pretext for the occupation of the islands was the same as that which justified the birth and existence of Sir James Brooke's principality: protection against pirates. When Marco founded his dukedom on the Archipelago, with Naxos as capital, he had it conferred on him by the Eastern Latin emperor, but he himself, like his companions, who had made themselves lords of other islands (some as his vassals, others on their own account), to all intents and purposes was still a Venetian noble.

The duke Marco was head of a feudal dynasty destined to last a good while in that Aegean archipelago, which nowadays represents an irresistible tourist attraction with its rocky isles dotted like mirages in the marvellous blue of Europe's most beautiful sea. But then it represented something both very distant and at the same time familiar, a myriad of scattered stages on the margin of the most frequented routes for Venetian merchant ships, innumerable anchorages, bays and ravines where those ships, after Marco Sanudo's expedition, were sure to find shelter from storms and pirates, but also a number of treacherous shoals, harsh coasts battered by the sea and the winds. Marco himself is an unusual figure, uniting and synthesizing the myth and reality of the medieval Mediterranean: from noble Venetian merchant he became a great feudal lord, but rather than settle down to a sedentary life he took to the sea again in search of new adventures. He landed in Asia Minor, conquered the city of Smyrna and made himself lord of it. However, he was attacked by the forces of the Greek emperor of Nicaea, the valiant Theodorus Lascaris, and was obliged to surrender his new conquests and follow him as his prisoner. Overcome in his turn by the charm of the noble adventurer, the *basileus* set him free again, and what is more, gave him the hand of his own daughter in marriage.

The duke Marco died in 1227 and was succeeded by his son Angelo. His direct line died out almost a century and a half later, in 1371, with Fiorenza Sanudo, who was married first to Giovanni dalle Carceri, a member of one of the families of *terzieri* of Negropont, and afterwards to her cousin Nicolò Sanudo.

On the great island, crammed with bleak but richly cultivated mountains (it was the most fruitful of the Cyclades as far as arable land and cattle farming were concerned: even today, it is probably the only one where good steaks of island beef can be eaten), Sanudo had his feudal court, like that of Villehardouin in Kyparissia or Otto de la Roche in Athens; or else, on a more modest scale, like that of the Ghisi family on Skiros, or the Querini family in their castle in Stampalia, or any of the other island lords of the Aegean. There were Venetian squires and sergeants, and there were the Greek villeins or *pareci* as they were known, whose circumstances seem to have been better under their Latin lords than when they were servants of the Byzantine empire. There were also craftsmen and merchants, pedlars and minstrels.

The partitio Romaniae *left Venice with the problem of making her authority effective over the parts of the Greek world which she had been allocated, and occupying the lands which she possessed only in name. The practical Venetian spirit found a simple and economical solution. Citizens of Venice were granted the title of many of the islands and other sites, so that they were absorbed into the Republic's sphere of influence without risk to the city, almost by delegation. In this way Marco Sanudo founded a strong duchy for himself and his heirs in the Cyclades, closely linked to the Republic.*

But the caprices of the sea made it difficult to enjoy the traditional pleasures of feudal society, hunts, tournaments, visits from troubadours and wandering poets such as Rambaldo di Vaqueiras (who appeared at the court of Conrad of Monferrato in Thessalonica). The constant tension with the Byzantine world, before and after the reconquest of Constantinople by the Greek emperor of Nicaea, did not allow for complete relaxation, and

Above: the capital of the island of Naxos, largest of the Cyclades, fortified around the castle built by Marco Sanudo. Left: Venetian fortress at Chalcis on the island of Naxos, built as a defense against the incursions of Barbary pirates.

there were other threats from within the Latin feudal world itself: the greed of the princes of Morea of the house of Villehardouin (who for some time succeeded in putting down the dukes of the Archipelago and in receiving tributes from them) and the belligerence of the Genoese. On one occasion, a knight from Negropont, a certain Licario, of Vicenza, went heart and soul over to the Byzantine cause and helped the Greeks to regain a number of islands which later had to be laboriously won back. The existence of these Venetian dynasties resembles that of Sir James Brooke in their isolation in a hostile world far from their homeland, while still maintaining indissoluble links with that home. James Brooke died on a Devonshire estate, where he retired after securing succession to the throne for his grandson. Marco Sanudo died in his castle at Naxos, the ruins of which still exist, eaten away and crumbling, facing out on to the port. However, at least once in their lives, his descendants, like those of the Ghisi, Dandolo, Barozzi and Zeno families, were to face the long sea voyage to Venice after the *serrata* of the *Maggior Consiglio* in order to uphold their right to belong to it and to exercise their right to vote.

Once the house of Sanudo had died out, having shaken off the tutelage of the princes of Morea with the help of the Venetian fleet, and having driven Licario's Greeks out again, another family entered the scene, one that was distantly related to the last duchess: this was the Crispo family, of uncertain origin, but probably Veronese. In spite of complicated family disputes, Turkish invasions and interregna, the great island fief survived more or less intact right up to the Turko-Venetian peace of 1540, laid down after Khair-ed-din, Barbarossa, the terrible Algerian pirate, had ravaged the islands in 1537, driven out the rulers and carried off many of the inhabitants as slaves. But the change from Venetian to Turkish sovereignty, blessed by the treaty of 1540, did not yet mean the end. Just like the families of Gozzadini from Folegandros, Sikinos and Sifnos, and the Sommaripa from Andros (houses that followed on by heredity or other reasons from the descendants of the conquerors), so the Crispo family remained on the island, and paid a tribute to the sultan. Eventually in 1566 Giacomo IV Crispo was obliged to renounce Naxos in favour of a very unusual

person, one of the strangest in the whole highly colourful cast of the Mediterranean. This was Josef Nassí, alias João Miquez, a Jewish banker from Lisbon who, fleeing persecution, had set anchor in Constantinople where he became the sultan Selim II's favourite, and personal councillor.

The story of this incredible character, to whom is attributed the enormous responsibility of having caused a war in Cyprus, as well as the far-sighted idea (a good 350 years before Theodor Herzl) of creating a national Jewish homeland in Palestine, has little to do with our subject. In any case this individual, who seems to have stepped from the pages of a novel, was given the fief of Marco Sanudo's dukedom. He administered it through a third person, a certain Francesco Coronel, who was none other than a "Marrano," a Jewish refugee who had fled from Spain 13 years before. He ruled very wisely too, from what little we know. The reign set up by Enrico Dandolo's grandson was to preserve some semblance of autonomy at least up until 1601, when a delegate of the Holy See reported to Rome on the existence

The island of Chios was taken by doge Vitale Michiel in 1172, but the Venetian presence was short-lived. The island was fought over by the restored Byzantine empire and by Turkish corsairs who infested this part of the Mediterranean, finally passing into the hands of Genoa. Below: the island of Chios in the 15th century (Biblioteca Marciana, Venice). The scroll at the base reads, "The island and city of Scio [Chios] which along with many other islands of the archipelago was for more than two hundred years a possession of the noble Giustiniano family of Genoa, and was occupied by the Turks in 1566. Its loss was made glorious by the entry of eighteen young Giustiniani into heaven. Through their faith in Jesus Christ they bore their deaths with fortitude."

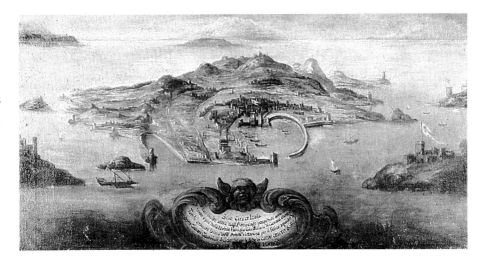

of a Greek duke, John Comnenus, who ruled over Naxos, Paros, Syra, Andros, Milos and Santorini, "as a good Christian and true Catholic," and who had obtained the fief by paying the Grand Turk a sum of 50,000 *zecchini* and 15,000 per year in tribute.

There followed centuries of oppressive Ottoman domination. Then liberation came again and absorption into the Greek state. Yet even today, a

visit to Naxos can recall something of the three or more centuries of Venetian feudalism. It is not just the ruins of the crumbling old castle, with its gates which still have the ancient wooden doors, or the little castles and towers scattered through the countryside, with Guelph or Ghibelline crenellations. Here and there on the narrow medieval streets little doors can be seen bearing the coats of arms of long ago; the names on the plaques attached to the doors (and on shop signs) are equally reminiscent of ancient times. According to a visitor 270 years ago, at that time there were still some members of the Crispo, Sommaripa and Barozzi families in the palaces clinging to Marco Sanudo's ancient walls. In 1814 a French visitor to Naxos met a group of descendants of what they called "castellan families:" in fact, just shortly before there had been the wedding celebrations of a Crispo, a descendant of the last duke of the Archipelago, who married a Coronello, a descendant of the man who governed the island on behalf of the only Israelite feudal lord ever seen in the Mediterranean. I myself once met a Sommaripa there, a probable descendant of the feudal lords of Andros, and a Dellarocca, according to tradition a descendant of the de la Roche family, ancient Latin lords and dukes of Athens.

Modon, the modern Methoni, in the south-west Morea, was an outpost and the cross-roads of the routes from Venice to the Levant. With Corone nearby it was one of the "eyes of the Republic." The Venetians turned the city into a center for navigational information, and every ship returning from the Levant stopped there to give and receive notice of the movement of pirates and other vessels. There are plentiful Venetian remains here, as can be seen from the two illustrations above. Left: the inner fortifications of the city with a column that supported the Lion of St. Mark. Right: the east gate of the Loredan bastion. Below, left: warriors assaulting a tower (from Livy's First Decad). Farther along the Levantine route, on the east coast of Morea, Venetian ships stopped at Nauplia where there is still a well-preserved Venetian fortress on the islet of Bourzi (opposite).

Crete and Cyprus

The Cretan writer Pandelís Prevelakis has been unjustly relegated to second place by the glory of his compatriot Nikos Kazanzakis, but in his delicious tales set in a calm, sleepy *fin de siècle* Rethimnon he tells us of a number of Candian gentlemen graced with high-sounding, Venetian surnames: Mocenigo, Dandolo and Contarini. One of the most respected poets of the island

ARSENAL

(naturally, a poet in demotic Greek) is called Marinos Falier, no less, like the celebrated and luckless doge who was beheaded in 1355. Are these descendants of Grecianized feudal lords, absorbed into the Cretan ethnic context? It would seem so. As time went by some of the feudal families returned, enriched, to Venice, but others instead were impoverished and were sucked into the world of the Cretan peasantry, at first so alien to them, and became part of it. Even now one may happen upon a typical Cretan farmer from Messara or the Lasithi plain, with breeches and moustache, who turns out to be a descendant of one of the old houses of the Venetian nobility before the *serrata* of the *Maggior Consiglio*, such as Muazzo, Zancaruol, Semitecolo or Baseggio.

Once the first two centuries of violence were over, the climate of hostility which separated the Venetian occupiers from the Cretan occupied was at an end. In Crete too, as in the rest of the Greek colonies, there were mixed marriages; and a number of Cretans came to study in Venice or at the state university of Padua. The most significant representative of this Venetian-Cretan cultural integration was Domenico Theotokopoulos, "El Greco," the Cretan painter of Madonnas that were exported to Venice (*madoner*, as they were called) and later a pupil in Venice of great painters, and eventually famous himself in Spain. Also, though at the moment of the Ottoman conquest, many Cretans of Venetian extraction chose to return to their city of origin, many others stayed on the island, where by now they felt they had deep roots.

In spite of the ravages of the Turks, of time, of town-planners (who for example razed to the ground the beautiful walls of Rethimnon) and of the bombings of the last war, Crete also retains in enormous quantity the vestiges of Venetian domination: fortresses and bastions, castles and strongholds, but civilian buildings as well: the lovely fountains of Candia, the loggia where Venetian merchants used to gather, their church of St. Mark and many other reminders of a daily life which, once the conflict was over, must have been quite peaceful and serene, though less stimulating than that of Venice.

In the Greek world there was, it is true, the problem of relationships between the official church, the Catholic church and the local church.

In a move that was extremely disagreeable to their Greek subjects, the Venetians had placed the Greek clerics in a subordinate position to that of Roman bishops, who were always Venetian. This was a political move, a guarantee of security in the face of the rabid nationalism which distinguished the Greek church. Freedom of worship was, however, for the Republic, a principle which was to be safeguarded wherever possible, even in the colonies, although (as happened in any case with regard to the Catholic church) the choice of heads of the ecclesiastic community fell to civil powers, whose firm stand as regards the Roman curia could hardly in any case have displeased the Orthodox clergy.

In this way Venice took under her own

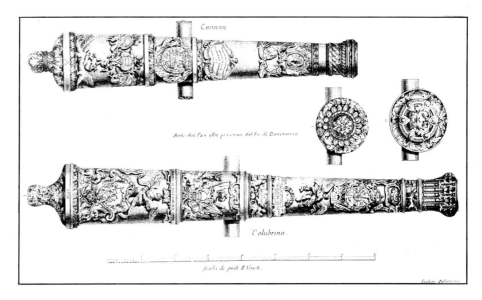

147

Below: Venetian watch-tower on an islet near Histiaia in Euboea. Bottom: the castle of Morea at Rhion, at the mouth of the Gulf of Corinth. During the 13th and 14th centuries Venice ruled a narrow strip of coast around the eastern Mediterranean, forming an empire of naval bases strategically situated at points essential for maintaining control of the sea.

protection Orthodox religious orders and bodies, starting with the convent of St. Catherine of Sinai, whose existing property in Candia had been enriched and exempted from taxes immediately after the conquest by the doge Pietro Ziani. The famous monastery of St. John on the island of Patmos also prospered for many centuries largely thanks to the protection of the Republic.

The principal problems arose from the decision of the Council of Florence on the union of the two churches, Catholic and Orthodox, in 1439. The Cretan clergy had no intention of renouncing its beliefs, and the Venetian Senate at first had no clear idea. What decided it to support the union was, more than anything else, the political situation, aggravated after the Turkish advance

and the capture of Constantinople, by the influx to Crete of refugees led by a clergy that was considered untrustworthy. The idea of union in any case, ended in failure, and is still discussed now, more than five centuries later. Its failure at least had the effect of normalizing relationships between the Venetian authorities and the Cretan religious world.

In Cyprus the long rule of the Lusignano family, who were strict Catholics, had installed and strengthened the Catholic hierarchy, introducing several religious orders to the island. Four hundred years ago the churches were transformed into mosques, but even today the architecture of the splendid Gothic cathedrals of Famagusta and Nicosia, built by architects from Champagne, bring to mind far better than any written account, the great adventure of the crusades. The Romano-Gothic Cistercian abbey of Bellapais instead, with its typically French shapes, set against a background of a violet-blue sea and a typically Mediterranean landscape, all olives and cypresses, could almost be a symbol of the Latin kingdoms of the Levant.

The annexing of Cyprus to the Venetian dominions was an operation in which the interests of the great Venetian capital found prompt response in the political action of the *Signoria*. The wedding of the king Giacomo di Lusignano with the beautiful Venetian patrician, Caterina Corner, in 1472, was only the last episode in a long-standing relationship between the ruling family of Lusignano and the great financial dynasty of the Corner family. Federico Corner, the man who declared to the Venetian exchequer in 1379 – in the midst of the war against Genoa – an income that was higher than any other citizen, had enormous business interests in Cyprus in cotton and sugar cane. After 1366 he lent huge sums of money to the king Peter I and received in return, for himself and his brothers, the district of Píscopi which was crossed by one of the few ever-open waterways of the island and could therefore be generally irrigated. There he set up a plantation and sugar refinery; sugar was a commodity much used in medicine and was therefore expensive and in great demand. Sugar-cane plantations already existed there, and these were enlarged by means of a great number of labourers, both freemen and slaves. The water was used not only for irrigation but also as the energy source for the mills which pressed the cane, and for subsequent processes to treat the juices and refine the sugar, for which purpose the Corner brothers had ordered from Venice two colossal copper cauldrons. If we consider also that Caterina's mother was Fiorenza Crispo, a descendant of Marco Sanudo and daughter of Valenza Comnenus, whose father was the Greek emperor of Trebizond, a network of relationships emerges in which economic implications knit closely with dynastic interests. All the more so, since another branch of the Corner family, resident in Candia, in 1306 took over the island of Scarpanto in the Dodecanese, so enlarging the area controlled by Venetian feudal lords in the Aegean.

The business relationship between the Lusi-

without making it too obvious: the fact that the person who supported him in driving out Charlotte and taking possession of Cyprus was the sultan of Egypt, the main supplier of spices to the Republic of the *Serenissima*, speaks louder than the documents which the Venetians put carefully under lock and key. The Venetian wedding of the new king cocked a snook at Genoa and the Visconti family, the duke of Savoy and the king of Naples, and Ferdinand of Aragon, who for a long while had had his eye on Giacomo, hoping to adopt him and so get his hands on Cyprus.

When king Giacomo died prematurely, a conspiracy set up by Ferdinand of Aragon himself wanted to have the young widow marry a relative of his, and her uncle Andrea was killed before her eyes. He was the procurator general for the affairs

Preveza in Epirus formed part of Venetian territory from 1499 to 1530, when it was occupied by the Turks. It was reconquered by Francesco Morosini in 1684. The redoubt (below) on the bank of the Azio is a relic of Venetian occupation. Left: bas relief from above the entrance to the fort.

gnano and the Corner family, and the blood relationships of the Corner family with the Latin feudal world and the Greek imperial family determined the choice of the bride destined for king Giacomo. But the real storm that broke out in the Mediterranean after this wedding is itself proof of the importance of the coup carried out in this way by the Republic. The Republic had a carefully prepared excuse: king Giacomo was not a legitimate son of his predecessor Giovanni II, being only the natural son; and the legitimate daughter of the king, Charlotte, wife of Louis of Savoy, had succeeded in expelling him, with the support of the Genoese, who were at that time subject to the rule of the Visconti family of Milan. This was enough for Venice to take his side, but of the family in the kingdom, and at this point the Republic sent the fleet to preserve order. While waiting for Giacomo's newborn, posthumous son to grow up, the Republic set by the mother's side a *provveditore* and two councillors, all three Venetian nobles, mentors and consultants, but who were in effect general dogsbodies, like certain "advisors" which today's superpowers place at the right hand of monarchs and dictators of the Third World. When the infant king then died while still in swaddling clothes, the queen found herself sole ruler of Cyprus, so the Republic immediately proclaimed it a protectorate, and in 1488 sent out her brother Giorgio, who persuaded her to make a spontaneous gift of the kingdom to the Republic. The poor queen dithered a little, but all happened predictably on cue, while the house of Corner received the investiture of 14 fiefs, or farmsteads, with which they continued and extended their fruitful industries of sugar and cotton farming, together with salt and potassium refining.

Once Venice had possession of the Cypriot kingdom (and the payment of an annual tribute to the sultan of Egypt was of no importance at all to her compared with the advantages she was gaining) she established her own administration on the island. In Nicosia, a *luogotenente* was installed, aided by two *consiglieri* "to represent the high court, and to judge feudal lords and gentlemen," plus two *camerlenghi* "who receive and dispense all the income of the kingdom with bills countersigned by the aforementioned *luogotenenti* and *consiglieri*." In Famagusta a captain and two castellans took over, at Paphos there was a captain, at Cerina a castellan, and another captain at Salines. The captain of Famagusta was called *capitanio del Regno*, "captain of the kingdom" and was the only one who could give capital sentences. Military defense was directed by a *provveditore generale*, but the office could be combined (as happened in the case of the famous Sebastiano Venier) with that of *luogotenente*.

One of the powers of the *rettori* was that of nominating the viscount of Nicosia, chosen from among the island feudal nobility (which Venetian sources describe as rather poor but proud). This man carried out various functions, both judiciary and administrative. Subject to him was the *mathessep*, a functionary elected by the people to

Left: resolution of the Senate of 1540. Below: Nicosia on the island of Cyprus besieged by the Turks in 1570. Venice never ceased to be a centralized state, with all important decisions being taken by the governing bodies in the capital in spite of the increase in the size of its dominions, or the fact that many of its territories were administered by private citizens. The good of the Republic prevailed over private profit. An example of this is Caterina Corner, who married Giacomo di Lusignano, the not unopposed king of Cyprus. The Senate hastened to declare her "adoptive daughter of the Republic," thus staking a claim on the island. It provided her with a rich dowry, and took her to Cyprus, where she was married in 1472.

The marriage of Caterina Corner (shown here in a portrait by Titian) was short-lived. The king died the year after their marriage, and his posthumous heir was no luckier, dying in infancy. Venetian influence was threatened by the outbreak of rebellion and intrigue, and the city hastened to lend the queen aid. It finally convinced the reluctant Caterina to give the island to the Republic of her own accord. She was received back in the lagoon with great honours and a handsome revenue, and then confined to Asolo, a gilded exile. Here she continued to hold court and entertain the famous personages of the day. Below: the court of Caterina Corner at Asolo; school of Giorgione (Attingham Park, Shropshire).

check weights, measures and prices of goods, as well as perform police duties. As symbol of his office he carried a silver-topped stick. Syrians, Maronites and Copts could initially take their disputes to a judge called the *rais*, an Arab name, but usually of western descent. After Venice's rise to power the Cypriot nobility found itself regimented into the *Maggior Consiglio* of the island, in which the Venetian patricians who had settled in Cyprus had the right to take part (originally Venice had thought of importing about a hundred of them and giving them fiefs, according to the Cretan example). The families of the Veneto mainland who had moved to Cyprus also had the right to be members of the *Maggior Consiglio*. At the time of the dramatic events and the battles which led to the loss of the kingdom, the *Maggior Consiglio* numbered 145. The Republic acknowledged their loyalty with a law in 1573, which fixed a public subsidy for all those who had managed to escape the horrible massacre with which the Turks celebrated their conquest between July and August 1571.

The Ionian Islands

At the fall of the Republic, the Ionian islands formed a unit which, along with Cerigo and Cerigotto and the Epirote strongholds of Preveza and Vonitsa, depended on the high command of the military fleet, that is, the *provveditore generale da mar*, who was resident in Corfu. This particular island, whose Venetian air in a Mediterranean setting we have already described, had fallen to Venice in the *partitio Romaniae* and Venice had also won it from the Genoese pirate Leone Vetrano, who was hanged from the top of the mast of a galley in Ranieri Dandolo's fleet, son of the doge Enrico. Later events took it away, restored it and took it away again from the *Serenissima*, until Charles III of Anjou, king of Hungary, died. He had owned the island, and the Citizens' Council voted that now it should be ceded to Venice. As the island, according to the resolution, was "bereft of help ... and coveted by rivals and neighbouring peoples, and virtually besieged by Arabs and Turks, and as her safety, protection and well-being are all equally desired," the councillors "with one accord, and no dissenters, have chosen,

Relations between the Venetians and the Greek inhabitants of the Ionian islands were harmonious, and both sides were equally interested in repulsing the constant Turkish attacks. Corfu, situated at the entrance to the Adriatic, was of special importance to the Venetians. It was acquired from the Anjou dynasty of Naples in 1386, with the consent of the local grandees. Heavily fortified, it became the seat of the Venetian naval command over the Gulf (left, the remains of the Arsenal). Corfu was heavily attacked by the Turks in 1537 and 1716, but the sultan's troops were unable to cross the walls. The island was saved from the second siege, which lasted 42 days, thanks to a Prussian general, count von der Schulenburg, to whose memory a statue by Antonio Corradini was erected in the fortress where he fought (below left).

instituted and ordained as defender, ruler and lord the honoured *Comune* of Venice . . ." It was 9 June, 1386. Shortly afterwards, an embassy of six councillors, one of whom was Jewish, presented themselves to doge Antonio Venier and gave a speech which ended with the expression of their certainty that, under Venice, "we shall live under our laws, under our own roofs, enjoying our own wealth: and Corcyra [Corfu] will have no fear with the Lion to guard her . . ." The reference to wealth leaves no doubt as to the social status of members of the embassy and the Citizens' Council; however, the latter had been influenced, it would seem, by the common people, who had demonstrated noisily in the public square in the few days preceding the resolution, waving banners depicting the Lion of St. Mark.

In the end, Venice accepted the submission and came to an agreement with the islanders on the conditions: protection and defense *erga omnes* and the assurance that it would not be transferred to any other sovereign. The administration of justice would be according to Venetian law and would be entrusted to Venetian *rettori*, who would

be aided by a council of local judges with the right of appeal to Venetian courts. Venice recognized the right to goods legitimately acquired by the local people as well as by their lords, and also recognized the rights of the Church of Corfu. Two clauses stand out among the many: one stated that anyone who was arrested by a feudal lord could not be tried by him but only by the Venetian *rettori*, and another stated that certain legal acts should be set down in Greek, so recognizing officially the two languages of the island.

Relationships with the Greek element came into being right from the beginning in an atmosphere of harmony. It was in connection with Corfu that the politician Gaspare Contarini spoke of "confederation" with Venice rather than colonization. Even religious differences and diffidences were overcome, if we consider that in Corfu, in the church of St. Arsenius, every year right up until 1797 an ecumenical rite was celebrated by Latin and Greek clergy, "in perfect time, so that while the one side sung the psalm the other side also intoned the verses." Sixteen years after the gift of the island, the Republic put in order her relations with king Ladislas of Naples, heir to Charles III and was all too pleased to hand over Corfu legally to him, on 24 August 1402, in exchange for 30,000 gold ducats in cash.

The acquisition of St. Maur (Levkas), Cephalonia, Ithaca and Zante was a far more complicated business. These islands were assigned to Venice in 1205 and had become a great fief of the Tocco (or del Tocco) family. While Leonardo del Tocco, the Palatine count of Cephalonia was still a child, Venice had tried in vain to get the islands back, partly by diplomacy, partly with money and partly by force. The Turks were also involved, perched menacingly at the mouth of the Adriatic. The spasmodic desire of the Senate to assure itself of the sea bases, and the harsh reluctance of the Turks to concede them, between them sealed the fate of the unfortunate population. In 1484, after diplomacy had prescribed the restitution of Cephalonia to the sultan, the Senate ordered the *provveditore* of Corfu to raze it to the ground, destroying "all that is good and useful on the island," even deporting the people, so that the Turk would find himself in possession of a desert and might decide to abandon it. The operation was concluded at the end of the century, in 1499:

Zante was occupied first of all, then Cephalonia – where now the Senate busied itself about repopulating the countryside, importing refugees from the Peloponnese and veterans, and supplying them with plants, seeds and building materials.

In Zante as in Corfu, the colony was modelled on lines that were by now traditional: there was a Great Council, or General Council and a Minor Council, elected by the larger Council and made up of 150 members (it was even called the "Council of the Hundred and Fifty"). Both were made up of local noblemen. In Zante, in 1683, a *serrata* limited the number of rightful members of the Great Council to 93, and the *provveditore*, Daniele Dolfin, underlined with a certain cynicism the antagonism and friction between nobles and common people, pointing out that this could be turned to the advantage of the subjects: "This must be tempered so that no grievous incidents arise, but should not be extinguished, since harmony between the members would be ... suspicious and dangerous." In Cephalonia instead, the Great Council, instituted in 1505, included only landowners, but "either by tacit

connivance by Venetian representatives ... or on one pretext or another" (as the *provveditore* Justinian wrote in 1608) it expanded to include 900 members, so that when some local office had to be elected, they had to gather in the street "and with a weapon in their hands, stand at the gates and stop the many, many people who wanted to enter by force." Worse still, according to the

The old fortress of Corfu. It was built by the Venetians in 1550, after the first Turkish attack, on a two-pronged promontory.

Above: San Giorgio on the island of Cephalonia. Below: view of Argostolion, founded in 1757 by the Venetians as the port of the ancient capital of San Giorgio (Benaki Museum, Athens).

actually more than 6,000 people who had the right to take part. It is significant that no one here mentioned the idea of a *serrata*: until the end of the Republic, this assembly, so heavily criticized by Venetian representatives who were aristocrats to the core, survived as a democratic rather than an aristocratic body. In its proverbial wisdom the Senate, though not actually approving the council, did not want to do anything which might antagonize the islanders, who had become extremely faithful subjects of St. Mark.

St. Maur (Levkas) at some point during the 14th century was conceded by the Latin duke of Athens, Gauthier of Ligni and Brienne, to *ser* Graziano Zorzi of San Moisè as payment for a debt he could not meet. Then it was lost, regained and lost again, and finally definitively reconquered by Francesco Morosini in 1684, and remained Venetian up until 1797. Here Venice installed a local government on clearly popular lines, represented by a single council which, under the tutelage of the Venetian *provveditore*, elected judges, civic officials and administrators. Yet it would seem that the inhabitants were not very scrupulous in the running of their autonomous government: faced with various cases of corruption, in 1760 the *provveditore* Nicolò Erizzo set up a Minor Council, in which there were 50 members elected from the population plus magistrates who no longer held office and, by right, those holding

provveditore generale da mar, Filippo Pasqualigo, "once a . . . peasant has been in the Council, he claims the right, with all his line, to be exempt from seizure of his possessions and galley duty:" in other words the Great Council of Cephalonia had become an assembly of small farmers and landowners, who took advantage of it to exempt themselves from forced labour inflicted on peasants. Some years later the number had risen to 1,000 voting members. In 1750 the *provveditore generale*, Vitturi, discovered that there were

Plan of the fortress of Asso (from a print of 1646). Although the inner fortifications were never built, the plan shows the importance which the Venetians attached to the defense of the Ionian islands. The political structure of Cephalonia and Zante followed models already successfully adopted by the Republic in other possessions. There were a Consiglio Maggiore *and a* Consiglio Minore *composed of members of the local aristocracy, in imitation of Venice's own constitution.*

degrees in law or medicine. Ithaca came under the direction of Cephalonia and was the cause of many headaches for the Venetian government, because its inhabitants were occasionally attacked by Barbary pirates and would regain their losses by turning to the continent and sacking the villages along the coastline. This was Turkish territory and so there was the risk of provoking diplomatic incidents or worse. In Cerigo (Cythera, the island of Venus) there still stands a spectacular Venetian town. (The ancient township was devastated by one earthquake after another). Here the Republic had driven out the feudal lords, the Veniers, after it was discovered that one member of the family had participated in the revolt of the serfs of Candia, and now the island was a front-rank stronghold. The English moved in after the fall of the Republic, and there still stand in their positions the bronze cannons with the initials of king George IV, with which they had armed the Attic fortress, positioned with admirable strategy at the extreme south of the Peloponnese.

Dalmatia

The populations of Corfu and the other Ionian islands saw in Venice the guarantee of efficient defense against the constant threat of the Turks. (The last Ottoman attack against Corfu was launched in 1716 and repelled after 42 days of siege.) So they were without doubt sincere in their numerous, rhetorical declarations of bonds with Venice. Certainly, this was more true of the nobles and middle classes than the villeins, who were not keen on obligatory service, decided by lot, on board Venetian galleys as a token of "good will." (They were, however, content with the limitations imposed on feudal lords, and the enriching of local agriculture by means of grants and the introduction of new crops). As for Dalmatia, the Dalmatian towns had given themselves to the Republic voluntarily. Struggles and tensions with the kings of Croatia and Hungary had occasionally strained relationships, but the experience of Hungarian rule tasted by the Dalmatians after the peace treaty of 18 August 1358 had obliged Venice to concede the Adriatic coast which she had owned for more than 350 years, had been such as to make

them feel that the government of the *Serenissima* was the best possible alternative. About two years later, someone wrote to the Senate: "Dalmatia is in such conditions that no one would credit if they had not seen and heard it. Almost everyone regrets the passing of your government and complains of the present one, saying that under your rule both the community and the individual were rich, and now it is quite the reverse." The truth is that integration into the Hungarian kingdom did not bring Dalmatia what only Venice was able to offer: the means to eat and live. It was the very same irrepressible rebels from Zara that now, having achieved their ideals, sent their laments to the *Signoria*, saying that the most basic necessities of life could not be satisfied since "*necessaria ad predicta non possunt habere nisi de civitate vestre Venetiarum,*" and it was the *bano*, the ruler in the king's name, who begged the *Signoria* to reactivate dealings with Dalmatia.

Abandoning Dalmatia had been a particularly sad necessity (even the doge had suffered the loss of his title of duke of Dalmatia and Croatia which was part of his ancient boast). It was all the more distressing in that the control of the eastern coast had been one of the conditions which allowed Venice to exercise the prerogative of which she was most jealous, and which to her was the most precious: dominion of the Gulf, *i.e.* the right to forbid the entry to the Gulf of Venice to any armed vessel that was not Venetian. Tradition attributed this right, real or presumed, but fiercely and tenaciously defended, to the gratitude of the pope Alexander III for the mythical victory of the Venetians at Punta Salvore in Istria against the armada of his mortal enemy, the emperor Frederick Barbarossa. In actual fact, it arose out of a number of circumstances and agreements, but above all from Venice's progressive assumption of the ancient Byzantine dominions. The same expedition of Pietro Orseolo II which gave birth to Venetian domination over Dalmatia had in a sense been carried out by proxy on behalf of the *basileus* of Constantinople, or at least with his blessing. Imperial requests for defense against Arabs and Normans had reinforced still further Venice's position as controller of the Gulf, and as for the rest, Venice had taken it for herself, by diplomacy or force. It was a perpetual battle however, because the other aspects of the

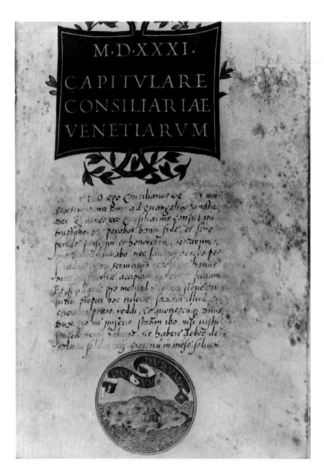

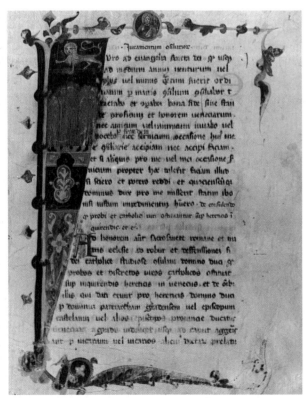

dominion of the Gulf were, on the one hand, acting as a kind of maritime police for the Gulf against local and foreign pirates (and, on this score, everyone was quite content to let Venice take the burdens, risks and dangers) but on the other hand, there was the stubborn claim to have a real monopoly of the Adriatic maritime trade, particularly with the Orient. As far as this claim was concerned, no one was in agreement.

Over the centuries then, an uninterrupted sequence unwinds of a contest with Venice on one side, and on the other all the powers which faced out on to the coastal territories. The Normans, Angevins and Aragons, who gradually took over the kingdom of Naples, were contained, but from a certain stage onwards Spain threatened the southern Adriatic. This was the first of the great modern national states to challenge Venice in the Gulf, and Venice held out against her with a staunchness which verged on the foolhardy, since there was a Hapsburg on the throne in Madrid as in Vienna and the Austrian Hapsburgs were just as hostile and eager to rid themselves of the Venetian presence on the opposite end of the Gulf, at Trieste and on the Quarnero where they fuelled and encouraged the persistent aggression of the Slav pirates, the Uzkoks, dread successors to the equally terrible Narentines. Then there were the Turks, who now and then broke through with all the weight of their enormous Eurasian dominion. There were also minor presences which were just as troublesome, such as the free merchants from Ragusa who, behind the walls of their fortified and elegant city, schemed with everyone in their constant battle for survival.

All these forces, in one way or another, focused on the Dalmatian coast, and this is the reason why Dalmatia's system was answerable to a high military authority, the *provveditore generale* for Dalmatia and Albania, the second principal naval office of the Republic, stationed at Zara. There was also the fact that the Dalmatian route, in spite of the storms of the Quarnero, was the most convenient and the safest of all, sheltered by a long series of islands which formed a kind of natural jetty with protected landing-stages and deep bays, almost right up to Corfu. It also had to be defended on the landward side where the Turks, who had occupied Macedonia, Serbia, Bosnia and Herzegovina, were bearing down on the other side

Two decrees of the councillors from 1531 (above), and 1396 (below), with the oaths sworn by these high officials when they took office (State Archives, Venice). The six councillors formed the Consiglio Minore, *and together with the three heads of the* Quaranta al Criminal Superior, *they constituted the Signoria. Their power was very great, and they oversaw all the doge's actions, but they were in turn subject to severe restrictions, not being allowed to take on any other office, leave Venice for even a single day without the permission of the doge, receive foreign ambassadors or envoys without the Senate's agreement, or distribute offices or appointments. Elected to act as a control on the doge, they were themselves controlled by the doge and the Senate. Opposite: view of the west coast of the island of Cephalonia.*

was a case of ridding herself of these pirates). They were barbaric and cruel, to the extent of feeding on the flesh of Venetian commanders captured in battle. To drive them out, it would be necessary to go to war with the Austrians and embark on interminable diplomatic discussions. Something of their ferocity and courage found an echo in the Dalmatian Slavs, by tradition more loyal to Venice. These were the Morlacks with their huge drooping moustaches and red berets fringed with black, and they were extremely rough-mannered, spartan in the face of suffering, and as courageous in battle as to seem almost foolhardy. Morlacks – *Bocchesi* from Cattaro and in general Dalmatian Slavs – made up the choice regiments of the Venetian army, together with Epirotes and Albanians from Camurlija. Giacomo Casanova, who happened to see them in quarters at the *castello del Lido*, where he was being held at the time, describes them as a 'horde of savages, gnawing all day long on cloves of garlic, like sweets. They were simple, loyal souls, and in 1797 wanted to fight the French in Verona and defend Venice against Bonaparte, and they would have done so had their commanders not prevented them.

As far as agriculture was concerned they were, alas, less effective, and Dalmatia was certainly not one of the most active elements of the Venetian balance of payments, at least in the later centuries. Venice herself had not lavished the same care on the Dalmatian lands as she had given to the development of the Levant: colonizing those arid, coarse lands was too arduous a task, quite out of proportion to the forces available to the Republic, not to mention her determination. In this poor but ancient country, social contrasts were perhaps more acute than elsewhere. In 1553 the *sindici inquisitori* Giambattista Giustinian and Angelo Diedo noted that between the common people, excluded from councils and offices of the city community, and the nobles there was "such pernicious and ancient hatred, that one day in most of that area, especially . . . in Cattaro, Lesina, Traú and Sebenico, some great tragedy will occur." This, as we have seen, had already happened in Lesina. It had also happened in Sebenico, and the fact that there were not uprisings and riots in all the other towns is due only to the skill of the Venetian *rettori* though in

The political center was always Venice itself. The colonnade under the Doge's Palace was the scene of patricians' meetings and even of electoral arrangements, as can be seen in the engraving by Domenico Lovisa from 1669. Broglio, or electoral intrigue, was frowned upon, but it proved impossible to extirpate it from Venetian political life. The word is itself Venetian in origin, coming from a garden (brolo), of which one existed in St. Mark's where the patricians made agreements and sold their votes before elections to offices. Those with a favour to ask would bow to the influential and "abassar stola" (lower their stoles), letting this symbol of their patrician status slip from their shoulder on to their arm as a sign of their request. The main influence on politics was, however, always trade. Every kind of vessel was used in this business, and two such are illustrated opposite, painted by Luca Carlevaris (Museo Correr, Venice).

of the strip of seashore. So there was a state of permanent warfare, alternating with phases of open fighting, and so it went on, right up until the last century of the Republic. (Venice, at a great sacrifice, established herself firmly in the fortresses of Clissa and Imoschi.) However, for many long years, between the last decade of the 16th century and the third decade of the 17th, the main bone of contention was the Morlacca canal, which goes down from the Quarnero, near Buccari, between the islands of Veglia, Arbe and Pago, up to Obbrovazzo and Novegradi. At Buccari and Segna the Uzkoks had their hideouts. They were descendants of Christian Slavs driven out by the Turks, and now lived by looting on land and at sea.

The house of Austria, which had high sovereignty over them, had made them a weapon against Venetian trade, which the pirates disrupted and damaged in every possible way. They were also a weapon against Venetian military forces, both on land and sea, that turned out to be cumbersome and heavy compared with the elusive swiftness of these adversaries who were even more ferocious than the Turks (and who in fact feared them to the extent of forgetting their hostility towards Venice and offering her support when it

the main these tended to favour the nobility, through a misguided sense of aristocratic solidarity.

At the time of the definitive annexing of Zara, an important Venetian politician, the *savio del Consiglio*, Antonio Contarini, had suggested involving a group of Zara nobles in governmental responsibilities. Ten young men could be given a military command each, and 18 more nobles could take charge of the government of 18 towns on the mainland, Istria and Albania. Such a measure, according to Contarini, would effectively bind Dalmatian nobility to the fate of the Republic, would attract other cities into the Venetian orbit and would be much more effective in keeping the loyalty of Zara's nobles than previous measures, *i.e.* keeping them "outside Zara with the permission to die of hunger."

His wise proposal was not taken up. In the *Collegio* and the Senate there prevailed the supporters of the most rigid patrician elitism, and a good opportunity was lost. As we shall see, a similar proposal, intended to link the fate of mainland nobles with that of the Republic, was to receive the same treatment some 300 years later. However, aristocratic composition of local governments, though long-established, was not yet

Illustrated on these two pages are views of the fort of St. Maur on Levkas. Above: the walls. Below: remains of buildings within the fort (left), and the Lion of St. Mark (right). Opposite: the eastern ramparts. The island of Levkas was ceded to ser Graziano Zorzi in the 14th century by the Latin duke of Athens, Gauthier of Ligny and Brienne, to pay off a debt which had not been honoured. It was lost and reconquered several times until its final occupation in 1684.

veditore generale or by local Venetian *provveditori*.

Like those in the Levant, Venetian representatives in Dalmatia were also subject to periodic inspections by the *sindici inquisitori*, but in the last two centuries of the Republic visits became so infrequent that public administration was severely damaged. The dishonesty of *rettori* was common knowledge, as was their negligence, bad judiciary administration, corruption and bias in public office. It was bitterly acknowledged that Dalmatian people, no longer feeling protected from the abuses of Venetian governors and the local privileged classes, tended to emigrate, even into Turkish territory, to escape these injustices. The first to denounce the scandal in the Senate was the knight Memmo in 1747, but the force behind the parliamentary battle for the setting-up of a formal inquest was Marco Foscarini, a famous diplomat and future doge. At first though, it was decided to nominate three *inquisitori* who would carry out their investigations from Venice, but it soon became clear that though the three were very able men (one of them was the illustrious historian, Flaminio Corner) they could not come to any fair conclusions from such a distance. Accordingly, on 6 September 1747 Marco Foscarini proposed in the *Pien Collegio* the nomination of three *sindici inquisitori* who, as in the good old days, would travel to be on the spot and make direct investigations that were not based on hearsay. The *Collegio* approved immediately, and the Senate too, by a majority of two thirds. The *Maggior Consiglio* however was not so inclined to

universal, for in 1786 at Arbe there was still a popular assembly, called the "University," which normally met once a year and could elect embassies to present requests and complaints to the *provveditore generale* and even the *Signoria*. Instead the noble council, or *Comunità*, had the privilege of nominating the *sopracomito* or commander of a war galley, which was maintained at the expense of the island.

The mountainous territories inland had been more recently won from the Turks. They had been declared state property, and had been assigned to the Morlacks, as colonies with certain special duties and a military organization. The leaders, colonels, *sardari* (from the Turkish word *sirdar*) and *arambassà*, were nominated by the *prov-*

Above: Galley cut in two from bow to stern in order to show its parts and proportions, presented to the most illustrious and excellent S. Sebastiano Sorano, procurator of St. Mark, by Master Coronelli, cosmographer to the Most Serene Republic of Venice, 1697 (*Biblioteca Marciana, Venice*). This section of a galley reveals the great capacity of the hold. Galleys were used for merchandise especially after the end of the 13th century, when the bireme was replaced by the trireme. This not only allowed the presence of a third oarsman per bench, but also increased the capacity of the vessel. *Below: an imaginary "war machine," illustration by Robertus Valturius from the Rei militaris libri XII (Biblioteca Capitolare, Padua).*

approve: here the nobles were more numerous, and for them, the lack of control over the regimens of Dalmatia had been a godsend, giving them the possibility of enriching themselves by means which though not exactly illicit, were not quite correct either. What is more, as always, there were the hawks, the supporters of force, who said that the only remedy for Dalmatia's evils was a

military government and martial law, in effect, a rule of iron. The first round of votes went badly. At this point, before voting took place for a second time, Marco Foscarini asked to be allowed to speak and gave one of the most brilliant speeches of his entire spectacular career.

He began by saying that 130 years had gone by since the *sindici inquisitori* were last in Dalmatia, and that the province was just emerging from 44 years of skirmishes and open warfare, which must have seriously disrupted administration, the economy and the judiciary, all of which had been in military hands. Instead, "as we well know, if we want the conditions of our subjects to be one and the same, the equality and temperance of the Venetian dominion must penetrate everywhere; everywhere, her holy laws should hold good." The *sindicato* was not offensive to the *rettori* who had been subjected to it, when the *sindici* were of exemplary virtue: there had been Jacopo Loredan who had been *provveditore generale* four times, but had to be buried at public expense because he had not left enough to pay for his own funeral; there had been Domenico Trevisan, who had taken on the supreme office *da mar* on condition that there should not be any corresponding emoluments; there had been Jacopo Foscarini who, as *provveditore generale* in Dalmatia, had spent a good 30,000 ducats of his personal inheritance for the good of his subjects. The list went on but, leaving sentiment aside the orator went into the substance of the matter: Dalmatia had quadrupled its area, and the public land register had not been completed because of the unjustified remonstrances of the local *rettori*, the tithes had been given on contract to a tithe-collector who harrassed the poor citizens, the tax on pasture was ruining sheep-farming. ... In short, there was a urgent need for radical reform. After other impassioned arguments, the future doge added in conclusion: "Unfortunately, *Serenissimo Major Consegio*, it is true that an infinite number of families, who shrugged off the Turkish yoke in hand-to-hand battle for the calm, tempered dominion of the Republic, in the last few years have been leaving ... their houses to return as beggars to flinch under Ottoman tyranny. They could do nothing else. The ways of the Venetian government used to be such as to enamour the people of them and make those people abandon

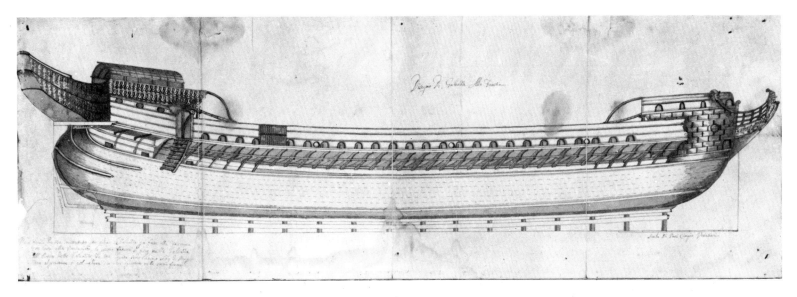

even the most comfortable and delightful homes to experience that dominion. If however we tolerate this state of affairs in Dalmatia, we must then deduce that traditional ways have been abandoned."

Foscarini won. Giambattista Loredan, Vincenzo Nicolò Erizzo and Sebastiano da Molin left for Dalmatia to examine, ask questions and make proposals. Taxes were levied on the iniquitous tithe-collectors, the soundness of the currency was given a new lease of life, fiscal subsidies were introduced that favoured Dalmatian products and other propositions adopted to make the lifestyle of the population more comfortable with less hardship. But it was late. The Republic was weary. The tenacity and dynamism of her heroic age were but a memory. The last 50 years of Venetian rule in Dalmatia were little more than nominal. But, for the Dalmatian peoples, this last gesture of active concern was enough to reawaken an affection which was to express itself in terms which reechoed to the honour and pride of the Republic at the moment of her fall: a farewell never to be equalled at the end of any other reign.

From the Quieto to the Adda

Istria, at one time prosperous, nearer to Venice and farther from the Turks (who had attacked it more than once in furious raids, but had never been able to establish themselves there) towards the end presented just as many problems. The coastal cities, Venetian through and through from their architecture to their dialect, were not distinguished by their activity (in 1786 it appears there was no industry there, and a magnificent woollen mill set up in Capodistria had gone bankrupt in no time: there were only a few tanneries and candle factories.) As for the countryside, though it produced oil and some very fine wines, it was often infested with smugglers and brigands. Fishing was prosperous, however, and there were salt-works and forests of great importance. The great woods of the Montona valley supplied the Venice Arsenal with timber, floated down to the sea on the waters of the Quieto.

From Muggia, Venetian Istria looked across to Trieste: this ancient city, raised and enriched by the rulers of the house of Austria, was to become Venice's most feared rival on the commercial level, and one of the main reasons for her economic decline. On the other side of the gulf of Trieste dominated by the castle of Duino, fief of the Torriani, a powerful family of imperial feudal lords, was Monfalcone, the start of Venice's mainland dominion.

The relations between the *Serenissima* and her mainland state, which was not limited to the Veneto, but also included a large part of Friuli (only the dukedoms of Gorizia and Gradisca were Austrian) and a quite substantial slice of Lombardy, are still the subject of discussion. Expansion inland had started late. Treviso was annexed in 1338, but for 65 years it remained the

Venetian galleass drawn by Stefano de Zuane, 17th century (Museo Storico Navale, Venice). The galleass was larger than the galley and more heavily armed, but also slower. The hull was completely decked over, and fitted with forecastle and quarter-deck. It was used as a combat vessel for the first time at the battle of Lepanto. The function of the oarsmen was essentially auxiliary; they allowed the vessel to maneuver more easily in port, overcame the need for it to tack when it was beating against the wind, and permitted it to move even in still weather. The long, tapering lines of the galley made it faster than other vessels.

own kingdom; nor were the rural feudal lords pleased to find themselves in their turn controlled by an external power that was stronger than its predecessors and, in addition, not at all inclined to concede freedom of action to feudal lords. The method of government did not differ at all from that employed in the territories *da mar*: maximum centralization, all decisional power as regards political and economic matters resting with the Senate and the *Maggior Consiglio* and therefore with the patrician class of the capital city, to which class belonged all the representatives, the *rettori* who had been sent immediately to govern the new territories. The *podestà*, captains and *provveditori*, were accompanied in the main cities by *camerlenghi* and castellans.

The ill-feeling of the city noblemen and feudal lords exploded on the arrival of the members of the anti-Venetian league set up at Cambrai. The mainland state seemed to melt away like snow in the sun: everywhere, almost all the nobles embraced passionately the cause of the emperor Maximilian of Austria, and his main representative was count Leonardo Trissino, a noble from Vicenza.

In Padua, the "citizens" (*i.e.* nobles) on 6 June 1509 raised the two-headed eagle of the Hapsburgs *cum maximo gaudio*, according to the account of a chronicler, who likens the liberation of Padua from the Venetian "yoke" to that of the Jews *de servitute Faraonis*. Flatly opposed, and indeed in open support of the Venetians, were the common people. Niccolò Machiavelli, who was in Verona at the imperial headquarters, did not conceal his amazement: not one day went by, he wrote, when one of them did not let himself be killed rather than deny the name of Venice. "Just yesterday evening," recounts the Florentine secretary, "there was a man in front of the bishop who said he was a *marchesco* (a follower of St. Mark and therefore of Venice) and *marchesco* he would die, for he did not want to live any other way; so that the bishop had him hanged ... it is impossible that the king can keep these lands with such countrymen living." In Treviso, one of the common people, Marco Pellizzaro, provoked an uprising that in effect obliged the nobles to declare themselves *marcheschi*. In the violent civil conflict which occured in Friuli between the followers of the patriarch and the emperor (the *strumieri*), and

Left: detail of the Romanesque entrance to the cathedral of Traú. Opposite: sculpture of a bishop from the screen of the cathedral of St. Mary at Arbe, by Andrea Alessi of Durazzo, born at the beginning of the 15th century. These are but two of a great number of works in which a common artistic tradition is revealed which linked the different cities of the Adriatic coast. The similarity of the work on both sides of the Adriatic does not imply a school created in Venice which spread throughout its domains, but stems rather from the inheritance of late Roman art, which persisted all over the huge coastal areas.

only Venetian possession in the Veneto. Then, within two years the following cities with their respective regions became Venetian: Vicenza, Feltre, Bassano, Belluno, part of the Polesine, Verona and Padua. Some joined voluntarily, some were bought, some conquered, as a lawyer noted shortly afterwards, "in a just war." The main adversary to Venetian mainland expansion had been the lord of Padua who paid for his stubborn resistance with his life. A long war with the Visconti family of Milan procured for the Republic Brescia, Bergamo and Crema, while the patriarch of Aquileia was expelled from the kingdom of Friuli and the Estensi were obliged to concede Rovigo. The last acquisition, in 1499, was Cremona, but this did not remain in Venetian hands for long. In effect the acquisition of most of the mainland state took place in no more than 24 years, between 1403 and 1427.

Almost everywhere, Venice took the place of rulers who had given the maximum power to local noble dynasties. So the latter hardly took kindly to the arrival of a power which wanted to govern directly and in its own name what it considered its

the followers of Venice (*zamberlani*), headed by the Savorgnan family, it was the common people, the peasants, who formed the shock troops of the *zamberlani* faction against the *strumieri* feudal lords.

Without seeking too many subtle reasons, it is obvious that the common people felt better protected by Venetian *rettori* than by noble councils in the towns or by feudal lords. These last had been firmly bridled (in fact, a specific controlling magistrature was instituted, the *provveditore sopra feudi*) while the former were relegated to purely minor roles, where before they had flaunted their power. In short, the justice administrated by the Venetian authorities with all its defects, had clearly been better than that of the

Carraresi, the Scaligeri, the Visconti, the Sforza, let alone that of the emperors or the Spaniards. The affection of the less privileged classes towards the Venetian government, which survived almost to the end (the very last days, even on the mainland, were sleepy, indecisive and based on the perpetual postponing of finding solutions to problems) could not have its roots only in the traditional hostility towards the rich, the nobles and the "citizens." To belong to a state which knew how to avoid famines and epidemics, how to defend its subjects and up to a point guarantee better conditions all round, without a doubt represented sufficient compensation for the lack of political decisional power; a lack which the common people shared with most if not all their counterparts in Europe.

Doubtless, it was a political error on the part of the Republic of Venice not to have channelled and exploited popular support against the aristocracy, and not to have turned to her advantage the cohesion of the under-privileged classes to dislodge the powerful ruling families of the Veneto and Lombardy. However, the Venetians of the 15th, 16th and 17th centuries can hardly be reproached for not anticipating the events of the future. Compared with the horrors perpetrated on the working classes by French and English industrialists in the last century, Venice, which carefully supervised child labour and firmly restrained abuses and harassments by the strong against the weak, the rich against the poor, was, three centuries ago, at least three centuries ahead of its time. It is not up to us at this point to conduct the official defense of the Republic against regionalist rancour and pettiness which came to a head over 200 years ago. The level of civil maturity reached by Venice compared with other regions speaks for itself, and it alone inspires the comparison which places the Venetian government on a much higher level than all the other rulers who shared out parts of Italy among them, up to the great reshuffling at the end of the 18th century.

Another political error is currently (though not coherently) laid at the door of the Republic of Venice. The arrogant ruling aristocracy, ignoring the tendencies of the plebeian classes, gave privilege as soon as it could to the aristocratic sections of provincial communities and collab-

The Dogana da mar or Customs House, situated on the point of the promontory dividing the Grand Canal and the Giudecca Canal. Here from 1414 goods which arrived by sea were unloaded and duty levied. The site of the earlier battlemented tower is today occupied by a 17th-century building containing huge warehouses and repositories, and surmounted by a tower on which two kneeling Atlases support a gilded sphere, which in turn supports the figure of Fortune that revolves with the wind (left). The Republic drew its revenue not only from customs duties, but also from its control of the trade in salt and grain. Together with the trade in exotic goods from the East, these combined to bring rapid commercial success to the city. (Opposite: the salt warehouses in the 16th century, near the point of the Dogana, from Jacopo de'Barbari's perspective view. Below: the public granaries in St. Mark's basin, nearly opposite the point of the Dogana, now destroyed, from an engraving by Domenico Lovisa). The proceeds to the state from the sale of salt in the 16th century amounted to 100,000 ducats, out of a total revenue of 1,150,000 ducats. Salt was under a monopoly by which producers were forced to supply their entire production to the Camera del sal. *This office granted licenses to exporters, and stated to who, and at what price, salt might be sold. The salt-pans were centered around Chioggia.*

Large quantities of salt were also imported from more distant lands such as Cyprus and the Balearic islands. Venice was also the largest grain market in north-east Italy. Unlike salt, grain was not monopolized and the price was fixed according to the laws of supply and demand. Grain came mainly from the areas surrounding the city, but when the harvest was poor it was bought in nearly every port in the Mediterranean.

orated with them to suppress the rest of the population. However, Venice did not actively involve them in her own politics, humiliating and alienating them, with the result that they did not identify with the Venetian *patria*, and abandoned her to her fate once more in 1797, facilitating her annihilation by Bonaparte and the *Armée d'Italie*.

In reality, even when Venice decided to expand into the mainland territories, she remained what she had always been, a city-state. She was capable of great plans and also capable of realizing them; her political horizons were vast. However, the spirit that moved her, even when commerce and finance were no longer the exclusive activities of the ruling class, continued to be mercantile, and therefore instinctively diffident. The Venetian

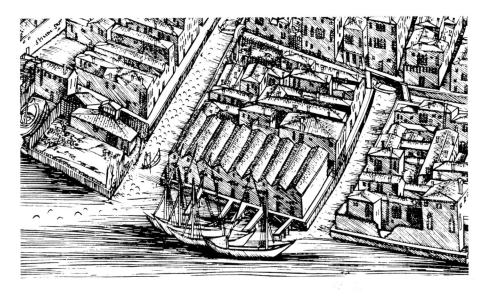

mentality (*i.e.* that of the social class holding power, the patriciate) combined two kinds of diffidence: one was that of the businessman, reluctant to hand over his powers to someone who did not take them seriously; the other that of the citizen of a town which for him was the center of the universe. In the case of Venice, it was also a unique city. So there was diffidence, plus what can be defined as insularity (a term which has also been widely applied to Britain which, like Venice, is an island). Besides being untrustworthy, the mainland aristocracies were also too "different." The diarist Girolamo Priuli gives an interesting account on this score. In 1509 a nobleman from the mainland, Girolamo di Savorgnan, happened to come to Venice. As he was a member of the Venetian patriciate (this had been conferred on his line in return for services to the Republic) he intended to take part in the parliamentary duties, as was his full right. A wave of enthusiasm (he had been an energetic and fortunate defender of Friuli against imperialist agents) elected him *pregado* (senator), and he accepted and participated in meetings. Priuli and his colleagues were worried by this. ". . . Such citizens," he wrote, "were made Venetian nobles to honour them and to enhance their reputation in their own cities and to keep them well-disposed and deserving of their office, not in order to confer any other office on them, and especially not the highest, secret offices of the Senate. It was not intended that such foreigners, not born in the city of Venice though they may be Venetian nobles, should be privy to the secrets of the Venetian Senate . . ." "Foreigners" because they were "not born in the city of Venice," *ergo* not to be trusted. The inevitable result of this attitude was obviously the exclusion of those who were "different" (in this particular case, the Senate resolved the problem by nominating Savorgnan *collaterale generale*, or head of General Staff of the army, a very high office, but one which was carried out in the field, far from the capital). Foreigners then, were excluded from secrets, not only at a high level, as in the Senate, but also at lesser levels, such as the government or administration of a city.

We have seen how the Senate in 1411 rejected the proposal to confer on the nobles of Zara certain offices normally due to Venetian nobles. In 1736 the marquis Scipione Maffei presented to the

Left: the Arneri Palace on Curzola. Above: view of Cattaro enclosed in its Venetian walls. Opposite: detail of the congregation in Bartolomeo Vivarini's Our Lady of Mercy *(Santa Maria Formosa, Venice). The relations between the suzerain Republic and its colonies were balanced and stable. In the 16th century the revenue from the overseas dominions amounted to 200,000 ducats, excluding the cost of the ships and fortresses necessary to their defense. In the same year the newly imposed direct taxation brought in 160,000 ducats.*

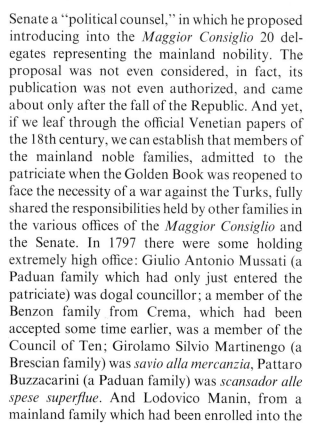

Senate a "political counsel," in which he proposed introducing into the *Maggior Consiglio* 20 delegates representing the mainland nobility. The proposal was not even considered, in fact, its publication was not even authorized, and came about only after the fall of the Republic. And yet, if we leaf through the official Venetian papers of the 18th century, we can establish that members of the mainland noble families, admitted to the patriciate when the Golden Book was reopened to face the necessity of a war against the Turks, fully shared the responsibilities held by other families in the various offices of the *Maggior Consiglio* and the Senate. In 1797 there were some holding extremely high office: Giulio Antonio Mussati (a Paduan family which had only just entered the patriciate) was dogal councillor; a member of the Benzon family from Crema, which had been accepted some time earlier, was a member of the Council of Ten; Girolamo Silvio Martinengo (a Brescian family) was *savio alla mercanzia*, Pattaro Buzzacarini (a Paduan family) was *scansador alle spese superflue*. And Lodovico Manin, from a mainland family which had been enrolled into the patriciate "for money," was actually the doge! (True, when he was elected, the nobleman Pietro Gradenigo, of a very old "native" family, exclaimed in Venetian dialect: "They have made a Friulan the doge; the Republic is dead." A prophetic murmur indeed.)

How can these apparent contradictions be explained? Leaving aside that 200 years had gone by since the Savorgnan affair, the fact is that these mainland nobles who had become patricians for money or for whatever merit, had totally "Venetianized" themselves and had transferred their homes to Venice. They had become integrated, and were no longer "different." In the provinces it was another story. There, the representatives of the *Maggior Consiglio* ruled, and they alone. Relegated to subordinate functions, the local privileged classes seethed, and were good and ready when the French arrived in 1797, to raise "banners of liberty" and proclaim the principles of the Revolution, not because they believed in them, but because they recognized the possibility of regrasping their lost power.

Then too, as at the time of the League of

Above: two scrolls in memory of Venetian governors on the walls of Capodistria.

The capitano generale da mar *was elected by vote of the* Maggior Consiglio. *Their nomination to the highest naval office was ratified in a ceremony in which he was entrusted with the baton of office, and in which the doge and the* Signoria *took part. The illustration by Giacomo Franco shows part of the proceedings.*

of the Venetian mainland the anti-French attitude of the common people and the peasants derived from seeing returned to power and ready to abuse it, those same lords that Venetian dominion, even in its most extreme state of decay and decline, had always restrained.

St. Mark on the Mainland

Long before the Venetian state expanded on to the mainland, there were already many private Venetian possessions there. Once dominion on land had been gradually acquired, as times changed and risks increased, the Venetians were ever more inclined to abandon mercantile and maritime investments in favour of real estate. The patricians invested in land to a vast extent: there were the very rich, such as the Contarini family of San Trovaso or the Pisani of Santo Stefano, who bought enormous territories – but most contented themselves with a few sunny fields. On those fields there grew up, little by little, villas that even today are symbols of a cultured and refined civilization. Andrea Palladio, Paduan by birth but who settled in Vicenza, was the most important architect and designed models that were to be immortalized under distant skies, such as those of England and the United States.

Private citizens' interest in the countryside was equalled by the Venetian state's interest in improvements, land reclamation and crops. Alvise Cornaro was a friend of Palladio and patron of the great Paduan comic author Angelo Beolco, known as Ruzzante. Cornaro was the author of a celebrated treatise on the merits of a sober life-style, and in the 1500s had been the champion of land reclamation, upholding the necessity of liberating the Venetian state from the desperate shortage of cereals that forced the government to pay dearly for imports from abroad. Among the many merits of the Venetian government there was, in fact, that of swiftly providing supplies of basic foodstuffs: corn was imported from Candia, Negropont or the Peloponnese, then, once those resources were wholly or partly exhausted, it was purchased, perhaps from Turkey, then stored and released on to the market as necessary, so as to avoid dizzy price rises which would in their turn have caused

Cambrai, it was the common people that rose up and cried "St. Mark!" Was this ignorance, superstition and backwardness, as has been suggested so often? It is difficult to believe. What happened in Verona, for example (where, however, there were at least two local aristocrats on Venice's side, Augusto Verità and Francesco Emilei, who paid for their allegiance with their lives) can certainly be explained by the harassment, insolence and brutality of the French military. The comparison with Venetian methods of government was stark. No doubt in other parts

Commandatore *and* capitano minore *(from Vecellio). Shipboard organization was remarkably favourable to the crew. In contrast to the modern principle by which the captain's authority is absolute, the powers of the admirals and commanders were circumscribed, and disciplinary measures had to be approved by a "council" consisting of all the commanders, unless they were ratified by the central power.*

the starvation of most of the least well-off.

Thanks to the enlightened work of this same government, crops essential to the survival of the population were brought to an adequate level of cultivation. The living conditions of the peasants, the poor despised villeins, hungry and badly treated in all Europe, in misery everywhere, were no different in the countryside of the Veneto, though here at least there was no starvation.

Venetian rule is often criticized for levying excessive taxes, which must have impoverished the countryside, just as the cities were impoverished by the protectionist policy which favoured the capital's industries and discouraged enterprise elsewhere. It does not seem that Venice's taxes were more rapacious in the country than those of equivalent rulers in other European states: certainly, the Venetian mainland never experienced the ferocious exactions which squeezed rural France dry under Richelieu or Colbert and which were accompanied by violence against the unfortunate rural communities. Even the most ill-disposed historians recognize the substantial fairness and comprehensiveness of the tax system. The main part of state income derived from indirect taxes, in particular import, transit and excise duties, from the state monopolies of tobacco and salt and levies on slaughtering and distribution of meat. Ominously, the Republic, in the last century of existence, handed over the task of exaction of a great number of these taxes to contractors, just as the Italian state was doing until a few years ago, and if this arrangement is to the advantage of the exchequer, the tax-payer never benefits. A document from 1773, quoted by M. Berengo, a historian who has made a special study of Venetian society at the time of its decline, brands these contractors and their agents with the following fiery words: "carnivores, thirsting for the blood of the productive classes, wringing them, oppressing them, ruining them to the fourth generation." In any age, it is always wise to keep a certain reserve concerning those who complain of taxes, and the archives of every government in the world are full of such complaints. Anyway, the exemptions enjoyed by certain fiefs and the special rights of redemption enjoyed by others were certainly unjust, though common to all the states of Europe. Of all the contractors, those of the tobacco monopoly were undoubtedly the worst:

real battles would break out between their agents and the peasants.

As far as direct taxes were concerned, the most remunerative was the *campatico*, which affected all fruit-growing land. There was also the *decima*, which affected all buildings, ship charterage and personal earnings, the *tansa* which fell generally on all income (and was so modest that it was popularly called the *insensibile*, "imperceptible") and the *taglione*, returned by the craftsmen or guilds. Contrary to what happened in several other states, direct taxes were demanded equally of all sectors, including the clergy, and the fact that there were no exceptions meant that in the dominions of the Republic a situation such as in the France of the *ancien régime*, when the greatest part of taxation fell on the rural population, could not come about. This was another merit of the Republic, which besides would impose severe and sometimes swingeing taxes on the incomes of those in public office, on merchants and on house owners. The patrician legislature, in short, proved to have little or no compassion towards itself, as for example when it voted for heroic measures at the time of the war against Genoa in 1379, which in effect reduced a large part of the nobility to poverty; among those who called for a moratorium, to save themselves from ruin (which was not conceded) was the doge himself, Andrea Contarini. It is fair to say that Venice did not ask anything of her mainland "subjects" that she had not demanded in far greater measure of her own ruling class.

It is yet to be demonstrated that Venice suppressed to her own advantage the industrial activities of the mainland territories (one of the favourite arguments in any anti-Venetian polemic). In any case, just to give a few examples, Brescia and its territory went on being one of the most prestigious centers of the European arms industry even after the territory was annexed to the Venetian state; and the textile industry, which had deserted the capital, made great headway in the mainland territories where, in the last century of the Republic, the woollen mills at Schio came into being through free enterprise. It is not possible to attribute to Venice the crises which struck various industries of the Veneto and Venetian Lombardy towards the end of the century. It would be more accurate to consider

Austrian competition and the general decline of the Venetian economy, the principal victim of which was in fact the capital herself.

There was even a kind of Venetian state aid to help workers stricken by the crisis, which functioned even at the lowest point of decline in the final century. It was very extensive in the capital and functioned quite well, backed up by pawnbrokers, charitable religious orders and welfare organizations in provincial cities too. It was less effective in the countryside. Here, right up until the fall of the Republic, lived thieves and bandits who were very often villeins who had been driven to become outlaws by necessity rather than innate vice. In any case, the phenomenon did not cease with the fall of the Venetian government. The most acute incidence occurred in the following century, in the years after 1849, when imperial Austria (which is still commonly held to have been the model of good government and wise administration) took violent and repressive measures against these unfortunate outlaws and, after proper trial but without mercy, ordered several hundreds of poor wretches that need had transformed into bandits to be shot.

On the subject of good government and wise administration, we should mention that the *sindici inquisitori* were also sent to the mainland, as to the Levant, regularly at first, then at ever longer intervals (though eventual abuses on the part of *rettori* were constantly investigated by the Council of Ten and the State Inquisitors).

As in the dominion *da mar*, the *sindici inquisitori*

invited to appear before them "anyone, of whatever status, grade or standing [who] had suffered as regards sustenance, goods or honour, any extortion, usury, fraud or tyranny of any kind," in order that he might feel "the true and proper effects of justice with the reimbursement of his damages at no cost to himself ..." (These words are taken from a proclamation by the *sindicato* for the Levant in 1635). Enquiries were extended to *rettori* "for trafficking, excessive gain, fraud and oppression of the common people," to chancellors and lawyers, tax-collectors, pawnbrokers and so on. In order to avoid intimidation of those who sought justice or were going to testify, *ser* Carlo Contarini, (one of the *sindici* for the Levant in 1635) ordered in a proclamation that: "... no-one should attempt by menaces, pleas or words, or in any other manner, to prevent, dissuade or in any other way, either with words, hints, facial expressions or gestures of the hands, or in any other fashion, hinder those who intend to appear before us for whatever cause ... on pain of death." The death penalty could also be applied to "lawyers, solicitors, legal representatives" who indulged in trickery. The Senate thought of everything: in the course of the inquisition, the *rettori* being investigated were not to be publicly discredited before their guilt or innocence had been proved, and so the *sindici* were advised to be cautious and "not look badly on *rettori* who have behaved strangely, nor show ill-will towards them." This, apart from anything else, could have jeopardized the fairness of the trial later on before the appropriate magistrates in Venice. When a *rettore* had been accused of embezzlement, abuse of power or any other serious crime, he had to present himself on the expiry of his term of office in order to defend himself. When the *sindici* served him notice of his charge, they also invited him to nominate a defending counsel. Only in cases where the gravity of the crime meant there was a risk of the *rettore* not presenting himself for trial, did they have the right to have him arrested and brought to Venice.

The last mainland *sindicato* probably took place in 1769, "in order to pinpoint and correct" (so reads the Senate decree) "with suitable provisions the abuses, frauds and intemperances unfortunately fatally committed to the detriment of the people and of the public economy as regards

Left: portico at Rab (formerly Arbe). Opposite: view of Rab with the bell tower of the church of Our Lady (center) and that of St. Justin (left). The island came into Venice's possession in 1409 and remained loyal to the Republic until its fall in 1797. The local government had a few individual features. A popular assembly called the università *met once a year to debate proposals or censure motions which were then submitted to the* provveditore generale, *or else straight to the* Signoria *of Venice by a specially elected ambassador. The people kept a war-galley at their own expense, the commander of which was nominated by the council of nobles or* comunità.

*Quàndo scomenza el scuro ogni contrada
Gha qua, e la'i so ferali; e mi li impizzo,
E tuta la Città xe inluminada.*

41

*Sechemo l'aqua, e prima la se ferma;
Da i rii cavemo el fango col bail,
E in burchiele el portemo in tera ferma.*

19

*Co sto bigolo porto un bezzo al sechio
L'aqua a boteghe, a chi no ha pozzo in casa
E assae dolce, e chiara co fa un spechio.*

all concerning duties, monies and taxes ..." The Senate did not draw any discreet veils over the unpleasant reality, nor had it ever done so. It happened quite often that some penniless patrician who had been sent as *podestà* to some outlying territory, might try to fill out his meager income by dipping into the public coffers (a crime of which *rettori* were most often guilty). It was not infrequent either for them to accept gifts or allow themselves to be bribed. This was a most serious crime and was severely punished, even on the grounds of suspicion alone. Yet in other European states, the practice of receiving gifts not only went unpunished, but was as common as enriching oneself on the profits of the territory under government. In short, what in France, for example, might be considered a recognized privilege, Venice looked upon as a crime.

Before leaving the mainland, we ought to glance briefly at certain anomalies of local government. Since 1077 Friuli had been the fief of the patriarch of Aquileia, who lived for a while in Cividale and then Udine. Apart from the wealth of St. Peter's, this was the largest church holding in the whole of Italy. A reminder of the temporal power of the patriarchs still exists in the annual celebration in Cividale of the "Broadsword Mass" as it is called, at the end of which the people are blessed with two strokes of a two-handed broadsword. A host of restless feudal lords, forever fighting among themselves and with the patriarch, divided the territory between them; but from the 13th century onwards Friuli had its own parliament, which had come into being specifically to regulate the relationship between the feudal lords and the patriarch. From this parliament was born an elected council which shared the responsibilities of government with the patriarch. In 1420 Friuli was annexed by the Republic, but the parliament survived, though the patriarch was confined to spiritual jurisdiction and a Venetian *luogotenente* was put in his place. Feudal lords, prelates and monasteries took part in this council, together with representatives from the most important cities. The *contadinanza*, *i.e.* a collective of free peasants, was admitted too; and what is more, it was the *Serenissima*, with a unique breadth of vision that, at the beginning of the 16th century, issued a series of edicts in favour of the peasants rather than the feudal lords. These included a law against depriving rural communities of the grazing rights they already enjoyed, a law against

Lesser trades of the alleys and canals of Venice, in engravings from Gaetano Zompini's Le arti che van per via nella città di Venezia *(Street Trades of Venice), 1789.
The lamplighter: "When dusk falls, I hang up my lamps in every street, and the whole city is illuminated." The canal-dredgers: "We stop up the water and empty it out; we dig out the mud from the small canals with shovels, and carry it in barrows to land." The water-carrier: "With my yoke I carry water to the shops and to those who have no well at home, sweet as anything and clear as a mirror."*

Remeto lastre, e veri a chi me chiama,
Comodo le fenestre, e pò a botega,
Ghe le fazzo da niovo a chi le brama.   50

Sti fassi forti, e dola mi all'ingrosso
Compro, che vien per mar, e per el Pò.
E per i rii li vendo a tanti al grosso.   36

In sti canestri gho del pesse aposta.
Da poco prezzo per la povertae,
Che in pescaria se vende quel che costa..   32

Further illustrations from Gaetano Zompini. The glazier: "I fit panes and glass for whoever wants it, I mend windows, and in my shop I make new ones for people to buy." The wood-seller: "These bundles of hard and soft wood I buy in gross from overseas and from the Po, and sell them on the rio *for so much a coin." The fishmonger: "In these wicker baskets I have good fish at a cheap price for poor people; it goes for a high price in the fish-shops."*

the judicial sequestration of work implements, and the constitution of a representative body of peasants who could defend their own rights, exact taxes and guard the arms of the territorial militia. These rights were taken away from the feudal lords. The *contadinanza*, besides having the right to enter parliament, was also allowed to have a permanent representative in Venice in the *Signoria*.

Another special case was the province of Feltre. There, as in all the cities of the mainland, large or small, there was a noble council of 70 members. However, it was accompanied by a "community unit" (*università di comunità*) made up of 36 delegates from 120 rural villages who elected four *sindici colmellari*. There were also the alpine communities: the Magnificent Cadore Community, the Seven Communes of Vicenza and a few others. Their independence was based on administration more than anything else, certainly not on politics. Nevertheless, they were independent, as was the Magnificent Community of the Garda Riviera.

So the Venetian and Lombard mainland had become a Venetian holding by the middle of the 15th century. Venice governed it more or less as she governed the colonies of the Levant and the territories *da mar* of Istria and Dalmatia. However, it is significant that Friuli, torn apart by the bad government of the patriarchs and the quarrels of the feudal lords, should be reborn in the 16th century and take on a new lease of life with the development of a civilization which had a feel and an individuality all its own.

Whatever comparison one might like to make with the Church states, the Savoy monarchy, the Medici grand dukes or Spanish Lombardy, all things considered, Venice emerges most favourably; this without mentioning the harrowing aspects of the lives of the people of southern Italy. Only after the advent of Maria Theresa and her sons, the "enlightened despots" of the house of Hapsburg, did Lombardy take its first leap forward towards greater prosperity. However, in many fields, Venice had been ahead of her time as regards her instincts and systems of government, even if occasionally the lack of adequate means and external circumstances prevented her from carrying them through.

Mercantile Enterprise

One day in 829 A.D. (the year after the purloining of the body of the evangelist St. Mark from Alexandria in Egypt, and its triumphant transfer to Venice) the Byzantine emperor, Theophilus, was looking out of the window of the Great Palace on to the waters of the Sea of Marmara. It was a day like any other. A large merchant ship was approaching slowly, heading for the port.

The emperor asked someone standing near by if they knew who was the owner of such a beautiful ship. It was more or less an idle question. However, when he found out who it was, Theophilus went into a rage. It was his wife, the empress! "God made me emperor, and you, woman, want to make me a sea-captain!" No sooner said than done, the order went out from the Great Palace immediately to burn the ship and all the merchandise aboard.

In his outburst of anger, Theophilus was adhering to the Roman law which forbade nobles to take part in business, "so that plebeians and merchants could carry out their business more peacefully:" the Byzantine emperor restricted himself to levying enormous taxes on those who were in business. The historian Roberto S. Lopez notes the episode, pointing out that for centuries Byzantine historians went on praising what they called Theophilus's "just action," and that the last to praise him was in fact a secretary of Alexius Comnenus, the emperor who found himself obliged to mortgage the economic future of the empire to merchants and Venetian shipbuilders.

In that same year of 829, Giustiniano Parteciaco, the doge of Venice, made his will. He left a quantity of lands, domestic animals, vineyards, fruit trees, houses and servants, in effect, what at that time usually made up the estate of a great lord. However, besides all this, there was also quite a substantial sum, 1,200 silver pounds, which he bequeathed with the proviso *si salva de navigatione reversa fuerint*, that they returned safely from the voyage. This means that this highly respectable personage gave no thought to the ancient Roman law, and had risked a part of his capital in maritime trade.

In February 853, Orso, the bishop of Olivolo and therefore of Venice (Olivolo was the island in the Castello quarter where the bishop's cathedral and palace stood, and where the church of San Pietro can be seen, which was Venice's cathedral until 1809) also made his will. Among the many legacies made to churches and monasteries figured in the document are a sack of pepper and another of *alivano*, a substance it is difficult to identify but which must be some other spice or drug. In other words, not even the bishop disdained trade or found it incompatible with his high moral and social standing.

The whole of Venice's history hinges on mercantile activity. The main commodities which fed maritime trade (and river trade: all the rivers of the Po valley carried Venetian ships) were salt, glass, and later on woollen clothing. Other products were wood for shipbuilding and iron, the former from the upper Veneto, floated down to the lagoon, and the latter mainly from mines in Styria and Carinthia. These products were sent to the Byzantine and Moslem Orient. The opposite route was taken by fine goods from the Orient, firstly spices, which were as indispensable as salt for preserving food at a time when there were no facilities for freezing, but which were also prized in Europe to add flavour to otherwise unrefined foods. Added to wine and other drinks, they also

A Venetian nobleman at the counting-house, from an 18th-century watercolour by Grevembroch. Banking and direct or indirect participation in commercial and shipping enterprises were the chief investments of the rich patricians for many centuries. Banking was for long a free activity and the domain of private citizens, the first public bank appearing only in 1587. The early banks were simple exchanges operating on tables or counters, which also lent surety. Banking operations extended at the beginning of the 14th century, and many banks began to give credit and keep their clients' books. These developed into true banks called de scripta, *since even cash transactions took place in writing. From this time we begin to find the suffix* del banco *attached to the names of noblemen involved in banking. Opposite: an office of the procurators of St. Mark (1391). As wealth was accumulated in the hands of the patricians, the needs of the treasury grew ever greater. This led to a complicated system of financing the national economy, sometimes involving fairly heavy levies, as when it became necessary to raise tariffs on overseas goods from one to three per cent, which affected purchase prices.*

took the place of many of today's stimulants which did not exist then. The Levant and the east also supplied basic foodstuffs which could not be found in adequate quantities in the lagoon islands: oil and corn above all, but also wine.

Another commodity which was part of the commerce of all Mediterranean trading cities, but which in the Middle Ages and 16th century was most important in Venetian cities, was that of slaves. The Christian Middle Ages had made no efforts to ban slavery, and trading in human beings was an ancient tradition in the Roman world. The church limited itself to disapproving of the sale of Christian slaves to infidels, and eastern and Byzantine monarchs disapproved of it only because it might increase military potential in the Moslem world. In any case Venice, along with Genoa, seems to have taken up this particular trade quite early on. After the fourth crusade and the fall of Constantinople, her main base for supplies was Azov, "the Lair," and the merchandise consisted mainly of Russians and Tartars. These might be sold in the Moslem world, but very often they were bought by other Venetians as a domestic work force in the city and as farmhands in the country, especially on Crete.

Azov also supplied a substantial proportion of the hemp for ships' cables (earlier this had come from the Po valley). Timber and hemp were the basic materials of the shipbuilding industry which was at the center of the survival of Venice itself, since it allowed the Venetian merchant sufficient freedom of movement not to have to limit himself to traffic to and from Venice, allowing him to develop profitable markets far away. Yet the capital continued to be the favourite clearing center, and a great part of her wealth was derived from this constant flow of goods. The truth was that she was in an ideal geographic position, at the head of the Gulf, linking the Mediterranean Orient and the European West, and her topographical features were ideal for use as a harbour. Gradually Venice became the great "entrepot," a vast warehouse for the Mediterranean, where anyone wanting to buy goods was sure to find them and anyone wanting larger quantities could order them. Alongside, industry and craftsmanship developed more and more, specializing in products of high artistic quality. There was also, though it may seem an anachronistic term, a

tourist industry. It was a kind of transit tourism: ships bound for Syria and Palestine took some pilgrims for the Holy Land, and these would embark at Venice. But increasingly, people came to Venice specifically to see the sights. This tourist industry was encouraged by the attraction of the extraordinary surroundings and the exotic elegance of famous buildings, the continual choreographic ceremonies in which Church and State vied with one another, and the profusion of holy relics, mainly brought in from the Orient but often also from the West. All this nourished the trade of inns and eating houses.

The history of Venice is full of astonishing episodes involving the theft and abduction of relics, which instead of incurring just punishment for the protagonists, were rewarded handsomely. It would be a mistake to think that Venetian tourists were all pilgrims, however: in the 16th century tourists could purchase cheaply from booksellers certain guidebooks with such suggestive titles as *Catalogue of all the principal and most famed courtesans in Venice; their names and the names of the procuresses and the rooms where they live; moreover this informs you of the district where they have their rooms, and also the sum of money that a Gentleman who wishes to gain their favours*

must pay. Gaming too had its place. From the Middle Ages, there was gambling virtually everywhere, even in the ante-rooms of the strictest tribunals and councils. In recompense for the capital lent to set up on the quay of the Piazzetta the two columns of the Lion of St. Mark and St. Theodore, one Niccolò Barattieri gained permission to run a gambling den in the open at the foot of the columns themselves. However, the fame of the *Ridotto*, the State gambling house,

Below: 18th-century register of legacies to the Republic (State Archives, Venice).

opened in the palace of San Moisè by the nobleman Marco Dandolo and closed in 1774, was similar to that of the casino at Monte Carlo at the height of the "belle époque."

Trade, in its turn, gave rise to financial activity, based mainly on commercial and shipbuilding enterprises. It appears that a very high proportion of the population, at least up to the middle of the 16th century were involved in the various forms of financial investment, all the more so because it was possible to invest small sums. The Venetian merchant shipbuilder never hesitated to accept money, and alongside those who risked enormous sums there was always someone who had invested as little as one gold piece. The Venetian gold currency (golden ducat or *zecchino*) had been coined relatively late compared to that of Florence and Genoa, under the doge Giovanni Dandolo in 1284. It is truly extraordinary that this coin was to remain constant in weight and fineness right up to 1797: 3.56 grams of 24 carat gold, apart from two insignificant alterations in the weight between 1491 and 1550 which brought it down to 3.49 grams. This, merely at today's prices for fine gold, would correspond to a value of $47 or £29. This solidity and stability of currency must have favoured the extraordinary enrichment of the city in spite of crises and reversals of fortune, right up to the first half of the 17th century.

The Commercial Routes

Inland, Venetian trade routes followed the course of the rivers, as far as possible, while long caravans crossed the Alps either on foot or on horseback. From the Friuli passes, they went on to Styria and Carinthia and beyond, to Vienna, Breslau and Cracow. Other passes, such as the Brenner and the Septimer led to continental Germany, to Augsburg, Nuremberg and Ulm. In fact, a large part of the German trade was set up by the colony of German merchants in Venice of whom there were a huge number on the Rialto. Ships too sailed in convoys, like sea-going caravans: these were the *mude*, convoys that were armed and escorted by a military force, and at variable intervals would set out, anything between one and four times a year, for the principal market-places. The most important *muda* was the eastern one that went to

The Venetian mint was famous throughout the world, and Venetian coinage was in circulation outside the borders of Europe. (Above: detail of the minting-press in the Doge's Palace.) When Venice was able to mint coinage without imperial permission she had become fully independent of the empire. The first truly Venetian coinage not to mention the emperor which is preserved is the half-denarius or marcuccio of Vitale II Michiel from 1156; this does not exclude the possibility that such coins were also minted earlier, however. Sebastiano Ziani introduced the small denarius between 1172 and 1178, and Enrico Dandolo (1192–1205) the large denarius or matapan, a silver coin weighing 2.18 grams, which circulated very widely and was stamped with the figure of the doge and St. Mark on the obverse and the Saviour on the reverse. Right, above and below: a later large silver denarius of Pietro Gradenigo (1289–1311). The silver ducat was first coined in 1561 by Girolamo Priuli (opposite, far right).

Constantinople and on to Azov, Trebizond and the other bases on the Black Sea. There were *mude* to Cyprus and Armenia, to Syria and Alexandria in Egypt. There was also one which went direct to the Maghreb lands, the Barbary *muda*. Another caravan limited itself to ports in Apulia, Sicily and Calabria, while yet another went to Marseilles and Aigues-Mortes in Provence.

From the start of the 14th century onwards there were regular *mude* for the Atlantic which reached Bruges, Antwerp and Southampton. When new routes were set up, better conditions could lead to the suppression of old ones. In 1282 all limitations were abolished on voyages directed towards Apulia, Calabria and Terra di Lavoro (beforehand, the armed caravan going to the Apulian ports would only gather together ships which carried aboard large sums of money so as to be able to buy huge quantities of corn: other ships had to make their own way).

The *mude* were organized by the State, which used to auction off to shipbuilders and private merchants the contract for the galleys that had this function: these were ships with oars and sails, with a narrow beam and were at first not large (on average, no more than 90 tons). Then gradually, particularly after the establishment of the Atlantic route, they reached about 300 tons in the 15th century. The volume of goods carried in the convoys of "merchant galleys" which, as we have said, represented Venice at sea and in all ports from the 12th to the 16th century, does not seem to have been enormous: from 3,000 to 5,000 tons a year in the 13th century, to between 7,500 and 10,000 tons per year in the 14th, and from ten to 12,000 in the 15th century. But the merchandise was extremely valuable. The chronicler Morosini, writing between the end of the 14th century and the beginning of the 15th, indicates the overall values of the cargo of each convoy on the outward and return journeys, as being on average 250,000 golden ducats (about £35,000 [$55,000] just for the value of the non-coined gold) with individual cases reaching double this figure. There were between six and ten annual *mude*, about 12 or 20 return voyages, so that the overall value of the merchandise transported could be calculated at between £50,000 ($80,000) and £170,000 ($270,000). These figures are nothing compared with those of the foreign trade of a great nation nowadays, but

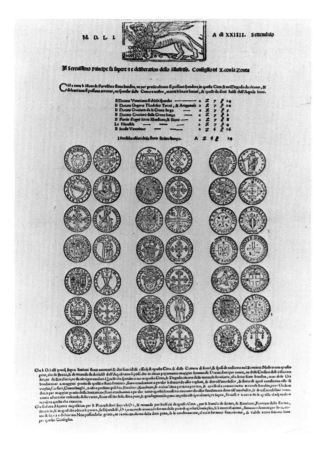

they were remarkable for the medieval economy.

Even though the State levied huge taxes, profits on the *mude* contracts were on average between ten and 30 per cent for each voyage (*i.e.* between 20 and 60 per cent for each return trip). Venetian maritime trade was not, however, limited to the *mude*. The bulk of less precious, but not necessarily less profitable goods, such as salt, timber and an infinite number of raw materials, were transported on unarmed ships. These did not follow prescribed routes and often would stay away from Venice for many years, working from one port to another. They were larger than the galleys: at the beginning of the 15th century there were a good 300 over 120 tons. Documents from the 13th century mention a sailing-ship, the *Roccaforte*, which had a tonnage of 500. (F. C. Lane has noted that the *Santa Maria* of Christopher Columbus had a tonnage of just 100 and the *Mayflower* which took the first pilgrims to North America, had a tonnage of 180). Compared to the merchant galleys it was like one of today's supertankers. There were all sorts of ships, to cover all kinds of routes, travelling back and forth on Mediterranean waters which were not always calm or safe, and also on the Atlantic ocean whose waters were safer but far from serene.

There were other routes, setting out from the main ports, which the tireless Venetian merchants sailed constantly. Trebizond, on the Asian coast of the Black Sea, and Laiazzo, on the coast of Cilicia, were the starting points for two branches of a caravan route, which converged at Tabriz in Persia, and then went on to the Persian Gulf at Hormuz, from where it was possible to reach India. It was also possible to reach India from Tana, crossing the Volga, coming down to Bokhara and Samarkand, climbing up the Afghan mountains as far as Kabul and down into the Indus valley, or else down through the Punjab to Delhi.

Political events and warfare which changed kingdoms and empires in the Asian world, as far as the Venetian merchants were concerned, only brought about changes in their itinerary. Tamerlane's warfare, for example, interrupted the "silk route," an interminable march from Tana to Astrakhan, along the coasts of the Baltic, then to Organdi on the coast of the Aral Sea, and thence across central Asia and the Gobi desert to

Left: printed list illustrating the impressions and values of different coins, dated 24 September 1551. Below: money-coiner (Grevembroch). Venice laid severe penalties on forgery in order to protect the reputation of its coinage. The techniques used in forgery combined both alchemy and expert craftsmanship, as can be seen from records of trials of forgers. From a deposition of 1499: "And I put an iron below, on which the impression of the marcello (a silver coin of the 15th century) was engraved, and on this I put a mixture of chalk, oil, and metal shaving, and then I placed another iron on top; and the marcello was well and truly done, both in word and deed."

Silver ducat of Girolamo Priuli (1561). From this period ducats were minted in silver, and the gold coinage began to be known as zecchini.

Kinsai (nowadays called Hangzhow, the capital of China and, according to those who had seen it, the most beautiful and richest city in the whole world). From here the route crossed the whole of China and arrived in Peking. From Peking to Tana, or Tana to Peking, a one-way journey took about ten months. After the destruction wrought by Tamerlane, it went from Laiazzo, or Antioch, or Laodicea, and the caravans followed the Tigris and Euphrates up to Baghdad, and reached Bokhara and Samarkand via Asterabad on the Caspian sea. The spices which reached Alexandria from India, via Jedda and Cairo by sea, or via Mecca and Medina by land, were only transported by Moslems, and the Venetian ships loaded up at the mouth of the Nile.

There is no point in discussing here at length the story of Marco Polo, the noble Venetian merchant who lived far from Venice for more than 25 years and served the Great Khan of the Tartars, the emperor of China, on important diplomatic and government missions. His fascinating story, dictated while he was a prisoner in Genoa, was enormously successful. He was not the only Venetian to have reached China and found his

The illustrations on these pages depict banking operations, in which Venice led the field. Below, left: detail of a painting by Canaletto, The Campo di Rialto, (Staatliche Museen Preussischer Kulturbesitz, Gemäldegalerie, West Berlin). Beneath the arches of the Campo di Rialto can be seen the bankers writing intently in the record-books on their counters, which resemble those depicted earlier by Carpaccio in the detail reproduced above, left, from his Embassy of Queen Hippolyta of the Amazons to Theseus, King of Athens, (Musée Jacquemart-André, Paris). The Rialto, the merchants' quarter, was both the banking center and the center of what we would call "credit transfer." The operation consisted in transferring credit from one account to another by writing on a client's order. There were no cheques as there are today: the party in question presented himself in person to the banker who noted down in his register the order to effect payment into the payee's account. Receipts were unnecessary, since the banker's register counted as an official notarial register. This method of business catered for the demand of Venetian merchants to transfer large sums of money with ease, avoiding the necessity of carrying money every time they wished to make a transaction, while sellers could feel secure in the credit of a well-known banker.

Above: The Banco del Giro on the Rialto *painted by Gabriele Bella (Fondazione Querini Stampalia, Venice). This was the second public bank opened by the Venetian government in 1619. The first was the Banco della Piazza, opened in 1587.*

fortune there. The missionary Odorico of Pordenone writes in 1325 that a large number of Venetians were living in Zayton, a large Chinese port just opposite the island of Formosa. Unfortunately we do not have many names or details of the lives and adventures of these men who had their homes and businesses so far from their native land, but countless Venetian merchants lived for years, or rather decades, far from Venice in Constantinople, Alexandria, Amman, Tana, London, Bruges or Augsburg, at the head of their own companies, waiting to return home after having passed on their business to a son or a relative, so that they could attend to the political demands of the Republic. We know however from Marco Polo himself that his father and uncle who accompanied him on his first voyage had curried favour with the Tartar Khan of the Golden Horde with the gift of certain crystal "jewels," which pleased him so much that he gave in return gifts of at least twice the value. We know of a certain *ser* Lorenzo Viaro and a Simeone Avventurato who had taken similar gifts to the Khan of Persia, but received nothing in return. Documents also men-

tion a *ser* Francesco Loredan, who left for China in 1344 with a capital of at least 300 pounds of precious metal, and one Andreolo Balanzano of San Felice, who also went to China before 1350, with a companion, *ser* Francesco Condulmer of San Geremia. We know also of other merchants, both patricians and commoners, who went even farther, to Japan, in other words as far as the boundaries of the known world at that time.

Normal commodities for trade, although luxurious in themselves, were supplemented by what we might now call "special offers." The most curious is perhaps the supply of eunuchs provided at least for a while by Venetian slave merchants for the harems of Moslem potentates. However, more commonly, it was crafted art, or luxurious *objets d'art* that provided the merchandise. The export of the talents of painters, sculptors and musicians has no place in a chapter on trade. (We might mention that even Mehmed II, the terrible sultan who conquered Scutari, Negropont and Constantinople, fell under the spell of Venetian painting and had Gentile Bellini as a guest in his court. Bellini, having had thrust under his nose the

THE POWER OF MONEY

The Venetian gold coinage was known first as ducats, and later as *zecchini*. The ducat was minted for the first time in 1284 with the same weight and fineness of the Florentine florin which had been in circulation for more than 30 years. The weight and fineness of the Venetian gold coinage never altered (1 and 2, golden ducat of Marco Barbarigo, 15th century). In 1455 the value of the ducat was legally fixed at 124 silver *soldi di piccoli*. With this the ducat became a standard unit, and silver ducats were struck. The gold coin did not change but became known as the *zecchino* from *zecca*, mint.

There were a number of silver coins, originally divided into two kinds of money, the *lira di grossi* and the *lira di piccoli*. The *grosso* was minted in the 13th century and was used in large transactions, whilst the *piccolo* was used in retail. Originally a *grosso* was worth 26 *piccoli*. There were 240 *grossi* in a *lira di grossi* and 240 *piccoli* in a *lira di piccoli*, whilst 12 *piccoli* made a *soldo di piccoli*. Later the *lira* too was minted (3 and 4, *marcello* or half-lira of Andrea Vendramin, 15th century; 5, *mocenigo* or half-lira of Pietro Mocenigo, 15th century; 6, *soldino* of Francesco Dandolo, 14th century).

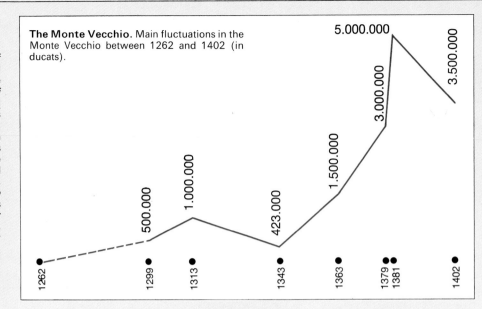

The Monte Vecchio. Main fluctuations in the Monte Vecchio between 1262 and 1402 (in ducats).

1   2   5   6

3   4

Throughout its history Venice financed itself through public borrowing. It could almost be said that it was the Venetian state which invented the public debt. All medieval governments financed their wars, which were the largest extraordinary expenses of the time, by borrowing on short loans at between 12 and 20 per cent. Venice was the first European state to consolidate its public debt, that is to say the loans made to the state, in what became known as the *Monte Vecchio* (literally the old pawnbroker's). Interest was paid regularly at a constant rate, initially a rate of 5 per cent to those who held titles of credit. The graph above shows the main fluctuations in the use of the Monte Vecchio from its inception in 1262 until the beginning of the 15th century.

The debt at the end of the second war with Genoa in 1299 stood at half a million ducats, while at the end of the war of Ferrara in 1313 it stood at more than a million. It was considerably reduced in the ensuing decades, but subsequently rose steeply. Within two years, from 1379 to 1381, at the time of the dreadful war of Chioggia, it rose by two million ducats to five million

ducats. The debt was sustained by compulsory loans, and the market value of the titles fell to 18 per cent. In 1381 payment of interest was suspended, to be resumed in the next year at 4 per cent. In 1402, when Venice was expanding on the mainland, the debt had been reduced to 3.5 million ducats, and the value of titles restored to 66 per cent.

Frederick C. Lane, the American scholar of Venetian history, devotes special attention to the economic and financial history of the Republic. The histogram shown here is taken from a table compiled by him. State revenues are shown in red and payments of long-term debts in blue, in ducats of account for various years between the beginning of the 14th century and the end of the Republic. Note that although the Venetian state made widespread use of public borrowing, the balance between income and repayments to its creditors remained favourable until the end, in spite of the decline of the city.

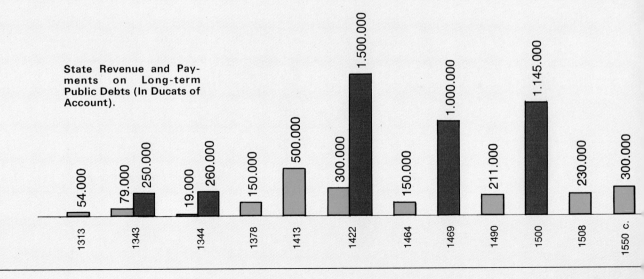

State Revenue and Payments on Long-term Public Debts (In Ducats of Account).

The *camerlengo di Comun* or Public Chamberlain (7, from the manuscript of Livy's *First Decad* in the Biblioteca Ambrosiana, Milan) was one of the earliest financial officials. Indirect taxation on consumption and goods in transit was long preferred to direct taxation.

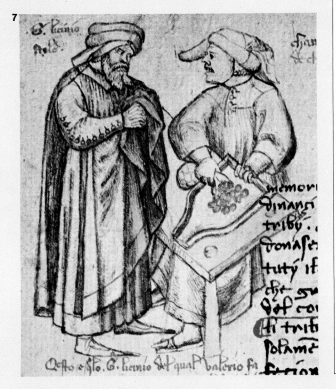

7

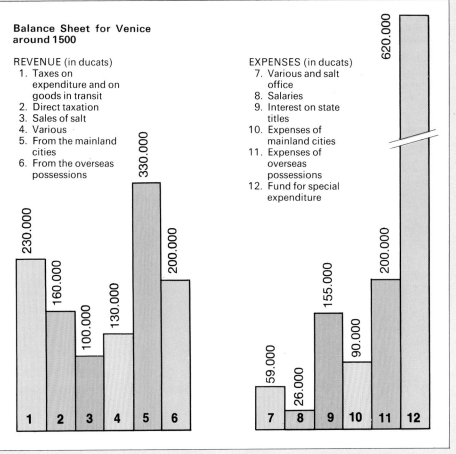

Balance Sheet for Venice around 1500

REVENUE (in ducats)
1. Taxes on expenditure and on goods in transit
2. Direct taxation
3. Sales of salt
4. Various
5. From the mainland cities
6. From the overseas possessions

EXPENSES (in ducats)
7. Various and salt office
8. Salaries
9. Interest on state titles
10. Expenses of mainland cities
11. Expenses of overseas possessions
12. Fund for special expenditure

1	2	3	4	5	6	7	8	9	10	11	12
230.000	160.000	100.000	130.000	330.000	200.000	59.000	26.000	155.000	90.000	200.000	620.000

The French ambassador Philippe de Commines was not alone in declaring at the end of the 15th century that Venice was the most wisely governed city. One of the reasons for this was the shrewd and impartial management of economic resources by the Venetian ruling class.

The balance sheet for the Venetian state about the year 1500, illustrated above was also compiled by Lane. At this time Venice had reached its zenith. It was the most powerful maritime presence in the Mediterranean and the largest state in Italy. Three points are worth emphasizing. Revenue and expenses for the overseas possessions are identical, while revenue from the mainland cities was considerably larger than expenditure. As Lane has pointed out, after the acquisition of the mainland domains, revenues from that source helped support the cost of overseas empire.

For the first time there is an entry for direct taxation. This system had been recently introduced because the system of financing wars through loans involved serious difficulties. In fact the raising of enforced loans amounted to direct taxation if the interest was cut (making the market value of titles fall). Note finally the huge sums available for special expenditure. This helps to explain how neither the League of Cambrai nor the Turks were able to destroy Venice's power.

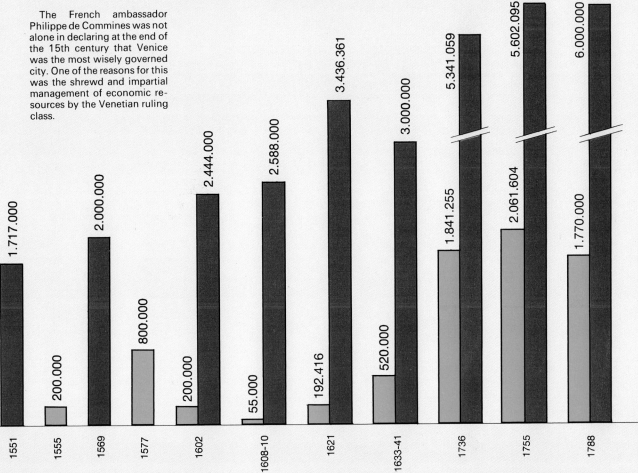

1551	1555	1569	1577	1602	1608-10	1621	1633-41	1736	1755	1788
1.717.000	200.000	2.000.000	800.000	2.444.000	2.588.000	3.436.361	3.000.000	5.341.059	5.602.095	6.000.000
				200.000	55.000	192.416	520.000	1.841.255	2.061.604	1.770.000

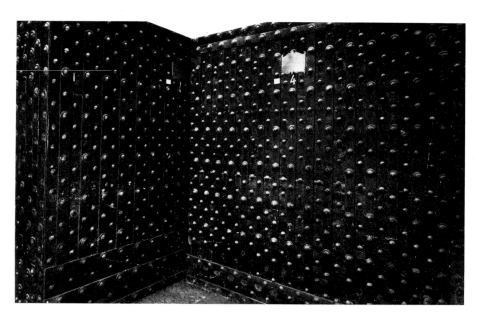

severed head of a slave by the sultan to show him exactly how he should paint the head of John the Baptist after his decapitation, preferred to return to Venice with the farewell gift of a lovely gold necklet).

We should mention the jewels supplied to Suleiman II by a company whose partner was the Venetian *bailo* in Constantinople, *ser* Francesco Zen: a gold ring with a repeating watch, and a spectacular helmet, encrusted with jewels, which was worth, as the chronicler Sanudo notes, "a great deal of money."

Even Ulugh Ali, the most daring of the Turkish admirals, who had miraculously escaped from the massacre of the battle of Lepanto and had become the patient organizer of a planned reprisal, had ordered at Venice for his wives a precious jewel-casket from the goldsmith Battista Rizzoletti who had a shop on the Rialto at the sign of Jesus. The casket arrived in Constantinople in 1598 after the death of the admiral, and was given by the *bailo* as a gift to the sultan, to his great wonder and pleasure, if diplomatic despatches are to be believed.

Above: detail of one of the early strongrooms in the mint. Below and opposite: two of the strange statues on the corners of the Palazzo del Cammello, which have given their name to the Campo dei Mori (Moors' square). According to popular tradition, these represent Moorish merchants who founded the palace in the 12th century, the brothers Rioba, Sandi and Afani. Below, right: arithmetical machine by the Venetian Giovanni Poleni, 1709, the precursor of the modern calculating machine (Museo della Scienza e della Tecnica, Milan).

Gold and Spices

We have already seen how diplomacy was concerned with sustaining trade, obtaining optimum market conditions and helping in every way the expansion of business for Venice and Venetians. Travellers had the same aim, whether they travelled, as was most usual from Marco Polo onwards, because they were themselves merchants, or whether they went for other reasons, like Odorico of Pordenone, who crossed the whole of Asia as a Franciscan missionary between 1318 and 1330. The list is endless: there was Marino Sanudo the Elder (1270–1343), a patrician. He made the great voyage to the Orient five times, and from his experiences wrote the curious book, *Liber secretorum fidelium Crucis*, a treatise on geography, nautical science, trade and economics, which proposes the annihilation of the Saracens and the annexing of Egypt, and, 500 years before Napoleon realized such a project at the expense of the British empire, also proposed a continental blockade against the Moslems. There was Niccolò Zeno who, bound for Flanders, was shipwrecked and discovered the Faroe islands, visited Greenland and was the first to describe the north American coastline, on the basis of reports from Scandinavian fishermen (this in the late 1300s). There was Niccolò de' Conti who in about 1424 explored Arabia, sailed in the Persian Gulf, explored the Malabar Coast, went up the Ganges and, once back in Venice 25 years later, recounted his adventures to the humanist Poggio Bracciolini. Together with Niccolò Michiel and Cristoforo Fioravanti, *ser* Pietro Querini reached the unknown Lofoten islands, after a terrifying experience in the turbulent Atlantic, and crossed the whole of Scandinavia. Alvise da Mosto is more famous: while in the service of the Portuguese *infante*, he discovered the Cape Verde islands in 1445. Only space necessitates the omission of a whole host of sailors, explorers and pioneers, some of whom won great renown.

One of the results of this ubiquitousness of Venetian merchants and sailors was the spread of the Venetian language in the Mediterranean basin and elsewhere. It is for philological specialists to decide how much of it survives not only in what was the dominion *dar mar*, but in the entire, enormous area covered by Venetian trade. The

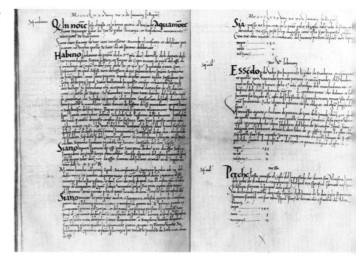

Above: state officials leasing out galleys to shippers in St. Mark's square, painted by Gabriele Bella (Fondazione Querini Stampalia, Venice). There were two distinct forms of sea-trade, that carried out in state-owned cargo vessels guaranteed and protected by the state, and free trade organized by private citizens in private cargo vessels. State vessels were leased out to private merchants who sometimes combined in association, since the expenses involved in loading with cargo, fitting out and manning the ships were enormous. Rent varied according to the length of the voyage and the demand of the market. On the right two documents are reproduced which are concerned with the lease of galleys from 1488–89. The upper example refers to voyages to Aigues Mortes, the lower to cargoes to the port of Beirut (Venice State Archives).

fact remains that, for example, a good half of the vocabulary used in spoken Greek today is virtually pure Venetian. Almost all words used in navigation are Venetian; even the notorious mistral wind, the *meltemi*, which in summer confines all boats to port, derives from the Venetian words for "good weather," because when this wind blows, the clouds disperse and the sun shines.

We have said that the government involved itself deeply in all mercantile matters. Besides the magistracies of the Senate which handled all major questions, there was an infinite number of lesser ones which dealt with every tiny detail. The law carefully regulated taxes and charges, intervened in brokerage, and the state saw to the contracting out of merchant galleys, their building and their safety amid the countless dangers of the Mediterranean, whose waters were infested with adventurers, pirates, plunderers, rivals and enemies. For a city whose power was based on economics, the subject of economics was important on all levels. Economic trends were always reflected, often dramatically, in the political actions of a nation which could not compete with larger or better organized states except by controlling markets or having vast sums of money at her disposal.

For this reason the expansion policy on the mainland started by the doge Francesco Foscari had been strongly opposed, because it could have taken away the Venetians' absolute priority over maritime activity (as was to happen). It was necessary to "cultivate the sea and leave the land alone," insisted the exponents of the party whose leader was the predecessor of Foscari, doge Tommaso Mocenigo. By avoiding involvement in the tremendous chaos of the Italian mainland, in the upheavals and battles between Italian potentates who were greedy and untrustworthy, would Venice be able to retain her greatness, and be "mistress of all the gold in Christendom."

Expansion on the mainland was inevitable, or almost inevitable, if for no other reason than to create a protective barrier behind the fragile boundaries of the lagoon dukedom and stop the formation of a huge continental state which might bear down on her. However, it is true that this policy brought with it a century and more of wars and expense of incalculable proportions, which seriously depleted the gold reserves of the *Serenis-*

sima and her citizens. Later the need to defend herself against the great warring, continental powers, again on the continent, by means of mercenary troops (demographic resources of the Republic were totally insufficient for the formation of a sizeable infantry) brought Venice to the brink of bankruptcy and many banks and bankers went under. All the same, the resources of the Venetian merchant were not destined to dry up as

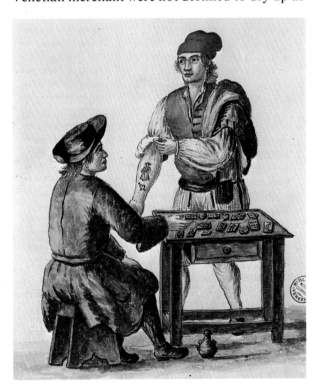

Above: Enlistment of the Crew *by G. B. D'Angelo, called Il Moro (Museo Storico Navale, Venice). From the middle of the 16th century officers, sailors, and galley oarsmen were recruited and provisions and ammunition for state bottoms organized by the* three provveditori all'Armar, *a branch of the College of the* Milizia da Mar. *When they were enrolling captains for the ships, the state officials set up a table on the Molo in front of the Doge's Palace, or under the colonnade of the palace itself facing the sea, and gave an advance, usually of three or four months' pay, to the men they hired. Left: tattooing, a practice which has always been in vogue among sailors of all countries (Grevembroch).*

rapidly as some determined enemies of the Republic might have hoped. The cardinal Ascanio Sforza was right when he replied in assembly to pope Alexander Borgia VI, who had given Venice up as economically lost: "Most blessed Father, the Venetians have more money than ever ... and if the banks have collapsed, this has come about through bad management on the part of the bankers, and not on account of deficiency of that State, and every day Your Holiness will hear news of the Republic."

Not even the attack unleashed by the Turks (and countered, at first, with no great energy and no great success) was enough to weaken the Venetian economy. Neither was the discovery of the route round the Cape of Good Hope by the Portuguese sufficient to weaken the Venetians a route which then became firmly established. From 1498 the Portuguese, by going round Africa on a route discovered by Vasco da Gama, were able to gain direct access to the sources of the supply of spices, load up their ships and carry the merchandise to Lisbon without incurring the high transport costs and heavy customs tariffs imposed by the intermediaries they were obliged to use, the Egyptian sultan being in the forefront.

Left: sailor being signed on. Below: crew embarking from the Molo, in a painting by G. B. D'Angelo, Il Moro. There was no real distinction between sailors of the merchant fleet and those of the navy, but warships carried a much larger crew. A large sailing-ship of 500 tons which would carry a crew of about 100 men on a normal trading voyage would carry several hundred when it was armed for battle. War galleys required a large number of oarsmen, who were mostly freemen until the 16th century. In cases of necessity an obligatory levy was raised by lot, but it was possible to buy exemption from the lottery for the price of six lire, to pay for a substitute oarsman. As well as soldiers and oarsmen, galleys carried a crew of a dozen sailors proper, who worked the sails and helm. The crews of both war and trading vessels had to be provided with arms and armaments at their own expense.

But the end of what had been a real spice monopoly, marked by the birth of the great Portuguese market, did not mean the end of Mediterranean trading in these precious products. Various factors contributed to keeping the Egyptian market afloat, which was Venice's mainstay by now.

Venice was to be excluded from trading in spices only in the 17th century, and it was not the Portuguese who stifled her but the Dutch, and the formation of the great East Indies companies. However, with Vasco da Gama's voyage and the arrival of the Dutch in the spice-producing countries, Venice had lost two enormous opportunities.

In the first case it is imprecise to speak of a lost opportunity. These are the facts: when in 1499 the news arrived in Venice of Vasco da Gama's ship docking in Lisbon laden with spices, the Republic immediately put diplomacy into action. The king of Portugal was cordial and obliging, and invited the Venetians to come and get their supplies of spices in Lisbon instead of Alexandria. Venice did not accept: first of all because in Lisbon she would not have been able to enjoy the advantages of a monopoly such as she had in Egypt, and also

because she did not want to give up all her trade in the Levant, which was still her main concern even without spices. The Senate decided it was better to try and improve the Egyptian trading conditions and set up in competition with the Portuguese. Here the Senate drew on all its proverbial breadth of vision and, as we have seen in other instances, seemed to act ahead of its time. For example, it even thought of digging a canal to take ships across the isthmus of Suez, thus shortening the route considerably and allowing Venetian ships to beat their Portuguese rivals. The project was discussed at great length in the *Pregadi* but could not be realized, although for reasons beyond the control of the *Serenissima*.

The second case however, does concern a missed opportunity. Between 1581 and 1585 it happened that the king of Spain, Philip II, who had conquered Portugal, in effect offered the Republic exclusive rights to the distribution of the enormous quantities of spices which he found at his disposal. The Senate was not at all keen: there was not the right kind of fleet, there were no shipbuilders or credit, and there was the danger on the sea from the enemies of Philip and of Spain. It still refused even when the offer was repeated with

Bill of loading for galleys from Barbary commanded by Giacomo Contarini (State Archives, Venice). State-organized commerce employed armed galleys which travelled in convoy at fixed times to Mediterranean and Atlantic ports. These convoys consisted in the 14th century of from eight to eleven galleys and were generally used only for valuable cargoes, because of the greater security they offered.

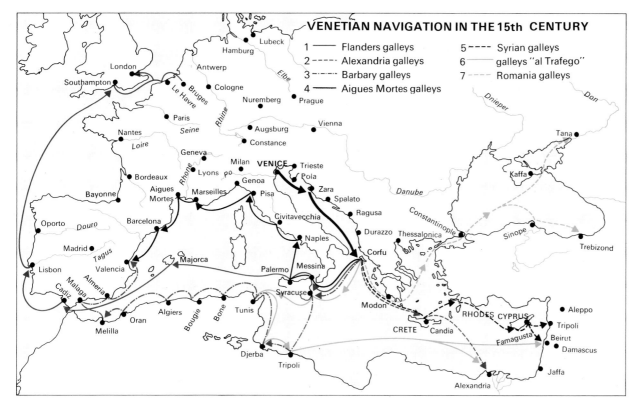

VENETIAN NAVIGATION IN THE 15th CENTURY

1 —————— Flanders galleys
2 - - - - - - Alexandria galleys
3 -·-·-·- Barbary galleys
4 —————— Aigues Mortes galleys
5 - - - - Syrian galleys
6 —————— galleys "al Trafego"
7 - - - - - Romania galleys

various guarantees, including military protection.

What an opportunity to relaunch the economic fortunes of the Adriatic capital! But was it really so marvellous? First of all, it meant giving up trade in the Levant, on which at least 4,000 Venetian families that had settled in the east depended. The volume of trade was still enormous: in 1603, a good 105 years after the voyage of Vasco da Gama, at Aleppo in Syria alone, the volume of Venice's business was valued at a million and a half gold ducats. Moreover the events which followed were to prove the Senate right, as the Genoese, Florentines and Milanese were proved right, who had also refused the king of Spain's offer. In fact, the great German bankers who at last said yes and invested fabulous amounts, failed to get the enormous gain they had hoped for and, as far as the guarantee of safety on the sea was concerned, offered by the Spanish navy, the catastrophic defeat of the Invincible Armada was to prove that the Atlantic was even more insecure than the Mediterranean for anyone carrying Spanish merchandise, whether directly or indirectly.

Piracy and Decadence

The Atlantic was full of pirates. While Spain was experiencing her golden age of literature and the arts, the ocean was the setting for the adventures of men such as Drake, Raleigh and Morgan, eager

Left: the theater of San Samuele, by Gabriele Bella. Opposite: from top to bottom, nobleman in a gambling house, Venetian singer, noblemen drinking coffee. Theaters, foyers, gaming-houses and coffee-shops were Venice's main meeting-places. In the 18th century there were no less than 14 theaters open to the public for the performance of operas, ballets and plays. The operas were especially famous for their lavish sets and costumes, and the singers were enormously well paid and looked after, and fanatically idolized. Comedians also gave excellent performances in Venice and were highly appreciated, but less well paid. Gaming tables were very common, and huge sums were hazarded on them, in spite of the Republic's disapproval. In order to control this evil, the state licensed a public gambling house in 1683, called Il Ridotto, but the cure proved worse than the disease, and the Ridotto was closed down in 1774 by order of the Maggior Consiglio. *Gambling retreated to private houses and coffee shops. The first coffee shop was opened in 1683 beneath the Procuratie Nuove, and soon the city was crowded with these centers of gossip, argument and gambling, which have been immortalized by Goldoni and Longhi. In the 18th century there were at least 27 coffee shops in St. Mark's square alone. Three of them survive, one of them with its original furnishings.*

to grasp the extraordinary riches arriving from the New World which had been discovered in 1492 by Christopher Columbus on behalf of the Spanish royal family. However, as far as the Mediterranean was concerned, pirates and plunderers on the seas had always been a plague and a problem for as long as anyone could remember. Plain banditry, when practised by a daredevil shipowner or the commander of a private ship, became "privateering" and was a recognized form of warfare even though outside the rules of the game. In this way, a republic or a ruler could make rich gains with little trouble, could spoil or ruin the fortunes of a competitor, or else drive dangerous rivals from certain areas. For some, it was a means of getting to heaven: the Saracens saw it as a tribute to the commandments of the Prophet, and the Knights of Rhodes (later of Malta) as a tribute to the principle of "holy war" permanently waged against the "infidel." The same principle inspired Moslem pirates, and more tortuously, the Uzkoks, who justified their plundering by the presence on board the pillaged ships of goods belonging to Jews and Moslems, the "infidels" *par excellence*. In the Middle Ages, certain great sea-bandits stand out, most of them from Genoa: Enrico Pescatore, who tried to hold Crete against the *Serenissima*, having become count of Malta; Leone Vetrano instead finished up swinging from one of the masts of the fleet of Ranieri Dandolo, for having taken over Corfu and trying to keep it for himself. Others included Guglielmo Guercio, Guglielmo Porco, Alamanno da Costa and Raniero di Manente (who in fact came from Pisa). This is only the tip of the iceberg. These are the greatest of the pirates. Behind them was a whole host of less famous, less important buccaneers. Sometimes they were merely captains of regular ships who hoped by their action to make extra gains for their state or sovereign. In later times inspiration (and financial backing) for privateering came from various sources. Personal initiative took second place. The archduke of Austria was behind the Uzkoks, and his actions, along with those of the king of Spain, were aimed at undermining Venice's Adriatic monopoly. If a Venetian admiral captured or sank a Barbary ship (the Berbers were Arabs from Maghreb, and incorrigible pirates right up to the end of the nineteenth century) it would be Constantinople that would

take offense and threaten reprisals. Spain, for whom Venice's independence was a thorn in the flesh, in her turn armed her pirates; but most significant was the initiative taken by the grand duke of Tuscany, who on the pretext of the "holy war" hoped to refurbish his market at Leghorn with slaves, a most precious commodity. In order to do this he founded a religious order, modelled on the example of that of St. John of Jerusalem (for which read Rhodes and Malta), and called it the Knights of St. Stephen. They pillaged under the banner of the cross, capturing galley slaves to be put on sale, as today one might put on the market a particularly sought-after kind of marine engine.

In the West from the 16th century onwards, the slave market altered. There were no more Tartar peasants to hoe Cretan soil, or Circassian girls to warm the beds of Venetian or Genoese merchants. Now the demand was for galley slaves; that is, power to drive galleys and (as far as Venice was concerned) galleasses, the super-armoured vessels of the time, extremely long and narrow, laden with armed men and guns, the principal protagonists and instruments of the victory of Lepanto which in 1571 put an end to Turkish dominion in the Mediterranean.

It had always been true that the life of anyone travelling by sea, whether merchant or helmsman, steersman or galley slave, noble crossbowman or pilgrim for the Holy Land, hung by a thread once pirates appeared on the scene. It was possible to die by the sword, but more probable to end up as a slave in Jedda, Saana, or more likely, Tunisia or Algiers. In order to secure the release of the "prisoners," two religious orders were founded, the *Mercedari* and the order of "the most Holy Trinity for the redemption of slaves." Its members wore on their breast a red and blue cross, and from the order's origin to the present day have given countless sums to rescue and restore to their families hundreds of thousands of poor wretches, most of whom were captured at sea.

Apart from the coastal pirates, there was also an imported variety, mainly English. The Mediterranean, which was already a dangerous and turbulent sea, now became impassable. In the 17th century the reburgeoning of piracy marked the beginning of the definitive decline of the Venetian economy.

MURANO: SEVEN HUNDRED YEARS OF GLASS-MAKING

A document of 1090 mentions one Petrus Flabianus phiolarius, (phial maker), but he was not necessarily the first Venetian glass blower. Excavations have shown that the glass industry flourished from the earliest times. In 1291 it was transferred to Murano because of the risk of fire. "Murano has become famous," says the caption to the drawings of Jan (Giovanni) Grevembroch in the 18th century, "for its craftsmen who make glass unrivalled by any other nation." This glass was made "on a continuous fire, by a workforce of some thousand men, who work half-naked, sweating as they move about, blow, run, and toil at this famous work.... They work for almost the whole year in shifts, except for August and September [the kilns were only allowed to go out on religious feast days, and the men worked night and day by turn]. At that time they divert themselves with bull-hunts and other rowdy sports, and on some of the carnival days sumptuous banquets with music and dancing are held." There were harsh rules protecting trade secrets. Any workman who took his craft outside Venice to the detriment of the state was first ordered to return, his family was then imprisoned, and he himself assassinated. A law of 1376 gave any male child born of the union of a patrician and a glass maker's daughter the right to sit in the *Maggior Consiglio*, revealing the importance which Venice attached to these early ventures in this industry.

Then as now, the Murano glass industry produced works of great artistic refinement, plates, bowls, goblets, cups, glasses and jugs in clear and coloured glass, decorated with enamel or cold-worked, in filigree or lace glass in millefiori and aventurine glass (the latter flecked with copper).

Mirror-glass and window-panes were also produced. The basic tool of the trade was the kiln, a famous engraving of which was made by Agricola, the German Georg Bauer, in his *De Re Metallica* in the 16th century, from which the illustration (left) is taken (3). There is no doubt that the kiln in question comes from Murano. Each working-hole in the oven contained a crucible from which the blower would lift a quantity of molten glass with his rod. The glass was shaped by blowing through the rod (2), as is still done today in the Murano glass-works, with the help of a marver or marble slab on which the glass was rolled

as it was blown. The glass-blowers' tools were fairly simple (7). First and foremost was the rod (a), a metal tube with a funnel-shaped end, with which the molten glass was lifted from the crucible, and a protective piece for the hands at the mouth end, through which the craftsman blew. Then there were metal tongs (b) with wooden handles (e), the *ferrabate* (d) with which the master glass-maker held the incandescent glass in order to round it out while he turned it on the marver, and lastly shears (c). These were used by the blower for cutting the base of goblets to the right size; the stem and the cup were then joined together with the help of an apprentice. The aid of an apprentice was also needed in pulling out glass tubes (4) to obtain glass of the right length and thickness.

One of the characteristic features of the Venetian glass industry was the production of

glass panes from blown glass cylinders, a method described as early as the 12th century by the monk Theophilus in his *Diversarum artium schedula*. Blown-glass cylinders sheared at both ends were slit along their length with a special red-hot splitting-iron (5). These cylinders were then reheated in flattening-kilns (6). They were placed in front of the kiln with the cut uppermost, and gradually pushed inside it. The cylinder opened up as the heat softened the glass, and the workman flattened it out with a pole.

There were other crafts dependent on the Murano glass industry which also survive today, such as the *margariteri* (8) and *perleri* (9), bead-makers. They are illustrated here after the 18th-century – drawings by Grevembroch. As the manuscript caption to these drawings tells us, this "diligent industry" consisted of "carefully heating, cutting, and shaping the [glass] sticks made in Murano." The resulting beads "are highly prized as far away as India." As for the *perleri* "the blast of a large bellows blowing strongly on a small flame melts the glass, and the workman carefully turns beads of incredible symmetry, and a thousand other transparent trifles."

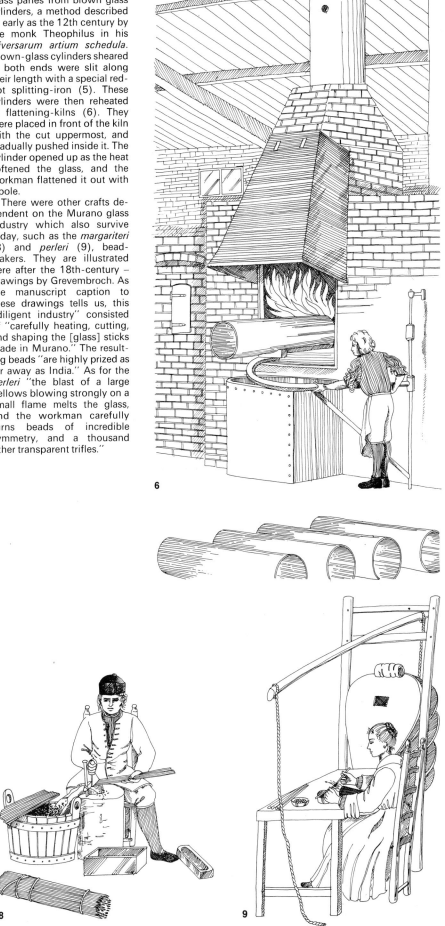

6

5

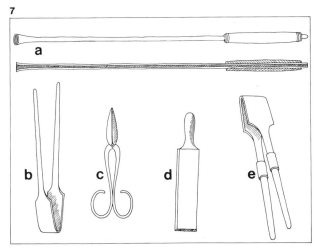

7

8

9

Let us go over the chronology of the history of Venice: there are pirates at every turn. In earliest times there were the struggles with the Slavs (though there is some doubt as to whether the pirate Gaiolo who, according to legend carried off the Venetian brides at Santa Maria Formosa and then was obliged to bring them back, was Slav or came from Trieste). Particularly troublesome were those from the Narenta, and Pietro Orseolo II did not hesitate to teach them a severe lesson. Then there were those from Ragusa (merchants by trade, but occasionally prone to bending the rules against rivals), the Almissans, and the Dulcignoti, all from the opposite Adriatic coast. The Saracens and the Normans were resisted and beaten on behalf of the emperor of Byzantium. Then there were the many Genoese and Pisan pirates, then Greeks, who took spoils on behalf of their rulers, sworn to hatred of the Latins and their ephemeral oriental empire. From a certain point onwards, however, the picture got worse. In the middle of the 14th century, Attica and surrounding areas were the victim of the pitiless onslaught of the Catalans: these were fearsome people, fierce adventurers without scruples. In order to drive them out, the Byzantine emperor, John Cantacuzene, was to commit the supreme error of bringing into Europe from Asia the first contingent of Turks. The Turks had already learnt their work well, and held to ransom unopposed islanders, sailors and the Venetian Aegean fiefs, most of which had been swept away by the attacks of the supreme pirate, the Algerian, Khair-ed-din, Barbarossa.

On behalf of the sultan, Barbarossa devastated more than half the Mediterranean (though at his own risk), and tested the strength of a great empire such as that of the Hapsburgs, over which the sun never set. Compared with him all others paled into insignificance, but his legacy went on for a long while: the last naval campaign of the Republic of Venice was fought by the *provveditore* extraordinary, Angelo Emo, against the Barbary territories of North Africa, between 1784 and 1786. It was in the 17th century however, that piracy made its name. We have already mentioned the Uzkoks elsewhere; the extent of the problem they presented can be gauged by the long list of *provveditori* against the Uzkoks and other military commanders who put themselves to the test on land and sea (and often lost their lives) against these Slavs who

Venice's economy was based on two foundations. It was a traditional center of exchange; and it had a high-quality manufacturing industry, which continued to flourish even when the city's sea power began to decline. Of the many industries which were a feature of Venice, we may mention sugar-refining (above, Grevembroch), and glass-making (below, a glass factory, Bertarelli Collection, Milan), which produced a huge range of items – bottles, goblets, mirrors, and window-panes. These became so common that it was said that every quarter had its own glazier. The most important craft was always ship-building, however, in which joiners and carpenters were employed. Opposite: the tools of a master-carpenter today, in one of the few remaining boat-yards.

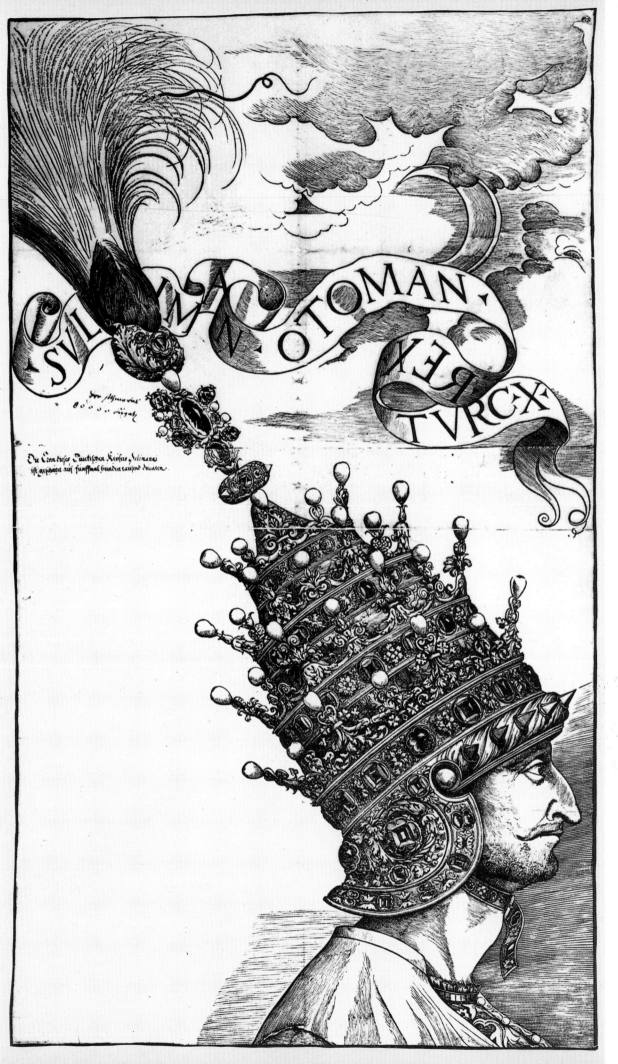

SVLIMAN · OTOMAN · REX TVRCX

Left: portrait of Suleiman the Magnificent wearing the extraordinary crown made by Venetian goldsmiths in 1532 (anonymous woodcut). Marin Sanudo mentions this unique work in his Diaries: "This morning I, Marin Sanudo, saw a remarkable and memorable thing in the Rialto. It was a most beautiful golden helmet, made by the Caorlini, covered with jewels and with four crowns, decorated with jewels of the highest worth, the golden plume most excellently worked, to which were attached four rubies and four large and very fine diamonds. The diamonds were worth 10,000 ducats, and the pearls were each 12 carats in size. There was a long and very fine emerald, and all the jewels were of great price. The plume was the plumage of an animal that lives in the air, with slender and colourful feathers, which comes from India and is very costly. It is said that this helmet has been made to send to the Turkish lord for more than 100,000 ducats. It was made by several associates, videlicet the sons of Sier Piero Zen and the Turkish orator, Sier Jacomo Corner, Sier Piero Morexini, and the aforesaid Caorlini, whilst others have made various other contributions. They are sending it to Constantinople with Sier Marco Antonio Sanudo, to whom they are paying 2,000 ducats for eight months, as well as all his expenses for the voyage and return, and they are selling it for 100,000 ducats and more, the said Sier Marco to have two per cent . . . They are to leave within the fortnight. They travel to Ragusa and thence by land to Constantinople with a great escort."

ventured on to the troubled waters of the Quarnero in long, narrow boats almost like the "drakars" of the early Normans. In the Mediterranean (as the historian A. Tenenti points out) in that century piracy was the most flourishing industry, and a document published by Tenenti paints a tragi-comic picture of the comings and goings of pirate ships, which were so numerous as to suggest the atmosphere of a railway station. The Venetian consul in Milos, in the Cyclades, sent the Senate in July 1607 a note of the *bertoni* (fast, manoeuverable pirate ships) that had passed under his nose from November onwards. On 12 November *The Golden Lion* had passed, with a crew of 150 and 50 cannon, under the command of a certain Antonio Carara. On 18 November, that of Antonio Rucaforte, a Genoese apparently, was sighted, armed with 30 cannon and 300 musketeers. December 10: two French ships with 20 artillery and 180 soldiers each. December 24: the Dutch bark *San Giovanni* passed, with 140 men and 40

cannon aboard, fitted out in Sardinia but commanded by a French knight, Monsieur de Roville. February 29 1607: the galleon *San Spirito*, commanded by Simon Galia, arrived, with 50 cannon and 400 soldiers aboard, escorted by three *bertoni* and a ship from Ragusa. April 13: the galleon *Il Sole* hove into Milos, commanded by a captain from Nice and followed by the ship *Zena*; and, the following day, the count Alfonso di Montecuccoli arrived with 14 vessels belonging to the grand duke of Tuscany. Shortly afterwards, 18 *bertoni* were sighted in the distance.

With such a state of affairs, maritime trade declined, the number of men taking up a career on the sea was visibly reduced as no one wanted to run such excessive risks. No more sailors were recruited in Venice, and only a few in Istria and Dalmatia. As for the patricians, now that they sensed behind them the green fields and gentle hills of the Veneto, Brescia and Bergamo, their atavistic, centuries-old vocation as merchants and

Above, left: acesèndelo, *a small lantern used for lighting one's way through the dark alleys. Right: plate with Apollo and the Muses. Both pieces are 16th-century Venetian work (Museo Vetrario di Murano, Venice).*

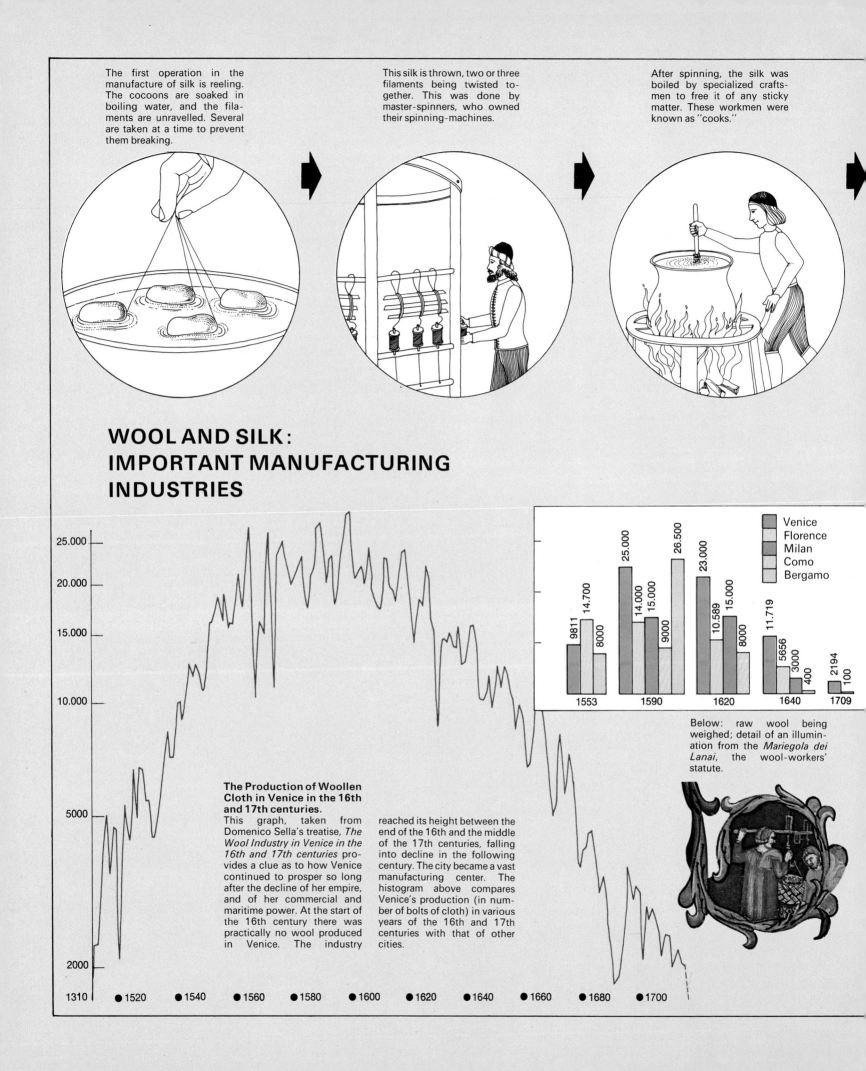

The first operation in the manufacture of silk is reeling. The cocoons are soaked in boiling water, and the filaments are unravelled. Several are taken at a time to prevent them breaking.

This silk is thrown, two or three filaments being twisted together. This was done by master-spinners, who owned their spinning-machines.

After spinning, the silk was boiled by specialized craftsmen to free it of any sticky matter. These workmen were known as "cooks."

WOOL AND SILK: IMPORTANT MANUFACTURING INDUSTRIES

Below: raw wool being weighed; detail of an illumination from the *Mariegola dei Lanai*, the wool-workers' statute.

The Production of Woollen Cloth in Venice in the 16th and 17th centuries.

This graph, taken from Domenico Sella's treatise, *The Wool Industry in Venice in the 16th and 17th centuries* provides a clue as to how Venice continued to prosper so long after the decline of her empire, and of her commercial and maritime power. At the start of the 16th century there was practically no wool produced in Venice. The industry reached its height between the end of the 16th and the middle of the 17th centuries, falling into decline in the following century. The city became a vast manufacturing center. The histogram above compares Venice's production (in number of bolts of cloth) in various years of the 16th and 17th centuries with that of other cities.

The skeins of dyed silk were then wound on to bobbins by *incannaresse*. This was one of the preparatory stages for weaving.

The silk obtained from the cocoons which the merchant-trader imported from Spain, Sicily and the East to be worked in Venice, was then dyed.

Before it was woven the silk was divided into batches by warpers. Today one batch usually consists of 80 strands but in earlier times the number varied.

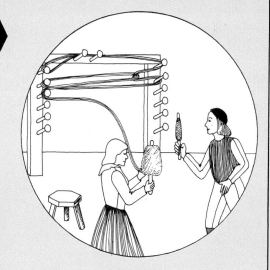

Below: Weavers (shown here on a painted banner belonging to the Guild of Weavers), were divided into velvet-makers and *samitari* or silk-makers. Groups of female workers called *imbarbaresse* and *levaresse* prepared the heald according to the design, for the production of worked textiles.

Together with the glass industry, ship-building and sugar and wax-refining, the manufacture of silk and wool were among the most important of Venice's industries. The woollen industry developed later here than in other Italian cities, not until the 16th century, but it grew to very important. The manufacture and export of silk was one of the main sources of this great mercantile Republic's wealth in the 13th century, and even more so in the next two centuries.

Wool and silk were home industries, the various stages of the work being performed by the workers in their own houses. In the usual fashion of the medieval economy, every worker was his own employer. In Venice, however, the merchant came to play the main economic role. The merchant was the true entrepreneur, buying the raw material and handing it on from one craftsman to another. He provided the capital and organized production, which was minutely subdivided. A 16th century document talks of silk having passed through "16 hands," that is having been worked by 16 craftsmen.

seafaring men crumbled in favour of the advantages of real estate: hail was less pernicious and dangerous than pirates, frost less risky than the Uzkoks, Algerians or the Knights of Malta or St. Stephen.

This was the ripening of the phenomenon which was the prelude to the economic decline of the Republic, the prelude in its turn to her political decline. The Venetian nobility had once gloried in being merchants: it was the provincial nobles who (foolishly, it was felt in Venice) considered trade *arte meccanica* and a reason for excluding those who practised it from their aristocratic councils. However, from the end of the 16th century onwards, the nobility turned in on itself, relying on the secure income from property and agriculture, forgetting the thrills of bold gains made in China, India, England or the Barbary territories, preferring to live on their interest, deserting the Rialto in favour of villas in the country. What had been the boast of the great doges, from Giuliano Parteciaco to Sebastiano and Pietro Ziani (the immensely wealthy doges, who could be compared, as the economist G. Luzzatto has suggested, to the Rockefellers and the Aga Khan), and what the Cornaro and the Mocenigo families had considered more than honourable, that is, trade, shipbuilding, finance, marine insurance, all this was repugnant to their descendants. The doge Nicolò Sagredo directed a timber business with members of his family and was criticized for it at the end of the 17th century, as if it were a mark of dishonour. Besides economic enterprise, 18th century patricians also abandoned the liberal arts: only law was practised with success and profit, but by a tiny proportion of nobles.

Worse still, interest in public office which had been passionate up to the end of the 17th century, began to diminish in the following century. In particular, offices that were considered uncomfortable, such as the *reggimenti*, attracted fewer and fewer nobles, with the exception of those with little or no fortune for whom even the most modest title of office was useful in order to get by. The fact was that the most important *reggimenti* were also the most burdensome. Only the richer nobles could take them on, since much of the expense, as was by now the established tradition, fell to the personal fortune of the *rettore*. Of those who could afford the position, ever greater num-

Below: view of Lizza di Fusina from where the Brenta canal flows into the lagoon. 18th-century engraving by G. F. Costa. The scene is enlivened by gondolas, Paduan or covered boats (center), and a large barge (right), used for transporting goods and passengers along the Brenta canal. Opposite, above: apparatus for hauling canal boats from one level to another. Below: Hunting in a Creek by Vittore Carpaccio. Because of its unique environment, Venice was one of the few cities which was not surrounded by walls. The lagoon acted as a defense, as a means of communication and a source of food.

bers preferred to pay the forfeit charge prescribed by the law for those who did not accept the office, rather than spend much more money, far from the capital, in Padua, Verona, Brescia or Bergamo.

It also came about that, in a system where it was necessary to be quite wealthy in order to hold an important office (the *dogado* was ruinous, but so were ambassadorships and the higher offices *dar mar*), rich patricians would almost automatically end up holding all or almost all of the main decisional offices. Whoever was not rich, but not actually poor either, would content himself with judiciary office, such as the *Quarantie* and certain *reggimenti* of middling rather than of the highest importance. The numerous and turbulent host of penniless nobles, the *barnabotti*, made up the greater part of the *Maggior Consiglio* and supplied all the lesser offices and the *reggimenti* of little significance. In this way an oligarchy was born within the aristocracy: the patrician equilibrium was disturbed, and this spelled the end.

But the decline was splendid, a marvellous Indian summer of riotously flourishing arts and culture, with strokes of genius even in politics and

waves of fervour in the religious field. The licentiousness, so criticized by moralizing historians commenting on the last stages of the Venetian Republic, was simply one of the characteristics of society all over 18th-century Europe. If anything, Venice stands out in that apparently frivolous, though seething world, for other features: her passion for music and the theater, pointed out by so many foreign visitors, her feverish building, the *mal della pietra*, or "stone fever" which has bequeathed us an infinite number of palaces and churches, her love of a style of painting which was destined to flourish, and illuminate all Europe. In the "conservatories," schools for orphan girls, set up and financed by the state, the girls learned to become virtuosos of song or instrumental music, under the guidance of such masters as Vivaldi, Porpora and Cimarosa. Giambattista Tiepolo carried to Milan, Würzburg and Madrid the imaginative skills with which he had decorated the historical scenes of the ceilings and walls of the Labia palace and villa Pisani. Goldoni took his plays to Paris, and for years their run was extended in competition with those of Gozzi and

Impressive Venetian church interiors. Left: side-aisle in San Giacomo dell'Orio. Opposite: detail of San Nicolò dei Mendicoli. Throughout its history, Venice was deeply and sincerely religious, but although Catholic orthodoxy was scrupulously upheld, the state was determinedly secular. In order to ensure the separation of the two powers and the freedom of debate of the organs of the state, a law laid down that whenever problems of ecclesiastical politics were being debated in the Maggior Consiglio *or the Senate, the so-called* papalisti, *that is those who were related to Cardinals or had personal links with Rome, had to leave the chamber. The minutes of the session were preceded by the formula* 'cazzadi i papalisti', "*the* papalisti *having been removed.*"

Chiari. Promoted by another Gozzi, Gasparo, modern journalism was born, right in Venice. In the unending festival of the Venetian Carnival – the great *kermesse* which lasted almost all the year, and attracted monarchs and adventurers from all over the world to the great feast which rendered everyone equal beneath their mask, rich and poor, honest and dishonest, men and women, Venetians and foreigners – the daily reality of a world that in spite of everything had preserved its original simplicity, was concealed and confused. The patrician Pisani family, at Stra, offered such feasting to king Gustav III of Sweden when he made a state visit that the family was ruined and the guest confessed openly that he would never be able to repay such magnificent hospitality in his own kingdom. At a ball in honour of king Frederick IV of Denmark and Norway, the pearl necklace of the lady with whom he was dancing the minuet, broke. The king made as if to bend down and gather the pearls, but the lady's husband, a Querini, came up smiling and trampled and scattered the precious beads with his feet. These were excessive and extreme displays; but there was also the worthy bourgeoisie of Goldoni's plays, law-abiding and prudent in their spending. There were also such people among the patricians, such as a certain Grimani who (according to a spy of the State Inquisitors) at the end of an important political meeting in 1787, lunched on a piece of hot polenta, standing up. Similarly, there were the numerous patricians who, dressed

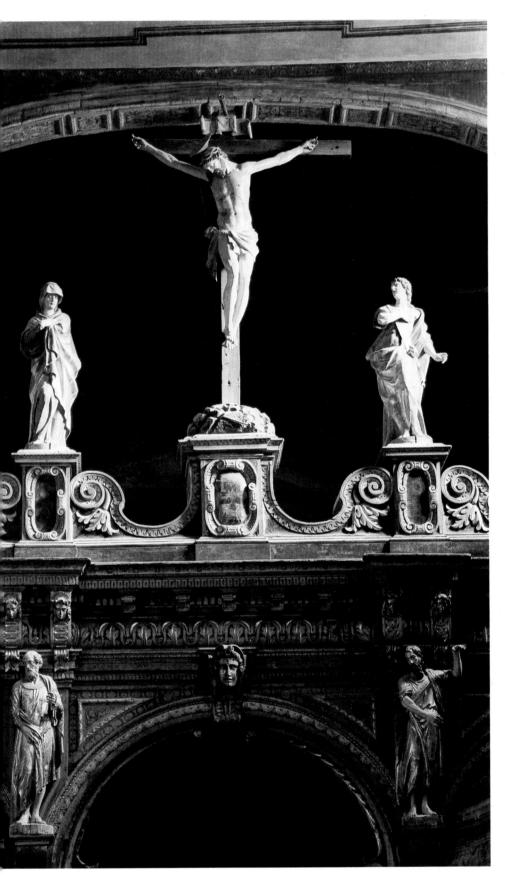

in gowns and wigs, used to take as refreshment, when meetings of the *Maggior Consiglio* ended, a good glass of Cyprus wine and a piece of cake at the renowned wine-shop on the Ponte del Rimedio.

Wars, Armies, Victories, Defeats

The pirates were not the only enemy that Venice had to contend with in the Mediterranean. Her entire history is a succession of battles: for the conquest of markets, the defense of markets, the acquisition of dominions, the defense of dominions, but, above all else, for survival.

We have seen the Franks turn to the lagoons, hungry for conquest; then the Hungarians, greedy for spoils. But the hardest struggle was in the hinterland, against *Comuni* and lords of the mainland who would have liked to drown Venice in her own salty waters. The lord of Verona, Mastino della Scala, tried to put together a great continental Italian state, but his first action was to place his markets and his customs officers on the borders of the *dogado*. The Visconti family of Milan hoped to conquer the whole of northern Italy including Tuscany, and, once they had taken possession of Genoa, also looked eastwards. However, the closest enemy, the most tenacious and the most treacherous, was the lord of Padua.

The Carrarese family had taken over Padua, having dislodged the Scaligeri family with the help of the Venetians. Very soon however, strengthened by the riches earned by the fertility of the land, the industry of craftsmen and the farsightedness of the bankers in this ancient city which boasted of being founded by Antenor (and was the birthplace of Livy, the great Roman historian), very soon, they also aspired to the creation of a continental state on a regional scale, lying behind the lagoons. Francesco il Vecchio, the "Carrarese fox," actually tried to strangle Venice economically through her most sought-after product, *i.e.* salt. Not only did he obtain it by land from the archbishop of Salzburg (who mined it from the rock-salt mines which gave his bishopric its

name), but he also tried to build salt refineries on the edges of the Venetian lagoon and in short, beat Venice on her own ground, or rather on her own waters.

Then there was the patriarch of Aquileia who coveted dominion over Istria, while the archduke of Austria cast greedy eyes on Feltre, Belluno and Treviso, which he considered rightfully his. There was the king of Hungary, who, as we have seen, considered Dalmatia to be his and in fact held it for a while.

On the mainland, the Republic could not rely entirely on its own resources. Only at the time of the League of Cambrai did the lagoon populace flow on to the mainland *en masse*, to the defense of Padua which was being besieged by the emperor Maximilian (who was to lose the war and with it his reputation). Otherwise it had to trust to allies who were not always reliable and mercenaries who were not always loyal. However, even on the mainland it was capable of grand undertakings. For example in order to beat the Visconti attack around Brescia, it transported an entire fleet over hills and valleys right up to lake Garda. It was the year 1438 and, it is said at the suggestion of a Greek naval engineer called Sorbolo, the ships were transported hauled along by oxen: two (but some reports say six) galleys, some frigates and about 20 large ships were transported in this way. It was a scheme that had never been witnessed before but, according to the calculations of the wise Venetian administrators, the total expenditure amounted to a figure which the *Signoria* did not think at all excessive considering the results gained.

The Republic fought the other wars in which it became involved by employing the best captains

Fragment of the tomb of Raimundo Lupi di Soragna (Oratory of San Giorgio, Padua). Now that she had become mistress of the Mediterranean, Venice had to fight hard to defend herself from the mainland cities at her rear, which were attracted by her wealth and situation. Mastino della Scala, lord of Verona, the Visconti of Milan, and the Carraresi of Padua all tried at various times to overpower the city. On the mainland the Republic entrusted its safety to allies who were not always reliable, and mercenaries who were not always loyal. Some of the most famous mercenary captains, Bartolomeo Colleoni, Bartolomeo d'Alviano, and the count of Carmagnola who was condemned to death for treachery, were in the pay of Venice.

in 1630, but usually they were highly efficient, though more used to sea campaigns than land warfare. Examples include Giovanni Dolfin, elected doge while under siege at Treviso: he left Treviso with banners unfurled right under the noses of the Hungarians in order to come to Venice and take possession of the dogal seat in 1356; there was Andrea Gritti who stopped at nothing in his endeavours to recoup the losses suffered by the members of the league of Cambrai. In the 15th-century wars, the Venetian militia went from victory to victory, and fought in Tuscany at Barberino di Mugello – quite a distance for people who were the butt of jokes (as we see from Boccaccio and Ariosto), because of their sea legs, which supposedly made them unable to ride horses or walk on dry land.

In the 18th century, at the height of her policy of neutrality, Venice entrusted her territorial defense to the *cernide*, or "home guard." The writer Ippolito Nievo wittily makes fun of them in his *Confessions of an Italian*. With all due respect to that great writer and patriot, we also owe a little respect to the ridiculous *cernide*: certainly, they were not particularly military or very efficient, they were a bit of a shambles, a little rascally; but, in a way they were the forerunners of the "national guard" which was to be the great democratic breakthrough in the years following the French Revolution. In short, they were a militia made up of ordinary townsfolk and peasants, that guarded the homes and fields of country folk.

Still in the 18th century, there were other militia, but these were specialized, consisting of artillerymen and *bombisti*. There was also a regular army, supplied by the mainland provinces with regiments of infantry bearing the names of the principal cities, plus cavalry divisions, dragoons and cuirassiers, all stationed in the major strongholds and fortresses of the dominion. (The main one was in Verona, where there was also the greatly esteemed military college of the Veneto).

However, Venice's fortunes, as always, depended on the sea. The attacks from the sea had been the most treacherous, the most dangerous. The Saracens and Normans had been resisted with the approval of the emperors of Byzantium, indeed, on their behalf; the putting to flight of the Narentines, however fraught with danger, was a part of the defense of mercantile routes and

available, from Bartolomeo Colleoni, who made Venice sole heir to the enormous riches accumulated during his fighting career and by hiring armies, to Bartolomeo d'Alviano, Renzo da Ceri, Niccolò Orsini and Francesco Bussone, count of Carmagnola, who ended up condemned to death for treason after a trial before the Council of Ten, and for whom the writer Alessandro Manzoni shed tears which nowadays we may consider inappropriate. The ruling patriciate was sometimes represented by *collaterali generali*, who were mainly honorary patricians such as Girolamo di Savorgnan, in whose family the office occurs several times. More often however, there were *provveditori* on the spot, who were sometimes inept, like Zaccaria Sagredo who fled to Valeggio

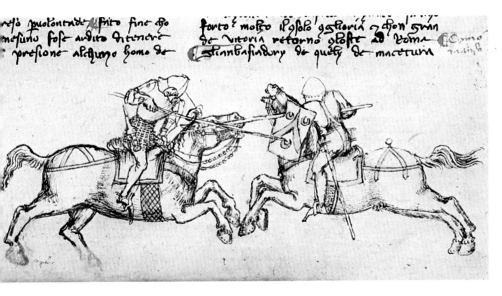

Knights fighting, from Livy's First Decad, *illustrated in the 14th century by the Venetian Giannino Cattaneo. By the beginning of the 15th century Venice had succeeded in overcoming her bitter rivals, the Carraresi of Padua, and had made herself mistress of almost the whole of the Veneto.*

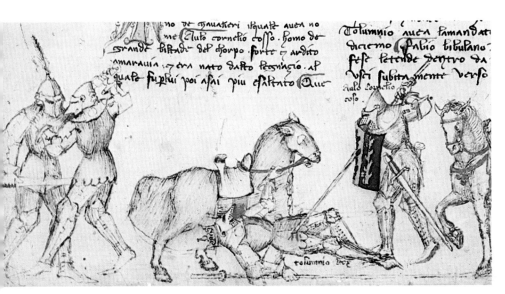

freedom of navigation and commerce. But Venice found herself for more than 200 years up against Genoa: this was mortal combat between two pitiless rivals.

After a series of devastating encounters, the battle shifted from the waters of Greece and Sardinia to the Adriatic. It was in the waters of Curzola, in Dalmatia, that Lamba Doria in 1298 inflicted on Venice the most bloody defeat in her history. Many Venetian galleys were captured, and Lamba burnt most on the spot, as he lacked the means to tow them to Genoa. The Venetian admiral, Andrea Dandolo, could not live with such disaster and crushed his skull against the side of the Genoese galley to which he was chained. In 1379 Genoa was threatening her rival right on Venice's doorstep: Genoese ships were sailing as far as Poveglia and Malamocco, within sight of the bell-tower of St. Mark's. The Genoese occupied and ruled Chioggia, while on land the forces of the lord of Padua, the patriarch of Aquileia and the king of Hungary were advancing. Venice mobilized her entire military forces as well as her economic and moral strength, and after many a dark hour, her victory in 1381 was definitive. From then on, though Genoa continued to be a great economic power, as a political power she disappeared from the scene for ever.

Hardly had Genoa been subdued than the Orient was in tumult. At first the troublemakers were the terrible Catalan adventurers, who had launched a looting raid on Greece. They were followed by the Ottoman Turks. Venice was to fight them for nearly 400 years, both on land and sea; and by the end, both adversaries found themselves worn out and still in their own corner of the Mediterranean "boxing ring" in which they had fought each other virtually without interruption.

Venice's relationship with the Turks was neither simple nor straightforward. From the middle of the 14th century onwards, the Turks advanced steadily into the Mediterranean basin. To the north they spread into the Balkans, to the south they drove the Mamelukes out of Egypt and took over all the Arab world, including north Africa. The inevitable clash with Venice recurred several times: from Smyrna, where the captain-general *da mar*, Pietro Zeno, was murdered at the foot of the altar while attending Mass, to Negropont and

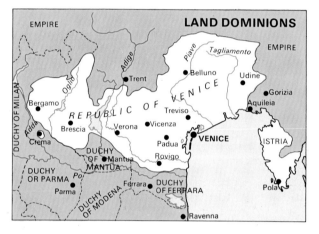

Constantinople, conquered by Mehmed II in 1453 (defending it to the end, the *bailo* Minotto perished along with thousands of his fellow-countrymen), to Scutari in Albania, in the first stage of the great Ottoman expansion. Later there were the horrors of the war in Cyprus, when the entire population of Nicosia was put to death by the sword; Famagusta was defended stubbornly so that more than 100,000 of Lala Mustafa's men were held up for months. (As revenge, he subjected the Venetian *provveditore* Marc'Antonio Bragadin to unheard-of tortures, after which he had him flayed alive.) The war on Candia was equally terrible, and once more, the overwhelming Ottoman troops were held at bay for years by relatively sparse Venetian forces. The war on Candia mobilized all the military resources of the Republic and actually obliged it to renounce its own aristocratic elitism and reopen the Golden Book of patricians of the *Maggior Consiglio* in order to scrape together money and troops. However, at every stage of this war with no holds barred, even at the most dramatic moments, Venice was painfully concerned to avoid situations in which negotiation could not provide a solution. In effect, she avoided the state of total war which the popes were dearly hoping for every

For almost 200 years, from the beginnings of the 13th century until 1381 an implacable war raged between Genoa and Venice on the sea, over the control of the Levantine trade-routes. At first veiled, the conflict finally broke out into bloody battles. The critical point of the long struggle was the war of Chioggia when the Genoese, already in sight of St. Mark's bell-tower, laid siege to their rivals inside their own lagoon. But the Venetians were able to fight back. Work went on day and night in the Arsenal to rebuild the shattered fleet; the entrances to the lagoon were blocked; the port of Lido, the only entrance to the sea which still remained free, was fortified; the Genoese, far from their base, were attacked by returning Venetian vessels, and began to give way, turning from besiegers into besieged, until in 1381 they collapsed. This was Genoa's end as a political power; Venice became richer and more powerful than ever. Fame was won on both sides in this bloody war, by the Venetian admiral Andrea Dandolo, who committed suicide after his defeat at Curzola; the Genoese Lamba Doria, who defeated him; Vittor Pisani, defeated at Pola and thrown into prison, to be released by popular acclaim and put at the head of Venice's last stand; and the aged Andrea Contarini, who was doge at the time of the final victory. The 15th-century miniature from a codex in the Biblioteca Marciana in Venice reproduced above refers to Vittor Pisani. Below: 14th-century map by Francesco Pizzigani showing the two great rivals, Genoa and Venice (Biblioteca Ambrosiana, Milan).

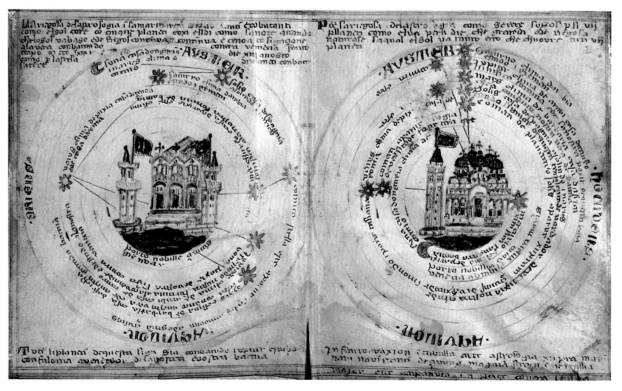

time they brought up the proposal of a crusade against the infidel. Venice fought and fought heroically, but she equivocated on the final aims of the war, and she always preserved the idea of transaction, agreement and a negotiated settlement. The reason was always the same: she did not want definitively to cut off trade with the Levant, the vital oxygen of the *Serenissima's* economy. She did not want to interrupt a flow of commerce which dated back to the origins of the Republic, and to which, when all was said and done, there was no valid alternative, since it would be mere wishful thinking to put herself in competition with the great national powers, Spain, France, England and Holland, in a contest in the far more distant, uncomfortable and dangerous theater of the Atlantic Ocean.

All this gave rise to an ambiguity which in the end created a strange relationship between the two rival powers, one of whom, in comparison with the other seemed totally swamped in terms of geographic and demographic proportions. It was a relationship almost of *frères ennemis*, as a reliable source states. For, if Venice depended on the Turks even for her supply of grain, in times of famine, the Turks saw in Venice a western civilization which their religion and moral code defined

as alien but which in their hearts they admired and would have liked to imitate. Francesco Morosini's undertaking at the end of the 17th century, setting up a kind of *Blitzkrieg* campaign against the Turks with the obvious intention of wiping them out, seemed almost to violate an ancient balance between two powers, of which daily confrontation was a normal element.

Venice and the Turks

The war against the Turks, even its most serious moments, was always counterbalanced by careful negotiations on the part of the *baili* and the special Venetian ambassadors, who tried to re-establish peace, and with it the commerce that was indispensable to the survival of the Republic. Nevertheless, and regardless of how one views this war, there were moments when Venice's military courage and military organization succeeded in achieving not superiority but equality of strength between the Republic and the over-sized Ottoman empire. The battle of Lepanto was fought at the beginning of October 1571 between the Ottoman fleet and that of the Holy League set up by papal diplomacy and under the command of John of Austria, the illegitimate son of Charles V, and therefore the brother of the omnipotent king of Spain, Philip II. It was won thanks to the substantial support of the Republic of Venice, which supplied most of the troops, plus the terrible galleasses which, by means of their concentrated

XIII XIV

"Everyone was weeping, no one was to be seen in the Piazza, the fathers of the College were gone, and our doge did not speak but stood as if struck dead." With these words Marin Sanudo described his city's distress at the defeat of Agnadello in May 1590. The year before, the League of Cambrai had united the "whole world" against Venice in a kind of crusade, which instead of moving against the enemies of Christendom, attacked Venice for usurping the lands of Christian powers. Once again, however, they were defeated by the "accursed pride of the Venetians" who divided the allies, beat the imperial troops in front of Padua, and recovered from a position which had threatened to bring an end to Venice's power. Illustrated here are two propaganda documents of the period. Above: proclamation of Maximilian of Austria to his "Venetian subjects," 1511. Below, left: engraving depicting the defeat of Venice and the triumph of Maximilian, which never took place.

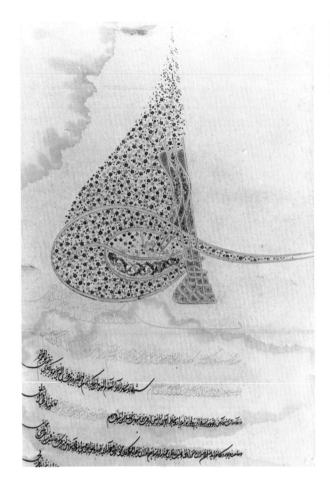

Venice's relations with the Turks were ambivalent. In spite of the long and bitter struggle between the two nations, the state of Venice maintained commercial relations with the Turks, and from 1621 onwards conceded one of the most important warehouses to the "infidel" merchants. They were still in possession of this in 1838, after the fall of the Republic. Thus interest proved stronger than old passions. The Turkish fashion was in vogue in Venice, and not only there but in Vienna too, where the terrifying troops of the crescent had been seen close at hand. The European attitude was one of fear and curiosity mixed with a certain degree of admiration. Traces of this can be seen in clothing, illustrations, music, and in day-to-day items such as baths and every kind of sanitation. The fashion was perhaps also caused by the Turkish love of luxury and luxury goods, and their artistic taste, some examples of which are illustrated on these pages. Above, left: finely executed firman or decree of sultan Murad III, dated August 1579 (State Archives, Venice). Right: 17th-century miniature showing a battle with the Venetians, seen from the side of the "infidels." The Venetians are reconquering the fortress of Lemnos which had fallen to the Turks (Biblioteca del Civico Museo Correr, Venice).

fire on the Ottoman ranks, shattered them. They also supplied the courageous and farsighted commanders, Sebastiano Venier and Agostino Barbarigo, as well as most of the men who were killed (about two thirds of the overall losses of the Christian forces). In effect, while on the continent it was the Austrian and Hungarian imperial forces that put up the greatest resistance to the Ottoman advance with the help of the brave Polish forces of king John Sobieski, on the sea there was no comparison between the fight put up by popes, Knights of Malta, grand dukes of Tuscany (and also the over-rich and over-powerful Spanish monarchs) and the Venetian Republic. If the victors' gains from Lepanto were short-lived, the aid supplied almost reluctantly by the king of France for the defense of Candia represented very little compared with the extent of Venetian involvement, the size of which was surprising if alongside it, we consider the size of the Turkish empire and of the flourishing, extensive and powerful states which, during 25 years of conflict,

brought such meager, modest and miserly aid to Venice.

An aspect which stands out in no less than 400 years of wars, guerilla combat, battles, skirmishes, frontal attacks and occasional forays, is undoubtedly the valour and breadth of vision of many Venetian commanders. Not all were like this: there was the *general dottor*, as the chronicler Sanudo calls the captain-general Canal, who was a highly-educated man but very hesitant commander, and the loss of Negropont can be attributed at least in part to him. (He had risen to the supreme command for purely political reasons, and when he was condemned to exile after his failure, Sanudo stressed that rather than his ineptitude, it was the irresponsibility of those who had elected him to the command that ought to be punished). Another example was Antonio Grimani, "ruin of the Christians," who lost to the Turks in the waters of Navarino in 1499 almost without fighting at all (he also was a political general, but his election had been supported by the fact of his

Turkish scenes of themselves from a 17th-century manuscript (Biblioteca del Civico Museo Correr, Venice). Above, right: a horse-market. Above, left: bazaar in Constantinople. Right: Turkish galleass of the 17th century.

didates by means of the ballot system). This was in 1657, and the intention was to take the war right into the heart of the Ottoman empire, to the capital where there were the military bases and the arsenals, and to try to force entry to the Dardenelles, the access point for the Sea of Marmara, the Bosphorus and Constantinople. However, just when the attempt was about to be successful, the standard hoisted on the top of the mast of the admiral's galley was shattered by cannon fire and split open his skull. His death put an end to the enterprise which had seemed on the point of success. The poet Gabriele d'Annunzio wrote a celebration of the admiral's death with verses which in my own opinion rise above his rhetoric. They occur in an ode in the book of Merops in the *Lauds of the sky, the sea, the earth and heroes*. Here is a translation of some of the lines:

"... on the very same galley/ bearing only the horror of the blackened debris/ on the same galley which witnessed the prow turn/ and plough to earth the coward Mehmed/ returned from the Dardenelles the victor Lazzaro Mocenigo./ And the standard from the mast/ which cleft with its shaft his skull,/ now creaks in the vigorous breeze...."

The same attempt had been made a while before by Lorenzo Marcello, who also died in the process. Later, others were to try with no success. However in Cyprus, Crete, Corfu and on the waters of the Aegean, the Ionian Sea and the Mediterranean, the commanders of the later naval wars proved to be no less outstanding than the legendary *condottieri* of the golden age. For examples there was the victor of the war for Chioggia against Genoa, Vittor Pisani, "father of seamen," the humane and generous *condottiere* who, at the will of his crews in 1380 was given supreme command once more, so as to influence the political alchemy of the *pregadi*. There was Carlo Zeno, the daredevil, adventurous seaman who was also the most refined of humanists; or there was the old doge Carlo Contarini who, well into his eighties, took command of the navy in person as the head of the state, to fight and drive out the invader.

There is no need to go on listing the great Venetian admirals, who can be admired in the commemorative paintings in the Doge's Palace or

having a great deal of liquid assets, the only candidate able to pay the crew in cash). There was also no shortage of weak admirals among the Venetian commanders, or those who lacked professional training or were simply cowardly. However, these negative examples are amply compensated for by a number of men who combined organizing ability with clear vision in strategic matters, ready reflexes in the field with a profound dedication and physical courage of the first order. The one who instinctively comes to mind is Lazzaro Mocenigo. He was a young, spirited commander who, once his term of office was over, returned to Venice and enroled in the fleet as a *venturiere* (which was the name given to commanders in the 17th century whose term of office had run out but who were willing to serve without a commission or rank). Later he was re-elected captain-general *da mar* (election was indispensable: the aristocratic *Maggior Consiglio* did not "nominate," it elected democratically even the commanders-in-chief from a number of can-

The first Sunday of October 1571. The League fleet and the Turkish fleet are shown drawn up for battle before Lepanto. The Italy League mustered 202 galleys with six Venetian galleasses in front (110 of the vessels were Venetian). The Turks had 208 galleys and 63 smaller vessels. By sunset 80 Turkish vessels had been sunk, 140 captured, whilst 8,000 men had been taken prisoner and 30,000 were lost. The League lost 12 galleys with 7,600 dead. These figures make clear the size of the Christian victory.

can be seen upright or stretched out on their tombs, in breast-plate and cuisses, fists clenched round the rod of command, on the sarcophagi in the churches of Santa Maria gloriosa dei Frari and SS. Giovanni e Paolo (San Zanipolo). We should mention just a few more: Pietro Mocenigo, victor at Smyrna and later doge (his tomb is in San Zanipolo, and beneath his statue, a Renaissance masterpiece, is the inscription *ex hostium manubiis* – paid for with spoils taken from the enemy); another Mocenigo, Alvise Leonardo, lies in a magnificent monument in the church of San Lazzaro dei Mendicanti: when he was seriously ill, carried by his men he led his troops out of the besieged town of Candia. Then there was Francesco Morosini whom we have already met con-

quering Attica and the Peloponnese, and who was the last doge to combine the office of head of state with that of supreme commander of the fleet. He died while still in office, doge and captain-general *da mar* in Nauplia in 1694. A curious series of pictures from his palace in campo Santo Stefano Museo, now in the Museo Correr, depicts the stages of his funeral, during which, as also occurred during the funeral of Alvise Leonardo Mocenigo, even the Turks, in spite of their different ideas of warfare, demanded a cease-fire so that a great and generous adversary might be adequately honoured.

It remains for us to consider the last of the series of victorious admirals of the *Serenissima*, Angelo Emo, the man who tried, little more than ten years

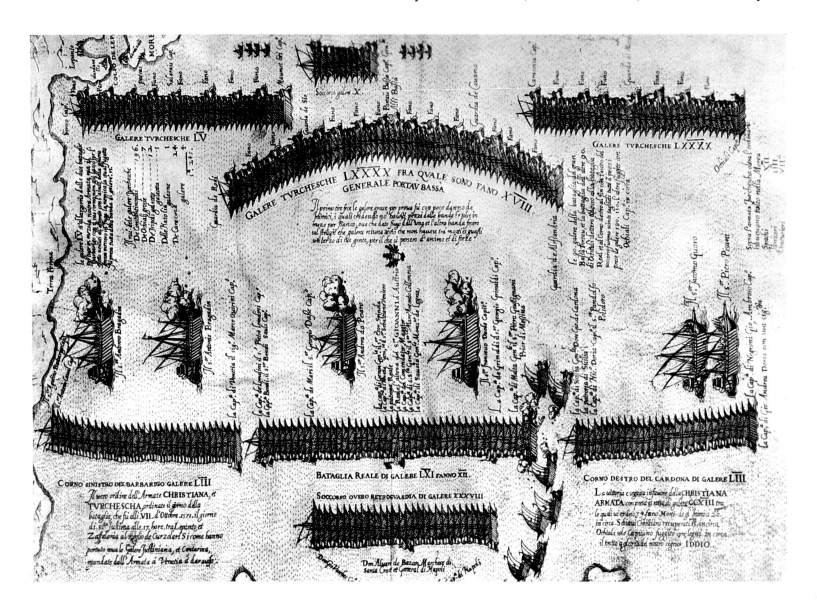

before the fall of the Republic, to impose peace and compliance on the Moslem plunderers of Maghreb. Of him we need only say that his mere presence, inspiring, authoritative and revitalizing, was sufficient to reawaken the flagging spirits of the Venetian armada, idly anchored in the port of Corfu, and to mobilize the enthusiasm of commanders and sailors and make out of an institution still turned towards the past (a recent past, but past nevertheless) an efficient and aggressive weapon. When he died, everything went back to the quiet *laissez faire*, waiting for an end which many felt to be near (and which some perhaps hoped for). Anyway, the story of this person who was so gifted with good qualities supplies a significant piece of information on the condition of the Republic in that century and at that moment: the massive drainage programme of the Valli Veronesi, proposed and encouraged by Angelo Emo when he was *inquisitore alle Acque*, could not be carried out because the finances set aside by the State had been swallowed up by the costs of the campaign against the Barbary pirates, which Angelo Emo had upheld and commanded in person.

The Venetian Armada

The structure of the Venetian armada (the war fleet) varied from one era to another according to customs and institutions. In ancient times, when the doge was still a sovereign even though elected, he was the commander: this was the age of the great warrior doges, from Pietro Orseolo II, Domenico Michiel, to Enrico Dandolo, the heart and the head behind the fourth crusade (he was very old and blind, but the French chronicles of Villehardouin and Clari, which certainly cannot be suspected of flattery, depict him as being at the peak of strength, full of physical and moral courage). When the doge could not do so, his son or some other relative would command the fleet. However, once the doge became definitively a magistrate, the top magistrate in the country, though many admirals became doges, very few doges became admirals once they had been elected to the supreme office. Examples of the former are Giovanni Soranzo who, before being elected doge,

At the end of the 17th century Venice's ancient glory seemed to be reviving. Francesco Morosini reconquered the whole of the Morea in a series of victories over the Turkish fleets. Shown here are some relics of his campaign. Left: a three-branched lantern from Morosini's galley. Below: painting depicting a naval battle between Venetians and Turks. Bottom: a prayer-book with a pistol encased in it which belonged to Morosini.

had devastated the Genoese colonies of Kaffa and Phocaea and had commanded the Venetian forces against Ferrara; Lorenzo Celsi who had been *capitano in Golfo*, or Marco Corner, and later Giovanni Bembo, Francesco Molin and Alvise II Mocenigo, who had all been captain-generals *da mar*. Of the doges who became admirals, Cristoforo Moro, at the time of the projected and later abandoned crusade of 1463–64 accepted the command of the fleet unwillingly: the death of Pius II,

which marked the end of the crusade also ended his military command – to his enormous relief, it would seem. The attempt to entrust to Francesco Erizzo, the tried and courageous general *da mar*, the naval command in 1645 failed because the poor doge was too far gone in years, and mounting responsibilities sent him out of his mind. So we come to Francesco Morosini, the "Peloponnesian," twice elected captain-general while doge, and who died during his second term of office as general. However, these elections, which incurred enormous constitutional complications given the mass of political duties which the doge had to neglect in his absence, were purely arbitrary. Morosini is an exception to this rule, in that his seafaring experience was deemed indispensable, and he exercised a charismatic power over the crews which it seemed opportune to take into account.

Normally the main naval offices in the last two or three centuries of the Republic were divided up as follows, in times of peace: at the apex there was the *provveditore generale da mar* (right up to the loss of Crete, there was also a *provveditore generale* in Candia). After him came the *provveditore generale* of Dalmatia and Albania, with a base at Zara, and the *capitano in Golfo*, who was responsible for the security of the Adriatic.

The Venetian armada was divided into two branches: the *armata grossa* and the *armata sottile*, the "greater" and "lesser" fleets, *i.e.* the sailing fleet and the rowing fleet (ships for the one and galleys for the other). The second in command of the rowing fleet, after the *provveditore generale*, was the *provveditore d'armata*. The *governator de' condannati* was a kind of commander of the crews. Each of the galleasses was commanded by a *governatore*, while the galleys were each commanded by a *sopracomito*. All these were patricians, elected by the *Maggior Consiglio*, as were the *nobili di galera*, the seconds-in-command of the oar-powered ships.

The sailing fleet was commanded by the *provveditore* extraordinary of the fleet, the admiral, and the *patrona delle navi*. Each sailing-ship had a captain aided by two other officers. Subaltern duties were not carried out by patricians and fell to *almiranti* (the commanders of general-bearing ships), *comiti*, helmsmen, and on galleys, *aguzzini* and *aguzzinotti*. They were responsible for the

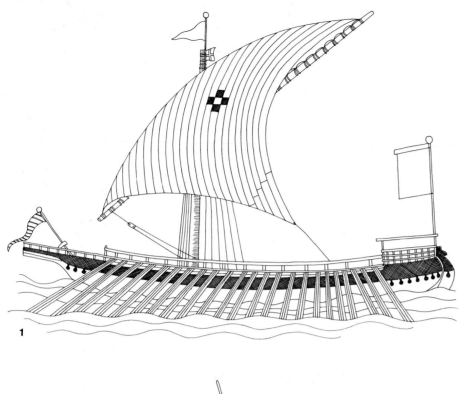

MASTERY OF THE SEA: LONGSHIPS

Two types of vessel were in use in the Mediterranean during the thousand years of Venice's history. These were cogs, and galleys. The basic difference between these two lay in their method of propulsion: the cogs proceeded only under sail, while the galleys used both sail and oar power. They were not of course rowed throughout the voyage, but only when manoeuvering in port, when the wind was light or slack, and when engaged in the rapid manoeuvers necessary in combat. The two types of vessel differed more than they resembled each other, and when technical improvements were introduced as a result of voyages in the Atlantic, the cog came to replace the galley. The main reason for this was that the cog could carry more cargo (or, in war, more cannon) with a smaller crew. Thus the galley slowly declined.

Until the 16th century the oarsmen in the galleys were free men. At the end of the Republic there were still galleys in the Arsenal but as early as 1783 the French ship *Pyroscaphe* had sailed up the Saône under steam.

5

The galley had long, slender lines, because long sides were necessary to accommodate the oarsmen: the more oarsmen, the greater the power.

In the earliest illustrations (1) the oars are grouped in twos or threes. The benches were set at a slightly oblique angle (2), and each bench sat two or three oarsmen, each with one oar. This method demanded equal strength and skill in all the oarsmen. Later, in the 16th century, it was found more convenient to put three or four oarsmen to a single oar (3). These oars were longer and heavier, but much less skill was required on the part of the crew.

Galleys carried one (1), two (7), or three (6) masts and were lateen rigged. Note that the 18th century galleass (7) was no longer armed with a bow ram. This had become outmoded as a weapon with the advent of cannon, and it was replaced by a bowsprit on which a jib could be hoisted forward of the foremast.

An important part was played at the Battle of Lepanto by the six galleasses which were positioned in front of the 202 Venetian and allied galleys. The galleass was taller, heavier and larger than the galley and although it was slower, it was heavily armed with cannon on the forecastle. Illustrated here are an 18th century galleass from a work by Coronelli (4), and another 18th-century one (6) voyaging under sail, with its oars raised. Figure 7 is a two-masted galley, also by Coronelli, showing its internal construction.

Galleys were also sometimes used for trade because of their ability to travel under oar-power when the wind dropped and because their large crew provided a strong defense in case of need. Around the end of the first quarter of the 14th century, the Venetians introduced the large galley which carried more than the normal type. It has been calculated that they could hold 200 tons of cargo, and carried a crew of 200. Figure 5 is an illustration of a large galley taken from an engraving by Reuwich in Breydenbach's *Peregrinatio* to the Holy Land (1483–4). Not all the details are perfectly clear. The enclosure on the starboard side near the stern was used to hold live animals, which served as a supply of meat.

7

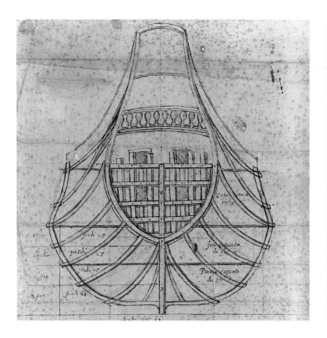

crews of oarsmen, who, from the second half of the 16th century were no longer volunteers, but slaves – apart from a tiny percentage selected by lot from among the inhabitants of Venice, Dalmatia and the Ionian isles, they were Turkish or Barbary prisoners, or common criminals who were condemned to the rowers' ranks in chains.

In times of war, a captain-general *da mar* was elected to be commander-in-chief holding wider powers. He was aided by the *provveditore generale*, the *provveditore* for the fleet and the other high naval officials, who were referred to as *capi da mar*, "commanders for the sea dominion," and with him made up the decisional council or *consulta*. The Senate in fact would send orders which would arrive at their destination at least ten or fifteen days later, but the commander-in-chief was ob-

liged to assemble the council for consultation in order to apply them (or if they had not arrived, in order to pass on his own decision). It depended on the authority and powers of persuasion of the captain whether his directives prevailed or not, and they became official once approved by the *consulta*. This then, was a democratic system of military leadership, and there were cases when consultation was extended to all the *sopracomiti* and *governatori*, even to all the crews.

Naval officers dressed in a breastplate and coat of mail, over which they wore a mantle called the *romana* which was more or less richly decorated according to their rank, and fastened on the shoulder with large, oval, metal buttons. On their heads they wore the characteristic flat hat, and in their hands carried the rod of command, which

Above, left: section of an 18th-century galley (State Archives, Venice). Above: model of the Capitana Savoina, *one of the galleys used as a combat vessel at the battle of Lepanto. Below: longitudinal section of a galley, drawing from 1747 (State Archives, Venice). There was no sharp distinction between warships and trading-vessels, and cargo galleys could be quickly armed for battle.*

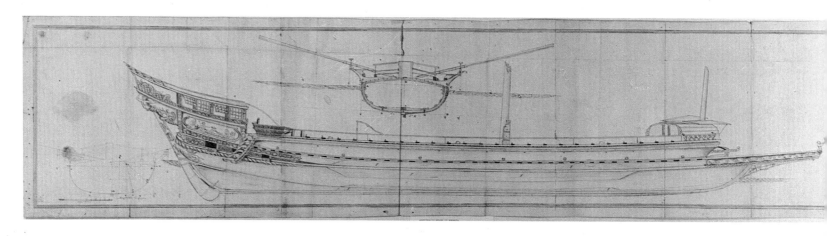

could be (like that of Francesco Morosini) made of tortoiseshell and gold, but was more often of ebony or ivory. Sebastiano Venier, the victor of Lepanto, went into the battle from which he was to emerge victorious in a strange garb: in slippers, because he had a bad leg, but carrying a pike in his hands, which he used with gusto in the assault on Ali Pasha's ship of command.

Normally, the captain-general sailed on a "mongrel galley" as it was known, because it was powered by sails and oars. It had an awning with scarlet and white stripes, and on the poop deck a beacon with three lights, to mark the captain's grade. The other *capi da mar* were also distinguished by the *fanò* on the poop deck of their ship or galley. The most beautiful that can still be seen today must be that of the captain-general Andrea Pisaro, who died in 1718 in the explosion which blew up the citadel of Corfu: it has three branches, and is very finely carved, and stands in the entrance to the captain's palace, now the headquarters of the Venice Conservatory of Music. There are others, some in precious metals, including silver. When their period of office was over, the *capi da mar* would take them home, together with the coats of arms from the poop deck and the pennants of the general's "mongrel ship," to decorate the entrance-hall of their palaces.

As far as the actual vessels were concerned, the most hardy, agile and aggressive was still the galley: it was very narrow in proportion to its length, and very low in the water. For this reason the decks were often swept by waves and it was one of the most uncomfortable vessels that could be imagined, all the more so in that besides the oarsmen, who were obliged to survive on a few square inches of wooden bench covered with cowhide, there were crossbowmen and landing parties – a whole crowd of people who ate, slept and attended to all their daily needs, on board. In such conditions, a long voyage on a rough sea must have been a real penance, though there were those who found the constant call of the helmsmen and the rhythmic thud of the oars restful or even pleasantly soporific. As for the galleasses, they were much longer galleys (more than 100 meters in length) and slightly broader, and they bristled with cannon.

Rations for the crews, slaves and sailors, as well as crossbowmen, arquebusiers and gunners con-

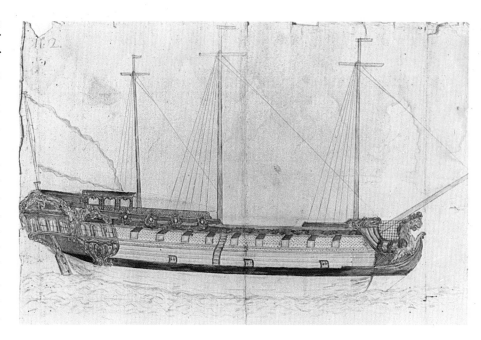

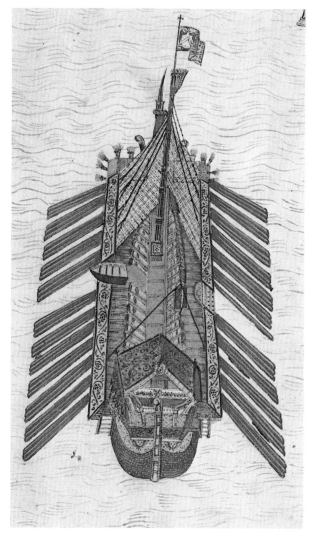

Above: drawing showing modifications to be made to a galley, enclosed in a despatch from the provveditore generale da mar, *1746 (State Archives, Venice). Right: Trireme (from Cristoforo Canal's* Milizia Marittima. *Biblioteca Marciana, Venice). The Arsenal was able to produce remarkable numbers of ships because of its excellent organization and the skill of its specialized workforce. The technical and industrial side of the Arsenal was under the supervision of the* magnifico armiraglio, *who oversaw the work of the* protomagistri *or foremen in charge of the main groups of workmen. The state-controlled enterprise of the Arsenal was administered by a council, the* Eccellentissima Banca, *consisting of three senators, the* provveditori dell'Arsenal, *and three* patroni, *members of the* Maggior Consiglio. *The* patroni *were on duty for shifts of a fortnight, sleeping in the Arsenal, keeping the keys of the storehouses and workshops, and inspecting the guards.*

MASTERY OF THE SEA: BROAD SHIPS

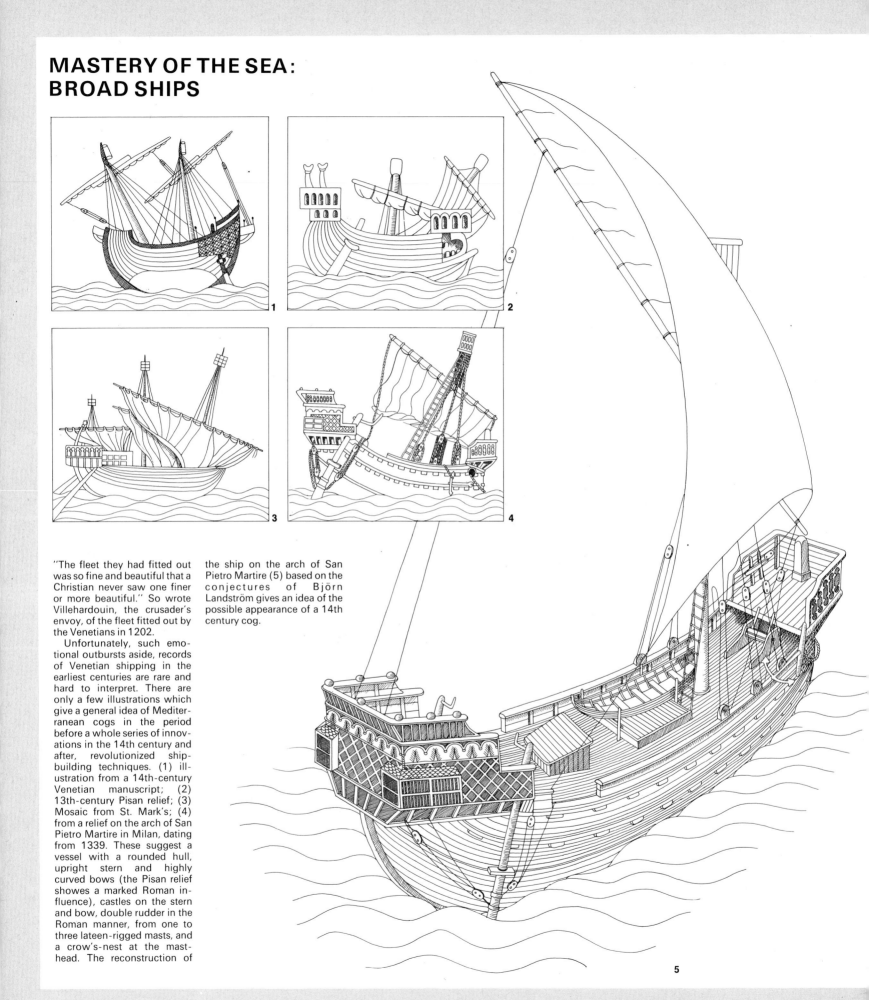

"The fleet they had fitted out was so fine and beautiful that a Christian never saw one finer or more beautiful." So wrote Villehardouin, the crusader's envoy, of the fleet fitted out by the Venetians in 1202.

Unfortunately, such emotional outbursts aside, records of Venetian shipping in the earliest centuries are rare and hard to interpret. There are only a few illustrations which give a general idea of Mediterranean cogs in the period before a whole series of innovations in the 14th century and after, revolutionized shipbuilding techniques. (1) illustration from a 14th-century Venetian manuscript; (2) 13th-century Pisan relief; (3) Mosaic from St. Mark's; (4) from a relief on the arch of San Pietro Martire in Milan, dating from 1339. These suggest a vessel with a rounded hull, upright stern and highly curved bows (the Pisan relief showes a marked Roman influence), castles on the stern and bow, double rudder in the Roman manner, from one to three lateen-rigged masts, and a crow's-nest at the masthead. The reconstruction of the ship on the arch of San Pietro Martire (5) based on the conjectures of Björn Landström gives an idea of the possible appearance of a 14th century cog.

5

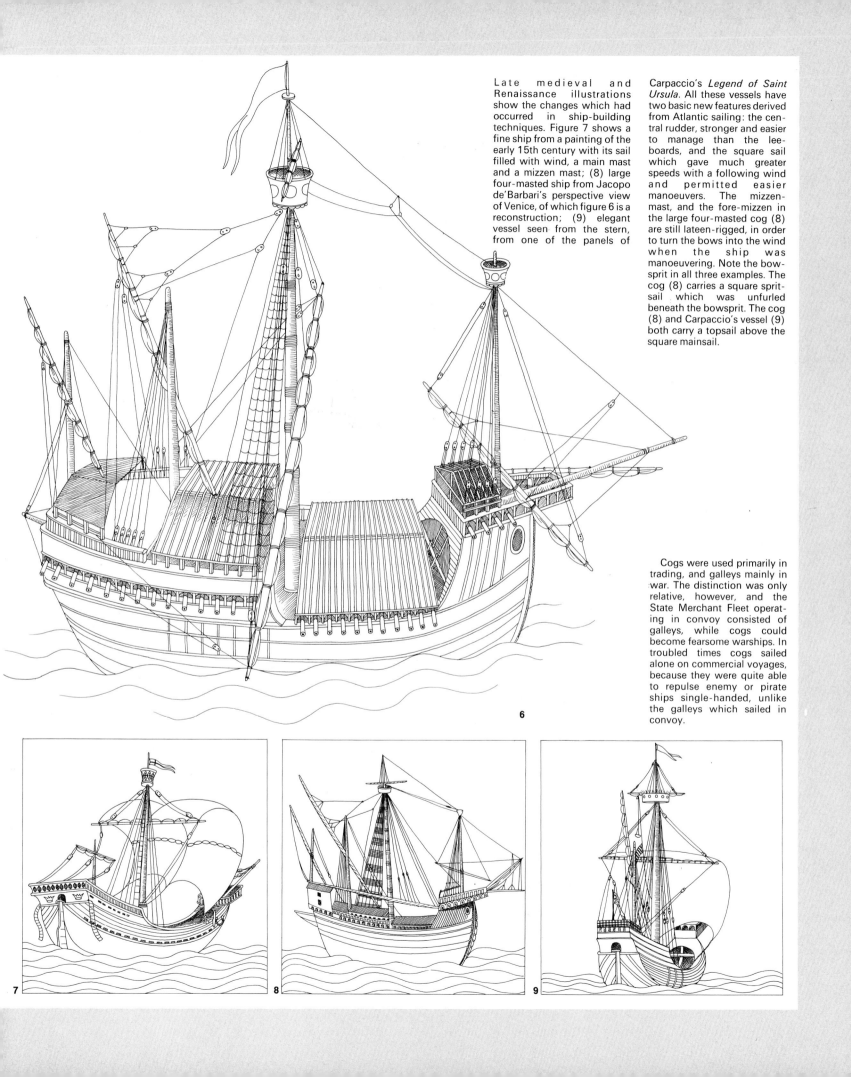

Late medieval and Renaissance illustrations show the changes which had occurred in ship-building techniques. Figure 7 shows a fine ship from a painting of the early 15th century with its sail filled with wind, a main mast and a mizzen mast; (8) large four-masted ship from Jacopo de'Barbari's perspective view of Venice, of which figure 6 is a reconstruction; (9) elegant vessel seen from the stern, from one of the panels of Carpaccio's *Legend of Saint Ursula*. All these vessels have two basic new features derived from Atlantic sailing: the central rudder, stronger and easier to manage than the lee-boards, and the square sail which gave much greater speeds with a following wind and permitted easier manoeuvers. The mizzen-mast, and the fore-mizzen in the large four-masted cog (8) are still lateen-rigged, in order to turn the bows into the wind when the ship was manoeuvering. Note the bow-sprit in all three examples. The cog (8) carries a square sprit-sail which was unfurled beneath the bowsprit. The cog (8) and Carpaccio's vessel (9) both carry a topsail above the square mainsail.

Cogs were used primarily in trading, and galleys mainly in war. The distinction was only relative, however, and the State Merchant Fleet operating in convoy consisted of galleys, while cogs could become fearsome warships. In troubled times cogs sailed alone on commercial voyages, because they were quite able to repulse enemy or pirate ships single-handed, unlike the galleys which sailed in convoy.

6

7

8

9

Above: panel belonging to the Guild of Carpenters (Museo Correr, Venice). The carpenters were numerically the strongest body of workmen in the Arsenal and their Guild was very important. The bell which summoned the workmen to their duties was known as the marangona *or "carpenter." Below: drawing showing different sections for galley-building, from Pre Todaro's* Instructione sul modo di fabricare galere, *a manuscript preserved in the Biblioteca Marciana, Venice.*

sisted mainly of the biscuit prepared in Venice in the bakeries looking out over the Riva degli Schiavoni near the Arsenal, but also in other establishments scattered throughout the Venetian empire. The contracts for the manufacture of this essential food, served in a broth, softened with oil and occasionally with sea water added, were often discussed in the Senate and the *Maggior Consiglio*: there were always suspicions of fraud on the part of the suppliers and of illicit profits made by commanders. Even the upright Leonardo Foscolo, who, as we have noted, was proclaimed doge by the sailors without being elected by the *Quarantuno*, was suspected of having made something on the supply of victuals. It was probably a false suspicion, since one of the constant characteristics of the long history of the Republic was the practice

of one faction or another accusing military commanders of incapacity, cowardice, insubordination, abuse of power, rashness, but above all, of embezzlement. This was an extreme consequence of a regime based on a parliamentary system and reciprocal controls. Naval commanders had to be very careful about what they did: some, such as the *general dottor*, the learned general Canal whom we have already described, arriving always just too late, at the time of the Negropont war, were so frightened by the possible consequences of their scant experience that they called the *consulta* together for every tiny decision, and on the whole, for fear of making a mistake, never decided anything. This did not prevent brave and self-assured commanders, such as Sebastiano Venier, Lazzaro Mocenigo or Lorenzo Marcello from taking very serious decisions on their own. The greatest example must be that of Francesco Morosini: abandoned by his few, meager French allies, he took the very grave responsibility for the surrender of Candia, which had been under siege for 25 years, and could no longer be held in any way. But he did not get away with it, in spite of the *a posteriori* approval of the Senate: the *avogador* Correr issued a decree calling him to trial on the counts of cowardice, desertion of his post, disobeying superior orders and all this was aggravated by the fact that he had lied by describing the stronghold as being in an extreme state whereas in fact it could have resisted for longer. A great parliamentary battle resulted in the *Maggior Consiglio*, because Morosini was defended by a great politician, Giovanni Sagredo, an expert on matters of the Orient. In the end, with a crushing majority, the *Maggior Consiglio* declared there was no case to answer. However, the common people were tenacious in their ill-feeling towards the man who, albeit with every good reason, had conceded what was left of the Cretan empire, and in their bitterness, boycotted the ceremony of Morosini's assumption of the high office of procurator of St. Mark.

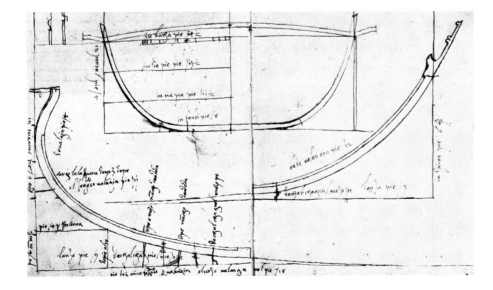

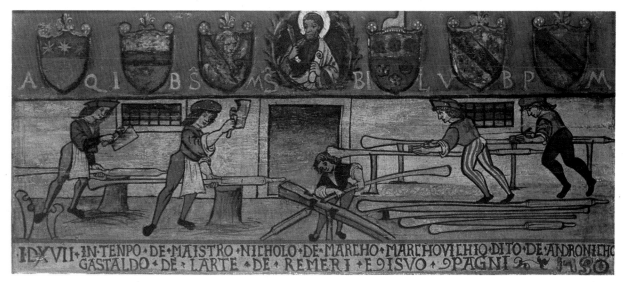

Left: panel depicting the Guild of Oarmakers. The various stages of oar-making are illustrated (Museo Correr, Venice). The Arsenal workmen were known as arsenalotti, *and their fame stretched far beyond the city; in 1696 Tsar Peter the Great asked for their work. The craft of ship-building was handed down from father to son. Beginners completed their apprenticeship aboard a galley; then they attended a school in the Arsenal where they learned reading, writing and the principles of arithmetic. Although wages were not especially high, the* arsenalotti *enjoyed a large number of privileges such as bonus payments, free housing for employees and master-craftsmen, free allowances of wine, and permission to use wood left over from their work.*

Fortresses and Generals

Among the Venetian magistratures were *provveditori* and inquisitors for the artillery and the fortresses, and I have quite a few times praised the Venetian fortified structures which to this day remain intact in Crete, Cyprus, Greece and Dalmatia. Many of these fortifications were the work of experts who came from mainland families which had been absorbed into the patriciate and which traditionally had the office of supervising military construction. In theory they were elected, but in practice the duty went from father to son. These were the Brescia family of Martinengo, mainly, and the Friuli family of Savorgnan. However, many patricians of ancient Venetian origin also understood military engineering. An example is Agostino Sagredo, to whom we owe the extraordinary fort of Palamede which overlooks the fortified city of Nauplia referred to by the Venetians as the Naples of Romania. In times of war the Venetian nobles were often voluntarily joined by mainland nobles, who would forget their resentments when faced with a common enemy, just as the Venetians would forget the supposed inferiority of their subjects. The families of Avogadro from Brescia and the Avogadro degli Azzoni from Treviso provided commanders for warships. The troops on land and, when necessary, those for combined action when the army had to back up the navy, were commanded by a whole series of *condottieri, i.e.* gentlemen who exercized the prerogative to recruit armed men and command

them. In effect they were the last vestiges of the Renaissance *condottieri* and were, in the main, feudal lords who handed down within the family this office which allowed them to direct troops bearing their names and coat of arms. They included the counts of Porcia, the Savorgnan, Colloredo and Strassoldo families, all from the Friuli, the Collato family from Treviso, the da Porto family from Vicenza, the Suardi from Bergamo, the Scotti and Martinengo from Brescia, the Pompei from Verona, and many others. There were also members of famous Italian families who traditionally served the Republic under arms: these included the Orsini from Rome, one of whom, Paolo Giordano, duke of Bracciano, commanded the Venetian infantry at Lepanto. On other occasions the Republic called on foreign generals such as the *general*, the count *da sbarco* Königsmark, a Swede, who commanded Francesco Morosini's troops (and ordered the famous cannonade that blew up the Parthenon, which the Turks were using as a powder store); or the Prussian general, von der Schulenburg, who was a most courageous defender of Corfu during the last siege.

Neutrality and the End

The unarmed neutrality which, in the last century of its existence, became axiomatic for the Republic in all the wars which ravaged Europe, transformed the continental territories into fields of manoeuver for foreign armies and contributed to creating the recipe for the final catastrophe. The events which led to this catastrophe are well known: the French armies, commanded by general Bonaparte, the future Napoleon I, descended on Italy and, after a first series of victories as swift as they were unexpected, they imposed surrender on the Piedmontese forces, the first opposition they had met. This was in 1796. The unexpected fall of Piedmont, considered the military power *par excellence* and the first line of defense for Italy, took everyone by surprise. But behind Piedmont was Austrian Lombardy, and the imperial armies were considered excellent and very well commanded (they were headed by an old, well-tried general, Marshal Beaulieu). Instead, Beaulieu too fell unexpectedly, and the unscrupulous French general hurled himself suddenly into the territories of the Republic. Moreover, his mentality rejected the traditional respect for the rules of the game. For him, Venetian neutrality was sacred until it no longer suited him, and then he was quite

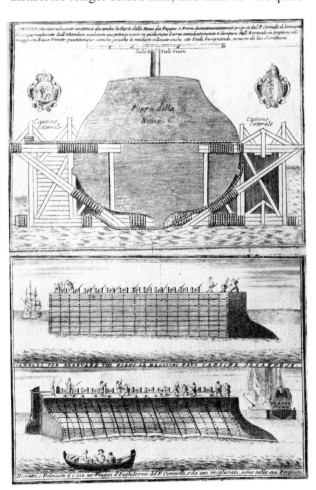

prepared to violate it, and did so with an unscrupulousness hitherto unknown, and always with an excuse at the ready.

There followed a very difficult period for the Venetian rulers, for the towns invaded by the French troops rose up against what they called "the Venetian yoke." In a sense this was a repetition of what happened at the time of the league of Cambrai: the local elite, who felt they had been excluded from the centralized system of Venetian government, now rebelled and took as their own the slogans of the French Revolution, raising the "banners of liberty" in their town-squares. Naturally the French aided and approved these demonstrations – when they did not openly provoke them, that is. The reaction of the rural peasants, who were almost always *marchesche*, or followers of St. Mark, now as in 1509 supplied Bonaparte with excellent motives for accusing the Republic of having been the one to violate its own neutrality by inciting the people against his army. In any case, Bonaparte required far more of Venice than normal respect of neutrality could provide – and what he wanted, he took: provisions, arms, munitions and even fortresses.

The government of Venice had been gradually reduced to the Collegio, then to *consulte* or special conferences: the Senate was phased out in its turn. The lack of adequate forces, and above all the awareness of the profound weakness of the Venetian state structure, led the rulers to adopt a policy of appeasement towards the hot-headed general, who always spoke to them in threatening, violent and imperious terms. Their only hope of a victory lay in the imperial forces, but every general produced by Austria was matched by the military talent of the young Bonaparte. Between badly conducted negotiations by men who were unsuitable and conditioned by prejudices, and the cunning of the general who, faced with the docility of his opponents, made ever wilder demands, the situation went from bad to worse. The popular insurrection of the "Veronese Easter," as it is known, which caused the killing of some French soldiers, and the incident provoked by a French ship trying to enter the port of Venice by force, whereupon, after the traditional threats, the soldiers guarding the city justifiably turned their cannon upon it and then boarded it, causing the death of the commander, all gave Bonaparte the

One difficulty in sailing on the lagoon was the shallowness of the waters, a problem which became increasingly serious as ships increased in tonnage. Illustrated on these two pages is the ingenious method devised for "lifting" ships by means of floating rafts known as "camels" which were attached to the sides of the ship. Left, drawing by Vincenzo Maria Coronelli, map-maker to the Republic (1650–1718), preserved in the Museo Storico Navale, Venice. The drawing opposite shows a sailing ship of 74 cannon hoisted by these devices. The ship is the Aquilea Valiera, *bearing the Valier family's coat-of-arms (Museo Storico Navale, Venice).*

cue for decisive action against the Venetian aristocratic government, which he accused of the worst possible crimes. The general wanted to defend his rear guard during the attack he was launching against Vienna, and so he wanted to ensure that the government in Venice was on his side, controlled and directed by men of his own choosing. This is how the painful final act came about: after a peremptory ultimatum from Bonaparte, the *Maggior Consiglio*, acting on the doge Lodovico Manin's proposal, decided to abdicate, suggesting as a remedy for the evils befalling the motherland, the election of a representative government. The gesture was a noble one, but the circumstances in which it came about were not noble at all: the sound of gunfire of Slavonian soldiers who were embarking to go back home (the Veneto government had in fact renounced all forms of defense) was mistaken for the beginning of an uprising, and the patrician Maggior Consiglio hurriedly voted in the end of its own reign, that had lasted 500 years.

All this happened in May 1797, when Bonaparte had already come to an agreement at Leoben with the emperor's officials to concede the Venetian mainland to Austria. This is not the place to analyze the factors which drove the daring general to finish off his handiwork with the concession to Austria of the city of Venice itself, as well as Dalmatia and Istria. It is a fact that, while he imposed a democratic constitution on Venice (though there was nothing democratic or representative about the choice of the members of the new government, the "Provisional Municipality": they were all people chosen by the general on the recommendation of the French diplomatic attaché in Venice), nevertheless, the general was already thinking of cancelling her out forever as an independent state from the map of Europe. When, in October 1797, the treaty of Campoformido officially sanctioned her destruction, the most stunned, the most wounded, were precisely those who in good faith had hailed the arrival of the French troops as the event which was to have opened up a new chapter in the history of Venice, that of democracy.

After Campoformido then, what remained of the Venetian empire passed under other authorities. Istria, Dalmatia and the mainland (apart from Bergamo, Brescia and Crema, which went to the Cisalpine Republic) went to the Austrians. The Ionian isles went to the French. Later they were to fall to the English before being attached once more to the Greek realm.

This brought to an end for ever the ancient Venetian order. The memory of the Republic was to be constantly maligned, first by the man who had subjugated it, then from those who took over after him. Austria held Venice from 1799 to 1806, then from 1806 to 1813 France came back in the form of the Kingdom of Italy, founded by Napoleon Bonaparte and entrusted by him to his stepson Eugène de Beauharnais, who was viceroy and governor-general. It was a black period: the sack carried out by the *armée d'Italie* in 1797 was followed by new looting, destruction and ruin of this marvellous city that was undergoing domination for the first time in its existence. Above all, there was a tragic impoverishment which affected all social classes and reached its nadir at the time of the continental blockade, decreed by Napoleon in order to strike and isolate England, but which had dramatic repercussions on the very subsistence of a city that was first and foremost a port. Then Austria came back and stayed until 1866, apart from the brief interlude of Daniele Manin's revolutionary republic: this was a heroic and maybe useless enterprise, but perhaps it was a necessary demonstration to the whole world, of the courage and vigour of the Venetian people, vindicating the fatal resignation of the aristocratic Republic, 50 years earlier.

As we have said, after its demise the Republic was discredited in all kinds of ways by its new rulers. The truth is that French and French-inspired propaganda sullied its memory on both a petty and a grand scale, count Daru, a faithful follower of Napoleon, took it upon himself to give a pseudo-scientific veneer to the worst calumnies concerning the aristocratic government, in his monumental *Histoire de la République de Venise* in which he did not hesitate to make recourse to false documents or ones skilfully adapted to fit his thesis. Austria however formal and correct in her own rigorous, rational structures, set about abolishing every memory of the Republic, which she felt was still too rooted in the minds of the citizens of the capital.

Thus, just as Napoleon had ordered when still general Bonaparte, that all the Lions of St. Mark

Sea-shore with jetty *by Marco Ricci, born in Belluno and raised in Venice (Museo Civico, Padua). The detail reproduced here is of the greatest interest, showing a ship lying on its side with workmen caulking its hull. Venice's greatness was built on the sea, and everything to do with the sea. Sailing, ships and the men who lived and worked on ships penetrated deep into the hearts of the Venetian people. Even a painter like Marco Ricci who normally avoided this kind of scene could not escape its temptations. His account is clearly and precisely rendered.*

carved in stone on walls and columns to indicate the presence of Venice's power should be chiselled away and destroyed, Austria made haste to wipe out everything that had traditionally marked out patrician rule, beginning with the title "N.H.," *Nobil Uomo*, (nobleman), the only distinction afforded to members of the *Maggior Consiglio*. Later, Austria required the ex-patricians to fit in with the rest of the nobles in her vast empire, taking as sovereign confirmation either acceptance of the simple title "noble" (without the addition of "man," something which gave rise to a certain amount of bitter humour) or ex-patricians could buy the title of count or prince of the Austrian Empire.

Austria set about running the new state by abandoning the methods of the old one. The peace and harmony of relationships between the Italian, Venetian and pro-Venetian elements, and the Slav element in Istria and Dalmatia had been one of the great successes of the Venetian rule. Imperial Austria rekindled old rancours without realizing what damage she was doing, particularly towards herself. In fact, the Italian element was strongly drawn to the appeal of the national *Risorgimento*, to which more than one Dalmatian and Istrian made considerable contributions in terms of ideas

and blood, and the Slav element was not slow in responding to the appeal of pan-Slavism and looking towards Serbia and thinking of a union of southern Slavs, with the tragic results which were to spark off the First World War and all the ensuing dramatic events.

These events, and especially those of the Second World War, were to bring about the definitive end of what remained of the Venetian presence on the Istrian and Dalmatian shores. Descendants of the inhabitants of cities of the Byzantine empire who had called upon Pietro Orseolo II for help, emigrated in the main to Italy. Even the names of the cities were made Slavic.

The official *damnatio memoriae* of the Venetian dominion has not stopped Yugoslav scholars researching that era with interest and success, an era which now seems remote. The same kind of study is being carried out in present-day Greece, where a fairly extensive historical period is officially entitled the "Venetocracy." In the ancient Venetian kingdoms, above all in the Ionian islands, the memory of the Republic is deeply rooted in the population, who recall it with a shade of nostalgia even after so much time and so many events.

Eleven Centuries
of Independence – why?

One hundred and eighty-two years have passed since the fall of the Republic of Venice and 1,282 since the election of the first doge, the fabled Pauluccio Anafesto. If we take the date of that election as the point of departure of the great period of history of which Venice was the main protagonist, we see before us more than 12 whole centuries, and only one of them, the 18th century, was a period of decline. Few states in the world have survived for such a long period of time.

It is not only a question of duration. There was the disconcerting phenomenon of a people made up of fishermen, salt-workers and boatmen, becoming central to the history of the Mediterranean. They built a city, as beautiful and as splendid as could be imagined, but with a population that never exceeded a maximum of 170–180,000 inhabitants, but which nevertheless exerted power over a territorial expanse that was vast and scattered: in Italy, from the Adda to the Isonzo and from the Alps to the Po; and outside Italy, Istria and Dalmatia, part of Albania, the Ionian islands, part of the Epirus, the Peloponnese and Attica, the Aegean islands, Crete and Cyprus, not to speak of the innumerable bases and concessions in cities and ports both far and near, from Ferrara to Constantinople, from Trebizond to Acre.

This city was also able to stand up against the great and powerful on land, against monarchs whose territories were at least a hundred times more extensive and highly-populated than hers. Venice influenced them, worried them, frightened them. With equal audacity, though professing and practising firm religious principles, she held out against the spiritual weapons of the popes in times when the popes used them as instruments in political battles, and with them were able to bend the most powerful and obstinate adversaries.

How was all this possible? We would like to analyze the phenomenon and isolate at least some of the rational explanations.

Let us first consider the constraints of nature. Right from earliest times, Venice's existence has been influenced by her natural environment (and still is today). The lagoon, a source of riches (salt) and sustenance (fish) was also a very valuable defense against invaders. However, it could be treacherous and dangerous. Changes in tides and currents could obliterate important towns, such as Malamocco, which, formerly the capital, was nibbled away and gradually destroyed by the lagoon, to the extent that we are not even sure exactly where it was. The rivers which flowed into the lagoon could bury the city with the silt they carried; by altering the balance of fresh and salt water, they could creak marshes, and render the air unhealthy and the environment uninhabitable. Moreover the islands and islets, on which Torcello was to rise up first, and later Venice, like others in the Venetian estuary on which people were living, were only rarely made of firm ground, and had to be banked up, strengthened and protected before any attempt could be made to build on them. The site of present-day Venice was achieved little by little, often by the most rudimentary means – fencing and palisades made from rushes, or the "land reclamation" carried out by the most far-flung inhabitants of the Veneto marshlands, in the dark night of prehistory.

This was probably the source of the habit of daily battle for physical survival. Long before the means were available for the huge hydraulic operations in which Venice was to become expert, the inhabitants of the lagoon busied themselves creating dams and diverting rivers and canals, in effect, adapting nature to their convenience. This was a way of life which probably hardened the ancient Venetian temperament, and trained men to twist circumstances to their own advantage.

Then there were human constraints. What lay beyond the lagoon, on the mainland, during the long period of Venice's emergence, was an ever more hostile and alien world. The refugees who reached the lagoon islands, though circumstances were probably less dramatic than those described by legend, made a choice which separated them from the social and political life of the hinterland, even though they maintained property and communications. As Venice gradually grew, asserted itself and became richer, the world beyond the lagoons became ever more hostile, more envious and more aggressive. After the Longobards, the Franks and the German emperors, there were the great feudal lords, then the great city-states and the signories, some more important than others but all deeply and instinctively hostile to Venice. She represented something "different,"

something elusive and impossible to subjugate, something intangible and powerful, in spite of everyone. Greed and envy were the basic attitudes of the many who attacked her lands (after the passing of the signories, there were the great national and international states). Her air of being different, though being the best way for her to defend herself, also aroused implacable hatreds and hostilities.

The sea was her only available kingdom and here the same thing happened. Venice's reliance on the sea was favoured by many factors: the nearness of forests, where there was an abundance of the basic materials for shipbuilding, the beaches which formed natural harbours, the port facilities offered by the lagoon and the distant location of the Moslem and Norman centers of aggression. All these advantages however, did not exempt her from the necessity of conquering land inch by inch against all manner of enemy and rival. Here too then a perpetual state of necessity, if not emergency existed, which bent the will and sharpened the wits, and allowed neither rest nor sleep.

So it was right up to the end. Even in later times, when the obsessive shadow of Spanish oppression had faded, it was Austrian aggression which obliged Venice to keep on the look-out and take care of herself, to be prepared for the worst, even on the commercial level, given the deadly competition of the Hapsburg ports, Trieste and Fiume, and with all the Mediterranean invaded by ships from the West (and not only these: the Russians were also to send a naval attachment to the Adriatic; not many years from the end, the Republic again thought of using the subtle weapons of diplomacy to gain the support of that enormous and expanding empire and so shake off the imminent Austrian menace). It was only in this last century that lucidity of vision was no longer equalled by the possibility of putting ideas into practice. The war against the Turks and the loss of most of the Levant had weakened the former queen of the seas too much, and the difference in size compared with the European states was by now excessive.

All the same, many centuries, indeed all the centuries of Venice's existence, passed in a state of constant emergency that must have contributed to the sense of total involvement which the Venetians in all that time dedicated to everything they touched: trade and politics, war and diplomacy. This involvement was motivated by the awareness that it was indispensable for survival, and that for survival it was not enough to keep one foot on home ground: they had to be capable of imposing their own will and if necessary of attacking before being attacked.

There was a second factor: the constant prevalence in all aspects of political and social life, of the "public" over the "private." In such a context as the Italian one, where everything was oriented towards what the Florentine historians called *il particulare, i.e.* the interests of the individual, with private interest superseding everything (there are notable and constant examples of this from the Middle Ages to the present day), the Venetian attitude stands out as an exceptional phenemenon. However, it is also an exceptional phenomenon in the larger context of Europe.

In effect, in the Venetian world the sacrifice of the *particulare* to what was considered the public good, was a rule from which no one was exempt, not even those individuals or social classes placed above the rest in order to exert power over society

as a whole. This goes back to remotest times, as far as the proto-history of the Venetian dogate: the alternation of the first rulers was imposed by the prevalence of this or that faction, or this or that political influence, but from a certain point onwards, it seems to have derived precisely from the subjection of the various dynasties and candidates to the requirements of the public good at that particular moment. In this way, the two dynasties of the Parteciaco and Candiano families seemed to alternate almost automatically depending on whether the city politics were in need of diplomatic flexibility or of a strong and strict military rule. However, these are only suppositions. It is instead a reality that the popular assemblies, when public service became their task too, adapted themselves to apparently contradictory decisions if the situation called for it: political parties, never by definition in agreement, would become united automatically when faced with danger or with a good opportunity to be grasped.

There is more. As we know, Venice was an aristocratic Republic for 500 years. This period is based only on the formal *serrata* of the *Maggior*

The Greek Favourite in the Harem, *by Francesco Guardi (von Thyssen Bornemisza Collection, Lugano). A nostalgic view of the East. In war and peace, from Byzantine to Turkish times, the Venetians were always irresistibly drawn to the East. The taste for the exotic which was widespread in 18th-century Europe had its roots in Venice.*

Below: gouache by Francesco Guardi showing the church of the Scalzi, the Grand Canal, and in the center a canal now filled in to form the present Rio Terrà Lista di Spagna (Ecole des Beaux Arts, Paris). Opposite: Interior of St. Mark's by Night by Canaletto (Royal Collection, Windsor Castle). No city has been celebrated by its painters with more zeal and affection than Venice. Paintings of the Venetian scene date back to at least the 15th century. There is always a feeling of intimacy between the painter and the scenes of daily life in the canals, squares and alleys he depicts, a feeling which became more common and affectionate as the Republic drew to its close.

Consiglio. In reality, the aristocracy actually ruled for at least a century and a half before this; indeed, to judge from the constant repetition of the same names in all the documents detailing a decision, the nobles ruled from the very founding of the Venetian state. We can calmly defy anyone to find another aristocracy which, once having gained power, was as concerned to limit, control and contain that power within precise boundaries which precisely coincided with what must have seemed to them the highest conception of the public good.

When one thinks of the harshness of the fiscal impositions on the patriciate, devised by a government made up entirely of patricians in a whole series of emergencies from the wars with Genoa and the Carraresi right up to the Cretan war or Morosini's campaign against the Turks, it must be admitted that for the Venetians, the exercise of power logically coincided with a burden of duties far heavier than those falling to men who exercised no power. The same fact emerges if we note that sanctions affected the patricians in a variety of fields far more severely than they affected the plebeian classes. This was all part of the same reasoning: first the public good, then the private good, which applied equally to the class in power.

Shrewd historians have observed that every discussion between governing bodies uses the adjective "our" to describe the Venetian state, and that therefore the Venetian patriciate had an "hereditary conception" of the state.

As many examples demonstrate amply, rather than a sense of "class possession" there was a sense of civic possession, that is, a collective possession in which not only the patricians but all Venetians considered themselves participants. The adjective "our" recurs in a number of documents regarding not only the patriciate: it resounds in the affirmations, contestations, acclamations and protests of the bourgeoisie and the populace. The fact that each Venetian over long centuries had considered the public cause as "his" cause, is undoubtedly another of the secrets behind the expansion, power and longevity of the Republic.

We have spoken of the severity of the patriciate towards its own members. This too was a logical

reason for Venice's survival in freedom and independence compared with the fate, for example, of her rivals Genoa and Florence. Both before and after the *serrata*, the patriciate always considered itself the depository of a delegated power: so much so that the last decree of the *Maggior Consiglio*, that of the abdication in May 1797, formally "restored" to the people the power it felt had been invested in it by them. It was this delegation of power which justified the severity with which the patrician government defended the people from its own class. This gave rise to a severity that can seem excessive, such as (to cite a single example) the sentence of death inflicted in 1500 on the son of senator Andrea Morosini, who had been found guilty of kissing a girl of the people in a public street and having stolen a jewel from her. But such severity reassured the people and offered them a guarantee against the privileged class becoming oppressive. Furthermore, since the suppression of any fantasies of domination of that class was guaranteed by the State Inquisitors and the Council of Ten, here we have the reason for the popularity of those two institutions, which pamphleteers and caricaturists from the past and the present have always depicted, mistakenly, as instruments of oppression used by the nobles against the common herd.

The absolute prevalence of public interest over private also explains a certain open-mindedness on the part of these two institutions, the Inquisitors and The Council of Ten. When private morality was found to be in opposition to the public interest, it was calmly sacrificed: the defense of Venice could authorize an assembly of good Christians and upright people to decree the suppression of a public enemy, a public danger (always by means of debate and voting). Public enemies, not class enemies: among the victims of these executions there figure a number of corrupt nobles, whose acts of oppression perpetrated against their own subjects had marked them out for a sentence carried out in secret but, which was always passed legally.

We may as well repeat once more: the law and the strictness with which it was observed was yet another of the ingredients which accounted for the longevity and the power of Venice. Goethe, who all things considered was not fond of the Venetians or of Venice, tells of having been present at a

Venice liked to portray herself as Justice. In this painting by Jacobello del Fiore from the beginning of the 14th century the city is depicted with the crown and attributes of Justice, the sword and scales, and with the lions symbolizing St. Mark (Gallerie dell'Accademia, Venice). Throughout the city's long history, the impartiality of its justice was a byword; undoubtedly the rigorous application of the law played an important part in preserving the life and power of the Republic. The personification of Venice opposite, from Giambattista Tiepolo's Neptune Offering the Gifts of the Sea to Venice *(Doge's Palace, Venice) three centuries later is softer and more forbearing in aspect.*

trial in which the morganatic wife of the doge then reigning, Paolo Renier, appeared and lost the case. He says that the Venetians seemed very proud that the wife of their lord was seated on a bench of the *Quarantia* with the other litigants, in conditions of absolute parity.

Compared with all the other Italian states, in any instance and before any tribunal the impartiality of Venetian justice is proverbial. The reader only has to look again at the many examples we have quoted, or else remember that four centuries after the son of the doge Antonio Venier died in prison for having offended the honour of a citizen and his wife, a member of the de Rohan family could have a fashionable, cultured man such as Voltaire beaten in Paris, with impunity.

The concept of the superiority of the public good over any other interest is also the basis for another fundamental moral principle of the Venetians: that which insists that bravery in the face of the enemy, administrative rectitude and fair use of justice are only duties and do not merit particular recognition, whereas incorrect behaviour was suitably publicized to the detri-

ment of whoever had been guilty of it, and the publicizing of the sanctions acted as a fitting deterrent. Everywhere, but above all on the outside walls of the Doge's Palace just under the porticos where gentlemen used to stroll, there are still commemorative tablets naming perpetrators of "enormous incursions" into the coffers of this or that state office, or commanders guilty of having "basely abandoned" some stronghold to the enemy. There are few, indeed there are only two in all, official monuments (to Sebastiano Venier and Francesco Venier) erected by the Republic in honour of great men. Great men had to have monuments set up at their own expense. They could be proud of what they had done, but as far as the state was concerned they had merely done their duty.

In conclusion, it is pointless to conceal a truth which can seem repugnant to our modern sensibilities as sons or grandsons of the French Revolution, brought up to respect the healthy principles of representative democracy (the worst form of government, as Winston Churchill said, but a better system has not yet been found). If Venice was able to maintain her independence 500 years longer than her rival Genoa, which suffered the dominion of other powers, Italian and foreign, right up to the end, if of those 500 years Venice was able to spend at least 400 at the level of a European power, and nearly 300 amid the ranks of the world powers, this is undoubtedly due also to the much deprecated *serrata* of the *Maggior Consiglio* in 1297.

The action taken in 1297 endowed Venice with strong, flexible and vigorous institutions, rescuing her from the chaotic demagogy which dragged Genoa beneath the heels of the Visconti family, the French and the Spaniards. It gave her the oxygen for centuries of prosperity and greatness, without local dictators or foreign lords ever being able to conquer her. This is not only our opinion: it should be enough to quote the pages of great historians whose opinions cannot be suspect, such as Yves Renouard or Frédéric Chabod.

Times were certainly not ripe for representative democracy, and the chaos of popular assemblies exposed to the influence of this or that leader, this or that demagogue, was certainly no terrain for the establishing of any long-lasting form of authentic democracy.

Left: the banquet given for
Clement, Duke of Bavaria and
Archbishop of Cologne in the
Casino Nani on the Giudecca
(School of Longhi,
Ca'Rezzonico, Venice).
Opposite, above: wedding
banquet for the Polignac
marriage in the Gradenigo
mansion at Carpenedo, watercolour by Francesco Guardi
(Museo Correr, Venice).
Below: Young Woman with a
Parrot (detail) by
Giambattista Tiepolo. She
might be the model of the
sumptuous feminine beauties
of whom Aretino spoke: "The
Venetians want solid stuff, not
Petrarchan fancies." With the
18th century, Venetian joie de
vivre became more intense
than ever. Famous visitors
came in greater numbers than
ever before and were
splendidly received. Frederick
IV of Denmark and Norway
was the guest of the Foscarini;
the king of Poland was
received by the Pisani, the
Corner and the Mocenigo
families, and other foreign
aristocrats were also
welcomed. Visits were made by
the duke of York, the emperor
Leopold II, the queen of
Naples, the emperor Joseph II,
pope Pius VI and many others.
It was as if the city was turning
its back on its lost glorious
past without regrets, in a
welter of feasts, festivities,
banquets and entertainments.
But behind the façade Venice's
spirit was troubled. There is an
air of regret about the
festivity, a tender, slightly
bewildered smile on the
woman's face in Tiepolo's
painting of Venice reproduced
on the preceding page, that
was possibly a premonition of
things to come.

The patrician Republic, besides, scored more than one point in finding of better ways of wielding power in favour of the poorer classes. It provided laws to protect the workers and the under-privileged. It listened to the needs of labourers and peasants with far more sympathetic and attentive ears than most of the sovereigns of Europe. When it collapsed it was mourned by the humble far more than by the gentlemen, for whom the end of the patrician regime meant the end of strict, daily controls from which most were only too eager to be free.

So it was in the cities and countryside of the mainland kingdom, and in the islands and lands in the dominion *da mar*. While there was an explosion of frustrated ambitions, aspirations, rivalries and vendettas among the privileged classes, the ordinary people recognized that, all things considered, they had been subject to the most humane rule that they could possibly have experienced. There were those who lamented its passing quite openly: in spite of the abusive rhetoric which has been levelled against it, the final leave-taking of the banner with the winged lion, by the *bocchesi* of Perasto when they buried it beneath the mensa of the high altar of their church, is recorded in an extraordinary document of devotion and love: "For 377 years our very substance, our blood, our lives have been all for you, St. Mark; and we have thought ourselves very fortunate, you with us and we with you...." We can only say again: which other rule in Europe could ever expect such an adieu?

This is yet another element of Venice's strength: her understanding of her subjects. It would have been better if the word "subjects" had not existed, according to today's sensitivities. However, it did exist, in Europe and in all the world. Many of the modern states inside and outside Europe came into being as a result of the rebellions of crushed and oppressed colonies. Once the conflicts in Crete and Zara had been settled, if there were rebellions in the Venetian states (and how modest they were), on the mainland and *da mar*, very few were revolts against the *Serenissima*. If anything, they tended to be directed against local lords and nobles.

One last factor: economic flexibility and mobility. Venice was born as a city of seamen and merchants, and, like her seamen and merchants,

she did not set herself preconceived boundaries; she was always ready for anything, with all due prudence, but with the necessary urgency and daring. Patriotic and religious idealism did not stem nor slow down that total willingness which is the mark of the great businessman. Unique in the world as a city, Venice was also unique as a state, in her constitution, her legislation and her history. What is left today of that uniqueness and that diversity which made her great?

It is difficult to perceive the Venice of yesterday in the Venice of today. In spite of the enormous, incredible destruction wrought, which those not actually involved cannot imagine (more than 70 churches demolished and more than 100 palaces destroyed, hundreds and thousands of works of art scattered all over the world: the Venice so much admired today is but a shadow of what it was before May 1797), nevertheless the unique setting remains, having survived many attacks from man and nature, and being exposed to many other very serious dangers which perhaps we do not do enough to avoid, in spite of the good will of many. However, the human ambience is deeply changed. Too many events have made a profound mark: the present exodus of the population that prefers the modern convenience of the horrible suburb, Mestre, to the discomfort of the ancient historical center was preceded by other mass exoduses, from the nobles who, no longer bound by the duty of residence, when the Republic fell, dispersed into the cities of the provinces which were less "different" and more comfortable, to the common people, who were obliged to flee the events of the Italo-Austrian war in 1915–18, which was fought in its last stages but a short distance from St. Mark's square.

Towards the 1880s port activities, which were impoverished and ruined under Napoleon and Austria, underwent a development which, however, involved the installations at Marghera on the edge of the mainland rather than the city maritime bases. There remains a lively exchange in the field of culture and the arts.

Between the end of the last century and the Second World War, a singular person, a Venetian businessman who was the topic of much discussion, Giuseppe Volpi, seemed to reincarnate the figure of the Venetian merchant of ancient times in the variety and vitality of his interests,

which were in part directed towards the oriental world. He was the focal point of the activities of other industrialists and financiers, one of whom, Vittorio Cini, was responsible for the creation of one of the most efficient cultural institutions of contemporary Italy, the Giorgio Cini Foundation. Present times do not favour the creation of new elites of this kind, nor the development of other elites, be they social or intellectual, of the kind which in the past made Venice a fashionable city for both artists and dilettantes. Yet if only for her misfortunes Venice has become a major focal point for the expression of international solidarity: from every corner of the world come proposals, ideas, money and expertise to contribute to the restoration of her monuments and works of art, to inspire and carry out these projects and to provide the necessary resources for her preservation.

This is a clear sign that the ideal of the Venetian empire still lives, extended over all the earth and seas, beyond the ruins of what was once her earthly empire; and that its profound appeal still reigns supreme over the hearts and minds of men, going far beyond a material greatness on which the sun has now set for ever.

Detail of Canaletto's Campo di Rialto *(Staatliche Museen Preussischer Kulturbesitz, Gemäldegalerie, West Berlin). A roof in the process of restoration. Two centuries after the fall of the Republic, Venice's very physical existence is in peril. Saving the city is a duty entrusted to the goodwill of mankind.*

Political Chronology, the
Doges of Venice, the Patrician
Families, "Regiments,"
Glossary, Index

Political Chronology

Historical outline

Venice's history as an autonomous state began some time during the early Middle Ages, after the collapse of the Western Roman Empire, and continued in all its originality for more than 1,100 years until the Napoleonic era. Venice lay at first on the fringes of the Byzantine empire, acting as a trading and shipping center on the lagoons and rivers up to the plain of Padua, and as a center of distribution for goods from the East. After the year 1000 Venice became a great Mediterranean naval power, and her role as intermediary between East and West was strengthened. With the conquest of Constantinople in 1204 she became the dominant power in the Levant. The Republican system of government developed in the city-state led it as well to supremacy in the Italian peninsula. At the beginning of the 15th century Venice made huge conquests on the mainland, although her interests lay only partly in this direction. The rise of the great modern monarchies transformed international politics, and spelled the end of the medieval states. In spite of pressure from the Ottoman empire in the East and from Spain (and later Hapsburg Austria) in the West, Venice was able to survive through diplomatic skill, by adapting her trade to the new conditions created by the opening of the ocean trade routes, and by developing her manufacturing industry, thus ensuring continued prosperity. Venice's complex history is more Mediterranean than Italian. It is bound up with developments in the Balkan peninsula, the Danube area, the Levant, and with the Islamic world as much as with the Holy Roman Empire, the Church, the maritime republics of the Tyrrhenian Sea and the powers of western Europe. The main turning points in her history are summarized here.

Origins

The inhabitants of the lagoon in the 6th century seem to have been boatmen, fishermen and salt-workers, according to a letter by Cassiodorus (537–38), in which he urged them to supply Ravenna. "Like water-fowl," he wrote, their houses were "now on land, now on sea," and their main source of income was salt, for "the man has yet to be born who does not want salt …" The Longobard invasion of Italy in 568 and their gradual occupation of the Roman (*i.e.* Byzantine) province of Venetia, eventually reduced to no more than the lagoon from Cavarzere to Grado, forced fresh groups of people to take refuge there. When the capital, Oderzo, fell in 639, the Byzantine governor transferred his seat to Cittanova on the lagoon, naming it Heracliana or Heraclea (after the emperor Heraclius). The foundation inscription of the church of Santa Maria in Torcello dates from these years, citing as it does the emperior Heraclius, Isaac, exarch of the Italian diocese, whose seat was at Ravenna, and the local governor, Maurizio. Venetia was on the fringe of the Byzantine Roman empire.

The first doge: 697

According to Venetian historical traditions, Venice was independent of Byzantium from the first, and the first doge or duke, Paoluccio Anafesto (or more commonly, Paulicius) was elected in 697. Roberto Cessi's rather more critical assessment identifies this figure with Paul, exarch of Ravenna.

Rebellion and reconciliation: 727–740

Pope Gregory II opposed the extension to Italy of the edict of the iconoclast emperor Leo III "the Isaurian" by ordering the destruction of the holy images in 727. The armies of Byzantine Italy proclaimed their own dukes; in Venice this may have been Orso, third in the traditional list of doges. The crisis was successfully overcome, however, and when the Lombard king Liutprand conquered Ravenna in 740, the exarch took refuge on the lagoon, from where he reconquered his capital with the help of the *venetici*.

From Cittanova to Malamocco: 742

At a time when Byzantine rule in Italy was threatened and the duchy's political state, so far as we can make out, was troubled, the doge's seat was tranferred from Cittanova to Malamocco. The inhabitants of Venetia, landowners, merchants, seamen and farmers continued their lives uninterrupted by the difficult circumstances of the time.

The attack of king Pippin and the Realtine islands: 810

By the end of the eighth century Italy's political situation had substantially altered, what with the Frankish conquest of the Lombard kingdom and the coronation of Charlemagne as emperor at Rome in 800, an event which the Roman emperor in Byzantium was unwilling to recognize. Charlemagne's son, Pippin, king of Italy, attacked Dalmatia and the lagoon, which belonged at least in name to Byzantium and the Byzantine Roman cultural tradition. Pippin was severely beaten by the *venetici* on the lagoon in 810. In the meanwhile a large number of refugees had left the settlements on the lagoon for the Realtine islands where they were defended by the castle of Olivolo. When Agnello Parteciaco or Partezipacio was elected doge, the duchy was also transferred there. In this way, the city of Venice was born. The territorial integrity of the duchy situated on the lagoon between Grado and Chioggia was guaranteed in the *pax Nicephori* concluded between the two emperors in 814.

The body of St. Mark the evangelist: 828

Two Venetian merchants, Rustico da Torcello and Buono Tribuno da Malamocco, purloined the body of St. Mark the evangelist from Alexandria and brought it back to their home town in 828. The relic was placed in the chapel of the doge's *palatium* and the first basilica begun in 829 and consecrated in 832, during the reign of Giovanni Parteciaco. The legend arose that St. Mark had landed on the lagoon and been forewarned of his final resting-place by an angel in a dream (*Pax tibi, Marce, evangelista meus*). At the synod of Mantua the previous year, Maxentius, patriarch of Aquileia, who belonged to the party of the Western Empire, had obtained the decision to suppress the patriarchate of Grado, a decision which was later reversed. The transfer of the body of St. Mark and its interment in the doge's chapel, with the legend of the foretelling of the event, was of political significance. It symbolized the independence of the church and community of Venice from both the Western Empire, to which Aquileia belonged and the Eastern Empire, not to mention Rome itself, by linking the city with one of the founding saints of Christianity who was neither Byzantine nor Roman.

Pactum Lotarii: 840

At the request of doge Pietro of Venice, the Frankish-Byzantine treaty of mutual respect of territory (814) was renewed by a decree of the emperor Lothair. It is significant that it was Venice, by now autonomous, and not Byzantium which was the signatory, and equally significant that the terms of the treaty entrusted the Venetian fleet with the defense of the sea (since there was no imperial fleet, and the Byzantine fleet was elsewhere), thus implicitly recognizing Venice's right of control over the Adriatic.

St. Mark asleep, with an angel. 13th-century sculpture from the central entrance to St. Mark's basilica. The incident refers to St. Mark's prophetic dream in which he was told of his eventual burial in Venice.

The sack of Comacchio: 866

As a Byzantine city on the edge of the Western Empire, Venice became the crossroads for trade with Constantinople, and its influence spread inland up river. Comacchio enjoyed the same potential from its controlling position over the Po after the fall of the Roman Adriatic ports of Aquileia and Ravenna. The Venetians eliminated this threat by attacking and sacking the city. In 932 they repeated the operation under doge Pietro II Candiano, this time deporting the inhabitants.

The rape of the brides: 946 or 948

Venice traded with Constantinople in precious goods from the East destined for the inland markets, as well as in basic commodities such as salt, fish, timber and slaves. As her maritime activity in the Adriatic expanded she soon came up against the Slavic pirates. The chief pirates' nest was at the mouth of the Narenta (Neretva), which gave its name to the Narentine pirates. As with the Byzantines and Turks, Venice entertained both commercial and warlike relations with these people, doge Pietro I Candiano perishing in an encounter with them in 887. The Narentines traded in slaves whom the Venetians bought and resold. Venetian tradition records the Narentine threat in the almost certainly mythical episode of the rape of the brides, on the occasion of a mass wedding in Santa Maria Formosa in 946 or 948.

Fire and revolt: 976

Doge Pietro IV Candiano was assassinated by the rebellious populace, and the *palatium*, the basilica of St. Mark, the church of San Teodoro and more than 300 houses, mostly built of wood, were destroyed by fire. The people then elected Pietro I Orseolo as doge in the church of San Pietro di Castello. This episode may have been caused by the political aspirations of the Candiano who employed foreign soldiers in their mainland conquests; this was seen as both oppressive and as the betrayal of Venice's vocation to trade and the sea.

Dux Dalmatinorum: 1000

A document from the end of the 10th century says of the Venetians, "This people does not plough, sow, or harvest grapes but buys its grain and wine in every port of the kingdom and in the market of Pavia." This somewhat surprised observation of a prosperity not founded on the land and agriculture fits in well with the guiding principles of Venetian policy. This is well illustrated by the reign of doge Pietro II Orseolo. On the one hand Venice lived in peace with the Ottonian empire, so that the movement of goods along the rivers Po, Adige, Piave and Livenza was guaranteed, routes whereby salt from the estuary, which was about to become a Venetian monopoly, was transported to the mainland. On the other hand, Venice made military efforts to control the Adriatic routes which formed the communication with the Levant. On Ascension Day 1000 a seaborne expedition left for Dalmatia. Pietro II Orseolo received homage from the Dalmatians at Ossero, Veglia, Arbe and Zara.

From Zara he fought the Croats, while at Spalato (Split) he forced the Narentines to negotiate, and took from them Curzola and Lagosta. He thus removed the Slavs from the sea, and placed the Byzantine Dalmatian coast under Venice's protection, assuming the title *Dux Dalmatinorum*.

The first Dogal Councillors: 1032

The Orseolo were overthrown in a revolutionary movement which carried Domenico Flabianico to power. At the same time two Dogal Councillors were elected for the first time, one from each side of the Grand Canal. This restricted the development of a monarchical type of government, which had been the tendency under the Candiano and the Orseolo, and laid the foundation for the ever-increasing limitations of the doge's power.

The new St. Mark's basilica

The church built by the Particiaci had been seriously damaged in the revolt of 976, and had been restored by Pietro I Orseolo, though it is hard to say to what extent. The present church was built in the second half of the 11th century and was founded by doge Domenico Contarini (1042–71) on the plan of the Church of the Apostles in Constantinople. A contemporary record says, "*consimili constructione artificiosa illi ecclesie, que in honorem duodecim apostolorum Constantinopolis, est constructa*" (resembling the marvellous construction of the church in honour of the twelve apostles in Constantinople).

Helping Byzantium: 1081

The Norman Robert Guiscard made himself master of the Apulian ports of Bari, Brindisi and Otranto, and launched an attack on the Byzantine empire on the eastern coast of the Adriatic. The emperor Alexius I Comnenus requested Venice's aid, which was granted because of the threat to its interests in the Adriatic routes and to trade with Constantinople. In 1081 a Venetian fleet appeared off Durazzo (Durrës) which Robert was besieging, and defeated the Norman fleet commanded by his son Bohemund. However the Normans took Durazzo, and further Venetian intervention in the waters of Corfu, in 1083, 1084 and 1085, did no more to resolve the situation. The Norman offensive was slowed down by Venetian action in spite of this, and in 1085 Robert died. In 1082 the Venetians had obtained a chrysobull from Alexis I Comnenus which increased the customs exemptions already granted to the Venetians in Constantinople in 992, extending to them many of the empire's trading posts and recognizing the Venetian quarter in the Byzantine capital.

The relics of St. Nicholas: 1099–1100

Only in 1099 did a Venetian fleet set out on the crusades, wintering in Rhodes. There it overtook Pisan ships which had the same plan, and the vessels of the two maritime republics did battle. The Pisans were defeated, taken prisoner and released after giving undertakings not to venture again into the waters of Romania (the Byzantine empire). The Venetian fleet left Rhodes at the end of May 1100. At Myra in Asia Minor it purloined the relics of St. Nicholas, patron saint of sailors, and at Jaffa the Venetians made an agreement with Godfrey of Bouillon to help him to extend the control of the crusaders over the coast, at the cost of granting them a colony (with a church, square, market, freedom to trade and tax exemptions) in every city conquered. Only Haifa was taken, and the fleet returned to Venice before the year ended.

The Arsenal: 1104

The Arsenal described by Dante, where "sticky pitch boils through the winter" was founded in 1104 in the reign of doge Ordelaf Falier. It housed an arms magazine, naval equipment and provisions, repair shops and a protected base, but even so occupied only a fraction of its present extent. It was enlarged for the first time in Dante's day, in the first quarter of the 14th century, when the fortified area was quadrupled. It was at this time that the Arsenal became a construction yard as well, although there were still dockyards scattered over the city and on the islands of the lagoon. The Arsenal was further enlarged during the Renaissance and later.

The voyage of Domenico Michiel: 1122–24

In late spring 1123 a strong Venetian fleet commanded by doge Domenico Michiel which had set out from Venice the preceding year appeared off Jaffa. During the 20 years which had passed since Venice's last expedition to the Levant, things had gone badly. The king of Hungary was establishing his rule over the cities of Dalmatia, which had been lost and reconquered; the last doge Ordelaf Falier had been assassinated near Zara (Zadar). The Byzantine emperor John Comnenus had refused in

1118 to recognize the privileges granted by his predecessors to the Venetians. A besieging Egyptian fleet had only just withdrawn from Jaffa. The Venetians gave chase, drew it into battle, and defeated it off Ascalon on 30 May 1123. Turning south, they captured some merchant ships laden with spices and precious cargo. Finally they took part in the crusaders' siege of Tyre, which fell on 7 July 1124, and obtained their usual privileges. On its way home the Venetian fleet sacked the Byzantine ports of the Aegean and the Adriatic. In response to this pressure the concessions granted by Alexius I Comnenus in 1082 were restored in 1126.

Consilium Sapientium: 1143

From this date we have records of a new body which had recently been instituted "for the honour and benefit and salvation of our country," the Council of Wise Men or *Consilium Sapientium*. This may have had 35 members as we know it did later, at the beginning of the 13th century. It was a deliberatory body, with the doge as president, and was the first nucleus of the later *Maggior Consiglio*.

Totius Istriae Dominator: 1145–53

Venice's relations with Istria were ones of protection, involving an obligation to provide defense by sea. These relations had been strengthened during the reign of Pietro II Orseolo, but dated from earlier than this. In 932 Capodistria had surrendered at the end of the economic war which the Venetians had begun in retaliation for various acts of provocation. This protectorate was transformed into submission in a series of accords, with Pola and Capodistria in 1145, and with Pola, Rovigno, Parenzo and Umago between 1148 and 1153. The cities had to swear *fidelitas* and recognize Venetian dominion over the mainland. The doge was given the title *Totius Istriae Dominator*.

The crisis with the Eastern Empire: 1171

The power of the Venetian traders in Constantinople was shared by the Genoese and Pisans, who were present in equal numbers. As diplomatic relations fluctuated, plunder and sacking were employed as means of exerting pressure and ensuring that privileges were renewed or extended. Greek resentment at this turned into open crisis in 1171 when Manuel Comnenus destroyed the Genoese quarter and dispersed the Venetian colony, arresting residents and confiscating their goods.

Doge Vitale II Michiel killed: Sebastiano Ziani elected: 1172

Faced with the hostility of the emperor Manuel Comnenus Venice reacted with force, and doge Vitale II Michiel sailed with a fleet to the Aegean. He returned with his crew decimated by plague and without having achieved anything. There were rumours of treachery, and rebels broke up the Council of Wise Men and pursued the doge, killing him near San Zaccaria. Sebastiano Ziani, the richest man in Venice was chosen to succeed him. An indirect method of election was used for the first time, 11 electors being nominated, and their choice made subject to the assembly's ratification. This was the beginning of the complex and famous method of election and lottery which was used in the later centuries.

Pope, emperor, and doge: The Congress of Venice: 1177

"Secure on all sides, fertile, abounding in all things, pleasant, and with a quiet and peace-loving people," such was Venice in 1177, when it witnessed the meeting between pope Alexander III and the emperor Frederick I Barbarossa, who were received by doge Sebastiano Ziani in St. Mark's. Here the war between the cities of northern Italy and the Church on one side, and the Hohenstaufen empire on the other, was brought to an end as a preliminary to the terms of the peace of Constance. Tradition has it that it was on this occasion that pope Alexander III presented the ring used in the ceremony later known as the "marriage with the sea," which had already been long in existence.

The six Dogal Councillors: 1178

The electoral procedure instituted in 1172 was completed in 1178 with the election of doge Orio Mastropiero, 11 men being designated to elect 40 electors of the doge. Six Dogal Councillors were now appointed from the six *sestieri* of the city.

A quarter and a half of the Eastern Empire: 1201–04

A treaty had been made with the Byzantine emperor in 1198, but when the tension in the East was eventually resolved as a result of the fourth crusade, the outcome was to prove surprisingly favourable to Venice. This crusade was undertaken by the count of Champagne and other great feudal lords of France. The crusader's envoys led by Geoffroy de Villehardouin settled the terms of transport with Venice in April 1201. More than 33,000 men were to be transported for a vast sum equivalent to 20,000 kilograms (44,000 lbs) of silver. The ships were ready by the spring of 1202,

but the crusaders were not as many as they should have been, neither had the agreed financial terms been completely honoured. Doge Enrico Dandolo agreed that the balance of the debt should be paid out of future booty, and while they were on their way, he requested the crusaders to help Venice recapture Zara (Zadar), which had rebelled with the support of the Hungarian crown.

In the winter they decided to attack Constantinople at the request of the pretender Alexius, son of Isaac II, who had been overthrown by his brother Alexius III and who wanted to regain the throne usurped by his uncle. It is now thought that Venice did not exert any particular pressure in this decision.

By this time the count of Champagne was dead, and the leader of the crusaders was the Marquis Boniface of Montferrat, a friend of Philip of Swabia, who was also his feudal overlord, and related to Alexius by marriage. Venice, by contrast, had begun diplomatic overtures to Alexius III. Nevertheless, in July 1203 the crusaders attacked Constantinople by land but were thrown back. The Venetians, fired by the 90-year-old blind Enrico Dandolo, sailed up the Golden Horn to attack the walls of the city, and took it. The new emperor Alexius IV was not welcome to the Greeks, and so proved extremely weak. Nor was the pressure of the crusaders and Venetians welcome. Finally Alexius (V) Ducas Mourtzuphlos proclaimed himself emperor with the aim of liberating the empire from the tyrant and from the foreign powers. Afraid of being crushed in the city by the uprising, the Venetians and the crusaders assaulted Constantinople for the second time in April 1204, took it, and sacked it for three days. The Venetians and the crusader barons drew up a new contract, forming the Eastern Latin Empire. The emperor was chosen by a council of six Venetians and six barons. Since Boniface of Montferrat was a former ally of the Genoese, the Venetians cast all their votes in favour of Baldwin, count of Flanders, who was elected. The emperor was given a quarter of the empire, and the remaining three-quarters were divided up between Venice and the barons, half going to each party. In this way the Doge became "Lord of a quarter and a half of the empire." The division was confused. With the fall of the empire, everyone who was able attempted to take what he could, whilst the Venetians were more interested in trade and naval bases than in territory. Apart from three-eighths of the city of Constantinople, their main gains were Negropont in Euboea, the two bases of Modon and Corone (Methoni and Koroni) on the southern tip of Morea (the Peloponnese), and lastly Candia (Crete). The latter had to be captured between 1207 and 1212 from the Genoese pirate Enrico il Pescatore, count of Malta, who had already made himself master of it in 1207. Marco Sanudo, a grandson of doge Enrico Dandolo, set up the duchy of Naxos as a fief of the empire on the Aegean islands.

The *Quarantia*: c.1220

A new council appears in Venetian government in the first decades of the 13th century, under the general heading "*pro proficuo et utilitatis Comunis Venecie.*" This was the *Quarantia*, the Council of Forty, which was elected in the same way as the Council of Wise Men, later to become the *Maggior Consiglio*, and consisting at that time of 35 members. Later the members of the *Quarantia* and the holders of individual magistracies and offices were made *ex officio* members of the *Maggior Consiglio*, and the elected portion of this body, the Council of Wise Men, was increased in size. In this way the stage was set for the laws of 1297, the so-called *serrata* ("locking") of the *Maggior Consiglio*.

Control of the Po: 1240

In 1240 the lord of Ferrara joined forces with the Hohenstaufen emperor Frederick II. At the pope's request the Venetians sent a naval squadron to besiege the city. The declaration of the citizens of Ferrara in favour of the Este family contributed to the city's fall. The Venetians concluded a treaty with the new lords of Ferrara, giving them control of all trade between the city and the sea, all merchandise coming from the Adriatic to Ferrara having to pass through the port of Venice. In order to exercise this right unobstructed they built the castle of Marcamò at the mouth of the Po di Primaro in 1258. Thus the Po, the great commercial route into the plain of Padua, fell under their control.

The *Pregadi*: 1255

From 1255 we have secure records of the *Consiglio dei Rogati* or *dei Pregadi*, those "invited" to give their advice and work. They were known in Venetian political life simply as the *Pregadi*, or classically as the Senate. The council was founded with a brief over naval material and certain international questions. It could meet either alone, or in conjunction with the *Maggior Consiglio*, in which it participated *ex officio*. Later, when the *Maggior Consiglio* had increased in size, the Senate was elected by the *Maggior Consiglio* and assumed the highest functions of state.

The maritime code: 1255

In 1255 doge Ranieri Zeno promulgated a code of maritime practice. The first statutes date back to 1242 in the reign of Jacopo Tiepolo. This regulated maritime affairs, the responsibilities of ship-owners, one of whom was designated as the ship's captain or "*patrono*" *de facto*, the rights of the crew, sailors and merchant-seamen, who were allowed to trade on their own account, and fixed the dates for contracts and the dates of departure of the *mude* (convoys).

The columns of St. John of Acre: the first war with Genoa: 1257–70

The Genoese position in Acre, as in Tyre, was as strong as the Venetian position, and a series of bloody incidents occurred between the citizens of these two maritime republics. In 1257 the Venetian Levantine merchant fleet was accompanied by a war fleet under the command of Lorenzo Tiepolo, son of the doge. The Venetians broke the chain which barred the port of Acre, and fired on the Genoese ships. Next year a large Genoese fleet appeared, but Tiepolo too had received reinforcements and the great naval battle which ensued at Acre in 1258 resulted in a heavy defeat for the Genoese. Half their ships were lost, and the survivors by land and sea retreated to Tyre. The Venetians returned home from Acre taking the columns which now adorn the southern side of St. Mark's. This was the beginning of the fight with Genoa which was to end only after four wars more than a century later. A few years after Acre, the Venetians suffered a reversal in the greatest center of their colonial power. The Byzantine emperor Michael Paleologus allied himself with the Genoese in the treaty of Nymphaion in 1261, took Constantinople in July 1261 and so put an end to the Eastern Latin Empire. The war at sea consisted of the harassment of Venetian shipping, which was forced to adopt the expensive procedure of sailing in convoy. This weighed heavily on the trading activities of the Venetians, who had been expelled from Constantinople where Michael Paleologus had conceded the suburb of Pera to the Genoese. In spite of this, the Venetians won the two main naval encounters, at Settepozzi in 1263, and at Trapani in 1266. Michael Paleologus again permitted the Venetians into Constantinople in 1268 although they were still at war with his Genoese allies, and peace was concluded in 1270. The Genoese took part in these negotiations more at the order of Louis IX of France, who needed their fleet for his ill-fated crusade, than out of conviction.

The Polos in the Far East: 1261–95

In the same year in which Michael Paleologus retook the city of Constantinople, 1261, two Venetian merchants, the brothers Nicolò and Matteo Polo, who had commercial interests in Sondaia (Crimea), set out to investigate the commercial possibilities of the hinterland in the new circumstances prevailing in Asia in the wake of the creation of the Mongol power. Failing to reach their goal of Tabriz in Persia by way of Sarai and Bukhara, they crossed central Asia to visit the Great Khan of the Mongols, Kubilai, who sent them back to the West with a message to the pope. The Mongols were interested in forming an anti-Moslem entente with the Christians. When they set out to return to the Mongol emperor in 1271 they were accompanied by two friars sent by the pope, who soon gave up the journey out of fear, and by Nicolò's son, the famous Marco Polo. They journeyed on through Laiazzo, a port in lesser Armenia which was to become an important point on the Asian caravan routes after the Mameluke conquest of Syria, and through Tabriz in Persia, the Pamir, and the oases of central Asia, the historical Silk Road, finishing up at Peking. Marco journeyed extensively in the far eastern parts of the Mongol empire, sometimes on official missions, eventually reaching Burma in 1285. The three Venetians returned home in 1295, 25 years after setting out, by the sea route from the straits of Malacca and the Indian Ocean, taking with them to Persia a betrothed Mongol princess, and then through Persia via Trebizond on the Black Sea. Marco Polo was subsequently captured in a naval encounter with the Genoese, and as a prisoner dictated his famous book, *Il Milione* (*The Travels of Marco Polo*) to another prisoner, the Pisan *littérateur* Rustichello. Fabulous and controversial though it was, it was substantially truthful. Marco Polo is alleged to have said on his death-bed in 1324, "*Non scripsi medietatem de hiis que vidi*" – I did not write half of what I saw.

The *Quarantaun*: 1268

The procedure for the election of the doge by the *Maggior Consiglio* was completed with the introduction of a series of stages of alternate voting and lottery, culminating in the selection of 41 electors (the *Quarantaun*) who nominated the doge. This method was used for the first time at the election of Lorenzo Tiepolo in 1268, and continued unchanged thereafter.

The Venetian gold ducat: 1284

The first cities in the West to mint gold coins were Genoa and Florence in 1252. This was because gold came mainly from the markets of North Africa. Venice used its own silver and gold coin minted in Byzantium. In 1284 she began to mint the gold ducat, later known as the *zecchino*, with the same weight and fineness as the Florentine florin. This was maintained until the fall of the Republic.

The second war with Genoa: 1294–99

The rivalry between the two maritime republics of Italy now became more intense than ever over the Black Sea trade. This was not calmed by the truce of 1270, and a new war broke out. This time it was the Genoese who started, and won, the great naval battles while the Venetians preferred to amass profits by plunder. The first Genoese victory was in 1294 off Laiazzo, which had become the most important Asian port after the fall of the crusaders' positions. The Venetians then made an incursion into Pera, and finally 80 ships under the command of Lamba Doria entered the Adriatic to ravage the Dalmatian coast. The Genoese won the ensuing great battle of Curzola (1298), but with such losses that they were unable to pursue the Venetians and carry the war into the lagoon. The peace of 1299 recognized Genoese supremacy over the coast of Liguria, which the Venetians had besieged with the help of Francesco Grimaldi, head of the Genoese Guelphs who had taken Monaco in 1297, and Venetian supremacy over the coast of the Adriatic. In the East their rivalry remained unresolved.

The "locking" of the *Maggior Consiglio*: 1297

With this reform in the reign of Pietro Gradenigo, admission into the *Maggior Consiglio* was restricted to all those who were members or had been members within the last four years, subject to the approval of the *Quarantia* with at least 12 votes. New candidates required the same approval. This more than doubled the number of members of the *Maggior Consiglio*, bringing it to more than a thousand. The rules for admission were subsequently made even more restrictive, with the quorum of votes from the *Quarantia* required for approval being raised first to 25, and later to 30. In 1323 membership of the *Maggior Consiglio* finally became permanent and hereditary. Bartolo di Sassoferrato remarked, "They are few in number in comparison with the whole population, though many when compared to those who rule in other cities, and so the people accept their government with a good will."

The war with Ferrara and the interdict: 1308–13

The chief reason for Venice's dominance over the Gulf of the Adriatic was to make sure that all goods passed through the market of Venice. Vessels of all countries could sail to Venice and merchants from every country did business there, but every transaction had to take place in Venice's market. The cargoes of merchants from Dalmatia, Zara and Ragusa (Dubrovnik) for example, bound for the plain of Padua, had to be unloaded in Venice. The Venetian castle of Marcamò on the Po delta made sure that trade bound for Lombardy from the Romagna passed through Venice. In 1308 the Venetians saw an opportunity to consolidate their control over the Po waterway by making themselves masters of Ferrara. They joined in an internal dispute over succession and sent troops to one side, eliciting from them the Castel Tedaldo, the fortress commanding the bridge over the Po. From Avignon the pope, overlord of Ferrara, placed Venice under an interdict, while the victims of Venice's commercial supremacy combined to plunder the Venetian markets and conquered Castel Tedaldo. Venice treated with Verona, and a waterway was planned to join the Adige and the Po, allowing access to the Po upstream of Ferrara. With this the interdict was eventually lifted in 1313.

The plot of Baiamonte Tiepolo and the Council of Ten: 1310

The architect of the expansionist policies in Ferrara which had led to the war with the pope was the doge, Pietro Gradenigo. Other families opposed this policy. This lay at the root of the conspiracy of 1310, the leaders of which were Marco Querini, Baiamonte Tiepolo, and Badoero Badoer. Three bands of armed men were supposed to attack the Doge's Palace, Querini's band by the Calle dei Fabbri, Tiepolo's from the Mercerie, and that of Badoer from the lagoon. The doge was informed about the plot, and by night summoned the families whom he could rely upon, gave the alarm to the Arsenal and ordered the *podestà* of Chioggia to stop Badoer. The rebels failed to synchronize their attack, and this together with the doge's preparations resulted in their defeat. Querini died, and the two other leaders were allowed to go into exile. The Querini and Tiepolo palaces were razed to the ground. The danger had been great, however, and it remained possible that the exiles might forge new alliances, a possibility which had occurred and was even then occurring in other cities. In order to prevent this and the formation of fresh conspiracies, the Council of Ten was established. Its members held office for a year, and one of three elected heads presided over them for a month at a time. The council was at first provisional, but because its small size allowed it to act with speed it was made permanent in 1335.

Galleys for auction: 1329

Between the end of the 13th and the beginning of the 14th century important innovations and considerable technical advances had been made in shipping. It now became possible, among other advantages, to sail during the winter months. The port of Venice "opened" in spring, but from the end of the 13th century it was open by February or even January. Towards the end of the 14th century the large galley came into use, which was capable of carrying more cargo. The same years saw the gradual introduction of the cog, a large, broad vessel with square sails. The state owned great galleys, and sailed on trading missions in regular convoy twice a year to four destinations, a system which reached full development at the end of the 14th century. These destinations were the Eastern Empire (the Aegean, Constantinople, and the Black Sea), Cyprus and Syria, Alexandria and Flanders. Alongside this system were the "free" merchant galleys and cogs, which were more numerous than the state-owned galleys. In 1329 the *Pregadi* (the Senate) decided to auction the state galleys and offer them on lease to the highest bidder voyage by voyage, on a given route and under binding conditions. The experiment began with the Eastern Empire galleys, and the success of the operation led to its being extended to the galleys bound for the other destinations. This system ensured work for the Arsenal, the largest state industry even in time of peace.

Treviso acquired: 1339

The first city of the Veneto mainland over which Venice asserted its rule was Treviso. At the rear of the lagoon the Della Scala family had risen to threatening proportions, ruling from Verona to Padua, Treviso and many other cities. The ambitions of these lords of Verona were cut down by a timely series of alliances and by a war. In Padua Venice lent its support to the rise of the Carraresi, while Treviso, which controlled the trade routes north, was directly taken over.

The Hall of the Maggior Consiglio: 1340

The number of those entitled to sit in the *Maggior Consiglio* had grown, and it was decided to build a hall worthy of the council. This project took ten years to complete, and occupied the part of the Doge's Palace facing on to the Molo. The Paduan artist Guariento painted it with frescoes depicting the *Coronation of the Virgin* or *Paradise* between 1365 and 1367.

The plague: 1347–48

The Bubonic plague which was raging in the Tartar army besieging the trading base of Kaffa in the Crimea, was brought to Italy by a returning Venetian vessel in the autumn of 1347. Within 18 months the city had lost three-fifths of its inhabitants.

The third war with Genoa: 1350–55

This began with a number of incidents connected

with the Black Sea trade. Venice was cast as the protector of the Byzantine empire against growing pressure from Genoa. In 1530 the Venetian fleet under Marco Ruzzini attacked a number of Genoese galleys in the port of Castro near Negropont, a few of which managed to escape because the Venetian crews, largely Greek and Dalmatian mercenaries (the Venetians having been decimated in the plague of 1347–48) began to plunder too soon. The Venetians gained reinforcements by hiring the allied fleets of Catalonia and Byzantium, and set out against Pera, the Genoese base close to Constantinople. Here the Genoese had a large fleet under Paganino Doria. The allied fleets failed to meet up, causing a series of delays and diversions, but eventually there was a bitter and bloody encounter in the Bosphorus in the winter of 1352. So great was the number of dead on both sides that the tactical outcome of the battle was uncertain; however, the Catalans and Venetians retreated, and Pera remained in Genoese hands. The following year, 1353, the Venetians under Nicolò Pisani together with the Catalans won a great victory over the Genoese off Alghero. Later, however, the Venetian fleet was surprised unarmed by Paganino Doria as it was wintering at Portolongo near Modon, and Pisani himself was captured. This victory proved of no advantage to Genoa. Racked with internal strife, the Genoese submitted to the lord of Milan, Giovanni Visconti, who engineered a compromise agreement in 1355.

The doge beheaded: 1355
Internal strife following the defeat at Alghero brought Genoa under Milanese subjection. The Venetian defeat at Portolongo led to an attempted dictatorship by the newly-elected doge, the septuagenarian Marino Falier. In Venice, however, the outcome was quite different. The Dogal Councillors were warned by denunciations, and summoned the Council of Ten. Among the conspirators who were at once arrested and condemned was Filippo Calendario, a building contractor, who has wrongly been credited with the construction of the Doge's Palace. When the doge's involvement was discovered, he was sentenced and beheaded on 17 April 1355. In the series of portraits of the doges in the Hall of the *Maggior Consiglio*, there is a black curtain in Marino Falier's place.

Dalmatia ceded: 1358
The cities, ports and islands of Dalmatia had been in Venice's possession since the profitable crusade of doge Pietro II Orseolo three and a half centuries before. However the kings of Hungary had cast their eyes on these lands in the course of their expansion over the Slav hinterland towards the sea.

The cities of Dalmatia were themselves turbulent and often rebelled against Venetian rule. At the end of 1355, after the peace with Genoa, Venice had to deal with the "whole of Slavonia in tumult." Arrayed against Venice in 1356 were the dukes of Austria, the patriarch of Aquileia, the Carrarese lord of Padua, and worst of all, the Hungarians, who were laying siege to Zara (Zadar). Zara fell, Traú (Trogir) and Spalato (Split) went over to the Hungarians, and in June 1358 Venice ceded her claim to the possessions in Dalmatia to the Hungarian crown.

The revolt of Candia: 1363–66
A local revolt led by John Kalergis was joined by a group of noble Venetians who had settled on the island, including members of the Venier, Gradenigo, Sagredo and Molin families. The rebels were thrown back but not eliminated by a Venetian fleet with the land army of Luchino dal Verme and the governor Pietro Morosini. The rebels reorganized in the mountains and made renewed attempts, until their leaders were captured and beheaded in April 1366.

The war of Chioggia, and the fourth war with Genoa: 1378–81
The origins of the fourth war with Genoa lay in rivalry over the conquest of the island of Tenedos, which was a potential base commanding the straits coveted by both Venetians and Genoese. The Venetians occupied it in 1376; war was not far behind. Against Venice were Genoa, the Carraresi of Padua, and the king of Hungary, while Dalmatia, ceded in 1368, could not longer be counted upon; indeed the Dalmatian bases and strongholds were now the preserve of Venice's enemies. In 1378 the Venetian fleet under Vittor Pisani sailed on an offensive war to the West, achieved a brilliant victory, and returned to winter at Pola. Here they were attacked by the Genoese in the spring of 1379. Pisani was lured into a trap, and his victory was turned into defeat. Returning home, he was thrown into prison. The Genoese were reinforced, and attacked the coast of the lagoon, taking Chioggia with the help of the Paduans on 16 August 1379. Never had Venice stood in greater danger. All reserves were mobilized. The populace and sailors forced the release of Vittor Pisani, "the chief and father of all the seamen of Veniexia." During the night of 22 December 1379, the aged doge Andrea Contarini and Vittor Pisani blockaded Chioggia, cutting off the occupying forces from both the Paduans and the Genoese fleet. Meanwhile another Venetian squadron under Carlo Zeno which had left on a plundering expedition before the battle of Pola was inflicting heavy damage on Genoese trade

in the Tyrrhenian and Aegean seas as far as Beirut and Rhodes. Zeno returned home on 1 January 1380, just in time to join the blockade of Chioggia. Failing in an attempt to subdue the mercenaries employed by the Venetians who were besieging them, the Genoese in Chioggia surrendered six months later in June 1380, allowing the Venetians to sally forth and regain control of the Adriatic. On land they tried to win over Gian Galeazzo Visconti as an ally, alarming the count of Savoy, who was in favour of a compromise. The peace of Turin of 1381 seemed to favour Genoa more than Venice, but Venice's greater political stability meant that she emerged victorious from the centuries of conflict. Thirty new families were admitted to the *Maggior Consiglio* after the peace, drawn from those who had most distinguished themselves in the war effort.

The occupation of Corfu: 1386
The island of Corfu was occupied with the consent of its rulers in 1386; legal rights of possession were later obtained from Charles, pretender to the throne of Naples. Corfu was strongly fortified and became a very important base, commanding the lower Adriatic. It remained in Venice's possession until the end of the Republic.

Expansion over the mainland of the Veneto: 1389–1420
Venice was a seafaring and mercantile power, whose main interests were trade and commerce. Just as in the Adriatic and in the Levant Venice's policy was to control ports, bases and trading-stations, so in the hinterland of the lagoon her policy was to keep the roads free so that her trade could flow unhindered. So long as there was only a sprinkling of communes to its rear, the Republic felt no great need to exert its rule over them, but with the flowering of the age of the great lords ruling over large stretches of land and ambitious to expand their territories, the situation was radically altered. The natural result of Venice's policy of playing off the ambitions of the different lords against each other was that Venice became involved herself in the struggle for territory, eventually becoming one of the five great states of the 15th century. There were three main pawns in Venice's game, the Scaligeri of Verona, the Carraresi of Padua, and the Visconti of Milan. Farther to the East were the lands of the patriarch of Aquileia, and here it was necessary to keep an eye on the ambitions of powers north of the Alps.

The first stage in Venice's expansion over the mainland was the recovery of Treviso, which had previously belonged to Venice but had been ceded to the dukes of Austria during the war of Chioggia, in order to keep the Carraresi at a distance. The alliance of Venice and the Visconti against the Carraresi in 1388 created the opportunity for the surrender of Treviso to Venice in 1389. On the other hand, although the Visconti were farther off than the Carraresi, they represented a far greater threat, especially when Gian Galeazzo ambitiously attempted to unite the whole of northern Italy under him. His death from the plague in 1402 left Venice facing Francesco Novello di Carrara. Vicenza, Belluno, and Bassano submitted to Venice in 1404. In 1405 Padua and Verona were conquered. Francesco Novello and two other members of his family were thrown into prison and strangled by order of the Council of Ten.

Within the lands of the patriarchate, the house of Savorgnan at Udine held firm with Venetian support, but here too the Carraresi had made attempts to expand, and Trieste had been given over to the dukes of Austria in 1382. When the emperor Sigismund of Hungary, with whom Venice was also fighting over Dalmatia, intervened, the military campaign of 1418–20 broke out. On 16 June 1420, Tristano di Savorgnan entered Udine bearing the banner of St. Mark. Venice now possessed almost the whole of the modern Veneto and Friuli.

Dalmatia regained: 1409–20

At the beginning of the 15th century there were two kings of Hungary, Sigismund of Luxembourg, son of the emperor Charles IV and himself emperor from 1411 (who effectively held the state), and Ladislas of Anjou-Durazzo, king of Naples, who was in possession of Dalmatia which he had conquered in an expedition against Zara (Zadar) in 1403 as part of his struggle to acquire the throne of Hungary. In January 1409 Venice regained its rights over Dalmatia, ceded in 1358, from Ladislas who was in difficulties. Less than a third of the intitial asking price of 300,000 ducats was paid. The little which Ladislas retained, principally Zara, was handed over to Venice, and the rest, Traú, Sebenico, Spalato, Cattaro, Curzola (Trogir, Sebenik, Split, Kotor, Korĉula), and the other islands she won in the war with Sigismund in 1420.

The election of Francesco Foscari: 1423

The formula, "If he is pleasing to you," with which the doge was presented to the populace recalled the fact that the election of the doge had originally been subject to the approval of the popular assembly, although it had long been a pure formality. In 1423 the formula was abolished; henceforth the *Maggior Consiglio* alone, and the patriciate which constituted it, was the sovereign master. In 1423 Francesco Foscari was elected doge to succeed Tommaso Mocenigo, who had in vain warned the

Maggior Consiglio not to choose him: "the said Francesco Foscari spreads rumours and many other matters without any basis, and stoops and climbs more than a falcon." The Foscari led Venice into costly wars with Milan to which Mocenigo had been opposed; meanwhile Turkey was growing into a great sea power. Thus while Mocenigo looked to the sea, Foscari looked to the mainland.

Thessalonica: 1424–30

The Turks had occupied nearly all the Byzantine Empire with the exception of Constantinople. The city of Thessalonica entrusted its defense to Venetian sea power, and the Republic dispatched a fleet there under Pietro Loredan. It was he who in 1416 had destroyed a Turkish fleet at Gallipoli in the first naval battle between the Turks and the Venetians. Thessalonica was soon lost, however (in 1430), while Venice was caught up in the wars in Italy against Milan.

The wars in Lombardy: 1425–54

"I counsel you to pray to the almighty power of God who has inspired us to make peace, as we have done, and to follow Him and render Him thanks. If you follow my advice, you will see that from now on we will be lords of all Christendom; the whole world will revere and fear you. Beware of the desire to take what belongs to others, and of making unjust war, for God will destroy you." These were the words of the aged doge Tommaso Mocenigo shortly before his death in 1423. Soon afterwards Venice was caught up in 30 years of war, precisely to "take what belongs to others," *i.e.* Lombardy. This carried Venice's frontiers to the Adda, convulsed the whole of Italy and ended in compromise with the Peace of Lodi in 1454 which brought 40 years of peace to Italy, but not to Venice. The prelude to the war against the rule of the Visconti house in the person of duke Filippo Maria (wars therefore of supremacy, or from the other point of view, to protect the balance of power in Italy which was threatened by the expansion of the Visconti), was the League between Venice and Florence of 4 May 1425. There were four wars. In the first, (1425–26), Venice took Brescia with an army led by Carmagnola, and the fleet on the Po advanced as far as Padua. The second (1427–28) saw a Venetian victory at Maclodio on 4 October 1427, and ended with Venice being granted Bergamo as well as Brescia. In the third war of 1431–33, the Po fleet was defeated at Cremona but Venice won a naval victory over Genoa, which was at that time a dependency of the Visconti, at San Fruttuoso on 27 August 1431. Carmagnola failed to act, and was suspected of having come to terms with the enemy.

He was recalled from the field by the Council of Ten for consultation, arrested in March 1432, and tried. A month later he was beheaded between the two columns of the Piazzetta.

The peace of Ferrara in 1433 left things as they stood. In the fourth war Venice's sea-captains were first Gattamelata, and later Francesco Sforza, while the Visconti side was led by Niccolò Piccinino. Sforza and Piccinino were in fact fighting a personal war in which the interests of the opposing powers were secondary. Piccinino laid siege to Brescia in 1438 and penetrated the Veronese defenses. Venice's response to this crisis was the famous transportation of six galleys and other lesser craft by land from the Adige to Lake Garda, more than 2,000 oxen being used in the operation (1439). On the field of Cavriana, Sforza acted as mediator between the two sides accomplishing the act for which Carmagnola had lost his head. No territorial changes were made in the ensuing Peace of Cremona of 20 November 1441.

None of these treaties was more than a truce, and no general accord between the Italian states was reached, as Venice would have preferred. Instead, important political changes occurred. Francesco Sforza entered the service of Visconti and married his daughter, while Florence took a new turn under Cosimo de' Medici. Visconti died in 1447, and in May 1450 Francesco Sforza entered Milan in triumph, after the demise of the short-lived Ambrosian Republic (in 1449 Venice had acquired Crema). Two coalitions were now formed, Sforza Milan with Medici Florence on the one hand, against Venice and Aragonese Naples on the other. The main theater of war was still Lombardy, where Venice clashed with Francesco Sforza. Worn out, both sides joined in the Peace of Lodi in May 1454, a peace which formed the basis for a general accord between the four contenders, Venice, Milan, Florence and Naples, under the leadership of the pope.

The Turkish advance: 1463–79

On 3 April 1463, ten years after the capture of Constantinople, the Turks seized the Venetian fortress of Argos in a surprise attack. A long war ensued from which Venice emerged defeated. At first the Venetians launched a counter-attack by sea and land with the help of their Hungarian allies, and gained some positive results (1463–68). In spring 1470 the Turks attacked the base of Negropont in force with both land and sea troops. Poorly supported by the naval squadron commanded by the hesitant Nicolò Canal, the base fell, along with the whole of Euboea. During the course of fruitless negotiations, Turkish squadrons sailed into Friuli in 1471, repeating the attack in 1477 and 1478.

Venice had meanwhile succeeded in drawing

the Shah of Persia into the war, and attacked the coast of Asia from the sea. However the Persians were put to rout (1472–74). The Turks began to press on the lower Adriatic, where the Venetians put up a tenacious resistance in Scutari. The peace of 24 January 1479 was humiliating: Venice lost Argos, Euboea and Scutari, and had to pay an annual tribute of 10,000 ducats. The Turks went on to attack peninsular Italy, landing at Otranto, but were unsuccessful in this attempt. The death of Mehmed II brought Turkey a period of crisis, which allowed Venice to take and hold Zante in the Ionian islands, and to improve the terms of the treaty. The tribute was abolished, duty was lowered from five to four per cent, and the privileges and immunities of the Venetian *bailo* in Constantinople were renewed.

Cyprus acquired: 1473

During the course of the disastrous war with the Turks, Venice managed to consolidate her hold on the island of Cyprus, where there were strong Venetian, and specifically Corner, interests. The king of Cyprus was Giacomo II Lusignano, who married Caterina Corner in 1472. A revolt against the queen broke out on the king's sudden death in 1473, with the aim of giving the throne to a natural son of Ferdinand of Naples. Venice reacted promptly and energetically, calling back Barbaro with his Venetian fleet from Asia to take charge of the island, and of the interests of Giacomo Lusignano's widow. The kingdom remained in the possession of Caterina Corner and of her baby son Giacomo III Lusignano, who died in 1474, under strict Venetian control until she was forced to abdicate on 24 February 1489. She ceded the island to the direct administration of Venice and was granted the signory of Asolo, were she continued to maintain a brilliant court.

The Polesine: 1484

The pope had sought Venice's help against the king of Naples, leaving her a free hand against Ferrara (1482). He subsequently became alarmed by Venice's success, however, and while Florence and Milan intervened in Ferrara's favour, Sixtus IV had recourse to an interdict in order to stop Venice. At the peace of 1484 Venice was allowed to retain the Polesine, which she had conquered. A year later The French ambassador, Philippe de Commines, wrote of Venice, "It is the most splendid city I have ever seen, and the one which governs itself the most wisely."

Between land and sea: 1495–1503

Charles VIII of France's descent into Italy in order to conquer the kingdom of Naples in 1494 is one of the turning points in Italian history. It marks the beginning of the crisis of Italian freedom. Venice was one of the architects of the anti-French league which, however, failed to destroy the French king's army at Fornovo in 1495 as it returned home. Nevertheless Venice occupied the Apulian ports, important strategic bases commanding the lower Adriatic and the Ionian islands. A few years later in 1499 Venice allied itself with Louis XII against Milan, and gained Cremona. In the same year the Ottoman sultan moved to attack Lepanto by land, and sent a large fleet to support his offensive by sea. Antonio Grimani, more a businessman and diplomat than a sailor, was defeated in the sea battle of Zonchio in 1499. The Turks once again sacked Friuli. Preferring peace to total war both against the Turks and by sea, Venice surrendered the bases of Lepanto, Modon, and Corone in 1499. Her supremacy in Italy seemed to be in peril, and her ambitions on the mainland won the day. Some believe that this decision, and this period were the critical point in Venice's fortunes.

The League of Cambrai: 1508–17

The area which had tempted Venice to divert her attention from her maritime position, with its promises of expansion, was the Romagna. This Venice hoped to remove from the control of the pope, now that the Malatesta lords of Rimini were passing through a period of crisis, and the meteoric career of the duke of Valentinois, Cesare Borgia, son of pope Alexander VI was over. Venice's power was at its height, but this brought her enemies. Eager to take some of Venice's lands, these all joined in the League of Cambrai in 1508. The pope wanted Romagna, the emperor Friuli and the Veneto, Spain the Apulian ports, the king of France Cremona, the king of Hungary Dalmatia, and each of the others some part. The offensive against the huge army enlisted by Venice was launched from France. On 14 May 1509 Venice was defeated at Agnadello in the Ghiara d'Adda; the city was in the gravest danger. French and imperial troops were occupying the Veneto, but Venice extricated herself by her efforts and her political skill. The Apulian ports were ceded in order to come to terms with Spain, and pope Julius II was placated when he perceived how much more dangerous Venice would be destroyed than powerful. The citizens of the mainland rose to the cry of "Marco, Marco." Andrea Gritti recaptured Padua in July 1509, and successfully defended it against the besieging imperial troops. Spain and the pope broke off their alliance with France, and Venice regained Brescia and Verona from France also. After seven years of ruinous war, Venice regained her domains on the mainland up to the Adda, which she held until the end of the Republic.

"Thanks to the virtue and wisdom of our ancestors": 1520–30

In 1544 Gasparo Contarini, politician and Venetian diplomat, and later a cardinal, wrote his *De Magistratibus et Republica Venetorum*. In this work he expressed the approval and interest which surrounded Venice's constitutional arrangements, not only among the patricians of Venice but throughout Italy and in foreign lands, where men were astonished at Venice's greatness, her long independence, her resistance to Italy's tragic loss of freedom and, not least, her emerging unscathed from the war against the League of Cambrai. In this work Contarini suggested that the secret of Venice's greatness lay in the co-existence of Aristotle's three types of government, monarchy, oligarchy, and democracy. In his opinion, the *Maggior Consiglio* was the "democratic" part, the Senate and the Ten were the oligarchy, while the doge represented monarchy. The combination of these three principles in the Venetian government came as close as was possible to perfection in the mechanism of government. At the same time the patrician Marino Sanudo, a politician who had a remarkable career, and a celebrated diarist, was bewailing the corruption which resulted from the great number of poor or impoverished patricians. "Votes are sold for money . . . . May God help this poor Republic . . . ." (1530).

Preveza: 1538

When the struggle for supremacy in Italy between France and Spain was resolved in favour of Spain, ruled by the emperor Charles V Hapsburg, Venice found herself caught between the Turks and Spain (and later between Hapsburg Austria and the Turks). To this her only possible response was to put up a long, tough, and often skilful defense. The interests of Spain and Venice were united against the Turks, though only in part. Venice's maritime aid was potentially useful to Spain, but not to the point of allowing her to reinforce her position in the Levant, which would increase her strength in Italy as well, where she was practically the only Italian state not subject to Spain. In the Turkish war of 1537–40, Venice was allied to Charles V. Andrea Doria was the emperor's admiral and commander of the allied fleets. He was unable to fulfil his instructions successfully, and was defeated at Preveza in 1538. In 1540 Venice made peace, and the Turks took the Aegean duchy of Naxos from the Sanudo family. After Preveza the supremacy of the sea passed to Turkey.

The three Inquisitors: 1539

The State Inquisitors, later known as the Supreme Tribunal, were instituted, and their duties laid

PALATII SENATORII APVD VENETOS CONFLAGRATIO
ANNO M D LXXVII.

down, in a law of 1539. There were three Inquisitors, one known popularly as *il rosso*, "the red one," who was chosen from the Dogal Councillors, who wore scarlet robes, and two from the Council of Ten, known as *i negri*, "the black ones." They began as a security body at the difficult time when Venice felt herself encircled by the Hapsburgs, and gradually assumed some of the powers of the Council of Ten. By means of espionage, counterespionage and internal surveillance, they made use of a network of informers and "confidants."

Enforced galley service: 1545
Until 1545 the oarsmen in the galleys were free sailors enrolled on a wage. They were originally Venetians, but later Dalmatians, Cretans and Greeks joined in large numbers. Because of the difficulty in hiring sufficient crews, Venice had recourse to conscription, chaining the oarsmen to the benches as other navies had already done. Cristoforo da Canal was the first Venetian to command such a galley.

The *provveditori ai beni inculti*: 1556
This office was founded in 1556, and was established for the improvement of agriculture by increasing the acreage under cultivation and encouraging private investment in agricultural improvement. The consistent rise in the price of grain during the 16th century encouraged the transfer of capital from trade to the land.

The loss of Cyprus and the battle of Lepanto: 1571
Venice's political situation now resembled that at the time of the battle of Preveza. Allied with Spain and the pope, she was able to assemble a grand fleet of 208 galleys, 110 of which were Venetian, equal in numbers to the Turkish fleet, under the command of John of Austria, half-brother of Philip II. The Venetians were commanded by Sebastiano Venier.

The Turkish fleet had sailed up the Adriatic as far as Lesina, and then returned to Lepanto in the Gulf of Patras for provisions. The Christian fleet had assembled at Messina and encountered the Turkish fleet off Lepanto on 7 October 1571. Lepanto was a great Venetian and Christian victory, and the victors divided up 117 galleys captured from the Turks. But the Venetians gained no strategic advantage. Philip II was concerned with the balance of power in the eastern Mediterranean and Africa, and was unwilling for the fleet to become involved in the Levant. Famagusta, the last stronghold on the island of Cyprus, had been attacked by the Turks in 1570 and had surrendered before Lepanto. The Turkish commander had had the Venetian *provveditore* Marcantonio Bragadin flayed alive. The loss of Cyprus was ratified in the peace of 1572.

The fire in the Doge's Palace: 1577

On 20 December a fire broke out in the Doge's Palace and destroyed the Halls of the *Maggior Consiglio* and the *Scrutinio*. The *Signoria* summoned the 15 greatest architects of the time. Palladio's proposed new building in the classical style was rejected, and the contract given to Antonio Da Ponte, who completed the reconstruction in under a year. Guariento's great fresco of *The Coronation of the Virgin* was beyond repair, and Jacopo Tintoretto's huge canvas of *Paradise* was placed over it (1588–90).

The public bank: 1587

The first public bank was set up by the Venetian government in 1587 after the collapse of a private bank, amid public outcry. It was known as the Banco della Piazza. A second public bank, the Banco del Giro, was started in 1619, and in 1638 the Banco della Piazza was abolished. These banks played a very important role in financing the Republic's wars, by issuing representative money.

The stronghold of Palmanova: 1593

After the war against the League of Cambrai, Venice had to cede Gradisca and retreat to the west of the Isonzo. Then came the Turkish incursions into Friuli. In order to reinforce the eastern border against the Turks and the Hapsburgs, Venice decided to build a fortress. In this way Palmanova was built to the design of Giulio Savorgnan, in a nine-pointed star. The first stone was ceremonially laid on 7 October 1593, on the twenty-second anniversary of the battle of Lepanto.

Paolo Sarpi and the interdict: 1605–7

The famous conflict between Venice and the Holy See began with the arrest of two members of the clergy who were guilty of petty crimes, and with a law restricting the Church's right to enjoy and acquire landed property. Paul V held that these provisions were contrary to canon law, and demanded that they should be repealed. When this was refused, he placed Venice under an interdict, which forbade priests from carrying out their religious duties and excommunicated the rulers.

Right: the first visit of the doge to the church of the Salute built as a thanksgiving for the end of the dreadful plague of 1630, and consecrated in 1687. Left: the dreadful fire in the Doge's Palace, 20 December 1577.

Tempio eretto alla B V Maria della Salute, per uoto fatto dall Ecc.mo Senato l'anno MDCXXX, difegnato da Marco Boschini conforme il modello di Baldafsare Longena e Pompa con cui procefsionalm.e si portò il Ser.mo Principe alla uisita del medesimo Tempio la prima uolta.

Per Domenico Lotifa à Rialto

The Republic paid no attention to the interdict or the act of excommunication, and ordered its priests to carry out their ministry. It was supported in its decisions by the Servite monk Paolo Sarpi, a sharp polemical writer who was nominated to be the *Signoria's* adviser on theology and canon law in 1606. The interdict was lifted after a year, when the French intervened and proposed a formula of compromise. Venice was satisfied with reaffirming the principle that no citizen was superior to the normal processes of law. In 1607 Sarpi was wounded in an assault by three ruffians, and said that in the dagger which wounded him he recognized "*lo stile* (= the style, *or* the dagger) of the Roman curia." To him Venice also owed two essays on *The Rule of the Adriatic* in which he defended Venice's jurisdiction over this "enclosed and restricted sea, which has since time immemorial been owned and guarded at [great] expense and labour."

The pirates and the war of Gradisca: 1613–17

"The whole house of Austria is displeased and disgusted at the just rule of the Most Serene Republic over the Gulf, and it appears to [us] that they are disturbing Venice's peaceful jurisdiction and possession with the frequent raids of the Uzkoks," so Venice wrote.

The Uzkoks were Christian refugees from Bosnia and Turkish Dalmatia who had been enlisted by the Hapsburgs to defend their borders after the peace between Venice and the Ottomans following the battle of Lepanto. They settled in Segna and lived as pirates in the Adriatic, causing Venice to worry that they would complicate relations with the Sublime Porte. When Venice acted against these *Uscocchi* in 1613, she found herself at odds on land with their protector, the archduke of Austria. An army was sent against Gradisca, which belonged to the archduke, and financial support was given to the duke of Savoy who was pinning down the Spanish army in Lombardy. The military operations on the eastern frontier were not decisive, but among the terms of the peace of 1617 the Hapsburgs undertook to solve the problem of the Uzkoks, whom they moved inland.

The war of Ossuna and the Marquis of Bedmar's conspiracy: 1617–18

Whether on his own initiative, or supported by his king, the Spanish viceroy of Naples attempted to break Venetian dominance in the Gulf by sending a naval squadron to the Adriatic. His expedition met with mixed success in 1617, and he retired from the Adriatic. Rumours of sedition and conspiracy were meanwhile circulating in Venice, and there were disturbances between mercenaries of different nationalities enrolled for the war of Gradisca. The Spanish ambassador, the Marquis of Bedmar, was wise to the plot, if not the author of it. Informed of this by a Huguenot captain, the Ten acted promptly. Three "bravos" were hanged, and the Senate demanded the immediate recall of the Spanish ambassador.

The Foscarini affair: 1622

Antonio Foscarini, a senator and ambassador to England, was accused of acting for foreign powers during his time as ambassador and of spying for Spain after his return. He was tried, acquitted of the first charge, found guilty of the second and hanged from a gallows between the columns of the Piazzetta in 1622. A few months later the Ten discovered that he had been the innocent victim of a plot. He was rehabilitated, and the news circulated around all the chancelleries of Europe.

The Mantuan succession and the plague: 1628–30

On the death of Ferdinando Gonzaga, duke of Mantua and Monferrato, the succession developed upon a French prince, Charles of Gonzaga-Nevers. This changed the balance of power in northern Italy, which had until now been controlled by the Spanish through Milan. In the ensuing war, Venice was allied with France against the Hapsburgs and Savoy. The Venetian army was defeated in an attempt to come to the aid of Mantua which was under siege by German troops, and Mantua itself was savagely sacked. The peace which recognized Charles of Gonzaga-Nevers as duke of Mantua and Monferrato was made practically without Venice's participation. War brought plague in 1630. In 16 months 50,000 people died in Venice, one third of the population. The first stone of the church of Santa Maria della Salute was laid as a thanks-offering for the end of the plague.

Valona bombarded: 1638

While the Venetian fleet was cruising off Crete, a corsair fleet from Barbary consisting of 16 galleys from Algiers and Tunis entered the Adriatic. When the fleet returned, the corsairs repaired to the Turkish stronghold of Valona. In spite of this Marino Cappello attacked the corsairs, bombarded the forts and captured their galleys, freeing 3,600 prisoners. The sultan reacted to the bombardment of his fortress by arresting the *bailo* Alvise Contarini. War was averted and the matter settled by diplomacy.

The sultan's harem: 1644

The Knights of Malta raided a Turkish convoy en route from Alexandria to Constantinople and captured part of the sultan's harem returning from Mecca. On their way home the Maltese landed on Crete. Christian pirates were no less active in the Mediterranean than Moslem ones, and Crete was an irritant to Turkish shipping. The sultan prepared a fleet to punish Malta, but it attacked Crete instead. So began the 25-year-long war of Candia.

The war of Candia: 1645–69

In the middle of 1645 the Turks attacked the frontiers of Dalmatia and landed on Crete. On 22 August, Khania was forced to capitulate. Dalmatia too was heavily attacked but the Venetians were able to save their coastal positions because of their command of the sea. The greatest Turkish effort was directed against Sebenico (Sebenik), to which they laid siege in August-September 1647, but the siege failed, and in the succeeding year the Venetians recovered several fortresses inland, such as Clissa. In Crete, however, the situation was more serious. The Turks attacked the capital of Candia, which held out for 20 years. Throughout the long war the Venetian strategy was to blockade the Dardanelles in order to surprise the Turkish fleet on its way to supply the troops on Crete. There were some signal successes, but they failed to alter the strategic situation. There were two victories in the Dardanelles, in 1655 and 1656. In the second of these battles on 26 August 1656, the Turks suffered their most crushing defeat since Lepanto, and the commander Lorenzo Marcello fell. The next year there was a three-day-long sea-battle (17–19 July 1657), in which the captain Lazzaro Mocenigo was killed by a falling mast. The battle was on the whole a defeat. With the end of the war between France and Spain in 1659, Venice received more aid from the Christian states than the small contingents which she had received in the first years. In 1666 an expedition to retake Khania failed, and in 1669 another attempt to lift the siege of Candia with joint action on land with the French contingent and by sea under Mocenigo, was also a failure. The French returned home, and only 3,600 fit men were left in the fortress of Candia. Francesco Morosini negotiated its surrender on 6 September 1669. The island of Crete was ceded, except for some small Venetian bases, while Venice retained the islands of Tinos and Cerigo, and its conquests in Dalmatia.

The line-of-battle ship: 1667

The backbone of the Venetian fleet had always been its galleys and galleasses. Naval battles were decided by boarding, as had been the case at Lepanto. But naval tactics had been revolutionized by the galleon, with rows of cannon on its sides, and by the line-of-battle ship, which derived from

Turkish forces attacking the fortress of Tenedos defended by the Venetians, during the 25-year-long war of Candia. Ottoman painting (Museo Correr, Venice).

it. Venice chartered some Dutch and British ships, and adapted merchant ships to military purposes. After this the first line-of-battle ship was built in the Arsenal in 1667, to the design of a British battle-ship. In the next half-century 68 line-of-battle ships came from the Arsenal stocks.

The Morea conquered: 1684–99

In September 1683 John Sobieski routed the Turks besieging Vienna. From this time the Ottoman power of expansion was broken, and the empire started the long course of its decline over the next few centuries. In 1684 Venice formed an alliance with Austria; Russia was later included in the league. Francesco Morosini occupied the island of Levkas and set out to recapture the Greek ports. Between June 1685 when he landed at Corone, and August when he occupied Patras, Lepanto and Corinth, he secured the Peloponnese for Venice. In September during the attack on Athens, a Venetian cannon blew up the Parthenon.

Venetian possessions were greatly increased in Dalmatia too, although the attempt to regain Negropont in 1688 was a failure. Morosini's successors failed to obtain lasting results in the next years, although large fleets were sent out, and in spite of some brilliant victories – at Mitylene in 1695. Andros in 1697 and the Dardanelles in 1698. The peace of Carlowitz in 1699 favoured Austria and Russia more than Venice, which failed to regain its bases in the Mediterranean taken by the Turks in the last two centuries, in spite of its conquests.

Neutrality: 1700

New conflict was brewing over the question of the Spanish succession. Both France and the Hapsburg empire, the two European powers which had been fighting in Europe for 200 years, attempted to gain an active ally in Venice, despatching envoys with authority there in 1700. The Venetian government preferred to remain neutral rather than accept hypothetical advantages offered by interested parties. The Republic remained faithful to this policy of neutrality to the end, caught in unavoidable decline but living out its life in enviable luxury.

The Morea lost: 1714–18

In December 1714 the Turks declared war when the Peloponnese (the Morea) was "without any of those supplies which are so desirable even in countries where aid is near at hand which are not liable to attack from the sea." The Turks took the islands of Tinos and Aegina, crossed the isthmus and took Corinth. Daniele Dolfin, commander of the fleet, thought it better to save the fleet than to

Pauiglione della Rep.ca di Venezia

the rest of the trade which comes from Germany." Even the cities of the eastern mainland up to Verona got their supplies from Genoa and Leghorn.

The sea walls: 1744–82

In 1744 the construction of sea walls was undertaken to protect the shore of the lagoon between Pellestrina and Chioggia to a plan drawn up by father Vincenzo Maria Coronelli, cartographer to the Republic in 1716. The thick wall of Istria stone, 14 meters (46 feet) wide and four-and-a-half meters (15 feet) above mean tide level were in two parts. The sea walls of Pellestrina were four kilometers (two and a half miles) long, and were finished in 1751, while the walls of Sottomarina were 1200 meters ($\frac{3}{4}$ mile) long and were finished in 1782. They were "a work which recalls the greatness of the Romans, outdoing men, sea, and time" (1777). They were the last great public work of the Venetian state, which had always devoted its skill, its persistance, and its money to the defense of the lagoon.

Tribunalisti and *querinisti*: 1762

Angelo Maria Querini, *avogador del Comun*, had "intervened" in a sentence of the Supreme Tribunal (the three Inquisitors of State), and was arrested by order of the Inquisitors. In protest the *Maggior Consiglio* refused to vote in the elections for the Council of Ten, nominating four "correctors" to revise the laws. The head of the party of reformers, known as the *querinisti* was Paolo Renier, while the *tribunalisti*, those who upheld the power of the Supreme Tribunal, were led by Marco Foscarini. The parliamentary battle concluded with the vote of 16 March 1762, in the *Maggior Consiglio*, in which the "conservative" proposals of the correctors were accepted by a majority of only two votes. Marco Foscarini and Paolo Renier were both subsequently elected doge.

The Barbary pirates: Jacopo Nani at Tripoli: 1766

Venetian trade with the western Mediterranean was seriously affected by the wars of the Barbary pirates on the coast of the Maghreb, who were only nominally under the control of the Sublime Porte. In 1750 the *savi* lamented that "the pirates are multiplying their arms, losses are unceasing, and we are reduced to either remaining in port, or to sailing with excessive expenses in crew and safeguards, or else losing our ships and disgracing our nation". Diplomatic delegations between 1761 and 1765 to Algiers, Tunis, Tripoli and Morocco, led to agreements for which the Venetians had to pay large annual indemnities. The bey of Tripoli

later caused further incidents, and Jacopo Nani's squadron was charged with undertaking military action. This turned out to be a simple demonstration of strength, since the bey hastily accepted the Venetian demands as soon as the fleet appeared. The goodwill purchased from the Barbary states bore fruit. From an original 40 Venetian vessels the number rose in 1774 to 303, and later to 405.

Attempts at reform: 1779–80

"All is in disorder, everything is out of control," exclaimed Carlo Contarini in the *Maggior Consiglio* on 5 December 1779. He was talking of a "commotion" in demand of a plan of reform also supported by Giorgio Pisani. The idea was to remove the monopoly of power enjoyed by the small number of rich patricians to the advantage of the very large number of poor ones. This gave rise to fears of "overturning the system" and the doge, Paolo Renier, opposed the plan. "Prudence" suggested that the agitations in favour of reform were a conspiracy. The Inquisitors took the arbitrary step of confining Pisani in the castle of San Felice in Verona, and Contarini in the fortresss of Cattaro.

The lament of "el Paron": 1784

On 29 May 1784 Andrea Tron, known as *el paron* (the chief) because of his political influence, said that trade "is falling into final collapse. The ancient and long-held maxims and laws which created and could still create a state's greatness have been forgotten. [We are] supplanted by foreigners who penetrate right into the bowels of our city. We are despoiled of our substance, and not a shadow of our ancient merchants is to be found among our citizens or our subjects. Capital is lacking, not in the nation, but in commerce. It is used to support effeminacy, excessive extravagance, idle spectacles, pretentious amusements and vice, instead of supporting and increasing industry which is the mother of good morals, virtue, and of essential national trade."

The last naval venture: 1784–86

The bey of Tunis's Barbary pirates renewed their acts of piracy following claims of compensation for losses suffered by Tunisian subjects in Malta, due to no fault of the Venetians. When diplomatic efforts to reach an agreement failed, the government was forced to take military action. A fleet under Angelo Emo blockaded Tunis and bombarded Susa (November 1784 and May 1785), Sfax (August 1785) and La Coletta (September), and then Sfax and Susa again, and Biserta in 1786. These brilliant military successes brought no com-

risk it for the Morea. When he eventually arrived on the scene, Nauplia, Modon, Corone and Malvasia had fallen. Levkas in the Ionian islands, and the bases of Spinalonga and Suda on Crete which still remained in Venetian hands, were abandoned. The Turks finally landed on Corfu, but its defenders managed to throw them back. In the meantime, the Turks had suffered a grave defeat by the Austrians at Petervaradino on 3 August 1716. Venetian naval efforts in the Aegean and the Dardanelles in 1717 and 1718 met with little success. With the peace of Passarowitz, of 21 July 1718, Austria, the conquering power, made large territorial gains, but Venice lost the Morea, for which her small gains in Albania and Dalmatia were little compensation. This was her last war with Turkey.

Losses from rivals: 1733

In 1733 the five *savi alla mercanzia* wrote, "We have many ports in the Mediterranean which cause losses to our trade." Trade passed direct to Lombardy and Germany from Genoa, Venice's old rival, and Leghorn, created by the grand dukes of Tuscany and a staging-post for English trade in the Mediterranean. Still more injurious were the papal town of Ancona and Hapsburg Trieste, a free port since 1719, in the Adriatic, which no longer constituted a Venetian "Gulf." "Apart from the residue which is left to us, Ancona robs us of the trade from both the Levant and the West, from Albania and the other Turkish provinces. Trieste takes nearly all parable political results in their train, and the Senate recalled Emo and his fleet to Corfu. After Emo's death on 1 March 1792, peace was made with Tunis by increasing the bey's dues.

The last doge: 1789

In January 1789 Lodovico Manin, from a recently ennobled mainland family, was elected doge. The expenses of the election had grown throughout the 18th century, and now reached their highest ever. The patrician Pietro Gradenigo remarked, "I have made a Friulian doge; the Republic is dead." In Valence Napoleon Bonaparte was serving the king of France as an artillery lieutenant.

The end: 1797

In spring 1796 Piedmont fell and the Austrians were beaten from Montenotte to Lodi. The Italian army under Napoleon crossed the frontiers of neutral Venice in pursuit of the enemy.

By the end of the year the French troops were occupying the Venetian state up to the Adige. Vicenza, Cadore and Friuli were held by the Austrians. With the campaigns of the next year Napoleon aimed for the Austrian possessions across the Alps. In the preliminaries to the peace of Leoben, the terms of which remained secret, the Austrians were to take the Venetian possessions as the price of peace (18 April 1797). Nevertheless the peace envisaged the continued survival of the Venetian state, although confined to the city and the lagoon, perhaps with compensation at the expense of the papal states. In the meanwhile Brescia and Bergamo revolted to Venice, and anti-French movements were arising elsewhere. Napoleon threatened Venice with war on 9 April. On 25 April he announced to the Venetian delegates at Graz, "I want no more Inquisition, no more Senate; I shall be an Attila to the state of Venice." Domenico Pizzamano fired on a French ship trying to force an entry from the Lido forts. On 1 May, Napoleon declared war. The French were at the edge of the lagoon. Even the cities of the Veneto had been "revolutionized" by the French, who had established provisional municipalities. On 12 May, the *Maggior Consiglio* approved a motion to hand over power "to the system of the proposed provisional representative government," although there was not a quorum of votes: 512 voted for, ten against, and five abstained. On 16 May the provisional municipal government met in the Hall of the *Maggior Consiglio*. The preliminaries of the peace of Leoben were made even harsher in the Franco-Austrian treaty of Campoformido, and Venice and all her possessions became Austrian. The accord was signed at Passariano, in the last doge's villa, on 18 October 1797.

Above: graceful 18th-century Venetian lady.
Left: colours of the "public ships" of the Republic
of Venice, from a nautical dictionary by a French author (1769).

The Doges of Venice

According to the traditional list, the series of Venetian doges comprises 120 names from Paoluccio Anafesto (or rather Paulicius), who is supposed to have been elected in 697, to Lodovico Manin, who witnessed the end of the *Serenissima*. Even the *magistri militum* are remembered, inserted into the traditional numbering, who governed the city from 737 to 742; the Caroso Tribune; the government of patriarch Orso (1031–32); Domenico Orseolo who was deposed after one day; the first election, which he refused, of Orio Mastropiero (1172); Jacopo Tiepolo, who according to chroniclers was acclaimed by the people, then escaped (1289); and Giovanni Sagredo, whose nomination was considered not to have taken place (1676). Names given in brackets are those attributed to some doges, without any particular foundation, by Venetian tradition.

1. Paulicius (Paoluccio Anafesto) 697–717
2. Marcellus (Marcello Tegaliano) 717–726
3. Ursus (Orso Ipato) 726–737
   Magistri militum: Leo; Felix Cornicula; Deusdedit; Jubianus Ypatus; Johannes Fabriacus 737–742
4. Deusdedit Ypatus (Diodato Ipato) 742–755
5. Galla Gaulo 755–756
6. Dominicus Monegarius (Domenico Monegario) 756–764
7. Mauricius (Maurizio Galbaio) 764–787
8. Johannes (Giovanni Galbaio) 787–804
9. Obilerius and Beatus 804–811
10. Agnellus Particiacus (Agnello Partecipazio) 811–827
11. Justinianus Particiacus (Giustiniano Partecipazio) 827–829
12. Johannes Particiacus (Giovanni I Partecipazio) 829–836
    Revolt of the Caroso Tribune
13. Petrus (Pietro Tradonico) 836–864
14. Ursus Particiacus (Orso I Partecipazio) 864–881
15. Johannes Particiacus (Giovanni II Partecipazio) 881–887
16. Petrus Candianus (Pietro I Candiano) 887

17. Petrus Tribunus (Pietro Tribuno) 888–911
18. Ursus Particiacus (Orso II Partecipazio) 911–932
19. Pietro II Candiano 932–939
20. Petrus Badoer (Pietro Partecipazio known as Badoer) 939–942
21. Pietro III Candiano 942–959
22. Pietro IV Candiano 959–976
23. Pietro I Orseolo 976–978
24. Vitale Candiano 978–979
25. Tribuno Menio (Memmo) 979–991
26. Pietro II Orseolo 991–1009
27. Ottone Orseolo 1009–1026
28. Pietro Centranico 1026–1031
    Orso Orseolo, patriarch of Grado 1031–1032
    Domenico Orseolo 1032
29. Domenico Flabianico 1032–1042/43
30. Domenico Contarini 1042/43–1071
31. Domenico Silvio (Selvo) 1071–1084
32. Vitale Falier 1084–1096
33. Vitale I Michiel 1096–1102
34. Ordelaf Falier 1102–1118
35. Domenico Michiel 1118–1130
36. Pietro Polani 1130–1148
37. Domenico Morosini 1148–1156
38. Vitale II Michiel 1156–1172
    Orio Mastropiero (elected in 1172, he did not accept but took up the position six years later)
39. Sebastiano Ziani 1172–1178
40. Orio Mastropiero 1178–1192
41. Enrico Dandolo 1192–1205
42. Pietro Ziani 5 August 1205–3 March 1229
43. Jacopo Tiepolo 6 March 1229–20 May 1249
44. Marino Morosini 13 June 1249–1 January 1253
45. Ranieri Zeno 25 January 1253–7 July 1268
46. Lorenzo Tiepolo 23 July 1268–15 August 1275
47. Jacopo Contarini 6 September 1275–6 March 1280
48. Giovanni Dandolo 25 March 1280–2 November 1289
    Jacopo Tiepolo (acclaimed by the people in 1289, he fled)
49. Pietro Gradenigo 25 November 1289–13 August 1311
50. Marino Zorzi 23 August 1311–3 July 1312
51. Giovanni Soranzo 13 July 1312–31 December 1328
52. Francesco Dandolo 4 January 1329–31 October 1339
53. Bartolomeo Gradenigo 7 November 1339–28 December 1342
54. Andrea Dandolo 4 January 1343–7 September 1354
55. Marino Falier 11 September 1354–17 April 1355
56. Giovanni Gradenigo 21 April 1355–8 August 1356

57. Giovanni Dolfin 13 August 1356–12 July 1361
58. Lorenzo Celsi 16 July 1361–18 July 1365
59. Marco Corner 21 July 1365–13 January 1368
60. Andrea Contarini 20 January 1368–5 June 1382
61. Michele Morsini 10 June–15 October 1382
62. Antonio Venier 21 October 1382–23 November 1400
63. Michele Steno 1 December 1400–26 December 1413
64. Tommaso Mocenigo 7 January 1414–4 April 1423
65. Francesco Foscari 15 April 1423–23 October 1457
66. Pasquale Malipiero 30 October 1457–5 May 1462
67. Cristoforo Moro 12 May 1462–9 November 1471
68. Nicolò Tron 23 November 1471–28 July 1473
69. Nicolò Marcello 13 August 1473–1 December 1474

Above: Oath of Doge Antonio Venier (1382–1400; State Archives, Venice). Opposite: the doges of Venice from a text in the Biblioteca Marciana. The doges from Paoluccio Anafesto to Tribuno Menio, and from Giovanni Soranzo to Leonardo Loredan are reproduced here.

70. Pietro Mocenigo 14 December 1474–23 February 1476

71. Andrea Vendramin 5 March 1476–6 May 1478

72. Giovanni Mocenigo 18 May 1478–4 November 1485

73. Marco Barbarigo 19 November 1485–14 August 1486

74. Agostino Barbarigo 30 August 1486–20 September 1501

75. Leonardo Loredan 2 October 1501–22 June 1521

76. Antonio Grimani 6 July 1521–7 May 1523

77. Andrea Gritti 20 May 1523–28 December 1538

78. Pietro Lando 19 January 1539–9 November 1545

79. Francesco Donà 24 November 1545–23 May 1553

80. Marcantonio Trevisan 4 June 1553–31 May 1554

81. Francesco Venier 11 June 1554–2 June 1556

82. Lorenzo Priuli 14 June 1556–17 August 1559

83. Girolamo Priuli 1 September 1559–4 November 1567

84. Pietro Loredan 26 November 1567–3 May 1570

85. Alvise I Mocenigo 11 May 1570–4 June 1577

86. Sebastiano Venier 11 June 1577–3 March 1578

87. Nicolò da Ponte 11 August 1578–30 July 1585

88. Pasquale Cicogna 18 August 1585–2 April 1595

89. Marino Grimani 26 April 1595–25 December 1605

90. Leonardo Donà dalle Rose 10 January 1606–16 July 1612

91. Marcantonio Memmo 24 July 1612–29 October 1615

92. Giovanni Bembo 2 December 1615–16 March 1618

93. Nicolo Donà 5 April–9 May 1618

94 Antonio Priuli 17 May 1618–12 August 1623

95. Francesco Contarini 8 September 1623–6 December 1624

96. Giovanni I Corner 4 January 1625–23 December 1629

97. Nicolò Contarini 18 January 1630–2 April 1631

98. Francesco Erizzo 10 April 1631–3 January 1646

99. Francesco Molin 20 January 1646–27 February 1655

100. Carlo Contarini 27 March 1655–30 April 1656

101. Francesco Corner 17 May–4 June 1656

102. Bertuccio (Alberto) Valier 15 June 1656–29 March 1658

103. Giovanni Pesaro 8 April 1658–30 September 1659

104. Domenico Contarini 16 October 1659–26 January 1675

105. Nicolò Sagredo 6 February 1675–14 August 1676

Giovanni Sagredo (his election was considered not to have taken place)

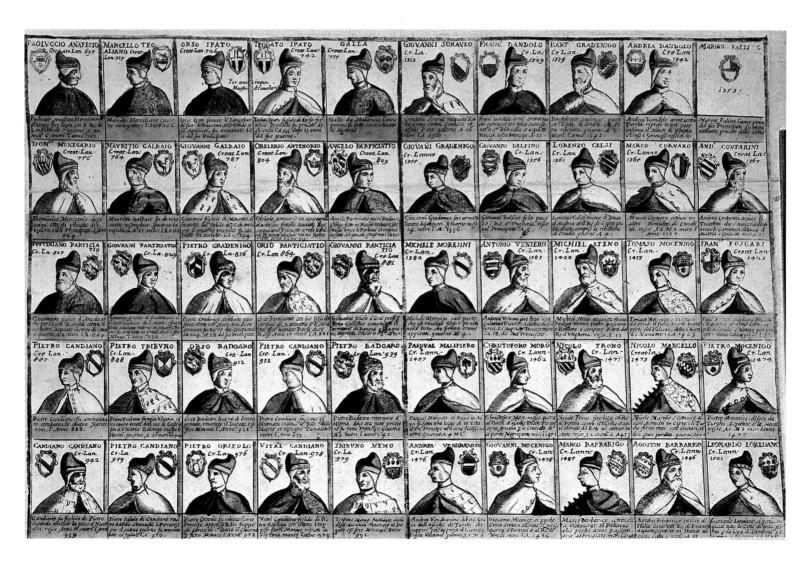

106. Alvise Contarini 26 August 1676–15 January 1684
107. Marcantonio Giustinian 26 January 1684–23 March 1688
108. Francesco Morosini 3 April 1688–6 January 1694
109. Silvestro Valier 25 February 1694–5 July 1700
110. Alvise II Mocenigo 16 July 1700–6 May 1709
111. Giovanni II Corner 22 May 1709–12 August 1722
112. Alvise III Mocenigo 24 August 1722–21 May 1732
113. Carlo Ruzzini 2 June 1732–5 January 1735
114. Alvise Pisani 17 January 1735–17 June 1741
115. Pietro Grimani 17 June 1741–7 March 1752
116. Francesco Loredan 18 March 1752–19 May 1762
117. Marco Foscarini 31 May 1762–31 March 1763
118. Alvise IV Mocenigo 19 April 1763–31 December 1778
119. Paolo Renier 14 January 1779–13 February 1789
120. Lodovico Manin 9 March 1789–12 May 1797

The Patrician Families

Families still in existence

Avogadro
Feudal house of Brescia, admitted to the *Maggior Consiglio* in 1438 for services to the Republic.

Badoer
Perhaps the oldest family, descended from the Parteciaci or Partecipazi who produced seven doges, including Agnello, who was elected after the Frankish invasion and the transfer of the capital on to the islands which form the Venice of today in 810. The family also produced eight procurators of St. Mark and one cardinal.

Baglioni
Family in the printing industry, admitted in 1716.

Balbi
Family which remained in the *Maggior Consiglio* after the *serrata* in 1297.

Barbaro
Famous family which produced, among other illustrious sons, the humanist and politician Marc'Antonio, and his brother Francesco, patriarch of Aquileia, both of whom patronized Palladio and Veronese.

Barozzi
"Old" house, one of the 12 "apostolic" families; The Barozzi produced a patriarch of Grado and were feudal holders of the island of Santorini in the Cyclades.

Bembo
"Old" house, descended from the tribunes, which produced one doge, Giovanni, a brave admiral (died 1618), and the famous cardinal Pietro, humanist and poet.

Bon
Admitted into the patriciate before 1297. They produced diplomats and two procurators of St. Mark.

Bonlini
Family from Brescia, two branches of which were admitted in 1667 and 1685.

Bragadin
One of the "old" families, which claimed doge Orso Ipato, of unknown family (died 737). They produced eight procurators of St. Mark, one cardinal and many other men of importance in the history of the Republic, including Marc'Antonio, who heroically defended Famagusta against the Turks in 1572.

Brandolini
Family of soldiers from the Romagna; admitted in 1686.

Buzzaccarini
Noble Paduan family, admitted in 1782.

Caiselli
Noble family from Udine, admitted in 1779.

Canal, or Da Canal
One of the "new" houses, which produced two captains general *da mar*, four procurators of St. Mark, and one of the most famous medieval chroniclers, Martino, who wrote his chronicle in the 13th century in the *langue d'oil*.

Cappello
"New" house, which produced ten procurators of St. Mark and many ambassadors and captains general *da mar*. Bianca Cappella was grand duchess of Tuscany (1578–1587).

Carminati
Family from Bergamo, admitted in 1687.

Cicogna
One of the *novissima* houses, admitted in 1381 for services in the war against Genoa; it produced doge Pasquale who died in 1595.

Civran
"New" house which remained in the *Maggior Consiglio* in 1297.

Collalto
Great feudal family from Treviso, admitted for services to the Republic before 1306. It produced several famous soldiers.

Condulmer
Patrician family from 1381. It produced two cardinals, one of whom became pope Eugenius IV in 1431.

Corner
One of the oldest houses in Venice, probably of Roman origin. It produced four doges, 22 procurators of St. Mark, nine cardinals, and many ambassadors and generals. Caterina, wife of king Giacomo II Lusignano, king of Cyprus, gave the kingdom to Venice in 1489.

Correr

"New" house, which produced seven procurators of St. Mark and two cardinals, one of whom became pope Gregory XII in 1406. In the last century the nobleman Teodoro Correr founded the Venetian municipal museum which bears his name.

Dolfin

One of the most illustrious "old" houses, which produced one doge, 14 procurators of St. Mark, six cardinals, and a great number of men distinguished in every walk of Venetian life.

Donà

"New" house, divided into two great lines, one of which was called *dalle rose* after the flowers in its coat-of-arms. It produced three doges, one of whom, Leonardo, was one of the greatest figures in Venetian history, eight procurators of St. Mark, one cardinal, and many important cultural figures.

Dondi dall'Orologio

Ancient Paduan family admitted into the *Maggior Consiglio* in 1653.

Emo

"New" house, which produced many important political figures including the famous admiral Angelo who commanded the Republic's last naval venture in 1784–6.

Foscari

This is one of the most famous families in Venetian history, and principally through doge Francesco, who was the guiding spirit behind Venice's expansion onto the mainland. He was forced to abdicate in 1457. His son Jacopo, whose unlucky history inspired Byron and Verdi, is also prominent in their annals. They ceased to be members of the patriciate from the end of the 18th century as a result of a marriage which the *avogadori di Comun* did not approve, but the title of count runs in the family, and was conferred on it by the Republic. It has produced many illustrious people up to our own day, and built the magnificent Gothic palace on the Grand Canal which today houses the University of Venice, and the villa of Malcontenta by Palladio.

Foscolo

Famous for the brave procurator Leonardo, who was captain general *da mar*. In the Middle Ages they were feudal holders of the island of Nanfio.

Gherardini

Veronese family of Florentine origin, admitted in 1652.

Gradenigo

One of the oldest and most important families, involved in all the major events in Venetian history from the beginning. It produced three doges (one of whom, Pietro, was the author of the "locking" of the *Maggior Consiglio* in 1297), 14 procurators, two cardinals and a great number of important diplomats and soldiers.

Grimani

One of the most illustrious "new" houses; three doges, 21 procurators, three cardinals, and important diplomats and admirals. The archaeological collection of Cardinal Domenico, patriarch of Aquileia, which he gave to the Republic, is famous, and forms the nucleus of the Archaeological Museum.

Loredan

Another of the great "new" houses; three doges, 12 procurators of St. Mark and many generals *da mar*. Doge Leonardo (died 1521) was the guiding spirit in the resistance against the League of Cambrai. He built the magnificent palace, later known as the Vendramin Calergi palace, on the Grand Canal.

Manin

Of Florentine origin, they later became important in Friuli, and were admitted into the *Maggior Consiglio* in 1651. They produced the last doge, Lodovico, the only one from a family which paid 100,000 ducats to the war expenses against the Turk to be admitted.

Marcello

"New" house, very probably of Roman origin; it produced one doge, and six procurators, as well as many brave admirals, including Lorenzo who died in the attempt to force the Dardanelles in 1656. Benedetto was a prominent musician of the 18th century.

Marin

Ancient family; the scholar Carlo Antonio was especially famous, and wrote a history of Venetian commerce.

Memmo

Very ancient "old" house, one of the 12 "apostolic" families. They produced one doge, Marcantonio, elected in 1612. Doge Tribune Memmo who was deposed in 991 probably belonged to this family. There were also five procurators of St. Mark, including Andrea, a distinguished diplomat and friend of Giacomo Casanova.

Mino

Family which "remained" in the *Maggior Consiglio* in 1297.

Minotto

"Old" house which produced Giovanni, *bailo* of Constantinople, who perished in the defense of the city against the Turks in 1453.

Moro

"New" house: One doge and six procurators of St. Mark.

Morosini

Very ancient house, one of the twelve "apostolic" families, which remained illustrious from the beginning to the end of the Republic. Four doges, 27 procurators of St. Mark and two cardinals. In the 10th century the Morosini, who belonged to a party which favoured the Byzantines, and the Coloprini, who favoured a rapprochement with the Holy Roman Empire, were the two factions in the city.

Mosto (Da)

"New" house, with many famous sons, including the famous navigator Alvise da Ca' da Mosto. In this family Andrea, the historian of the doges and famous paleographer, added luster to the family.

Nani

Novissima family, admitted in 1381; produced six procurators of St. Mark. Battista, diplomat and historian of the 17th century, should be mentioned.

Orio

Very ancient house, which owned part of the land on which the present quarter of the Rialto was built in the 12th century.

Pasqualigo

One branch entered the *Maggior Consiglio* in 1297, another in 1381. Three procurators of St. Mark, several admirals and ambassadors.

Persico

From Bergamo, admitted in 1685.

Pizzamano

"New" house. Domenico, who defended the port of Venice against the French in 1797, belonged to this family.

Priuli

One of the most illustrious "new" families; produced three doges, 14 procurators of St. Mark and five cardinals.

Querini

"Old" house, claiming descent from doges Maurizio and Giovanni (764–804), to whom the surname Galbaio was attributed by Venetian tradition. They were connected with all the events in the life of the Republic until the end, and were the guiding spirit of the conspiracy of 1310. They produced 15 procurators of St. Mark and one cardinal. Giovanni, last of the line which were feudal holders of the island of Stampalia in the Dodecanese, established a cultural foundation in 1878 which is still in existence.

Redetti
From Rovigo, admitted to the *Maggior Consiglio* in 1698.

Renier
Admitted in 1381; they produced three procurators and the last doge but one, Paolo (died 1789). Giustina, wife of Marcantonio Michiel, was a learned writer and brilliant polemicist in the last century.

Romieri
Admitted in 1689.

Sandi
From Feltre, admitted in 1685. Vettor was was a famous historian of the 18th century.

Soranzo
"Old" house; produced one doge and 16 procurators of St. Mark.

Spatafora
Sicilian feudal house, admitted in 1409. It moved in part to Venice, and took part in the political life of the city.

Tiepolo
One of the 12 "apostolic" families, and one of the most powerful and famous. It produced two doges and seven procurators of St. Mark. Baiamonte, called "the great knight" headed the revolt of 1310.

Trevisan
One line "remained" in 1297, another was admitted in 1381, whilst a third was inscribed into the Golden Book in 1689. One doge and ten procurators of St. Mark.

Valier
"Old" house, one of the 12 "apostolic" families, according to some, and of undoubtedly Roman descent. It produced two doges and two cardinals.

Van Axel
Family of wealthy Flemish merchants, admitted in 1665.

Venier
Another great "new" house; with 21 procurators of St. Mark and three doges, including Sebastiano, victor of the battle of Lepanto.

Veronese
Noble family from Chioggia, admitted in 1704. Produced one cardinal.

Zorzi
"Old" house that produced one doge, 11 procurators of St. Mark, one cardinal, and the feudal lords of Curzola in Dalmatia, Lampsacus and Karistos in Greece, and Levkas in the Ionian islands.

Some of the chief families now extinct

Barbarigo
One of the most important "new" houses. Two doges, ten procurators, four cardinals, one of whom, Gregory, bishop of Padua, was canonized by pope John XXIII.

Barbo
Four procurators and one cardinal, afterwards pope Paul II.

Bernardo
"New" house; produced four procurators and built two fine Gothic palaces, one of which is on the Grand Canal.

Cavalli
Novissima family, known for three ambassadors of note, Jacopo, Marino, and Sigismondo, and for a brave general also called Jacopo.

Celsi
Two procurators and one doge, Lorenzo (died 1365).

Contarini
One of the 12 "apostolic" families, and one of the most important throughout Venetian history. It produced eight doges and 44 procurators of St. Mark. Gasparo, diplomat and cardinal, was one of the forerunners of the Counter-Reformation.

Dandolo
One of the noblest houses of Europe. Four doges, including Enrico, conqueror of Constantinople and leader of the fourth crusade, and Andrea, chronicler and *littérateur*, a friend of Petrarch. The family also produced 12 procurators and one patriarch of Grado.

Diedo
"New" house; three procurators of St. Mark and many other distinguished figures.

Duodo
"New" house; four procurators of St. Mark.

Erizzo
"New" house; one doge, four procurators. Paolo defended Negropont against the Turks. Niccolò Guido was one of the few capable and courageous politicians in the last days of the Republic.

Falier
Very old house; one of the 12 "apostolic" families, probably of Roman descent. Three doges, including Marino, beheaded in 1355 for having tried to make himself lord of Venice. Five procurators, one patriarch of Grado.

Foscarini
"Old" house; one doge (Marco, *littérateur* of some merit, died 1763), 14 procurators, several generals, diplomats and politicians.

Gritti
"New" house that produced doge Andrea, who had been the victorious general in the battles against the League of Cambrai and has been immortalized in a famous portrait by Titian.

Labia
Family admitted to the patriciate in 1646, famous for the magnificent palace in which Giambattista Tiepolo painted the frescoes, and for the saying, *l'abia o no l'abia, sarò sempre Labia*, "wealthy or not, I shall always be Labia," said by a Labia as he threw a gold plate out of the window.

Lando
One doge, four procurators, and several famous bishops.

Lezze (Da)
Family of diplomats and soldiers; produced seven procurators of St. Mark.

Malipiero
"New" house; produced one doge and three procurators of St. Mark.

Michiel
Another very ancient house, famous for three doges, twelve procurators of St. Mark, one cardinal, and many politicians and soldiers. Marcantonio acted with strength and fortitude in the last days of the Republic.

Mocenigo

Very great "new" house that produced seven doges, 25 procurators and, among a host of others, the brave admirals Alvise Leonardo and Lazzaro, hero of the wars against the Turks. Only recently extinct.

Molin (Da)

One doge, nine procurators of St. Mark, and many politicians, generals and prosperous merchants.

Navagero

Famous for Andrea, diplomat and poet, and for cardinal Bernardo.

Orseolo

Famous dynasty which produced doges Pietro I (later to become a Camaldolese monk and a saint), Pietro II, conqueror of Istria and Dalmatia, Ottone, and Orso, patriarch of Grado and regent of the duchy. This family was closely connected with the Byzantine ruling family, and with the family of St. Stephen, king of Hungary. It became extinct in the 14th century.

Paruta

Novissima house; it produced Piero, historian and procurator of St. Mark.

Pesaro

One doge, seven procurators, and the superb palace on the Grand Canal, the masterpiece of Baldassare Longhena.

Pisani

Rich family of merchants and bankers, which produced diplomats and soldiers including Vittor Pisani, national hero and Supreme Commander in the war of Chioggia against Genoa. Sixteen procurators of St. Mark and one doge, Alvise, who built the grand villa of Stra.

Polani

One of the "apostolic" houses; produced one doge, Pietro (died 1148).

Polo

Famous for the travellers Nicolò, Matteo, and Marco; The latter was author of a famous book on his travels, known as *Il Milione*.

Ponte (da)

Produced doge Nicolò, a superb diplomat (died 1585), and three procurators of St. Mark.

Rezzonico

Family from Como, admitted to the *Maggior Consiglio* in 1687, produced two cardinals, one of whom became pope Clement XIII (1758–69), and

two procurators of St. Mark.

Ruzzini

"Old" house, produced two procurators and doge Carlo, one of the shrewdest of diplomats (died 1735).

Sagredo

Gherardo, abbot of San Giorgio Maggiore, evangelized Hungary and died a martyr's death in 1047. He was later canonized. The family also produced one doge and seven procurators, including Giovanni, historian and man of letters. In the last century, Agostino was a famous scholar of Venetian affairs.

Sanudo

Very ancient house, which claimed descent from The Candiani who produced five doges in the ninth and tenth centuries. Marco, nephew of doge Enrico Dandolo, conquered the duchy of Naxos in the Cyclades for himself. Marino the Elder called Torsello was a merchant, writer and geographer. Marino the Younger who lived at the turn of the 15th and 16th centuries wrote the vast *Diarii* (*Diaries*), which are a masterpiece of Renaissance chronicle writing.

Steno

Three procurators and one doge, Michele, the first to take the opportunity to expand on the mainland.

Tron

One doge, and seven procurators of St. Mark, including Andrea, *savio del Consiglio* (sage of the Council), who exercised immense power in the Venice of the mid-18th century.

Vendramin

Novissima family, very wealthy; produced one doge, Andrea (died 1478), three procurators of St. Mark and one cardinal.

Zane

Very ancient and very wealthy house that produced five procurators of St. Mark.

Zeno

"Old" house, only very recently extinct in the male line, one of the most active throughout Venetian history. One doge, 13 procurators of St. Mark, cardinal Giovanni Battista who has a fine tomb in St. Mark's basilica, and the navigators Niccolò, Antonio and Caterino, as well as Carlo, a national hero in the wars against Genoa in the Middle Ages.

Zustinian (or Giustinian)

One of the greatest "old" families, only recently extinct. It produced one doge, 27 procurators, and

a great number of important personages including Paolo, forerunner of the modern reforms in the Roman Catholic church; and Leonardo, one of the finest Venetian poets. Angelo Lorenzo, *provveditore* in Trieste in 1797, bravely stood up to Napoleon Bonaparte.

The main non-Venetian families admitted to the patriciate at various times

At various times European ruling houses were inscribed in the Golden Book, such as the Bourbons of France, the Bourbons of Parma, the Wittelsbachs of Bavaria and the dukes of Brunswick. So were various families of Italian princes, including the house of Savoy, the Estensi, dukes of Ferrara and later Modena, the Gonzaga, Marquises and later dukes of Mantua, the Medici of Florence, later grand dukes of Tuscany, the Cybo Malaspina, Marquises of Massa, the Pico della Mirandola, the Pio da Carpi, the Sforza, dukes of Milan, and the Pallavicino, Marquises of the so-called "Pallavicino state." The honour was sometimes extended to families who possessed lordships in the Veneto, such as the Carraresi, lords of Padua, and the Scaligeri of Verona, as well as to soldiers loyal to the Republic. Papal families were often inscribed; such were the Albani, Aldobrandini, Altieri, Barberini, Boncompagni, Borghese, Chigi, Colonna, Conti, Corsini, Ludovisi, Odescalchi, Orsini, Pamphili, Pignatelli, Rospigliosi, and Savelli. None of these families ever played an active part in the parliamentary work of the *Maggior Consiglio*, with the exception of the Bentivoglio of Aragon, an extinct branch of the family which held the lordship of Bologna, and the Pepoli, also from Bologna.

"Regiments" at the Fall of the Republic (1797)

Listed below are the administrative bodies and the respective titles of the domains of the Venetian Republic.

Dogado

CAORLE, *podestà* (16 months)

CAVARZERE, *podestà* (16 months)

CHIOGGIA, *podestà* (16 months); *saliner* (16 months); *castellano* (16 months)

GAMBARARE, *provveditore* (24 months)

GRADO, count (16 months)

LIDO, *castellano* (16 months)

LOREO, *podestà* (16 months)

MALAMOCCO, *podestà* (16 months)

MARANO, *podestà* (16 months)

MURANO, *podestà* (16 months)

TORCELLO, *podestà* (16 months)

Sea regiments

ALBONA, *podestà* (32 months)

ALMISSA, *provveditore* (24 months)

ARBE, count and captain (32 months)

ASSO, *provveditore* (24 months)

BRAZZA, count (32 months)

BUDUA, *podestà* (32 months)

BUIE D'ISTRIA, *podestà* (32 months)

CAPODISTRIA, *podestà* and captain (16 months); 2 *consiglieri* (16 months)

CASTELNUOVO, *provveditore* (24 months); *castellano* (24 months)

CATTARO, governor and *provveditore* (24 months); *camerlengo* (32 months)

CEPHALONIA, *provveditore* (24 months); 2 *consiglieri* (24 months)

CERIGO, *provveditore* (24 months); *castellano* (24 months)

CHERSO, count and captain (24 months)

CITTANOVA, *podestà* (16 months)

CLISSA, *provveditore* (24 months)

CORFU, *bailo* (24 months); *provveditore* and captain (24 months); 2 *consiglieri* (24 months); *capitano della cittadella* (24 months); *castellano della cittadella* (24 months)

CURZOLA, count (32 months)

DIGNANO, *podestà* (16 months)

ISOLA D'ISTRIA, *podestà* (16 months)

KNIN, *provveditore* (24 months); *castellano* (24 months)

LESINA, count and *provveditore* (24 months); *camerlengo* and *castellano* (24 months)

LEVKAS, *provveditore* (24 months)

MACARSCA, *provveditore* (24 months)

MONTONA, *podestà* (32 months)

MUGGIA, *podestà* (16 months); *castellano* (16 months)

NONA, count (32 months)

NOVEGRADI, *provveditore* (24 months)

PAGO, count (32 months); *camerlengo* (32 months)

PARENZO, *podestà* (16 months)

PIRANO, *podestà* (16 months)

POLA, count and *provveditore* (16 months); 2 *camerlenghi* (16 months); *castellano di San Felice* (16 months); *castellano di Castel Vecchio* (16 months)

PORTOLE, *podestà* (32 months)

PREVEZA, *provveditore* (24 months)

RASPO, captain (32 months)

ROVIGNO, *podestà* (16 months)

SCIM, *provveditore* (24 months)

SEBENICO, count and captain (24 months); *camerlengo* and *castellano* (32 months); *castellano di San Nicolò* (24 months)

SPALATO, count (32 months); *camerlengo* and *castellano* (32 months)

TRAÚ, count (32 months)

UMAGO, *podestà* (16 months)

VALLE D'ISTRIA, *podestà* (16 months)

VEGLIA, *provveditore* (32 months); *camerlengo* and *castellano* (32 months)

VONITSA, *provveditore* (24 months)

ZANTE, *provveditore* (24 months); 2 *consiglieri* (24 months)

ZARA, count (24 months); captain (24 months); *camerlengo* and *castellano* (24 months)

Land regiments

ADRIA, *podestà* (16 months)

ANFO, *provveditore* (24 months)

ASOLA, *provveditore* (16 months); *castellano* (24 months)

ASOLO, *podestà* (16 months)

ASSO, *provveditore* (24 months)

BADIA POLESINE, *podestà* (16 months)

BASSANO, *podestà* and captain (16 months)

BELLUNO, *podestà* and captain (16 months)

BERGAMO, *podestà* (16 months); captain (16 months); 2 *Camerlenghi* (32 months); *castellano della cappella* (16 months)

BRESCIA, *podestà* (16 months); captain (16 months); 2 *camerlenghi* (16 months); *castellano* (16 months)

CADORE, captain (32 months)

CAMPOSAMPIERO, *podestà* (16 months)

CANEVA DI SACILE, *podestà* (16 months)

CASTELBALDO, *podestà* (16 months)

CASTELFRANCO, *podestà* (16 months)

CENEDA E TARSO, *podestà* (16 months)

CHIUSA, *castellano* (24 months)

CITTADELLA, *podestà* (16 months)

CIVIDALE DEL FRIULI, *provveditore* (16 months)

COLOGNA VENETA, *podestà* (16 months)

CONEGLIANO, *podestà* and captain (16 months)

CREMA, *podestà* and captain (16 months); 2 *camerlenghi* (32 months); *castellano* (24 months)

ESTE, *podestà* and captain (16 months)

FELTRE, *podestà* and captain (16 months)

GRISIGNANO, *podestà* (16 months)

LEGNAGO, *provveditore* and captain (16 months)

LENDINARA, *podestà* (16 months)

LONATO, *provveditore* (16 months)

LONIGO, *podestà* (16 months)

MAROSTICA, *podestà* (16 months)

MARTINENGO, *podestà* (32 months); *provveditore* (32 months)

MESTRE, *podestà* (16 months); *castellano* (32 months)

MONSELICE, *podestà* (16 months)

MONTAGNANA, *podestà* (16 months)

MOTTA DI LIVENZA, *podestà* (16 months)

NOALE, *podestà* (16 months)

ODERZO, *podestà* (16 months)

ORZINUOVI, *provveditore* (16 months)

PADUA, *podestà* (16 months); captain (16 months); 2 *camerlenghi* (16 months); *castellano della Saracinesca* (16 months); *castellano di Castel Vecchio* (32 months)

PESCHIERA, *provveditore* (16 months); *castellano* (16 months)

PIOVE DI SACCO, *podestà* (16 months)

PONTEVIGODARZERE, *castellano* (32 months)

PORDENONE, *podestà* and captain (16 months)

PORTOBUFFOLE, *podestà* (16 months)

PORTOGRUARO, *podestà* (16 months)

QUERO, *castellano* (32 months)

ROMAN, *podestà* and *provveditore* (32 months)

ROVIGO, *podestà* and captain (16 months); 2 *camerlenghi* (16 months)

SACILE, *podestà* and captain (16 months)

SALÒ, *provveditore* and captain (16 months)

SERRAVALLE, *podestà* (16 months)

SOAVE, captain (16 months)

TREVISO, *podestà* and captain (16 months); 2 *camerlenghi* (16 months)

UDINE, *luogotenente* (16 months); 2 treasurers (16 months); *miniscalco* (32 months)

VERONA, *podestà* (16 months); captain (16 months); 2 *camerlenghi* (16 months); *castellano di San Felice* (16 months); *castellano di Castel Vecchio* (16 months)

VICENZA, *podestà* (16 months); captain (16 months); 2 *camerlenghi* (16 months)

A Short Glossary of Venetian Place Names

Abate: the corte dell'Abate is a courtyard in San Gregorio, so named after some houses which belonged to the abbey of San Gregorio. The pedestal holding the standards which decorated Venice's *campi* was once known as an *abate*.

Abazia: abbey. The name, from the abbey of Santa Maria della Misericordia, extends to the neighbouring *fondamenta*, portico, *campo*, and bridge.

Accademia: the Academy of Nobles for the education of young patricians was founded in 1619. It was on the Giudecca, and gave its name to a *calle*. The Academy of Fine Arts gave its name to the ugly wooden bridge over the Grand Canal which was built some 40 years ago to replace an even uglier cast iron bridge built by the Austrians.

Acqua dolce: the barges which brought fresh water from the mainland to fill up the city's wells halted at a canal in the Santi Apostoli district, to which they gave their name.

Acquavita: aqua vitae. Coffee shop owners were also spirit-sellers. A bridge and a *calle* are named after one of these merchants' shops.

Acque: "spirit-shops" was the old name for cafés. There is a calle delle Acque in San Salvador.

Altana: wooden belvedere on the roof of a house. Here families would spend summer evenings. Venetian women would sit on the *altane* wearing a *solana*, a kind of crownless straw hat, to bleach their hair.

Anatomia: the theater of anatomy was established in 1761 and gave its name to a courtyard and a bridge near San Giacomo dell'Orio.

Arsenale: the complex of shipyards and workshops where the Venetian fleet was built. The name may derive from the Arabic word *darsina'a*, a workshop, or from the Italian *darsena*, dock, or else from *arginato*, a place enclosed by dykes.

Arzere: dam, dyke. There are a bridge and a *calle* of this name.

Aseo: vinegar. A *calle* and a bridge in San Marcuola are so called after a vinegar works which stood there in the 15th century.

Assassini: the *rio* and *calle* of this name in San Beneto are said to take their name from the frequent murders which were committed there in remote times. The government forbade the wearing of false beards, which criminals were in the habit of using, for reasons of public security, and ordered *cesendoli*, or lanterns to be hung by night in unsafe streets.

Avogaría: Ministry of Justice. There are a bridge, a *rio*, a *ramo* and a *calle* so named in San Barnaba, because the Zamberti who lived there held office in the *Avogaria di Comun*.

Bacino: sheet of water, wide part of a canal, used for mooring ships, as in St. Mark's basin, or gondolas, as in the Orseolo basin which was dug in the 19th century near St. Mark's square.

Balanze: weighing scales. The *calle* of this name in San Luca was named after a workshop where these were made.

Banco Giro: the state bank founded in the 17th century and known as the Banco del Giro gave its name to an arcade on the Rialto.

Bande: parapets. One of the first bridges to be so protected near Santa Maria Formosa still bears this name.

Bando: the *pietra del bando* from which the *bandi* or decrees were announced is the stump of a column of Syrian porphyry situated on the south corner of St. Mark's basilica.

Barbacani: these were wooden corbels which supported upper floors projecting out over the street. In the calle della Madonna in San Polo there was a stone corbel of this type supporting a huge projection.

Barbaria delle tole: wooden planks (*tole*) may have been planed, removing their "*barbe*" (beards) in this *calle*, giving it this name.

Bareteri: beret or cap-makers. There are a bridge and a *rio* of this name in San Salvador.

Beccarie: butchers' shops. The public butchery consisted of rented rooms in the houses on the Rialto belonging to the rebel Guerini, and gave its name to a *calle*, a *campo*, a bridge, and a *rio*.

Bergama: the inn, *La Bergama* where foreigners from the city of Bergamo stayed, gave its name to a *calle* and a bridge next to San Simeone Grande.

Biasio: this was the name of a pork-butcher who according to some accounts killed small boys to make the *squazzeto alla Boechera*, a pork delicacy still appreciated in Venice today. The *riva* at San Simeone Grande is supposed to be named after him.

Bisati: eels. There was a business which sold eels in a passage of this name in the Gesuati.

Bissa: snake. The calle della Bissa in San Bartolomeo is so named either because it is very windy, or because shops selling the silk cloth known as *bisso* fronted on to it.

Bo: ox. In the calle del Bo on the Rialto there was an apothecary's shop under the sign of a golden ox. Before this there was a hostelry under the same sign.

Bocca di Piazza: this is the broadway at the eastern entrance to St. Mark's square.

Boteri: coopers. A *calle* in San Cassiano is named after them.

Bovolo: spiral staircase. The Palazzo Contarini del Bovolo in San Luca is so called after the fine spiral staircase in its courtyard.

Bragora: the name of the church of San Giovanni in Bragora may perhaps derive from the Greek *agorà*, market-place, or else from the Venetian dialect words *bragolà*, market-place, or from *bragolare*, to fish.

Bressana: this place name in San Zanipolo comes from the official representative of the city of Brescia. Like Bergamo, Chioggia, Vicenza and Badia Polesine, subject cities of the Republic, the Patria del Friuli and Feltre, Brescia also had a nuncio and a residence in Venice.

Buranelli: the inhabitants of Burano. There is a *calle* named after them.

Burchielle: small barges. There are a *rio* and a *fondamenta* named after them in Sant'Andrea.

Ca': house, used also in the sense of family.

Ca' di Dio: the Ca' di Dio *riva*, bridge and *rio* are reminders of a hospice which was founded in the 13th century to house pilgrims from the Holy Land.

Caffettier: coffee-shop keeper. The *calli* of this name recall old coffee-shops.

Calcina: the lime-sellers' shops were on the Zattere. A bridge and a *campiello* are named after them.

Calderer: coppersmith. There is a *calle* del Calderer in San Marcilian.

Calegheri: shoemakers. The *ramo* dei Calegheri in San Tomà is named after the fine *scuola* of the guild of shoemakers which faced on to the *campo*.

Callesella: small *calle*.

Calletta: small *calle*.

Calle: from the Latin *callis*. Streets in Venice are known as *calli*, *calli larghe* (wide streets), and in the diminutive, *callette* and *calleselle*, except for a few which preserve the old Italian form *ruga* and its diminutive *rughetta*, and a very few other wide, recent streets, which are known as *vie* (streets).

Campanati: bell-founders. A foundry in the *sestiere* of Castello (or perhaps a Campanati family) gave its name to the *ramo*.

Campazzo: large *campo* (square). There are a *campazzo* San Sebastiano and *campazzo* dei Tolentini.

Campiello: little square.

Campo: squares in Venice are so called, the term *piazza* being used only for St. Mark's square (Piazza San Marco). From *campo* come *campazzo* and *campiello*.

Canalazzo: popular term for the Grand Canal.

Canal Grande: the Grand Canal is the largest canal in Venice and with its double bend divides in two the Realtine islands on which the city is built. It is an old river course, perhaps that of the Rivus Businacus.

Canali: the canals separate the islands on which the city stands, forming a network of waterborne communication ways. There are some hundred canals, the smaller of them being known as *rio*, and a few as *riello* and *rio menuo* (tiny *rio*). The canals in the lagoon are navigation channels excavated in the shallows, and are marked out by *bricole* or wooden posts.

Cannaregio: from the Latin *cannarecium* or rather *canaleclum*, a marshy zone with reeds. It is one of the city's *sestieri*.

Capitello: the merceria del Capitello, which links St. Mark's square and the Rialto, is named after a little walled shrine (*capitello*) which stands there.

Carampane: the Venetian family of Rampani, known in everyday speech as Ca'Rampani, owned houses in San Cassiano where there are a *calle* and a *rio terrà* of this name. The popular term derives from the large number of courtesans or *carampane* who were originally to be found in the Castelletto on the Rialto, but later moved to this street.

Carbon: coal barges moored along the Grand Canal in San Luca to sell their goods wholesale, gave their name to the *riva, calle, ramo, sottoportico* and *traghetto*.

Cariole: barrows. There are a *sottoportico* and a *corte* in San Zulian named after a shop which made barrows.

Carità: the campo della Carità takes its name from the church and great *scuola* of Santa Maria della Carità.

Carmini: name given to the church of Santa Maria del Carmelo on the campo dei Carmini.

Carrozze: carriages. Strange as it may seem, carriages for use on land were made in Venice until the end of the 17th century. A carriage-maker of 1661 gave this name to a *calle* in San Samuele.

Casaria: market for dairy produce on the Rialto. The term derives from the Latin word *caseus*, cheese, and the Venetian word *casarol* derived from it.

Casin dei Spiriti: literally, "house of ghosts." Villa on the lagoon, on the Sacca della Misericordia, in the garden of the Palazzo Contarini Dal Zaffo so called either because of its echo, or because of its isolation.

Cason: prison. Each *sestiere* had its own prison for debtors and minor offenders. There is a *campiello* della Cason in Santi Apostoli.

Casselleria: the *calle* of chest-makers in Santa Maria Formosa, where chests were made for sending goods and for dowries.

Castello: the name of this *sestiere* derives from a Roman fort which was probably situated on the island of Olivolo, which was one of the earliest settlements on the lagoon, and where the bishop had his seat in San Pietro di Castello.

Cavallo: the workshop in which the equestrian statue of the Colleoni was cast was in the corte del Cavallo in Madonna dell' Orto. The bridge and calle del Cavallo in San Zanipolo are also named after this monument.

Celestia: *campo* and *rio* near the place where the now demolished church of Santa Maria della Celestia once stood.

Cenere: ash. Soap and lye were made from the ash deposits of Istria and Slavonia. This gave its name to a *calle*.

Cerchieri: coopers. There are a *ramo* and a *calle* of this name in San Barnaba.

Cereri: candle-makers. The term is found in the name of a *fondamenta* in Santa Maria Maggiore.

Chiovere: there is a campiello delle Chiovere in San Rocco. *Chiovere* were stretches of ground where cloth was dried after dyeing. Earlier they were enclosed meadows, *clauderiae*, from which the Venetian word is derived.

Colonne: the two granite columns at the end of the Piazzetta facing the Molo, one of which is pink and the other grey. On their tops they support the Lion of St. Mark and the statue of San Todaro (St. Theodore), the first patron saint of the city. They come from the East.

Coltrera: perhaps named after a manufactory of blankets (*coltri*). There is a *corte* in the *sestiere* of Castello with this name.

Corazzeri: armourers. The streets, a *calle*, *ramo*, and *sottoportico*, between Sant'Antonin and San Martino di Castello, where the armourers worked.

Cordaria: rope-factory. This place-name is found in the Rialto where there were many rope-shops.

Corli: wool-winders (also tramps and worthless people). There is a *calle* in San Tomà with this name, either because of shops of people of this profession, or else on account of the prostitutes who lived there.

Corte: small square surrounded by houses, with a single entrance.

Crea: clay. There are *calli* of this name in Spirito Santo and San Giobbe where there were clay deposits used in brick-making.

Crosera: place where several streets begin, crossing.

Cuoridoro: craftsmen in gilded leather, which was used for covering walls, chairs and books. There are a *sottoportico* and a *corte* in San Fantin of this name.

Dai: dice. Dice-playing and the sale of dice were commonest in the San Marco *sestiere* where there are an arcade, a bridge, a *rio*, and a *fondamenta* with this name. According to a more romantic interpretation, the name is derived from the cries of the people who pursued one party of Baiamonte Tiepolo's conspirators, fleeing across St. Mark's square after their attempted coup d'état of 10 June 1310.

Diamanter: diamond worker. The *diamanteri da duro* worked diamonds, and the *diamanteri da tenero* other precious stones and coloured gems. A *corte* in Santa Fosca bears this name.

Diavolo: there are an arcade and a *corte* of this name ("devil") in Santa Maria Mater Domini, perhaps, according to the learned Tassini, because of the almost devilish darkness of the spot.

Doaneta: small customs house. The Doaneta dell'Ogio where oil for sale in the city was stored and measured had given its name to a *ramo* in the Frari.

Donna onesta: there are a *calle*, a bridge and a *fondamenta* of this name in San Pantalon. According to a traditional story two gentlemen were debating the honesty of women on this bridge, when one of them ironically pointed to the small head of a woman on the wall of the neighbouring house as the only honest woman. The name may also be derived from a married woman who killed herself after being raped, or else from a prostitute who was called an honest woman because of the discretion with which she plied her trade.

Dorsoduro: "hard ridge," one of the *sestieri* of Venice. So called perhaps because it stands on ridges which were harder than the others.

Dose: doge. Doge Nicolò Marcello was born in a palace in Santa Marina, an event which gave the name to a *calle*, a *corte*, and the *fondamenta*. The name is found elsewhere, and refers to other houses and palaces, or business premises under the doge's arms.

Due Aprile: there is a merc, of this name in San Bartolomeo recalling the events of 2 April 1849, when the Venetian assembly determined to resist the Austrians at all costs.

Erberia: market in the Rialto selling fruit and vegetables from neighbouring islands and the mainland.

Fabbri: the calle dei Fabbri in San Moisè is so named after the *scuola* of the smiths.

Fava: according to some the calle della Fava in San Lio is so named after a miracle, while others say that it refers to an old pastry-shop renowned for its *fave dolci*, a special sweet eaten on All Souls' Day. In the next *campo* there is the Church of Santa Maria della Consolazione or della Fava.

Felzi: a *felze* is a movable cabin placed over the main seat of a gondola in winter. The fondamenta dei Felzi, named after the *felze* makers who worked there, is in San Zanipolo.

Ferali: street lamps. The bridge and *rio* of this name are in San Zulian.

Fiubera: buckle, pin. A *calle* and an arcade in San Zulian are so named after the shops which sold them.

Fondamenta: these are the streets which run alongside the *rii* and canals, so called because they form the base of foundations for the buildings.

Fontego: factory, building used as a warehouse, and sometimes also a dwelling place by the various foreign communities of merchants, *e.g.* the Turkish, German and Persian factories. The name is found in various parts of the city.

Formagier: cheese-seller. There is a *salizzada* (paved street) of this name in San Canciano.

Formosa: this term appears in the name of the church of Santa Maria Formosa, traditionally founded in the seventh century by St. Magno, bishop of Oderzo, to whom the Virgin had appeared in the form of a beautiful matron (Latin, *formosa*).

Forner: baker. This is a common name, and indicates the site of bakeries.

Forni: the calle dei Forni in San Giovanni in Bragora takes its name from the 15th century military bakeries which stood there, where the biscuit for the Venetian armada was made.

Frari: the large church of Santa Maria dei Frari stands in the campo dei Frari *i.e.* the Franciscan Friors Minor, for whom it was built.

Frezzeria: arrow-factory. The Frezzeria is a busy commercial street in San Marco.

Frutarol: fruit-seller. There are a number of calli del Frutarol, one of which is in San Fantin.

Furlane: Friulan. The campo and calle delle Furlane in the Castello *sestiere* may also be named after the *furlana*, a dance which was performed there.

Fuseri: spindle-makers. The name is applied to a *ramo*, a bridge, a *rio*, and a *calle* in San Luca.

Gatte: a corruption of *legate* or papal nuncios, who lived nearby, where there are a *salizzada*, a *ramo*, and a *campo* named after them, until they moved to the *Nunziatura* in San Francesco della Vigna.

Gesuati: this is the name of the church of Santa Maria del Rosario on the Zattere, built in the 18th century on the site of a religious house belonging to the abolished order of *gesuati*. The Jesuit church is considerably older, and still in existence.

Ghetto: the Jewish quarter of Venice stands on the site of old foundries, where arms were cast (*gettare*). The German-speaking Jews who were the first to settle there pronounced the word *getto*, foundry, with a hard *g*.

Giudecca: the large island south of the main part of the city is so called because it was inhabited by the Jews for a certain period. Others consider, though without much evidence, that the name comes from *zudegà*, the Venetian for *giudicato*, the judgment whereby lands were awarded to families recalled from exile at the end of the 11th century.

Giuffa: the riga Giuffa in San Lorenzo is perhaps named after the Armenian city of Julfa, merchants from which resided in the quarter. It is more likely that it comes from *gajuffi*, louts or gypsies.

Gobbo di Rialto: this is a 16th-century statue of a kneeling man supporting the steps leading to a column in the campo di Rialto from which the *comandador* proclaimed laws and made other announcements.

Gorna: gutter, drain. There was a drain taking rainwater into the lagoon on the calle della Gorna on the Fondamenta Nuove.

Guerra: street battles with fisticuffs or staves between the inhabitants of different districts were a very popular sport, and were held on a number of bridges. The ponte dei Pugni and the ponte della Guerra in San Zulian commemorate them.

Guglie: the ponte delle Guglie on the Cannaregio canal is named after the four small obelisks on its parapets.

Incurabili: there are a bridge and a *campiello* named after the Hospital for Incurables where St. Ignatius Loyola and St. Francis Xavier worked.

Indorador: gilder. A *sottoportico* and a *corte* in Santa Marina recall the existence of a gilder's shop there.

Lavadori: wool dealers. The calle dei Lavadori is in the Tolentini.

Leoncini: the two red marble lions gave their name to the *piazzetta* facing St. Mark's basilica which is now known as the Piazzetta Giovanni XXIII.

Librer: bookseller. The *campiello* of this name is in San Polo, and called after one of Venice's many bookshops.

Lista: the area of street in front of an ambassador's residence marked out by white stones, within which diplomatic immunity prevailed. The term is found in the Lista di Spagna where the embassy of the Catholic king stood.

Liston: at the beginning of the 18th century the paving of St. Mark's square was renovated with slabs of trachyte from the Euganean hills and white Istria stone. The latter gave the name *liston* to the public way.

Loggetta: the building designed by Sansovino at the foot of the Campanile (St. Mark's bell-tower). In the 17th century it was the guardroom of the Arsenal workers who kept public order during sessions of the *Maggior Consiglio* under the command of a procurator of St. Mark.

Luganegher: pork-butcher. This is a common name in Venice, occurring in the Frezzeria, in Sant'Aponal and elsewhere.

Lustraferri: polisher of the *ferri*, the iron ornament which decorates the prow of gondolas. The bridge of the Lustraferri is on the Fondamenta degli Ormesini.

Madoneta: the rio della Madoneta is named after a bas-relief of the Madonna on the façade of the Donà palace.

Malvasia: a sought-after wine which came originally from Malvasia in the Morea. There are several calli della Malvasia around Venice.

Mandoler: almond-seller. There is a calle del Mandoler in San Tomà.

Manganer: mangler, *i.e.* a cleaner of silk and woollen cloth. There is a calle del Manganer in Santi Apostoli.

Marangon: ship's carpenter and, by extension, carpenter. There are calli del Marangon almost everywhere in Venice.

Marangona: this was the name of one of the bells in St. Mark's bell-tower which gave the signal for the start and end of work for the carpenters of the Arsenal.

Margaritera: the *margariteri* made small beads of enamelled glass called *margarite*, pearls. The corte Margaritera is in San Martino di Castello.

Marzer: draper. There is a calle del Marzer in San Polo.

Megio: millet. The *fondamenta*, bridge, *sottoportico* and *calle* of this name in San Giacomo dell'Orio are so called after the millet and grain stores which the Republic maintained here in case of shortage.

Mendicanti: the *fondamenta* and rio dei Mendicanti are named after the hospice and church of San Lazzaro dei Mendicanti.

Mendicoli: mendicants. The name is found in the places connected with the church of San Nicolò dei Mendicoli, one of the earliest churches in Venice.

Mercerie: the five different stretches of the shopping-street joining St. Mark's square and the Rialto.

Milion: the house of the Polo family, nicknamed "Milion," stood in the corte del Milion in San Giovanni Crisostomo. *Il Milione* is the name given to Marco Polo's *Livre des merveilles*.

Miracoli: these place names refer to the church of Santa Maria dei Miracoli, built in the Renaissance to house an image of the Madonna which was held to be miraculous.

Misericordia: these place names refer to the Scuola Grande di Santa Maria Valverde or della Misericordia, one of the largest *scuole* in Venice.

Mistra: Mistress (of a *scuola* or guild). The corte della Mistra is in San Barnaba.

Molo: the quay by the Piazzetta and the Doge's Palace.

Mori: there is a campo dei Mori in Madonna dell'Orto, named after the three sculptures of the Mastelli brothers, traders from the Morea dressed in the eastern manner. The two bronze figures which strike the hours on the top of the clock-tower in St. Mark's square are also called the *Mori*, as are the four figures of the tetrarchs in red porphyry on the southern side of St. Mark's basilica.

Mosche: black taffeta beauty spots used by women in order to bring out the whiteness of their skin.

There are a *campo*, *ramo* and *campiello* delle Mosche in San Pantalon which are named after the place where these ornaments were made.

Muneghe: nuns; *muneghette*, young nuns. The names are found in a number of place names commemorating nunneries in Sant' Alvise, Santa Marina, San Maurizio and elsewhere.

Murer: builder. There is a calle del Murer in the Incurabili. The builders had a very fine *scuola* in San Samuele.

Naranzeria: orange market and warehouse on the Rialto.

Nomboli: the hindquarters of cattle. The rio terrà and calle Dei Nomboli are in San Tomà.

Nonzolo: sacristan. There are a *sottoportico* and *corte* del Nonzolo in San Moisè.

Ole: pots and pans. The calle delle Ole is in Castello.

Oresi: goldsmiths. The *ruga* and *sottoportico* with this name are on the Rialto.

Orio: the word is found in the name of the church of San Giacomo dell'Orio, perhaps named after a laurel tree (Italian, *alloro*).

Ormesini: the name is derived from Ormuz, and refers to the cloth which was first imported, and later imitated in Florence and Venice. The *fondamenta*, *calle*, and bridge with this name are in San Marcilian.

Ostreghe: oysters. The bridge, *rio*, *fondamenta*, and *calle* della Ostreghe are in Santa Maria Zobenigo.

Paglia: straw. The ponte della Paglia on the riva degli Schiavoni is so named after barges carrying straw which moored there.

Palada: dwelling built on piles. The *fondamenta* on the Giudecca was once built on piles, and has retained the name which has spread to the adjacent bridge and *rio*.

Papa: pope. The corte del Papa is the birthplace of Pietro Barbo, later pope Paul II.

Paradiso: paradise. According to the scholar Tassini, the district of Santa Maria Formosa was known as "el Paradiso," because of its splendid illuminations on Good Friday. There are a *calle* and a bridge which have this name.

Parangon: paragon. The name is found on the Rialto and commemorates the silken cloth which was produced here to strict standards, and which served as a point of reference, or paragon, for all contemporary work.

Parrocchie: parishes. There are little more than 30 parishes in Venice today but at one time there were about 70, all with their own district and grouped in the six *sestieri*. The parish name is indispensable in locating a house, even when it is in the dialect form, as for example San Trovaso for Santi Gervasio e Protasio, since the houses are numbered not by streets but by *sestieri*; Santa Croce, the smallest *sestiere*, has more than 2,000 houses, and Castello, the largest, nearly 7,000.

Pescaria: fish-market on the Rialto after which several places are named.

Pestrin: milkman. There are a *calle*, a bridge, and a *rio* del Pestrin in Santo Stefano.

Piazza: in Venice the squares are called *campi* or *campielli*, and the name *Piazza* stands only for St. Mark's square (Piazza San Marco).

Piazzetta: there are only two *piazzette* in Venice, the Piazzetta San Marco between the Libreria Sansoviniana and the Doge's Palace, facing on to St. Mark's basin, and the Piazzetta dei Leoncini, on the north side of St. Mark's basilica, now called the Piazzetta Giovanni XXIII.

Pietà: the blessed Peter of Assisi founded a shelter for foundlings and illegitimate children in some houses on the riva degli Schiavoni. This was the beginning of the Conservatorio della Pietà of which the Venetian composer Vivaldi was musical director.

Pignate: pots. The Ponte delle Pignate is in San Luca.

Pinzochere: pious women. The corte delle Pinzochere all'Angelo Raffaele is named after the tertiary order of Franciscan women. There is another in Santo Stefano named after Augustinian tertiaries. Other examples of the name recall hospices where elderly women with no family were given free lodging until some 20 years ago.

Piovan: parish priest. There are many streets of this name, and also a fondamenta del Piovan in San Martino.

Pirieta: tin-workers. The sottoportico and corte del Pirieta are in San Bartolomeo.

Pistor: bread-maker, more precisely dough-kneader, as distinct from the *forner* or baker. There are a *calle* and a Ponte del Pistor in San Lio.

Ponti: bridges: there are almost 400 of these in Venice, nearly an eighth of which are private property. Some are still wooden, some 18th century ones are of iron, and the majority are stone, dating from the end of the 15th century. At one time they had no parapets. Every bridge has a name.

Procuratie: this is the name of the colonnaded buildings in St. Mark's square. Looking towards the façade of the basilica, the Procuratie Vecchie are on the left, and the Procuratie Nuove on the right. They were the residences and offices of the procurators of St. Mark.

Proverbi: proverbs. In the calle larga dei Proverbi in Santi Apostoli the following proverbs can be seen on the cornices of two balconies: *Chi semina spine non vadi descalzo* (He who scatters thorns should not go barefoot), and *Di de ti e poi de me dirai* (Speak for yourself, and then you can speak for me).

Pugni: the Ponte dei Pugni was the site of the mock battles between the Castellani of Castello and the Nicolotti, from the parish of San Nicolò dei Mendicoli, of Dorsoduro. This sport came too close to rioting, with attendant serious consequences and was abolished in the 18th century.

Quartarolo: the Ponte del Quartarolo was the original name of the bridge del Rialto, when it was built on barges, and a fee of one *quartarolo* (a quarter of a *denaro*) had to be paid to cross it.

Ramo: short *calle* joining two streets.

Rasse: black cloths used for covering the *felzi* or gondolas which came originally from Rascia (Serbia). The calle dell Rasse is in San Provolo.

Redentore: the campo del Redentore is named after the church built to honour the vow made for the ending of the plague of 1576.

Regina: the palazzo Corner della Regina which belonged to Caterina Corner, queen of Cyprus, gave its name to a *calle* and a *ramo* in San Cassiano.

Remer: oar-maker. The *campiello* and *sottoportico* del Remer are in Sant'Agostino near the house of the rebel Baiamonte Tiepolo. A corte del Remer faces on to the *Canalazzo* in San Giovanni Crisostomo.

Remurchianti: bargees who towed other vessels. The *campiello* and *calle* dei Remurchianti are in San Nicolò.

Renghiera: this was the name of one of the bells in the Campanile, used for calling together the *arengo*, the old popular assembly.

Rialto: the historical commercial center of Venice. Its name is the Italianized form of Rivoaltus, which was the Latin name of the group of islands on which the city is built.

Ridotto: public gambling house opened by Marco Dandolo in his palace in 1638, and closed in 1774. The calle del Ridotto is in San Moisè.

Riello: small *rio*.

Riformati: this was the name of the Franciscans who officiated in the chapel of St. Bonaventure. The name has spread to the *calle*, *rio* and *fondamenta*.

Rio: the name given to smaller canals.

Rio menuo: very small *rio*.

Rio terrà: *rio* which has been silted up to make it into a street.

Riva: the banks of canals or quays where goods were unloaded in Venice (riva degli Schiavoni, del Carbon, etc.). *Riva* also denotes the steps on a *fondamenta* or in front of houses facing on to a canal where boats moored and cargo and passengers disembarked.

Ruga: some streets in Venice are called by this old Italian word for "street," similar to the French *rue*.

Rughetta: small *ruga*, alley.

Salute: the campo della Salute is named after the church of Santa Maria della Salute, built as a thanksgiving for the end of the plague in 1630.

Salizzada: paved street. The name is derived from *salizo*, paving, and is still used to denote the earliest paved streets.

San Basegio: Venetian for St. Basil.

San Boldo: Venetian for St. Ubaldo.

San Lio: Venetian for St. Leo.

San Marcialian: Venetian for St. Martial.

San Marcuola: Venetian for the church of S.S. Ermagora and Fortunato.

San Pantalon: Venetian for St. Pantaleone.

San Paolo: Venetian for St. Paul. The *sestiere* of this name is named after the church.

San Stae: Venetian for St. Eustace.

San Stin: St. Stefanino. The church of this name, now demolished, gave its name to a *campo*, a bridge, and *rio*.

Santa Croce: the church of Santa Croce was built and demolished at the same time as the convent adjoining it, and gave its name to one of the *sestieri*.

Sant'Aponal: Venetian for St. Apollinare.

Santa Ternita: Venetian for the Holy Trinity.

San Tomà: Venetian for St. Thomas.

San Trovaso: the Venetian name for the church of S.S. Gervasius and Protasius, and the associated place names.

San Zan Degolà: Venetian for St. Giovanni Decollato.

San Zanipolo: the Venetian name for the church of S.S. John and Paul, and for the associated place names.

San Zulian: Venetian for St. Julian.

Saoneri: soap-makers. There is a calle dei Saoneri in San Polo.

Sartori: tailors. There are a *fondamenta, calle,* and *ramo* dei Sartori in the Gesuiti.

Scaleter: pastry-cook. The "scalete" (pastries) bore the pattern of the steps of a small staircase ("scala.") The *calle* and *corte* del Scaleter are near the Frari.

Schiavine: large woollen blankets. The calle delle Schiavine is in San Luca.

Schiavoni: the inhabitants of Dalmatia, formerly known as Slavonia or Schiavonia, after whom the *riva* facing on to St. Mark's basin between the parishes of San Zaccaria and San Giovanni in Bragora is named, and where they moored to trade.

Scoacamini: chimney-sweeps. The *calle* and *rio* dei Scoacamini are in San Marco.

Scoazzera: from "*scoazza,*" cleaning. These were enclosures walled in on three sides where rubbish was collected. There is a campiello della Scoazzera in Sant'Aponal.

Scuellini: crockery-makers. The *campiello* of this name is in San Barnaba.

Scuola: the *scuole* in Venice were religious and charitable societies, some of which were also trade guilds. The *Scuole Grandi,* with their names of their patron saints are found in Venetian place names, for example the Scuola di San Rocco, as are the trade *scuole* such as the Scuole dei Varotari; and the *scuole* of national communities such as the *scuola* of Albanians. Synagogues were also called *scuole.* The campo delle Scuole in the Ghetto is named after the synagogues around it.

Sestieri: each of the six parts into which the city is divided. There are three *sestieri* on one side of the Grand Canal, San Marco, Castello and Cannaregio, and three on the other, Santa Croce, San Polo and Dorsoduro. The latter includes the island of the Giudecca.

Soccorso: succour. The *fondamenta* and bridge of this name commemorate a hospice for fallen women founded by the poetess and courtesan Veronica Franco in Santa Maria del Carmine.

Sospiri: sighs. The Bridge of Sighs connects the Prigioni (prisons) to the Doge's Palace. The name is a piece of romantic imagination; the prisoners were supposed to sigh as they passed the windows pierced in the bridge and gazed on Venice for perhaps the last time.

Sottoporteghi: *sottoportici,* arcades. These are passages covered by an arch of greater or lesser depth, which lead under private buildings for the benefit of the public.

Spezier: apothecary. There is a calle del Spezier in Santi Filippo e Giacomo.

Squartai: although history does not record the fact, tradition relates that in very distant times the bodies of various criminals were quartered (in Italian, "squartati") and hung as a warning from the bridge of this name in the Tolentini.

Squero: builder's yard. The calle del Squero is in San Moisè.

Stagneri: tinsmiths. The calle dei Stagneri is in San Salvador.

Stramazzer: mattress-maker. The calle del Stramazzer is in San Giovanni Crisostomo.

Strazzarol: rag-and-bone man. The calle del Strazzarol is in San Zulian.

Strazze: rags. The calle delle Strazze, also called dei Strazzeri, is in San Marco.

Stretto: narrow passage.

Stua: hot bath, public bath-house. There is a sottoportico della Stua in San Giovanni Nuovo, where there was one of these ill-famed establishments.

Tagliapietra: stonemason. Many streets in Venice are named after this trade.

Tana: the rio della Tana which passes through the Arsenal is named after the Casa del Canevo (hemp), where ship's ropes were made. This was also known as the Tana, from Tana (Azov) where the hemp was imported from.

Tentor: dyer. Many places are named after this flourishing trade.

Testori: silk-weavers. The calle dei Testori is in Sant'Andrea.

Tette: breasts. According to legend, the bridge and *fondamenta* of this name in San Cassiano are so called because prostitutes used to show themselves at doors and windows with uncovered breasts.

Toletta: small plank. The bridge and *calle* della Toletta in San Trovaso are named after a gangway made of small planks over a *rio* which once stood there.

Trottiera: this is the name of one of the bells in the Campanile; when it sounded, the patricians put their horses to the trot in order to arrive on time for political assemblies.

Turchette: Turkish girls. The bridge, *calle* and *fondamente* delle Turchette are named after some Turkish girls kept prisoner in the area.

Varotari: tanners. The Scuola dei Varotari, the guildhall of this profession, is in the campo Santa Margherita.

Vecchi: old men. A *corte* of this name in San Sebastiano is named after a hospice for old men who had to be "good-living, and with no sons or wife, either Venetian or subject."

Ventidue Marzo: the calle larga Ventidue Marzo in San Moisè commemorates the expulsion of the Austrians from Venice on 22 March 1848.

Vento: the wind. It is said that the wind blows more strongly in the calle del Vento in San Basegio than elsewhere.

Vera da pozzo: well head. These were often highly decorated, and were to be found – and in some cases still are – in many of Venice's *campi, campielli* and *corti.*

Vergola: silk snood, also twist of silk used as decoration for clothes. The calle della Vergola is in San Geremia.

Veriera: glazier's shop. The *sottoportico* and *corte* della Veriera are in San Zanipolo.

Volti: arches joining houses across *calli.* There is a calle dei Volti in the Gesuiti.

Volto Santo: the corte del Volto Santo was the center of silk-workers from Lucca who moved to Venice, and is named after an image of Christ, which was the silk-workers sign.

Zattere: the *fondamente* of this name running along the canale della Giudecca are named after the rafts used for carrying timber, which moored there.

Zavater: cobbler. There is a calle del Zavater in San Marcuola.

Zirada: bend. The ponte della Croce in the Tolentini is also known as the ponte della Zirada because at this point in the Grand Canal a stake was placed, round which boats turned in the regattas before starting on the return lap.

Zitelle: the fondamenta delle Zitelle on the Giudecca is named after the church of Santa Maria della Presentazione, called delle Zitelle (maidens), because of the nearby conservatory for girls founded in 1561.

Zobenigo: the church of Santa Maria del Giglio is also known as Santa Maria Zobenigo, because it was founded by the Iubanico family.

Zudio: Jew. The calle del Zudio on the fondamenta degli Ormesini is named after an apothecary's shop under the sign of a Jew.

Zueca: Venetian for the Giudecca, the southernmost island of Venice.

Bibliography

Armao, E., *In giro per il Mar Egeo con Vincenzo Coronelli*, Florence, 1951.

Berengo, M., *La società veneziana alla fine del Settecento*, Florence, 1976.

Braudel, F., *La Méditerranée et le monde méditerranéen a l'époque de Philippe II*, Paris, 1966.

Braunstein, Ph. and Delort, R., *Venise, portrait historique d'une cité*, Paris, 1971.

Brunelli, V., *Storia della città di Zara dal 1409 al 1797*, Venice, 1913.

Cessi, R., *Venezia ducale: Duca e popolo*, second edition, Venice, 1940.

Damerini, G., *Le isole Jonie nel sistema adriatico*, Milan, 1943.

Da Mosto, A., *I Dogi di Venezia*, second edition, Milan, 1960.

De Benvenuti, A., *Storia di Zara dal 1409 al 1797*, Milan, 1944.

Dudan, B., *Sindicato d'oltremare e di terraferma*, Rome, 1935.

—, *Il dominio veneziano di Levante*, Bologna, 1938.

Fotheringham, J., *Marco Sanudo, the Conqueror of the Archipelago*, Oxford, 1915.

Gerola, G., *Monumenti veneti nell'isola di Creta*, four volumes, Venice, 1905–32.

Guerdan, R., *Vie, grandeur et misères de Venise*, Paris, 1959.

Guerrini, E., *Venezia e la Palestina*, Venice, 1928.

Kretschmayr, H., *Geschichte von Venedig*, three volumes, Gotha-Stuttgart, 1905–34.

Lane, F.C., *Venice, a maritime republic*, New York, 1973.

Lopez, R.S., *La révolution commerciale dans l'Europe médiévale*, Paris, 1974.

Lunzi, E., *Delle condizioni politiche delle isole Jonie sotto il dominio veneto*, Venice, 1859.

Luzzatto, G., *Storia economica di Venezia*, Venice, 1961.

Molmenti, P.G., *Storia di Venezia nella vita privata*, three volumes, Bergamo, 1929.

Renouard, Y., *Les villes d'Italie de la fin du Xe siècle au début du XIVe siècle*, edited by Ph. Braunstein, Paris, 1969.

Romanin, S., *Storia documentata di Venezia*, ten volumes, Venice, 1853–60.

Tenenti, A., *Venezia e i corsari*, Bari, 1961.

Thiriet, F., *La Romanie vénitienne au Moyen Age*, Paris, 1959

Various Authors, *Venezia e le sue lagune*, five volumes, Venice, 1847.

Ventura, A., *Nobiltà e popolo nella società veneta del '400 e '500*, Bari, 1964.

Zorzi, A., *Sua Serenità Venezia*, Milan, 1971.

Index
of Names
and Places

Picture Sources

The abbreviations a, b, c, l, r refer to the position of the illustration on the page (above, below, center, left, right).

Listed below are some interesting sources relating to Venetian history, costumes from which are illustrated in this book.

Breydenbach, Bernard von (or Breitenbach or Breidenbach), *Peregrinationes in Terram Sanctam*, 1486. The author was canon of Mainz and travelled in Palestine between 1483 and 1484. He wrote an account of his journey which was illustrated with woodcuts by his travelling companion Erhard Reuwich of Utrecht (illustrations pages 9a, 10a).

Franco, Giacomo, *Habiti d'huomeni et donne venetiane*, Venice 1610. The author (1550–1620), a painter, engraver, writer and publisher, ran a bookshop at the sign of the "Sun" in Frezzeria (illustrations pages 30, 58b, 67, 70c, 70br, 71a, 74a, 170).

Grevembroch, Jan (Giovanni), *Varie venete curiosità sacre e profane*, a collection of drawings in the Museo Correr. The author (1731–1807), from a family of Dutch origin, may have been born in Venice and was employed in the service of the Gradenigo household (illustrations pages 28ar, 34, 36a, 37bl, 48c, 49c, 63, 72b, 75, 128b, 178, 181bl, 189b, 190a, 193, 196a, 202a).

Jacopo de' Barbari, *Pianta prospettica a volo d'uccello*, 1500. Woodcut using six different kinds of wood, measuring 1·35m × 2·82m (4ft 4in × 9ft 2in). The original is preserved in the Museo Correr (illustrations on pages 12, 76, 77, 146, 167a).

Vecellio, Cesare, *Degli habiti antichi e moderni di diverse parti del mondo*, Venice. The author (1521–1601) was the cousin of Titian. A painter and draughtsman, he also published three books on costume (illustrations pages 47ar, 47br, 48bl, 1271, 171).

Zompini, Gaetano, *Le arti che van per via nella città di Venezia*, 1753. The author (1700–1778) was born at Nervesa and was a painter and engraver. In 1784 John Strange, an Englishman living in Venice, bought the plates of the book from Zompini's heirs and had a second edition published (illustrations pages 174, 175).

Livy's *First Decad*, a 14th-century illuminated manuscript by the Venetian Giannino Cattaneo. Milan, Biblioteca Ambrosiana (illustrations pages 40b, 40ar, 46br, 47al, 47bl, 144b, 185, 209).

Registro catastico del monastero di San Maffeo di Murano, (Register of Landed Property of the Monastery of San Maffeo) 1391. Illuminations similar in style to those of the Bolognese school, preserved in the Seminario Patriarcale, Venice (illustrations pages 51r, 112, 179a).

Museums, Churches and Collections

Amsterdam: Rijksmuseum 59.
Asolo: Museo Comunale 24ar.
Athens: Benaki Museum 154b.
Attingham Park, (Shropshire), courtesy of the National Trust 151b.
Bassano del Grappa: Museo Civico 39b.
Bergamo: Private collection 40a.
Berlin: Staatliche Museen Preussischer Kulturbesitz, Gemäldegalerie 182b, 240; Munzkabinett 180bl.
Castagnola (Lugano): Thyssen-Bornemisza collection 233.

Florence: Fondazione Horne 216b; Galleria degli Uffizi 151a.
Hartford, Connecticut: Wadsworth Atheneum 72a.
Istanbul: Imperial Palace 103a.
London: British Library 101a; National Gallery 20.
Madrid: Museo del Prado 6.
Milan: Biblioteca Ambrosiana 40b, 46ar, 46br, 47al, 47bl, 144b, 185, 209, 210b; Biblioteca Nazionale Braidense 203; Museo del Castello Sforzesco 133; Museo Nazionale della Scienza e della Tecnica 130l, 186br; Raccolta delle Stampe Bertarelli 196b; Raccolta Numismatica del Comune 180br, 181r.
New York: Metropolitan Museum 198; Public Library 61b.
Oxford: Ashmolean Museum 239; Bodleian Library 9b, 101b.
Padua: Biblioteca Capitolare 162b; Museo Civico 44b, 229; Oratorio di San Giorgio 208.
Paris: Bibliothèque Nationale 100a, 103b; Ecole des Beaux-Arts 234; Louvre 24b, 25bl; Musée Jacquemart-André 192a.
Prague: Národní Galerie 128a.
Ravenna: San Giovanni Evangelista 102.
Rome: Galleria Doria Pamphili 232; Galleria Nazionale, Palazzo Corsini 176.
Toledo (USA): Museum of Art 52bl.
Venice: State Archives 28al, 28c, 29bl, 94b, 95, 126, 134, 150a, 156, 179b, 181al, 188c, 188b, 191a, 211a, 212l, 220al, 220b, 221a, 258; Biblioteca Marciana 8a, 9a, 10a, 11, 30, 31a, 32ar, 39a, 47ar, 47br, 48bl, 58, 61al, 61ar, 67, 105b, 110c, 110b, 115, 127l, 143, 162a, 170, 171, 186a, 210a, 221b, 224b, 259; Ca' d'Oro, Galleria G. Franchetti 51l; Ca' Rezzonico 50a, 91, 238; Museo Ebraico 129a; Gallerie dell'Accademia 25br, 52br, 53, 62, 88, 89, 139, 236; Museo Correr 22, 23, 27, 28ar, 28b, 29br, 31b, 32al, 32b, 34, 36, 37a, 37bl, 46al, 46bl, 48c, 49c, 63, 64al, 65b, 68, 69, 70, 70–71c, 71l, 72b, 73, 74a, 75, 127r, 128b, 130r, 131, 132, 135, 146, 158, 159, 167a, 178, 181bl, 184, 189b, 190a, 193, 196a, 200, 201, 202a, 212r, 213, 215a, 215b, 224a, 225, 239a, 252, 255; Museo Storico Navale 25a, 38a, 114b, 116, 138, 147a, 163, 189a, 214, 215c, 226, 227; Museo Vetrario di Murano 199; Doge's Palace 3, 19bl, 26, 44a, 60, 104, 115, 119, 147b, 216a, 237; Pinacoteca Querini Stampalia 41, 48cr, 48–49a, 49b, 183, 188a, 192; St. Aponal 18al; St. Mark's 15, 17, 18ar, 19c, 64b, 66, 96, 97r, 106b, 107b, 108, 109, 113, 244; St. Mark's, Museo Marciano 2; Treasury of St. Mark's 19al, 106a, 107a; S. Maria Formosa 169; S. Maria Gloriosa dei Frari 50b; Seminario Patriarcale, Pinacoteca Manfredini 51r, 112, 179a; Torcello, Cathedral 14, 18b, 19br.
Windsor Castle: Royal collection. By gracious permission of Her Majesty the Queen 235.
Woburn Abbey: Duke of Bedford collection 37br.

Photographs and Photographic Agencies

Anders, Berlin 182b, 240.
Böhm, Venice 18al, 18b, 19al, 46al, 46bl, 53, 62, 65a, 70, 71, 74a, 75, 118b, 119b, 236, 239a.
Bulloz, Paris 182a, 234.
Cameraphoto, Venice 129a.
Caprioli, Venice 127a.
Carrieri, Milan 107b.
Costa, Milan 36b, 37a, 49c, 110a, 135, 178, 193c, 193b,

212r, 213, 255, 259.
De Biasi, Milan 52a, 52br, 167b.
Edition Robert Laffont, Paris 101b.
Electa Editrice, Milan 106a, 107a.
Emmer, Venice 2, 25a, 38a, 51l, 138, 147a, 169, 215c, 224a, 225, 227, 237, 244.
Fabbri Editore, Milan, 96b, 162b.
Farabola-Alinari, Milan 118a.
Farabola-Anderson, Milan 102.
Fleming, London 151b.
Foto Cine Brunel, Lugano 233.
Foto Labor Color, Bergamo 40a.
Giacomelli, Venice 31b, 32al, 32b, 51r, 64al, 65b, 68, 69, 112, 147b, 179a, 200b, 201b, 202b.
Kodansha, Tokyo 20.
Lotti, Milan 129b, 220ar.
Lucchetti, Bergamo 24ar.
Lufin, Abano Terme 44b, 208, 229.
Magnani e Baroni, Milan 203.
Mairani, Milan 111a.
Marzari-Emmer, Venice 106b.
Mori, Milan 24b, 25bl, 50a, 50b, 72a.
Nicolini, Milan 14, 15, 17, 33, 45, 56–57, 60, 73, 80, 81, 84, 85, 90, 92, 94a, 166, 180a, 186bl, 187, 197, 204, 205, 206, 217, 230.
Pineider, Florence 216b.
Pizzi e Chiari, Milan 199.
Pucciarelli, Rome 105a.
Renard, Venice 28al, 28c, 29bl, 94b, 95, 126, 134, 150a, 156, 179b, 181al, 188c, 188b, 191a, 211a, 212l, 220al, 220b, 221a, 258.
Ricciarini-Bevilacqua, Milan 25br, 28ar, 28b, 29a, 29br, 37b, 41, 48c, 48–49a, 49b, 72b, 181bl, 188a, 189, 190b, 193a, 196a, 202a, 215b.
Saporetti, Milan 133.
Savio, Rome 176, 232.
Scala, Florence 3, 96a, 97r, 104, 108, 113, 151a, 238.
Swaan, 103a.
Tortoli, Tavarnuzze 98, 99, 117, 120, 124, 125, 136, 137, 140, 144a, 145, 148, 149, 152, 153, 154, 155, 157, 160, 161, 164, 165, 168, 172, 173.
Toso, Venice 8a, 10a, 11, 22, 23, 30, 31a, 32ar, 39a, 47ar, 47br, 58, 61al, 61ar, 67, 91, 105b, 110c, 110b, 115, 116, 127l, 131, 132, 162a, 170, 171, 183, 186a, 210a, 215a, 221b, 224b.
Woolfitt, 26.
Zorzi, Rome 142.
Mondadori Archives, Milan 9, 13, 18ar, 19c, 38b, 39b, 44a, 52bl, 59, 64b, 66, 74b, 78, 79, 88, 89, 100b, 109, 114, 119a, 128a, 129c, 139, 143, 150b, 151a, 159, 180b, 192, 196b, 214, 252, 253, 256, 257.

The publishers would like to thank the following for their help with the picture research for this book: the State Archives, Venice and the director Dr. Giustiniana Colasanti and all those who provided photographic material from the Archives; the Biblioteca Nazionale Marciana and Signor Mario Favaretto; the Library of the Seminario Patriarcale, Venice, Monsignor Giuliano Bertoli, and the curator Don Antonio Niero; the Fondazione Giorgio Cini; the Fondazione Scientifica Querini Stampalia; the Museo Correr, its director Dr. Lucia Casanova Bellodi and Signor Mario De Fina; the Museo Storico Navale and its curator G. B. Rubin de Cervin.